Kindergarten

PROGRAMS AND PRACTICES

Kindergarten

PROGRAMS AND PRACTICES

MARJORIE E. RAMSEY

Professor and Head, Division of Education,
Georgia Southwestern College, Americus, Georgia

KATHLEEN M. BAYLESS

Associate Professor, Early Childhood Education,
Kent State University, Kent, Ohio

with **125** illustrations

Merrill Publishing Company
A Bell & Howell Company
Columbus   Toronto   London   Sydney

All rights reserved. No part of this book may be reproduced in any form, electronic or mechanical, including photocopy, recording, or any information storage and retrieval system, without permission in writing from the publisher. "Bell + Howell" is a trademark of the Bell & Howell Company. "Charles E. Merrill Publishing Co." and "Merrill" are registered trademarks of the Bell & Howell Company.

Copyright © 1980, The C. V. Mosby Company

Copyright © 1986, Merrill Publishing Company
Columbus, Ohio 43216
A Bell & Howell Company

Library of Congress Catalog Card Number: 80-11478
International Standard Book Number: 0-675-20603-0
Printed in the United States of America
2 3 4 5 6 7 8 9 10—91 90 89 88 87 86

To all the kindergarten teachers and
about-to-be kindergarten teachers and the
five-year-olds with whom they share the joy
of learning, we dedicate this book.

Preface

This book began in 1972 with the decision to team-teach the undergraduate kindergarten education course at Kent State University. From that point to this, together with students aspiring to be teachers and with kindergarten teachers in area schools and in schools throughout the country and overseas, we have observed and studied the five-year-old in many settings and worked with those responsible for the care and education of that "symphony of movement and sound" we describe in the chapters you will read.

We have attended and presented workshops, participated in national and regional conferences, developed a graduate-level kindergarten education course, and sought the counsel of many nationally known figures in early childhood education. We have supervised student teachers as they worked with master teachers in the kindergartens of Ohio. From the kindergarten classrooms of Iowa, Maryland, Tennessee, Michigan, Texas, Utah, Minnesota, and North Carolina, and from the teachers we have met about the country, have come the materials, ideas, and activities—enough to fill several filing cabinets—a veritable storehouse!

No single book would be comprehensive enough to encompass the wisdom shared with us about the kindergarten and the children nurtured there. If you, the reader, know a five-year-old or work with a group of fives, you know the delights we have experienced in coming to know them. You will also know that not all the ideas and activities we describe will "match" all fives. Because five-year-olds are so individual, with wide ranges of ability and potential, materials of varying levels of difficulty are included in the content. Our intent is not that you cover or incorporate all ideas or materials with a group of children. Richness of resources offers flexibility and choice. You, too, must sort, adapt, study, and select from the programs and practices.

We elected to concentrate on the fives—not the threes and fours or the sixes and sevens—although most early childhood programs and sources encompass all of these ages. Many fives are like fours; many are like sixes or sevens; but, because this age *is* special and kindergarten is a beginning, we thought that prospective teachers and those already experienced needed a resource that concentrated on the fives. In our research we found relatively few curriculum guides or source books that offered enough information about kindergarten to meet the needs of our classes or workshop groups. There is so much to learn, so much to share about this age!

The text is organized to facilitate planning for the school year, such as a teacher new to the kindergarten situation might sit down to do. To plan the total environment that is the kindergarten, one begins with the children, the setting, and the resources; the curriculum evolves about that framework.

This book is also a beginning. We invite your reactions and notes in the margins as you read. Study the photographs—vignettes of life in the kindergarten. The fives you know and work with are special, and we want to become acquainted with them. Find out what works for those "why-ers" in your charge.

Note on terminology: In relation to the current concern with the use of pronouns, we have elected to use *he* or *she* in whatever manner it first occurs to us to use them in each instance and hope for the understanding of the reader.

Also note that the names of children and teachers have been fictionalized in the narrative examples given to illustrate particular points.

Because this book evolved over a period of several years, to attempt to mention individually all those who shared with us ideas, thoughts, materials, and feelings about what kindergartens should be (including parents, psychologists, pediatricians, colleagues, and yes, even the five-year-olds) would be impossible—our deep appreciation is extended to all.

Undergraduate and graduate students, colleagues in the Department of Early Childhood Education, and other professionals within Kent State University and within and outside the community participated extensively in the book and are noted specifically in some sections. Special thanks go to Dr. Ambrose A. Clegg, Jr., who contributed Chapter 6 on social studies.

Kindergarten teachers of Northeast Ohio offered materials, permitted us to visit their classrooms, came to the University as resource speakers, and welcomed us graciously for picture-taking sessions. Here we thank, particularly, the Hudson, Ohio Public Schools; Kent City Schools; Orange Schools; Euclid Schools; Warren City Schools; and the Kent State University School.

We are deeply indebted to the members of the Ohio Ad Hoc Kindergarten Guidelines Committee, with whom we worked for four years in the development of Recommended Kindergarten Guidelines for the state. Each committee person shared unselfishly with us their time and curriculum ideas.

Professional educators throughout the country reacted to our materials in this book and offered constructive criticism as they attended workshop presentations at several national conferences.

The office staff in the Department of Early Childhood Education and Student Personnel Services merit our thanks. Mrs. Mazella Janecek contributed excellent secretarial help and a superbly typed manuscript. Photographers Jack Ulman and Doug Moore capably captured the personality of the five-year-old, and Mrs. Marilyn Spelman, a personal friend, spent many hours in library research to compile an excellent listing of children's books. The patience and support of our families was invaluable and provided the incentive to complete the task.

Working with the book and with all of the individuals mentioned has been a rich, learning experience for us. We hope that as you use the text, the five-year-old will flourish.

Marjorie E. Ramsey
Kathleen M. Bayless

Statement of beliefs

Most educators now agree that kindergarten is one of the most important and influential experiences a child can have. In our years of work with children, teachers, and parents, we have developed several strong convictions about kindergarten that we would like to express before you pursue the chapters in our book. May these beliefs serve as a basis for helping you better understand our thinking on quality kindergarten programming.

We believe:

- That each child who attends a quality kindergarten program should be helped in developing as a curious, intelligent, caring, self-confident, and responsible person
- That kindergarten children need the guidance of a professionally qualified, caring teacher—a teacher who remains a constant learner
- In a mutual interdependence of the home and school
- In respect for each individual kindergarten child and in the necessity for providing activities, experiences, materials, and equipment that are appropriate to each child's maturity level and developmental need
- In a rich, multisensory environment
- In kindergartener's active participation in their own learning experiences
- In a program that nurtures the development of social interaction, including the awareness, understanding, and appreciation of the richness of cultural variations within society
- That children should be motivated and encouraged to "stretch their minds" and use their bodies to the degree to which each is capable
- That divergent and creative expression should be encouraged
- That kindergarten is not first grade; that it is not intended to hurry up the maturation process or pressure children to perform at a superior level when they reach first grade
- That kindergarten should be a place where children feel comfortable, where their minds and bodies are stimulated, where they enjoy learning, and where they look forward to coming each day

Contents

1 **TODAY'S KINDERGARTEN,** 1

   Program, 2
   Models, 2
     Traditional, 2
     Montessori, 2
     Open, 3
     Follow-through, 4
     Eclectic, 4
   Kindergarten timetable, 5
   Purpose and philosophy, 8

2 **THE FIVE-YEAR-OLD AND THE TEACHER,** 11

   Characteristics of the five-year-old, 11
   Needs of the five-year-old, 12
   Characteristics of the teacher, 13

3 **BEGINNINGS,** 19

   Before school begins, 19
     Orientation to kindergarten, 19
     Home visits before school begins, 20
     Staggered entrance, 20
     Knowing the community, 20
     Basic planning, 21
   The first day, 21
   Separation anxiety, 24
   The next few days, 24
   Kindergarten screening, 25

4 **ORGANIZING FOR INSTRUCTION,** 29

   Equipment and instructional materials, 29
   Room arrangement and organization, 32
   Outdoor environments, 36
   Scheduling for the kindergarten day, 37
   Program planning, 40
     Curriculum guides, 41
     Long- and short-term goal planning, 42
     Lesson planning in the kindergarten, 42
     Work time–activity period, 44
     Learning centers, 47
     Grouping, 48
   Summary, 48

5 **THE WELL-BEING OF THE FIVE-YEAR-OLD,** 51

   Play, 51
   What is play? 51
   Contributors to play, 52
   Values and purposes of play, 53
     Play promotes physical growth, 53
     Play provides children with a sense of power, 53
     Play nurtures problem solving, 53
     Play fosters emotional growth, 53
     Play provides an opportunity to acquire concepts, 54
     Play provides a means for playing out roles and encourages self-expression, 54
   Kinds of play, 54

Group games, 55
The teacher's role, 56
An added thought, 57
Health, 57
Health examinations and forms, 58
  Chart of communicable diseases of childhood, 59
Detecting health problems, 59
  Vision, 59
  Hearing and speech, 59
  Other perceptual problems, 67
  Special problems, 68
Proper food and nutrition, 70
Kindergarten snack time, 70
Rest, 70
Emotional health, 71
Physical fitness and activity, 72
Safety, 88
Maintaining a safe school environment, 88
  Safety to and from school, 89
  Emergencies, 89
  Special hazards, 89
Safety: a priority, 89
Safety activities, 90
Child abuse and neglect, 93
Child abuse and neglect defined, 93
Child abuse and neglect reporting, 94
Causes of abuse and neglect, 94
The teacher's role, 95
Behavior, 96
Teachers who care and are in control, 96
Setting limits, 98
When children misbehave, 98
  Denial of the activity, 98
  Conferences, 98
  High degree of expectancy, 99
  Isolation, 99
  Redirection, 99
  Positive reinforcement, 99
  Teacher's voice and remarks, 99
Summary, 100

6 LEARNING TO LIVE TOGETHER: THE SOCIAL STUDIES, 107

Ambrose A. Clegg, Jr.

The domain of knowledge, 108
  Knowledge about individuals, 110
  Knowledge about groups, 111
  Knowledge about human beings, 112
  Knowledge about human culture, 113
Abilities and skills in social studies learning, 123
  Gathering information, 123
  Forming concepts, 123
  Defining concepts, 124
  Complex concepts, 125
  Relational concepts, 125
  Other thinking skills, 127
Valuing, 128
  Basic values, 129
  Other values, 129
  Moral education, 132
  Democratic behavior, 133
  Teaching strategies, 136
Social participation, 138
Summary, 141

7 THE EXPRESSIVE ARTS, 143

Music and movement, 143
Music, 143
  The teacher's role, 145
  Listening, 146
  Singing, 148
  Instruments, 153
Movement, 155
  Materials to enhance movement, 156
  Tips for promoting movement exploration, 157
  Summary, 157
The dramatic arts, 157
Stories, 157
  Choosing and using books with five-year-olds, 157
  Presenting stories, 158
  Bibliotherapy, 161
  Books: the lifetime investment, 161
Dramatic play, 162
  Creative dramatics, 164
  Pantomime, 165
  Puppetry, 166
Poetry, 167
Art and woodworking, 171
Art, 171
  The teacher's role, 173
  Establishing an art center, 175

Art activities, 176
Woodworking, 182
   Establishing a woodworking area, 182
   Example of a program utilizing woodworking, 183
   Teacher-made wooden puzzles, 184
Summary, 185

8 THE COMMUNICATION ARTS, 191

Language, 191
Planning a language program, 192
Listening, 195
Speaking, 198
   Bilingualism and a second language, 199
   Summary and additional thoughts, 201
Writing, 202
Reading, 208
Readiness, 210
Approaches to reading, 211
Summary, 213
Television, 222
Concerns, 222
Benefits, 223
Guidelines, 223
Summary, 224

9 DISCOVERY: ORDER AND FORM, SCIENCE AND NUMBERS, 231

Science, 231
Planning, 231
Goals, 233
Activities and experiences, 234
Numbers, 241
Planning, 242
Goals, 243
Activities and experiences, 244

10 PARENTS AND THE TEACHER, 259

Parents as partners, 259
Patterns of involvement, 260
   Parents as paraprofessionals, 260
   Parents as volunteers, 261
   Parents as resources, 261
   Extensions of involvement, 262
Printed communications, 263
School visitation in kindergarten, 268
   Observation, 268
   Conferences, 269

11 THE STATE OF THE ART, 277

Organization, 278
Enrollment, 279
Evaluation, 279
Retention and promotion, 281
Legislation, 282
The curriculum, 282
Research directions, 283
Trends in kindergarten education, 284

APPENDIXES

A Children's books, 286
B Information forms for children entering kindergarten, 298
C A brief annotated bibliography on kindergarten screening, 302
D Films, 304
E Resource materials, 307
F Some programs used with kindergarten children, 309
G Transitions, 311
H Guides, 314

Kindergarten
PROGRAMS AND PRACTICES

CHAPTER 1
Today's kindergarten

> Early childhood education is obviously in ferment—a ferment comparable to that at the turn of the century. The issues, too long left unresolved, are plaguing kindergartens today. Never before has the education of young children assumed greater importance in the eyes of the general public. (Weber, 1969, p. 207)

Expressed a decade ago, Weber's words are even more potent and intensive today. New demands are being placed on kindergartens. Each year finds more women with school-age children in the labor market; the need for quality day care and educational programs impacts on all levels of schooling. The kindergarten presents particular challenges as the child of a single-parent family, the child of a culturally different family, the "mainstreamed" child with handicaps (physical, social, emotional, or learning disability), the bilingual child, the child who has attended nursery school or several day care programs, the child of a migrant family, the child of the "jet set" or "latchkey" generation, and the child of the executive transfer syndrome all find their way into the same kindergarten class.

Today's kindergartens exist in infinite variety throughout the country—yet not all five-year-olds are participating. Kindergartens may be an integral part of the public school system; they may be privately operated; or they may be included in an early education unit. Attendance may be compulsory or voluntary—schedules may encompass 2½ hours, a half day, an extended day, all day, every day, or alternate days. The children may be housed in a unit separate from the elementary school, in a church basement Sunday School room, in a community facility, within the elementary school, or in one of the many types of private facilities.

The teacher of the five-year-old may be a highly trained, specially certified graduate of a four-year university program, a "retrained" elementary or secondary school teacher, or the holder of the Montessori certificate—or this person may hold no certificate at all.

Supportive services, aides, volunteers, grandparents, subject specialists, special personnel (nurses, librarians, psychologists) may be found in profusion or not at all.

Today's kindergarten child may be a member of a class of one, may be privately tutored, may attend an isolated rural or mountain school with a group of two or three, may attend an American school overseas, or may be one of 20 or 25—or in some situations, one of 45—vying for the teacher's attention.

In some communities, kindergartens are considered a frill, the first program to be eliminated when budget cutbacks are mandated. In others, public kindergartens are carefully nurtured, broadly supported, and encouraged, with equipment and materials in abundance. Commercially operated and Montessori-type facilities are an option, usually with a high fee structure.

PROGRAM

In assessing the learning potential of a kindergarten program, one must consider many issues. Programs range from low-pressure, permissive child growth and development approaches to highly structured, carefully programmed approaches.

The more permissive child growth and development programs stress socialization, creativity, traditional principles of child growth, parent involvement, and utilization of a wide variety of materials along with allowing children great diversity in their use. The emphasis is on process rather than content.

The highly structured programs stress language and mathematics, have clearly defined objectives in behavioral terms, select materials, and prescribe ways of using them. The teachers work in small groups. The emphasis is on content rather than process.

Several approaches between the permissive child growth and development approach and the more highly structured behaviorist approach stress the responsive environment; learning activities are Piaget based and are self-rewarding and self-pacing.

All of these approaches are oriented toward child growth and development, and all have established objectives and procedures. All are concerned with helping children learn, and all are concerned with content. They have all demonstrated their effectiveness with young children.

All of the approaches also require some structure, although the structure itself varies in kind. The programs vary in procedures and objectives; therefore, the accomplishments vary according to the objectives that are emphasized (Early Childhood Education in Illinois, 1970).

MODELS
Traditional

Today's kindergarten may be of the "traditional" type, with one teacher solely responsible for 25 to 30 children, a 2½-hour daily or alternate-day schedule, and/or two sessions daily. Preparation for first grade characterizes the activities—leaving little freedom of choice—and reading readiness materials predominate. Teacher planning and directing may be the mode. Classroom management and specific scheduling are prized, with children often occupied with worksheets or workbooks in total-group instruction.

Group instructional goals are usually stressed in the traditional kindergarten. Expectations for being "ready to read" and ready for first grade are high. The "basics" are emphasized with report cards carrying A-B-C evaluations. In one such situation, I (M.R.) heard the comment that "this is such a good kindergarten; everybody is so quiet." Play has given way to work in such classrooms.

Montessori

Today's kindergarten may be a private Montessori facility where children engage in carefully laid out, specific activities sequenced according to difficulty, with control of movement, independence, self-discipline, concentration, and satisfactory completion of a task as goals. Sensorial materials, cylinders, geometric forms, color spools, and sandpaper letters and blocks are found in abundance—the responsibility of the teacher to create the best possible controlled environment for each child in keeping with individual stages of development is emphasized. Self-selection of tasks and voluntary work offer each child an ever-widening span of responsibility.

Practical life exercises (dressing, bathing, brushing hair, buttoning, tying, sweeping, dusting, preparing vegetables, caring for plants, orderliness, etc.), techniques of observation, and crystallization of basic ideas through exact terminology also characterize this model. Diligence and respect for the rights of others are cultivated. Careful observation of the children and their behavior determine the procedures chosen.

Usually, heterogeneous groupings of children from ages three to six are the mode. Formal class teaching is dispensed with, along with the usual desks, benches, and fixed chairs.

Work experiences for the child are paramount, with desire to learn a compelling factor. Children's literature, field trips, outdoor play, excursions, and dramatic play tend to be minimized. The teacher is trained as a technician in the use of Montessori materials—since much of the material is formal and must be used in a prescribed manner—and tends to be more directive and active in planning a calm, quiet, total environment for the child. The program demands reinforcement of certain responses and ways of utilizing materials and nonreinforcement of other approaches.

Open

Today's kindergarten is often an "open" or informal British infant school–type of setting, called an integrated day, with an individualized program for each child promoted through extensive learning and interest centers and team teaching. Children are grouped in clusters that sometimes include ages four to seven and work with several adults or older children. There is usually no established formula for the day. The teacher serves as guide and facilitator and is much less visible than in the usual classroom. Exploratory and experimental behavior is encouraged; a wide array of manipulative materials is in evidence and children make decisions about their own learning. There is no work-play dichotomy. Individual learning styles are developed through interaction, exploration, and observation. Extensive records or anecdotal "jottings" are kept on individual children. Volunteers, a blending of work and play, self-pacing, and movement to indoor and outdoor spaces characterize a rich program developed through joint responsibility of adults and children.

Proponents of the open kindergarten strongly advocate the richness of the program. Extensive use is made of the out-of-doors and area resources. The fact that it becomes everyone's program and that constant evaluation, problem solving, reorganization, planning, and flexibility promote maximum growth are other strengths. Children accept the responsibility for their own learning, and productivity depends on the skill of the teacher in planning and organizing learning centers. Children may spend as much as three years with the same group of adults. The environment becomes the product of

everyone's thinking and cooperation. There is a wide latitude for school personnel to plan the curriculum. The choices a child could make and the fact that freedom of movement is encouraged help the child develop a strong sense of responsibility, and discipline is seldom a problem. Reading, creative writing, cognitive growth, and strong social skills mark the progress of most children. A high level of attainment in the arts is also reported.

Other advantages for the open classroom cited in the literature include the freedom given the teacher, the avoidance of artificial incentives, the apparent lack of obsession about the children's future with the current learning situation paramount, and the development of a kind of accountability for each child's learning.

The principal disadvantages of the open kindergarten, as reported by those involved, are the burdens of planning, overcrowded rooms, setup, preparation, record keeping, and sometimes the numbers of children. Providing ample materials could become a problem. However, the advantages and growth possibilities for children appear to outweigh the difficulties.

Follow-through

Today's kindergarten may be a "follow-through" model that provides continuity of program for children of urban or inner-city locations. From a background of Head Start or day care and nursery classes, the child has experienced an intensive skills orientation prior to kindergarten. Specially structured language development activities, socialization and self-concept, self-care, and the beginnings of independent action have been concentrations. The teacher's activities are specifically geared toward seeing that every child masters a common body of cognitive content, and strong attention is given to reading and mathematical concepts.

Sometimes called the Bereiter-Engelmann model, originating in Illinois, this approach offers a "no nonsense" academic curriculum with little of the esthetic or appreciative. Children usually work in groups of five, with 20-minute time modules devoted to each skill area. Unison response to the teacher's questioning begins the instruction of patterned responses, and rapid pacing is the mode.

Follow-through kindergartens may also be characterized by the use of individualized learning modules—individual programmed instruction (IPI)—with a token or ticket system for the child's selection of activities, self-pacing for part of the day, and the remainder of the schedule taken up with art, music, and enrichment activities.

Heavy community involvement is an integral part of the Head Start effort and often continues into the follow-through kindergarten. Parents and other adults volunteer services through commitment of specified time blocks involving a broad variety of responsibilities and transactions with the children. A particularly strong component of this model is the availability of health care services to all children, with an emphasis on nutrition, dental, and overall physical needs. Strongly emphasized is the need for continuity—a continuation into a type of follow-through first-grade or primary experience.

Eclectic

Although not labeled as "eclectic" in the literature, many kindergarten programs today borrow from all the models described. Montessori-type materials are in use, and scheduling patterns and organizational plans are flexible and designed to fit a particular school or community situation. The all-day, everyday kindergarten is developed in some systems. Class sizes vary; both small- and large-group activities are provided; and blocks of time for certain work projects are scheduled. Most kindergartens of this type feature a somewhat similar curriculum, including reading readiness activities, socialization centers and sharing, dramatic play, attention to play and work time endeavors, story telling, manipulative materials, block corners, interest centers, and the like. Usually one teacher and sometimes an aide or other volunteer work with the group of five-year-olds.

• • •

That there is no one best or most popular model of kindergarten operation is evident as one visits the many school systems and facilities for young children. That the quality of programs is uneven is also evident. As Goodlad and his associates (1974, p. 83) state:

Our data lead to the firm conclusion that the overwhelming majority of our classrooms—in organization, subject matter, materials, and mode of instruction—were geared to group norms and expectancies rather than to individual differences in learning rate and need. Judging from our sample, childhood schooling is more vanilla than pistachio or neopolitan.

Goodland and his associates (p. 92) make the additional comment that "although the kindergarten, in general, appeared to be more open, flexible, and permissive than others, a block of them deviated markedly toward a strong academic orientation and marked teacher control."

Discussing the "distortions" in kindergarten, Harris and Fisher (1969, p. 283) list:

1. Readiness for admission
2. Grouping or tracking plans
3. Teaching of subjects
4. The academic curriculum
5. Work sheets
6. Readiness tests for grouping purposes
7. Pressures for achievement
8. Preparation for grade one
9. Interference with creativity
10. Written report cards
11. Retention
12. Kindergarten graduation (Now he goes to work!)

Writing in the same vein, Harris and Fisher (p. 279) state: "Old fashioned, child-centered, supportive non-hurried kindergartens now seem to be on the defensive. They are called 'the Establishment.'"

After more than a decade, strong differences appear to prevail, with individuals taking positions along a rather uneven continuum. The same "distortions" cited by Harris and Fisher need to be confronted.

KINDERGARTEN TIMETABLE

Study of young children began in the sixteenth century and has continued in intensity to the present day. Emphases have shifted and attitudes have changed from the view of the young child as a miniature adult to that of the young child as a unique being, living and growing through developmental stages.

The timetable of early efforts for young children (Table 1) reveals many milestones significant to the development of the kindergarten.

The reader interested in studying the historical growth and chronology of the kindergarten is referred to Weber's (1969) discussion of the movement. Contemporary programs and practices are the focus of succeeding chapters of this text.

As Cohen and Rudolph (1977, p. 5) state:

Kindergartens became a definite part of American society during the last decades of the nineteenth century. They were regarded as corrective for affluent children . . . and as beneficial for lower class children, who were sufficiently hurt by street influences to need the orderliness and social morality of the kindergarten.

From simple beginnings, today's kindergartens, diverse in program and purpose, have grown. In the 1960s, according to Cohen and Rudolph (p. 7), "the problems of

Table 1. Early educators

	Dates	Nationality	Contributions
John Amos Commenius	1592-1670	Moravian	Developed graded school system Recognized need for experience first Wrote *School of Infancy* and *Orbus Pictus*—first picture book
Jean Jacques Rousseau	1712-1778	French, Swiss	Advocated freedom and experience, and natural development of children Wrote *Emile*
Jean Frederick Oberlin	1741-1826	French	Originated infant school, or "creche" Emphasized moral education
Johann Heinrich Pestalozzi	1746-1827	German, Swiss	Saw need for activity program Started first outdoor education Founded demonstration school—Yverdun Wrote *How Gertrude Teaches Her Children*
Robert Owen	1771-1858	Welsh, English	Founded infant schools for mill children in Scotland Stressed importance of environment in early childhood
Freidrich Froebel	1782-1852	German	Father of kindergarten (1842) Bestowed 20 gifts for kindergarten Encouraged mother play with child Wrote *Education of Man*
Elizabeth Palmer Peabody	1804-1894	American	Founded private kindergarten in Boston (1860) Started teacher training in kindergarten Wrote *Moral Culture of Infancy*
Susan Blow	1843-1916	American	Founded first public kindergarten, St. Louis, 1873 Started teacher training—Midwest, 1874 Translated Froebel's work into English Wrote *Educational Issues in Kindergarten*
Kate Douglas Wiggan	1856-1923	American	Founded Silver Street Kindergarten in San Francisco, 1880 Started teacher training—West Coast Wrote *Kindergarten Principles and Practices* and books for children
John Dewey	1859-1952	American	Applied pragmatism to education Advocated progressive education Wrote *School and Society*
Margaret MacMillan	1860-1931	English	Started nursery school movement Provided public support for preschool education, Fisher Act Wrote *Nursery School Education*

Table 1. Early educators—cont'd

	Dates	Nationality	Contributions
Patty Smith Hill	1868-1946	American	Freed kindergarten from Froebelian pattern Advocated progressive education in kindergarten (1910-1930) and use of large blocks, libraries, and mental tests in kindergarten IKU became ACEI
Maria Montessori	1870-1952	Italian	Stressed special methods for slow-learning children Created Casa du Bambini (Houses of Childhood) Developed sensory training equipment and Montessori method
Jean Piaget	1896-	Swiss	Developed intelligence stages of learning and conceptual development Foremost contributor to field of intellectual development

the country inevitably turned the spotlight on the beginnings of learning, and the kindergarten, long separated from the problems and anxieties of the total school community, was jolted out of its isolation to face new concepts of children and new demands for children's learning."

Today's kindergartens are pressured to adopt less play and more "basics"—less free time and more academic programs. Specialists in early childhood education urge balance and consideration of alternatives—a thoughtful discussion of the learning modes of children and the goals of early education. Differing opinions and values abound. As Robison (1977, p. 419) states:

> Educators continue to be perplexed as to the most appropriate stress for this age grade. If the school chooses family, interage, or vertical grouping (i.e. for four, five, and six year olds or five, six, and seven year olds) program decisions seem to be easier.

Perhaps the only constant is change. The key to quality, emphasis, and program rests with individual kindergarten teachers, administrators, and the community. Decisions are critical and *now*. The five-year-old is at the threshold.

PURPOSE AND PHILOSOPHY

Froebel, the "father" of the kindergarten, wrote in about 1840:

> It (the kindergarten) shall give them employment suited to their nature, strengthen their bodies, exercise their senses, employ their waking minds, make them acquainted judiciously with nature and society, cultivate especially the heart and temper, and lead them to the foundations of all living—to unity with themselves. (ACEI, 1960-1961, p. 1)

A handbook developed by the Ohio Association of Classroom Teachers (1971, p. 4) provides a philosophy:

> There shall be no single standard toward which all pupils work—rather the child shall be encouraged to work according to his own ability.
>
> There shall be a stimulating atmosphere to arouse the child's interest and curiosity.
>
> A concept of self-reliance shall be developed within the child.
>
> A child shall be encouraged to develop a worthwhile relationship with his peer group.
>
> The child shall be encouraged to improve his basic body management.

Early childhood educators, kindergarten teachers, and adults concerned with the five-year-old need to scrutinize critically the total dynamics of the learning environment, establish priorities for each child, and garner the best resources to meet the task of developing the potential of a diverse group of children. A creature of the television age—of instant replay—oblivious to tomorrow and a "playful" learner, the five-year-old must be nurtured in *today's* kindergarten.

REFERENCES AND SUGGESTED READINGS

Almy, Millie. *Young children's thinking: studies of some aspects of Piaget's theory.* New York: Teachers College Press, 1966.

Association for Childhood Education International. *What are kindergartens for?* 1960-61 Membership Service Bulletin A. Washington, D.C.: The Association.

Association for Childhood Education International. *What about kindergarten?* Washington, D.C.: National Educators Association, undated.

Auleta, Michael S. Preschool and kindergarten overview. In *Foundations of early childhood education: readings.* New York: Random House, Inc., 1969, pp. 127-208.

Boegehold, Betty D., Cuffaro, Harriet K., Hooks, William H., and Klopf, Gordon J. *Education before five.* New York: Bank Street College of Education Publications, 1977.

Broman, Betty L. *The early years in childhood education.* Chicago: Rand McNally & Co., 1978.

Brophy, Jere E., Good, Thomas L., and Nedler, Shari E. *Teaching in the preschool.* New York: Harper & Row, Publishers, Inc., 1975.

Cohen, Dorothy H., and Rudolph, Marguerita. *Kindergarten and early schooling.* Englewood Cliffs, N.J.: Prentice-Hall, Inc., 1977.

Day, M. C., and Parker, R. K. *The preschool in action.* Boston: Allyn & Bacon, Inc., 1972.

Early Childhood Education in Illinois. *Focus on Kindergarten,* 1970.

Evans, Ellis D. The Piagetian mystique. In *Contemporary influences in early childhood education* (2nd ed.). New York: Holt, Rinehart & Winston, Inc., 1975, pp. 193-252.

Furth, Hans G. *Piaget for teachers.* Englewood Cliffs, N.J.: Prentice-Hall, Inc., 1970.

Ginsburg, Herbert, and Opper, Sylvia. *Piaget's theory of intellectual development.* Englewood Cliffs, N.J.: Prentice-Hall, Inc., 1969.

Goodlad, John I., et al. *Looking behind the classroom door.* Worthington, Ohio: Charles A. Jones Publishing Co., 1974.

Harris, Bucher H., and Fisher, Robert J. Distortions in the kindergarten. *Young Children,* 1969, 24(5), 279-284.

Leeper, Sarah Hammond, et al. *Good schools for young children* (3rd ed.) New York: Macmillan Publishing Co., Inc., 1974.

Ohio Association of Classroom Teachers. *Recommended kindergarten guidelines.* Columbus: Ohio Education Association, 1971.

Piaget, Jean, and Inhelder, Barbel. *The psychology of the child.* New York: Basic Books, Inc., Publishers, 1969.

Robison, Helen F. *Exploring teaching in early childhood education.* Boston: Allyn & Bacon, Inc. 1977.

Robison, Helen F., and Spodek, Bernard. *New directions in the kindergarten.* New York: Teachers College Press, 1968.

Singer, Dorothy G. Piglet, Pooh, and Piaget. *Psychology Today,* June 1972, pp. 71-73; 96-97.

Sund, Robert B. *Piaget for educators.* Columbus, Ohio: Charles E. Merrill Publishing Co., 1976.

Weber, Evelyn. *The kindergarten: its encounter with educational thought in America.* New York: Teachers College Press, 1969.

Weikart, David P., et al. *The cognitively oriented curriculum.* Urbana: University of Illinois, 1971.

Wills, Clarice, and Lindberg, Lucille. *Kindergarten for today's children.* Chicago: Follett Publishing Co., 1967.

Kindergarten models*
Traditional

Isaacs, Susan. *The nursery years.* New York: Schocken Books, Inc., 1968.

---

*For in depth study of various models of kindergarten, the reader is referred to these sources.

Isaacs, Susan. *The children we teach.* New York: Schocken Books, Inc., 1971.

Reed, K. H., *The nursery school: a human relationship laboratory* (3rd ed.). Philadelphia: W. B. Saunders Co., 1960.

Sears, P. S., and Dowley, E. M. Research on teaching in the nursery school. In N. L. Gage (Ed.), *Handbook of research on teaching.* Chicago: Rand McNally & Co., 1963.

Weikart, David. A traditional nursery program revisited. In Ronald K. Parker (Ed.), *The preschool in action: exploring early childhood programs.* Boston: Allyn & Bacon, Inc., 1972.

Montessori

Evans, Ellis D. The Montessori method. In *Contemporary influences in early childhood education* (2nd ed.). New York: Holt, Rinehart & Winston, 1975, pp. 255-290.

Lillard, Paula Polk. *Montessori, a modern approach.* New York: Schocken Books, Inc., 1972.

Montessori, Maria. *The absorbent mind.* Madras, India: Theosophical Publishing House, 1949.

Montessori, Maria. *The Montessori method.* New York: Schocken Books, Inc., 1964.

Orem, R. D. *Montessori, her method and the movement: what you need to know.* New York: G. P. Putnam's Sons, 1974.

Standing, E. M. *The Motessori revolution in education* (6th ed.). New York: Schocken Books, Inc., 1971.

Open

Cazden, Courtney, and Williams, S. M. *Infant school.* Newton, Mass.: Educational Development Center, 1968.

Day, Barbara. *Open learning in early childhood.* New York: Macmillan Publishing Co., Inc., 1975.

Evans, Ellis D. Open education. In *Contemporary influences in early childhood education* (2nd ed.). New York: Holt, Rinehart & Winston, 1975, pp. 291-326.

Featherstone, Joseph. *Schools where children learn.* New York: Liderwright Publishing Corp., 1971.

Hertzberg, Alvin, and Stone, Edward F. *Schools are for children: an American approach to the open classroom.* New York: Schocken Books, Inc., 1974.

Neill, A. S. *Summerhill: A radical approach to child rearing.* New York: Hart Publishing Co., Inc., 1960.

Taylor, Joy. *Organizing the open classroom: a teachers' guide to the integrated day.* New York: Schocken Books, Inc., 1972.

Weber, Lillian. *The English infant school and informal education.* Englewood Cliffs, N.J.: Prentice-Hall, Inc., 1971.

10 *Kindergarten: programs and practices*

Follow-through (Bank Street model)

Biber, Barbara. *Preschool education.* New York: Bank Street College of Education Publications, 1964.

Biber, Barbara. A view of preschool education. In B. Boegehold, H. Cuffaro, W. Hooks, and G. Klopf (Eds.), *Education before five.* New York: Bank Street College of Education Publications, 1964.

Biber, Barbara. The developmental-interaction approach: Bank Street College of Education. In M. C. Day and R. K. Parker (Eds.). *The preschool in action* (2nd ed.) Boston: Allyn & Bacon, Inc., 1976.

Biber, Barbara, Shapiro, E., and Wickens, D.: *Promoting cognitive power: a developmental interaction point of view.* Washington, D.C.: National Association for the Education of Young Children, 1971.

Cuffaro, Harriet. The developmental-interaction approach. In H. Cuffaro, W. Hooks, and G. Klopf (Eds.), *Education before five.* New York: Bank Street College of Education Publications, 1977.

CHAPTER 2

The five-year-old and the teacher

A five-year-old is a symphony of movement and sound (Widmer, 1968, p. 20)

Anyone who has ever observed that "symphony of movement and sound" that is the five-year-old knows the quicksilver-like quality of the kindergarten child—knows that the five is also a wriggler, a bundle of restless energy, and a creature of feeling who laughs and cries easily, loves to talk, and changes direction and behavior in the blink of an eye. As one five said, "I'm a why-er; you're a becauser!"

Because the "why-er" is such a bundle of curiosity, a seeker of information who responds with spontaneity and likes to make decisions and choices, the adult who works with the five-year-old needs to capitalize fully on all available resources and, most important, become an astute observer.

CHARACTERISTICS OF THE FIVE-YEAR-OLD

To accurately describe the five-year-old who enters kindergarten is a demanding task. Many kinds of descriptions are found in the literature. A leaflet published by the Association for Childhood Education International (ACEI) states:

1. Most fives can skip smoothly and well and keep time to music. They are deft in handling small objects.
2. Most fives can solve simple problems, like to finish what they are doing, and put away their toys in orderly fashion. They can carry a plot in a story and count to ten intelligently, are eager to know realities, but cannot always distinguish fact and fancy; can carry play from one day to another and have fairly vivid appreciation of today and tomorrow.
3. Most five-year-olds can answer questions more or less to the point.
4. Most five-year-olds are relatively independent and self-reliant, dependable and obedient, and protective toward younger playmates and siblings. (Fowler, undated, p. 1)

Other characteristics of the kindergartner are often mentioned: this child is eager, active, curious, questioning, investigating, untiring, and yearning, with a tremendous drive for physical experiencing.

McFadden (1972, p. 33) tells us that the kindergarten child functions as a psychological whole and that "behavior is screened through the fine meshes of his image of himself in a particular setting at any specific moment."

Those who work with the kindergarten child know that this is a period of slow growth as the child grows taller and the hands and feet grow larger. The five-year-old is also beginning to be capable of self-criticism, and is eager and ready for some responsibility. Yet the child still needs assurance of being loved and valued while he is learning to do things independently and is developing his own powers.

Perhaps the most perceptive observations are those made by Hymes (1968, pp. 25-36), who describes the child as:

1. Young
2. Not a good sitter
3. Not good at keeping quiet
4. Shy
5. Highly egocentric
6. Wanting to feel proud, big, and important
7. Having a private dream world
8. Very tender
9. A beginner
10. Hungry for stimulation
11. Earthy, practical, concrete minded
12. Acquiescent
13. Illiterate

What do such qualities mean? What are the implications for program development and a nurturing environment for learning? A long-time advocate of young children, Hymes (p. 25) contends that "young children are a special breed. Three- and four- and five-year-olds are exceptional children. They have their own kind of exceptionality that marks them off and demands special approaches."

An extended discussion of the fives can be found in the works by Cohen and Rudolph (1977) and Leeper et al. (1969). An excellent developmental level chart is offered by Todd and Heffernan (1977).

If you have ever worked or lived with a five-year-old, each descriptive term should bring to mind an incident or illustration. The five-year-old may be young, a beginner, and illiterate, but comments about immaturity, such as those so often heard ("John is so immature"), indicate lack of understanding on the part of the speaker, lip service to the principles of individual differences, or perhaps an individual ill suited for involvement with the child of this age. Yes, the five-year-old kindergartner *is* a tender beginner—a beginner at life—and kindergarten should be, for that child, a propitious beginning.

NEEDS OF THE FIVE-YEAR-OLD

What are the needs of this child we have just described? What expectations should rightfully be met? Many professional position papers express the belief of and need for:

1. Respect of the individual child
2. A rich, multisensory environment
3. A caring teacher who is professionally qualified
4. Active participation of the child in the learning experience
5. A curriculum that nurtures, through social interactions, awareness, understanding, and appreciation of the richness of cultural variations within society
6. Interdependence of the home and school
7. A support system, including personnel, facilities, and finances, to implement the program

A 1960-1961 brochure issued by ACEI (pp. 1-2) states in answer to the question, "What does a kindergarten child need?":

1. He needs a friendly teacher and a homelike classroom.
2. He needs opportunities to explore and understand his world.
3. He needs a maximum of freedom and physical activity.
4. He needs protection, too.
5. He needs help in learning to live with other people.
6. He needs to "act his age." Growing up is the child's main business.

These priorities are *still* priorities after almost two decades. The young five-year-old still needs caring, security, continuity, and support; the child also needs to "experience" and to be five years old!

Recall the characteristics or descriptions expressed earlier. Most early childhood authorities agree on several significant needs:
1. Opportunities for dramatic play—expressive activities
2. Opportunities to use imaginative and creative talents
3. Time to observe, experiment, listen, and talk
4. A gradually evolving, balanced curricular program
5. A calm, tension-free, yet stimulating, challenging, and welcoming environment
6. Problem-solving, choice-making situations at the child's own level
7. Opportunities to achieve in terms of maturation and acceptance at the child's own level of accomplishment
8. Caring, transactional adults—nurturing in attitude and action
9. Time for action and participation, as well as time for quiet and solitude

The five-year-old is acquiescent, with faith in the adult caregiver whether teacher, parent, or concerned "other." Eagerness is easily squelched. The ego is fragile. The power of words—the power of the adult model—are great.

Let us consider, then, the teacher of the five-year-old.

CHARACTERISTICS OF THE TEACHER

As was true with the five-year-old, the task of defining a *good* teacher is difficult. Studies of the characteristics of a good teacher are legion. Articles abound in the research literature and in popular literature. Most of us have experienced good teachers; and as kindergartners, we probably had "good" teachers. Most of us have definite opinions about good teaching—but a teacher of kindergarten is special.

What do we know about the kindergarten teacher? In 1974 an Ohio Kindergarten Sur-

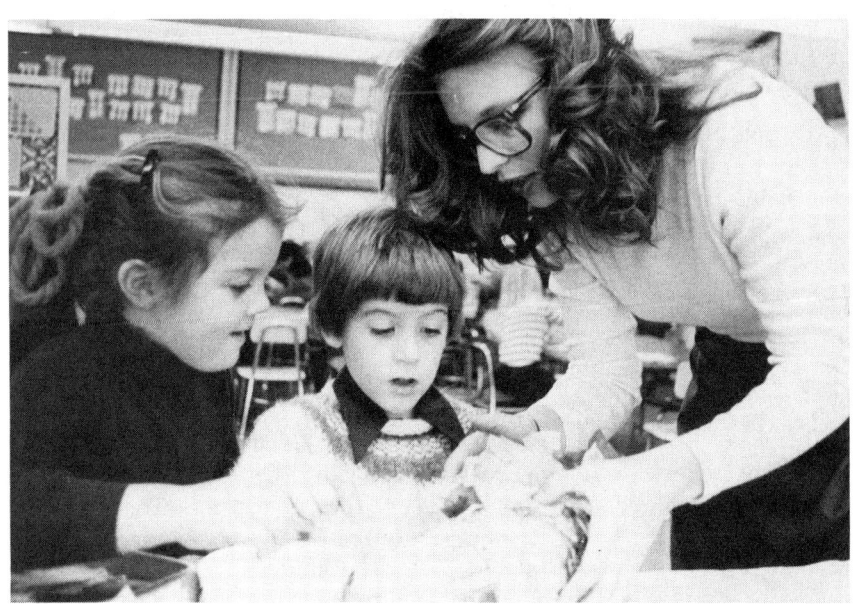

vey Questionnaire sent to 333 Ohio kindergarten teachers, with 272 responding, revealed in part:

1. A little over half of the teachers had seven or more years of experience.
2. Fifty-four percent of the Ohio kindergarten teachers were 40 or older.
3. About 10 percent of the kindergarten teachers were black.
4. Twenty-one percent reported that they held an elementary rather than a kindergarten-primary certificate and a college degree. (Ad hoc Kindergarten Guidelines Committee, 1976, p. 3)

There are probably similar findings to be reported throughout the country.

A somewhat different approach is taken by Hymes (1968, pp. 82-85) in a discussion of the many faces of a teacher:

1. A teacher must be an astute purchaser. . . .
2. A teacher must be a persnickety picker-and-chooser. . . .
3. A teacher must be a scavenger. . . .
4. A teacher must be a community planning engineer. . . .
5. A teacher must be a safety engineer. . . .
6. A teacher must be a maintenance specialist. . . .
7. A teacher must be a cautious, thoughtful manager.

How most would-be or "already" kindergarten teachers can chuckle in agreement!

In another vein, Hymes (pp. 24-25) emphasizes that good (kindergarten, early childhood) teachers:

1. Keep their goals utterly clear.
2. Are child-centered.
3. Are society-centered.
4. Are subject-matter centered.
5. Have the tools they need to do their jobs.

Again, recalling the characteristics and needs of that vital kindergartner who has such high hopes and brings such eagerness, if we had our "druthers," what qualities would we hope for in a teacher? From extensive experience in kindergartens and from conversations with administrators, parents, and, yes, even children, we have gathered the following descriptions. (Does your list include at least some of these?)

1. A fully certified, professionally competent, experienced individual
2. A caring, aware, patient, and warm person
3. A consistent, flexible, and secure person, with genuine liking for children
4. A person acquainted with, accepting of, and appreciative of the different cultures, customs, and languages children bring
5. A person with initiative and resourcefulness in working with children and adults in developing and adapting a program to meet individual needs and preferences
6. A creative person who enjoys the challenge of designing and developing materials to "match" each child
7. Someone willing to spend the necessary time to work with parents and others through the critical kindergarten year
8. An energetic, physically fit person possessing a sense of humor and a positive attitude toward life
9. A "growing" individual
10. A responsible role model
11. One who knows that all five-year-olds are special and in turn is special to all five-year-olds

As we consider the kindergartner and the kindergarten teacher, we are reminded that some children naturally stand out, some children must be sought out, and some children literally blend into the group. A personalized, empathetic relationship between teacher and five-year-old is of high priority in this contemporary society.

The kindergarten teacher would do well to read extensively, observe critically, listen selectively and keenly, question, consider thoughtfully, and walk in the moccasins of the five-year-old. A very astute and perceptive teacher would know, or be aware of, all of the dimensions of the life of the kindergartner.

We need to provide stability; we need to help children understand themselves; and we need to understand the value systems of the fives. We need to take children as they are *at present*.

The basic characteristics and needs of the five-year-old remain essentially the same. However, in contemporary society, anyone involved with the kindergartner must be aware of and informed of the changing sociological structure and value systems. The reader is urged to thoughtfully consider statements of Chamberlin and Girona (1976) in their provocative article in *Educational Leadership* and an analytical statement by Cohen (1974) in *Childhood Education*. Both articles are generalized to the condition of the young child, yet strong implications are evident for the teacher of the kindergarten. We need to ask ourselves as Cohen does, "Who is today's child? Who is the five-year-old?"

As we consider the learning environment, the qualities and expectations of the fives, as well as our own competencies and expectations, the answers we give are critical. We know that the five-year-old is the child of *today*.

The following account was shared by a kindergarten teacher. We appreciate her willingness to permit its inclusion in the text.

My first days as a kindergarten teacher

Alicia Jimenez

What does it take to be a kindergarten teacher? A lot of organization, planning, patience, creativity, adaptability, a genuine desire to really focus on a child and listen to what he has to communicate . . . these are only some of the qualities necessary to survive and to succeed in the kindergarten classroom.

My first days as a kindergarten teacher were as interesting as I expected them to be. I was mildly surprised (and somehow elated) to find that many circumstances in a kindergarten classroom elicited a kind of spontaneous mothering, to which I responded without second thoughts. I found myself tucking in Brad's shirttails, fixing Estelle's loose braids, wiping several wet noses, and reading or talking to a child who thought nothing of, and required no invitation to, making himself comfortable on my lap.

The children in my class are a variety of little people. Pam is a child with the physique of a two- or three-year-old. She is retarded . . . how severely, I cannot tell. She cannot distinguish colors or shapes. She cannot draw, though she makes little squiggles on her paper. She cannot cut. She does not speak . . . she only smiles. She does not have the blank facial expression common to many retardates, but somehow her response to her environment is very bland.

On my fourth day with the children, I read *Henny Penny* to them. They really enjoyed the story. As they were getting ready for home, I could hear Pam repeating all the way to the

Continued.

My first days as a kindergarten teacher, cont'd

coatrack, "Luck-ky Duck-ky, Luck-ky Duck-ky." It was the first time I heard her speak at all! She responded to the stories I read in class, but the responses were so subtle they were hardly there.

The other children "mother" Pam. They hold her hand in line, they wait on her, they play with her. They even cut for her! I find spontaneous peer tutoring going on at Pam's table without any encouragement from me. The children respond to her as an equal. It is a sad thought that some of these children may learn prejudice as they grow up. They have none at this stage.

Derek wears a patch over his left eye because he has amblyopia (lazy eye). He participates in class activities, but he can be found lying down on the corner of the rug during sharing time at the end of the day with a mild complaint that he is tired.

Then there is Abe. He is very self-conscious and hesitates to join dancing activities. He would rather paint or draw or cut. He is such a creative child. He adds his own touch to simple art projects. (He made high-heeled shoes for his Halloween witch instead of the plain old triangles the project called for.) He creates things out of blocks, Lego, boxes, etc. He is very independent in class. He is also articulate. This rather independent child sits on his father's lap and sucks his thumb when the lengthy church services make him sleepy. He also yells, "Hi, Teach!" across many rows of seats in church when he spots me and enjoys making conversation after service is over.

And there are the bright children who are verbally proficient. Three girls are just about ready to read. They and a few others are the clean, loved, attractive children whose happy home lives are evident in the laughter in their eyes. Every class has children like them who are so easy to love.

The children respond very well to songs, both live and recorded. One early morning I was testing a record on low volume so as not to distract the children from whatever they

REFERENCES AND SUGGESTED READINGS

Ad hoc Kindergarten Guidelines Committee. *Recommended kindergarten guidelines, state of Ohio*. Columbus: Ohio State Department of Education, 1978.

Association for Childhood Education International. *What are kindergartens for?* 1960-61 Membership Service Bulletin A. Washington, D.C.: The Association.

Broman, Betty L. *The early years in childhood education*. Chicago: Rand McNally & Co., 1978.

Chamberlin, Leslie J., and Girona, Ricardo. Our children are changing. *Educational Leadership*, 1976. 33(4), 301-305.

Cohen, Dorothy. This day's child in school. *Childhood Education*, October 1974, pp. 8-15.

Cohen, Dorothy, and Rudolph, Marguerita. What are kindergarten children like? In *Kindergarten and early schooling*. Englewood Cliffs, N.J.: Prentice-Hall, Inc., 1977, pp. 23-44.

Fowler, Marie. *What to expect of the fours and fives*. Leaflet No. I. Washington, D.C.: Association for Childhood Education International, undated.

Hymes, James L., Jr. *Teaching the child under six* (2nd ed.). Columbus, Ohio: Charles E. Merrill Publishing Co., 1974.

were doing. I was amused to see several children dancing to the music without taking time out from what they were doing. Some were swaying, some were nodding, others were tapping their feet in rhythm to the music.

I introduced the song "Half the greatest sounds in the whole wide world . . ." to the children. We did it several times, and I asked the children to think of a sound that we could make together as a group and to say it when I pointed to them in the course of the song. One little girl snapped her fingers, opened her eyes wide and sang, "Give me a cow." The children responded, "Moo, moo," without making fun of her. They just kept right on going.

Being with kindergarten children opens one's mind to other possibilities of thought. During a field trip to a supermarket, the children were taken to the various preparation rooms of the store. A child asked me what the things were that were hanging on the meat hooks. I said, "Meat. That's what your mom makes into steaks and roasts." He was silent for a moment, took a deep breath, and repeated his question: "I know, but what was it when it was still walking around?"

Being with kindergarten children also awakens one's sense of humor, however dormant it may have become through the years. I overhear comments such as this girl's remark to her "family" at the housekeeping area: "Don't believe everything that's said . . . [dramatic pause] unless they say it like it's really true."

At the end of the day we walk the children to the buses. On my second day with them, Danielle came up to me with outstretched arms and said, "I like you," and gave me a kiss. Twenty other children followed suit. I looked around, embarrassed because the buses were waiting and all the bus drivers were smiling. As I hesitated, another (more experienced, mischievous) kindergarten teacher said, "Just pucker up, lady!"

Teaching kindergarten is a refreshing change. There are no defense mechanisms to penetrate, no pretenses. The responsibility is great, too, for it is easy to hurt these trusting children. This year sets the tone for all their future schooling.

Leeper, Sarah Hammond, et al. Working with exceptional children. In *Good schools for young children.* New York: Macmillan Publishing Co., Inc., 1969, pp. 422-437.

Looking toward learning. Handbook. Hudson, Ohio, Public Schools, undated.

McClinton, Barbara Sweany, and Blanche, Garner Meier. *Beginnings: psychology of early childhood.* St. Louis: The C. V. Mosby Co., 1978.

McFadden, Dennis N. (Ed.). *Early childhood development programs and services: planning for action.* Washington, D.C.: National Association for the Education of Young Children, 1972.

Todd, Virginia Edmiston, and Heffernan, Helen. Understanding preschool children. In *The years before school: guiding preschool children* (3rd ed.). New York: Macmillan Publishing Co., Inc., 1977, pp. 33-78.

Widmer, E. L. In kindergarten. In Joe L. Frost (Ed.), *Early childhood education rediscovered.* New York: Holt, Rinehart & Winston, 1968.

CHAPTER 3

Beginnings

BEFORE SCHOOL BEGINS

Today, most states are mandating that school districts provide kindergarten programs. As more kindergartens are being added, renewed interest in upgrading kindergarten programming and providing the best possible orientation and school beginning for our nation's five-year-olds is evident.

For some children, stepping foot into kindergarten is exciting and long awaited. They are eager and ready to begin. For others, it may be the first experience away from home. As Spodek (1972, p. 241) points out, "The beginning of school is always fraught with some fear, for the new situation raises a set of questions for the child who does not know exactly what to expect." Before the kindergarten year begins, careful consideration needs to be given to planning effective orientation programs for children and their parents.

Orientation to kindergarten

There are many ways of orienting entering kindergarten children and their parents to school. Some schools plan a springtime visit (sometimes called "Kindergarten Roundup") wherein children visit the kindergarten room for an hour or so while their parents talk with the principal, school nurse, school psychologist, and other team members. In some school districts a short screening assessment is administered to each incoming student. At this time, parents are sometimes asked to fill out an information sheet on their child (see Appendix B for example). This visit, carefully planned, is not a time when the class shows their visitors *all* the things they know how to do; instead, the teacher, with the assistance of the class, might share some of the regular activities with the visitors. These might include working with puzzles and blocks, creating a picture, and singing songs. Serving juice and cookies and having story time is a good way to end the visit to the kindergarten.

One school system we know has the parents of entering kindergarten children register their children early in the spring. Soon after registration, a child who is presently enrolled in kindergarten invites a neighbor child who will be entering kindergarten in the fall to attend a class session. This is carefully planned by the kindergarten teacher and the parents of the children involved. Spacing the visitations of the children allows the visitor to see a typical day in kindergarten. It also makes it possible for the children to take responsibility for helping the guest get involved and feel comfortable. To show how eager some children are for their visit, the following incident is related. On one occasion in late spring while supervising a student teacher, a kindergarten teacher discovered an extra little girl in the class. There on the floor, gathered around the student teacher, were the afternoon kindergarten children plus a young visitor. The little girl was smiling and looking as if she were in seventh heaven. Without saying a word to the child, and knowing quite sure who the child was, the teacher went swiftly to the office and called the mother. The mother remarked, "You must be mistaken that Karen is at school; she's playing in the front yard." The teacher asked the mother to look again. Sure enough, Karen was not in the front yard playing. She had seen the bus pull up in front of her friend's house next door, and, being anxious to visit school, got on the bus with her friend and came to school as if it had been planned that way. (Previously, Karen's mother had told her that she would soon be visiting the kindergarten.) The bus driver, observing the happy, waiting child, thought this was Karen's day for visitation. The kindergarten teacher, after taking everything into consideration, allowed Karen to spend the remainder of the session with the children.

Home visits before school begins

Home visits are one way for children, parents, and teacher to get acquainted. Some teachers visit the children's homes within the days allotted before the opening day of school. These kinds of visits are time-consuming but often very rewarding. Some parents are pleased to have teachers come to their homes—others are hesitant and reluctant. (If you are considering making home visits, be sure and check on the advisability of this with your administrator. If home visits are made, the time for the visit should be mutually agreed on by you and the parents.) Home visits should not be lengthy, drawn-out affairs. Visits are a time for getting acquainted and sharing information. In some school districts kindergarten handbooks are distributed to the parents at this time. Handbooks could also be given to parents at registration or orientation time. (See Chapter 10.)

Staggered entrance

One of the most popular methods of helping kindergarten children become acquainted with their teacher and school is to have staggered entrance of the children during the first week of school or during the week prior to school opening. Some schools have two children and two parents visiting every half hour. In this way, much closer attention can be given to the children and their parents. The children can explore the room; the teacher and parents can exchange information. The room should be colorful, warm, and inviting, but not overstimulating. Puzzles, books, and other appropriate activities can be made available for the children to handle and explore.

Some teachers have staggered entrance in which ten or more children come in the morning session, and ten in the afternoon session on the first day (Monday) of school. On Tuesday and Wednesday, this procedure is repeated. (In some schools parents attend the session with the children on the first day. They fill out information forms and observe general kindergarten routine.) On Thursday, the total group attends the entire session. Before planning any type of staggered entrance, however, one must be sure to check state regulations in regard to required days of attendance for kindergarten children.

No matter what method or combination of methods are used to help children become acquainted with school, it is important that the introduction be as smooth and pleasant as possible for all involved.

Knowing the community

One of the best ways for a teacher new to a school system to learn about the community is to drive around and observe the various neighborhoods from which children will be coming to school. Another useful approach is to ride the school buses the first few days of school if it can be arranged. This not only helps the teacher become acquainted with the school district, but also may make kindergarten children feel much more secure—knowing that their teacher or another kindergarten teacher will be on the bus to help them. Before attempting such a procedure, however, one should check with the principal and local superintendent in regard to the legality of teachers riding buses for educational purposes. State laws may differ on such matters.

It is often helpful to talk to members within the community in regard to socioeconomic factors, and also geographic-demographic factors, that have or might have an influence on the education provided for the children under one's care. It is also a good idea to become familiar with community resources and agencies (both people and places), such as family services, the health department, dairies, the fire department, and the like. Community members can often give clues and understandings that could be helpful in designing a program and planning for the year ahead.

Basic planning

Long before school begins, a teacher needs to plan and prepare for the year ahead. Following are a list of suggestions that may be helpful:

1. Check supplies. Keep a running account so that supplies can be reordered before they are depleted.
2. Work to make the room attractive but not overly stimulating.
3. Check and arrange for necessary repairs on equipment.
4. Try to picture children in the room and arrange the furniture and equipment according to the type of program you plan, the number of children you will have, and the most efficient ways of working together.
5. Know the building, personnel, and resources available to you and the children. Know the rules about the school's operation—bus schedules, fire and tornado drills, snack provisions, etc.
6. Develop a system for keeping records. Have file folders ready and labeled. Keep records on each child.
7. Be sure each child has a cubby or place to leave clothing, possessions, and school papers.

THE FIRST DAY

It is only natural that kindergarten teachers (and in particular first-year teachers) have anxious moments about the first day and the first week of school. The new teacher, lacking experience, is apt to be a bit tense and unsure; and "seasoned" teachers often indicate that they too experience some anxiety until the children's immediate needs are met and all feel reasonably comfortable. Although situations differ, and because many schools do not provide kindergarten guides, the following suggestions may be of help, especially for the beginning teacher. Remember that these are only suggestions; adapt them to fit your situation.

Greet the children at the door. If possible, call each child by name. (Some children will appear at the door with name tags pinned on them by their parents. Many teachers have an appealing name tag ready for each child. Some teachers prefer to pin the tags on the backs of the children's clothing with safety pins. Another way to make and distribute name tags is at registration time. As children are registered, their names can be printed on a tagboard that has been precut. This is then given to the parent for use on the first day of school. Whatever system is used, care should be taken that the tags do not get in the children's way or make them feel uncomfortable.) Invite each child to sit on the rug or at a designated area with others until all have arrived. At this point it might be risky to permit the children to explore the room, since you may have difficulty getting them all back together without a great deal of confusion. In cases where buses might be arriving at different times, permit the children to explore the room, look at books, draw a picture, etc.

When most or all of the children have arrived, sit down with the group. Congratulate them and welcome them to kindergarten. Introduce yourself by saying, "I am _____. What is your name?" Do not insist that children tell you their names. Some may be reluctant to do so. Assure them if they came by bus or car that they will be picked up later.

Briefly discuss what it is like to be in a group and explain that you will be getting together in groups each day. If a child is clutching something, be sure to ask about it. For example, if a child is holding a teddy, ask him to show it to the other children. The child may even want to talk about it. This will encourage other children to share possessions they might have with them. It is extremely important to be sensitive to ways that will help each child feel comfortable and accepted. Talk about some of the things in the room while you are seated on the floor. Before leaving the rug, establish some signal for bringing the children back to the same location. A chord struck on the piano would provide a good signal. Then take the children on a short tour of the room, indicating where things are located. During the tour of the room, be sure to show the children where the bathroom is, explain when they may go, and how they can tell when it is in use. Some teachers provide a string of colored beads or use some object or picture to hang on the outside of the toilet door when it is in use. (This would apply to a toilet that is located within the room setting.) Show them light switches, how controls operate, how to flush the toilet, and where to wash their hands. In cases where toilets are located in another part of the building, take the children to the location early in the session. Children should not have to worry about this aspect on their very first day of school. More than one child has had an accident or worried unduly because of not knowing what to do about using the bathroom. If the children are taken as a group to the bathroom, this is a good time to allow them to get drinks.

After the children have been shown the kindergarten room, assemble back on the rug. At this time, they may choose something in the room to try out, such as blocks, puzzles, drawing with crayons and making a picture, using clay, etc. Be sure puzzles do not contain too many pieces, since children may become embarrassed or frustrated if they cannot get the pieces back together in their proper places. Allow about 30 minutes for this. Avoid making a lot of rules on the first day. Simply tell the children that materials and equipment are put back where we find them.

If a child starts to cry, comfort the youngster. Speak in a quiet voice. Be confident. Have patience, remain calm, and try to divert the anxious child.

As children choose an activity, move freely about the room, helping them get acquainted and involved. Introduce them to materials and interest areas. When possible, label materials properly. Let this part of the first day be one of mainly trying out and experimentation.

Give the signal, previously established, to return to the rug. Sing some songs the children already know. Teach a finger play or two.

Sometime during the session, take the children outside. Instead of using the playground on the very first day, it might be wise to choose a grassy area and play a game such

as "Duck, Duck, Goose" or a circle game that involves using a large rubber ball. This suggestion is made because some playgrounds are so large that they may be overwhelming to children on the first day. However, show the children where the playground is and indicate that they will be able to play on it in a day or two. Before allowing them to use the playground equipment, be sure they know how to follow directions and that you have made very clear any rules regarding such use. Ideally, choose a time to use the playground when other classes are not outside.

If the children have cubbies or lockers, you may need to help them identify their own in some way. For example, the children could look through a magazine and cut out a picture they especially like. (Some may need help here. This activity might be appropriate on another day.) Put a loop of masking tape on the back of the picture and have each child place it on his cubby or locker. Later, each child's name could be placed by the picture. Some teachers prefer to have each child's name already on the cubby when school begins. Children are proud and happy to have a place for their possessions. Having a compartment of their very own on the first day of school helps promote a feeling of belonging and develops responsibility for caring for school materials and personal treasures. If children come to school with sweaters or other wraps, show them where to place them when they first arrive.

Sometime during the session, a light snack might be served. Before the children leave for home, read them a carefully selected story. This is a delightful way to draw the day to a close. Also, discuss with the children some of the things that they did on their very first day. This will help them remember what

they did so that they can share their experiences with their families. It is also the early stage of evaluation of accomplishments. Tell the children you will be looking forward to seeing them tomorrow (unless there is a plan for staggered entrance). Be sure you have spoken to each child in a personal way sometime during the session. Bid the children goodbye at the door. Try to end the session in a relaxed, unhurried way.

SEPARATION ANXIETY

As more children attend day care and nursery school programs, there seems to be a lessening of separation anxiety between parents and children on that first day of kindergarten. Since many school systems have developed orientation programs in the spring, this has helped to decrease fears on opening day. Nevertheless, teachers need to be aware of and sensitive to the feelings of both parents and children, since it is only natural that some anxieties may appear at this special time. In cases where parents leave their children at the kindergarten door on the first day, teachers should be prepared to deal with separation problems if they occur.

Of course, we need to remember that the independent five-year-old may be very eager to leave mother for the new "world"!

Most kindergarten teachers report, in the case of a crying child, that the child will usually "settle in" once attention becomes diverted to the day's activities. The teacher says goodbye to the parent, asks the child to do the same, takes the youngster's hand, and tries to foster interest in a toy or puzzle. In a few instances, when separation anxiety becomes intense, the parent might be asked to stay for a short period of time in another room of the school until the crying child seems settled. (A cup of coffee or tea would be much appreciated by the anxious parent.)

There is no best way of dealing with separation anxiety. Individual children will require different approaches. When possible, it is helpful to have a student teacher, an aide, or other person available to assist with the myriad problems and details that occur on opening day.

THE NEXT FEW DAYS

The following are suggestions for the next few days.

Discuss with the children some of the basic rules they will need to remember. Be natural and confident in your presentation of rules before each activity is initiated. In this way, the children will know what is expected. Anticipate that reminders of these rules will be necessary until they are firmly established. Many discipline problems can be averted if this procedure is followed. Establish a routine and adhere to it as closely as possible. Demonstrate with the children how they should leave the building to get to the playground. If this route is the one designated in case of a fire, you might tell them that this is the way to leave the building should the fire alarm sound. Check with the principal concerning all procedures and rules regarding fire drills. Without creating any anxiety, practice going through the fire drill procedure. Choose a capable and reliable student to lead the line. Later, train other children to do the same.

During the next few days you might also take the children on a tour of the building. Do not try to visit all areas. On one day, include the library and the principal's office. On another, make a visit to the custodian's quarters and perhaps the nurse's office. You might want to ask the nurse to come to the kindergarten room first. This helps to eliminate some of the fears children might have about the clinic. When visiting the nurse, you might ask her to weigh and measure a few of the children. The remaining children could be told that they would be having their turns in the next few days.

Another important point to remember on these beginning days is to limit the number of materials and pieces of equipment available to the children in the room. Too much, too soon can be overwhelming and often leads to confusion. It is also wise to refrain from using the larger wheel toys until the children are well acquainted with the room and know proper usage. Spacing out introduction of equipment and materials also adds interest and variety.

It is imperative to be understanding and responsive to the children during these first days, because what occurs during this time often colors the attitudes and impressions of the children and parents concerning the school and may well influence a supportive or nonsupportive learning environment for both teacher and children.

KINDERGARTEN SCREENING

Observation and experience indicate that prevention is more effective than remediation. To develop appropriate and effective educational programs for children, one must have pertinent information on each child. Identification and early diagnosis of possible learning difficulties or related conditions provides baseline data and greatly facilitates the process of accurately prescribing and planning an educational program wherein optimal development can take place. Screening of kindergarten children not only helps identify those with health problems as possible learning difficulties, but also may be beneficial in identifying the more advanced or gifted youngster.

Screening brings parents to a higher level of awareness concerning their child's competencies. It also provides early identification of problems, so that referrals can be made early to appropriate specialists, team members, and agencies. Most important, it gives the kindergarten teacher more information concerning the competency levels of the children.

Many school systems throughout the country have developed kindergarten screening programs. Often, initial screening conducted in the spring of the year preceding kindergarten includes testing in such areas as speech and hearing, vision, and motor skills. Systems differ in regard to test areas and criteria. Usually, more comprehensive testing is conducted in the fall after school has begun. If problems or potential problems are discovered in the spring, the summer months can be used to work on these deficiencies. Some schools provide kindergarten parents with lists of helpful suggestions and activities to do with their children during the summer preceding school. If some method of screening is used, however, it is imperative that parents be aware that undue pressure on children after initial screening should be avoided. The school and parents must work closely together in finding ways to correct deficiencies before they become major problems. We also strongly recommend more cooperation and communication between specialists (outside the school) and the school team. For screening to be truly effective, better communication between the schools, the home, and other agencies is necessary.

In some systems kindergarten teachers do a major share of the screening. Working with children on a one-to-one basis is invaluable. Close observation of them becomes possible as they respond to test items. Many teachers report that by administering a good portion of the screening program themselves, immediate prescriptive measures and adaptations of curriculum can be programmed to help each child.

A survey of professional organization position papers reveals common agreement on a multifaceted screening design. Any comprehensive kindergarten screening program includes an assessment of the child's:

1. General health, including allergies and/or diseases
2. Vision, including ability to see nearby objects and screening for amblyopia
3. Hearing; including acuity and discrimination between sounds.
4. Oral language patterns and enunciation
5. Fine and gross motor abilities
6. General family information
7. Visual perception, visual memory, visual discrimination, and visual sequencing
8. Auditory facility (of spoken word), auditory memory (such as for directions), auditory discrimination, and listening comprehension
9. Basic early skills (e.g., knowledge of numbers, letters, and colors; ability to categorize things; vocabulary; common cultural referents—animals, social roles, school roles; ability to follow oral directions; knowledge of relationships of words)
10. Social and emotional maturity

Skills and knowledge needed by the child for a successful kindergarten experience serve as the basis for screening. The teacher and curriculum specialists should assume the primary role in the development and implementation of the screening, and a team approach (nurse, psychologist, speech therapist), should be part of the overall evaluation process. "Ideally, all persons involved in the education of the child should have input in the development and administration of the screening device to assure that useful information is derived and that the individuals dealing with the child will have an opportunity to observe his performance," (Ad Hoc

Kindergarten Guidelines Committee, 1978, p. 44).

Results of screening should be understandable to the teacher. In addition, children should have an opportunity to adjust to the school experience prior to screening (assessment of social behavior may be an integral part of the screening process after the child passes this adjustment period).

The limited predictive value of standard intellectual assessments (i.e., IQ tests) for very young children, the limited diagnostic information derived from these tests, and the dangers of abuse of the information taken from these tests suggest that standard intellectual assessments should be avoided as a routine part of screening procedures. When results of screening procedures suggest severe and uniform deficits, the use of standard intellectual assessments should be considered. Parental consent is necessary before a specific assessment can be performed (Ad Hoc Kindergarten Guidelines Committee, 1978, p. 45).

The value and meaningfulness of screening for both school and home increases in direct proportion to parental involvement in the screening process. There is also an obligation on the part of the school to share any results with parents. As previously indicated, parents may be provided with at-home activities for their children. Parents must especially be informed of any suspected deficiencies, such as in vision or hearing.

Written information derived from screening is confidential, as are any other test data. Only those professionals in the school demonstrating a need to know should have access to the child's files. Written parental consent is necessary prior to release of data to outside agencies.

Developmental screening in early childhood: A guide, by Samuel J. Meisels (1979), has been published by the National Association of Young Children. Schools will find this publication a helpful source in designing kindergarten screening programs.

By way of summary, it is important to state that there is no substitute for a competent, professional teacher observing children carefully and systematically and then translating those astute observations into an individualized curriculum for each child, thus ensuring maximum opportunity for a successful kindergarten experience.

REFERENCES AND SUGGESTED READINGS

Ad Hoc Kindergarten Guidelines Committee. *Recommended kindergarten guidelines, state of Ohio.* Columbus, Ohio, 1978.

Cohen, Dorothy H., and Rudolph, Marguerita. *Kindergarten and early schooling.* Englewood Cliffs, N.J.: Prentice-Hall, Inc., 1977.

Hildebrand, Verna. *Introduction to early childhood education* (2nd ed.). New York: Macmillan Publishing Co., Inc., 1976.

Meisels, Samuel J. *Developmental screening in early childhood: a guide.* Washington, D.C.: National Association of Young Children, 1979.

Spodek, Bernard. *Teaching in the early years.* Englewood Cliffs, N.J.: Prentice-Hall, Inc., 1972.

Todd, Virginia Edmiston, and Heffernan, Helen. *The years before school—guiding preschool children.* (3rd ed.). New York: Macmillan Publishing Co., Inc., 1977.

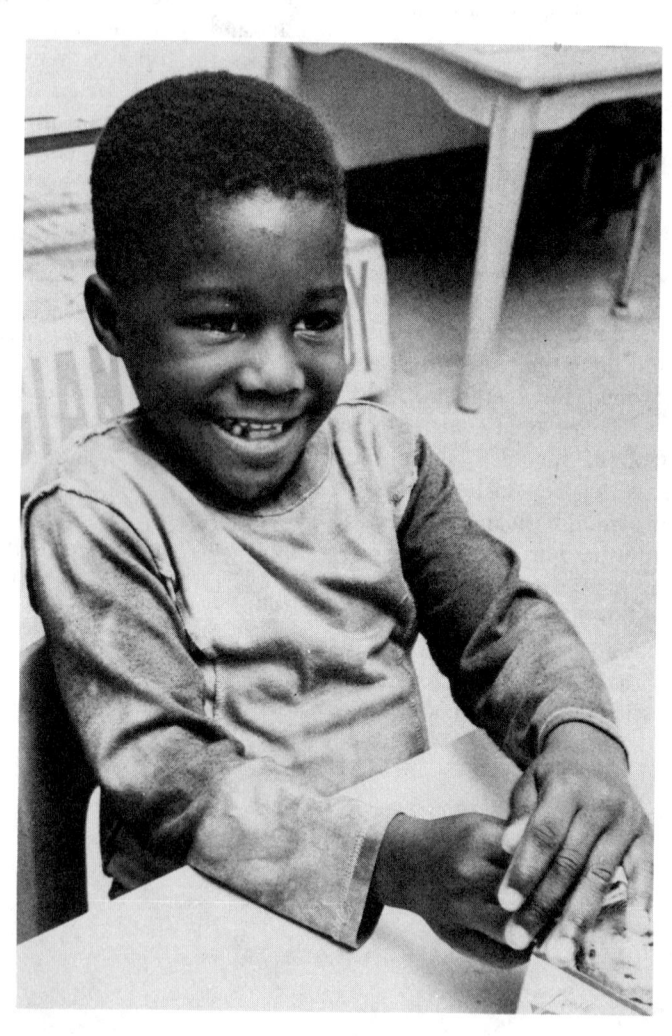

CHAPTER 4
Organizing for instruction

Perhaps the most critical and demanding task of the kindergarten teacher is organizing for instruction.

Organizing for instruction embodies much more than arranging furniture, setting up goals, and developing a curriculum. So many times, such great emphasis is placed on these aspects that the organization and management of the environment both indoors and outdoors becomes neglected. Preplanning is essential in preparing the total environment in order that optimal learning can take place. After the children arrive at school and the teacher assesses their interests and needs, it is often necessary to rearrange and reorganize equipment and materials. How well the teacher "sets the stage" often determines the quality of learning and the attitude of the children toward school.

EQUIPMENT AND INSTRUCTIONAL MATERIALS

The Ohio Ad Hoc Kindergarten Guidelines Committee (1978) offers the following recommendations for the use of equipment and instructional materials:

Learning for the kindergarten child takes place through a variety of concrete sensory experiences and through the use of all the materials in his environment to better understand himself and his world. All types of equipment and instructional materials must be carefully selected to aid the child in playing, learning, and growing, with the teacher and administrator aware of the potential values the child will derive from each. Well-established criteria must be used as a guide in the selection of equipment and instructional materials for the kindergarten, as the degree to which a child expands his knowledge and experience is dependent upon the teacher's understanding and use of appropriate materials and equipment. Materials and equipment, matched to the varied interests, developmental levels, abilities, and learning styles of the young child should be provided in all kindergartens.

Children should have access to a variety of materials, both structured and unstructured, to learn through looking, touching, hearing, smelling, and tasting. Kindergarten children are limited in their ability to deal in abstracts; therefore, they learn best through concrete experiences.

It is desirable to provide a balance between active and passive activities and commercial and teacher-made materials. Kindergarten children have an abundance of energy, but because of their inability to attend to an activity for a prolonged period of time, they tend to tire easily. Children need to change activities often and need a variety of activities and materials to nurture and sustain their interest in learning.

Five-year-olds should have materials and equipment that are durable, easily cleaned, and safe. These ought to be adaptable to many uses and parallel the child's social, physical, mental, and emotional levels of development. Although the patterns of growth are common to all children, the rate of growth is unique, and wide variations in the rates of individual children exist. Varied materials challenge, stimulate new interests, and make the child aware of his creative abilities.

Community Playthings* publishes an excellent pamphlet entitled *Criteria for Selecting Play Equipment for Early Childhood Education*. Criteria are listed and rationale is given for selecting the proper play equipment for young children.

In addition to the basic furniture and furnishings in a kindergarten classroom, the following list of supplemental materials is presented. The materials are grouped according to activity areas or learning centers and are merely *suggested* listings. Each teacher will want to design and equip each center according to the needs and interests of the fives involved.

Block center

Accessory block materials
Airplanes
Boards of different lengths
Hollow blocks
Trains
Trucks and trailers
Unit blocks of various shapes and sizes (maple or hard wood)
Wooden animals
Wooden human figures

Housekeeping and homemaking center

Baby dolls and doll clothes (both sexes and various ethnic groups)
Cooking utensils
Cupboard
Full-length mirror
Ironing board and iron
Doll beds
Dress-up clothing for dramatic play (both sexes)
Lamps
Laundry materials
Refrigerator
Rocking chair

---

*Write to Community Playthings, Rifton, N.Y. 12471.

Table and chairs
Telephone
Sink
Stove
Wooden clock with movable hands

Manipulative center

Bean bags
Clock
Counting blocks
Counting cubes
Games
Geometric form boards
Hand puppets
Large dominoes
Lincoln Logs
Pegboard and pegs
Picture dominoes
Plastic interlocking and snap-in blocks
Snap-together toys
Tinkertoys
Wooden beads for stringing
Wooden puzzles and puzzle rack

Motor center

Balance beam
Balls of various sizes
Basketball hoop
Bean bags
Climbing equipment
Jump ropes
Hoops of various sizes
Parachute
Push-and-pull equipment
Record player and records
Ring toss games
Swings for out-of-doors

Music center

Autoharp
Colored scarves
Music books
Hoops
Piano
Pitch pipe
Record player
Records
Rhythm and melody instruments
Tape recorder and tapes
Tuning fork

Art center*

Brushes (different types and sizes)
Chalk (assorted colors)
Charcoal
Clay (as well as garbage can, plastic, and liner for clay)
Cloth of different types
Collage materials
Crayons (assorted sizes)
Easels and easel clips
Felt-tipped pens, markers
Glue
Paints (tempera, finger, water color, spray)
Paper (for drawing, painting, finger painting, coloring; newspaper and newsprint)
Paste
Pencils (variety of shapes and sizes, also colored)
Pipe cleaners
Scissors
Sponges
Stapler
String
Wire
Yarn

Woodworking center

Brace and bits
C-clamps
Crosscut saws
Dowel rods
Glue
Hammers
Nails (large heads, assorted sizes)
Pliers
Ruler
Screwdrivers and assorted screws
Sandpaper (assorted grades)
Tape measure
Wood (soft pine)
Workbench
Yardstick

Language arts center

Boards (felt, flannel, cork, chalk, peg. magnetic, small bulletin board)
Bookcases
Books

Filmstrip projector and filmstrips
Language games
Listening stations
Pictures and picture file
Primary typewriter
Projector and films (or access to)
Puppets
Record player and records
Tape recorder and tapes
Wipe-off cards

Science center*

Aquarium
Cages for animals
Calendar
Collections
Compass
Exhibits
Magnets
Magnifying glass
Measuring containers
Plants
Prisms
Pulleys
Scales, weights, balances
Seeds
Terrarium
Thermometers (inside and outside, Fahrenheit and Celsius)
Tubing
Tuning fork
Watering can

Mathematics center

Attribute blocks
Calendar
Counting blocks
Counting frames and sticks
Cuisenaire rods
Dominoes
Flannel or felt board and cutouts
Magnetic board and materials
Measuring and weighing materials
Math games (commercial and homemade)
Parquetry blocks
Play money
Scales

---

*A more detailed list of art materials is presented in Chapter 6.

*More detailed lists of science and mathematics materials are presented in Chapter 9.

The ACEI publication *Selecting Educational Equipment and Materials for School and Home* (1976) gives many helpful suggestions for equipping new classrooms and also lists criteria for selecting equipment and materials. In addition, it gives suggested lists of equipment and materials for various age groups and for specified numbers of children.

ROOM ARRANGEMENT AND ORGANIZATION

To motivate and challenge the active five-year-old, the kindergarten classroom should be a warm and inviting place, reflecting the children's interests and ongoing activities. Paintings, experience charts, and displays carefully arranged in the room help make the environment attractive and stimulating. A survey of the entire kindergarten room will often reveal the kind of learning that is taking place.

A rectangular room containing 40 square feet per child is desirable. Some authorities suggest 50 to 100 square feet per child. In localities where colder weather exists for longer periods of time, kindergarten rooms need to be larger to accommodate large-muscle activities during times when children cannot use the out-of-doors. Space needs to be provided for individual, small-group, and large-group activities.

Generally, the kindergarten room is divided into activity areas or learning centers such as those listed on pp. 30 and 31. The activity-learning areas ought to be distinct in themselves, yet should blend into the "whole" of the room. It is imperative that activity areas be placed in relation to each other. Quiet activities need to be grouped together, and the same holds true for the more noisy activities. Painting and cooking activities should be near a sink. Each area should be designated by a word, picture, or symbol to make it easier to locate. Some teachers hang designations (signs) from the ceiling that can be recognized from across the room.

Many kindergartens provide a cubby (within the classroom) for each child. Cubbies are usually grouped together. Children attending morning sessions generally share cubbies with children attending afternoon sessions. Providing space for belongings helps develop early in the year a sense of responsibility in the children for taking care of wraps, papers, and other personal items.

Equipment and materials ought to be readily available on open shelves. It is important that all materials and equipment have a specified place in the room. Materials and shelves may be color coded and coordinated. The rule that "we put materials and equipment back where we got them when we finish using them" should be reinforced. By having specific jobs and tasks assigned on a daily or weekly basis, the children will get into the habit of keeping the room tidy and neat. Children like a cheerful, tidy room. A sense of order helps them feel more secure. If the teacher insists on an orderly room, equipment and materials can be easily found by all.

When arranging the kindergarten room, one should consider the flow of traffic from one activity to another. Drawing the room arrangement on paper is often helpful; however, one needs to have children engaging in various activities and moving about the room in order to see what arrangement works best. Additional space is needed for those activities that require "wiggle room," such as block building, woodworking, music, and housekeeping.

Each teacher must arrange the equipment and materials in a way that provides for the best possible learning environment. Figs. 4-1 and 4-2 illustrate the kindergarten room arrangements of two teachers.

Fig. 4-1 is the kindergarten room of Ann

Organizing for instruction 33

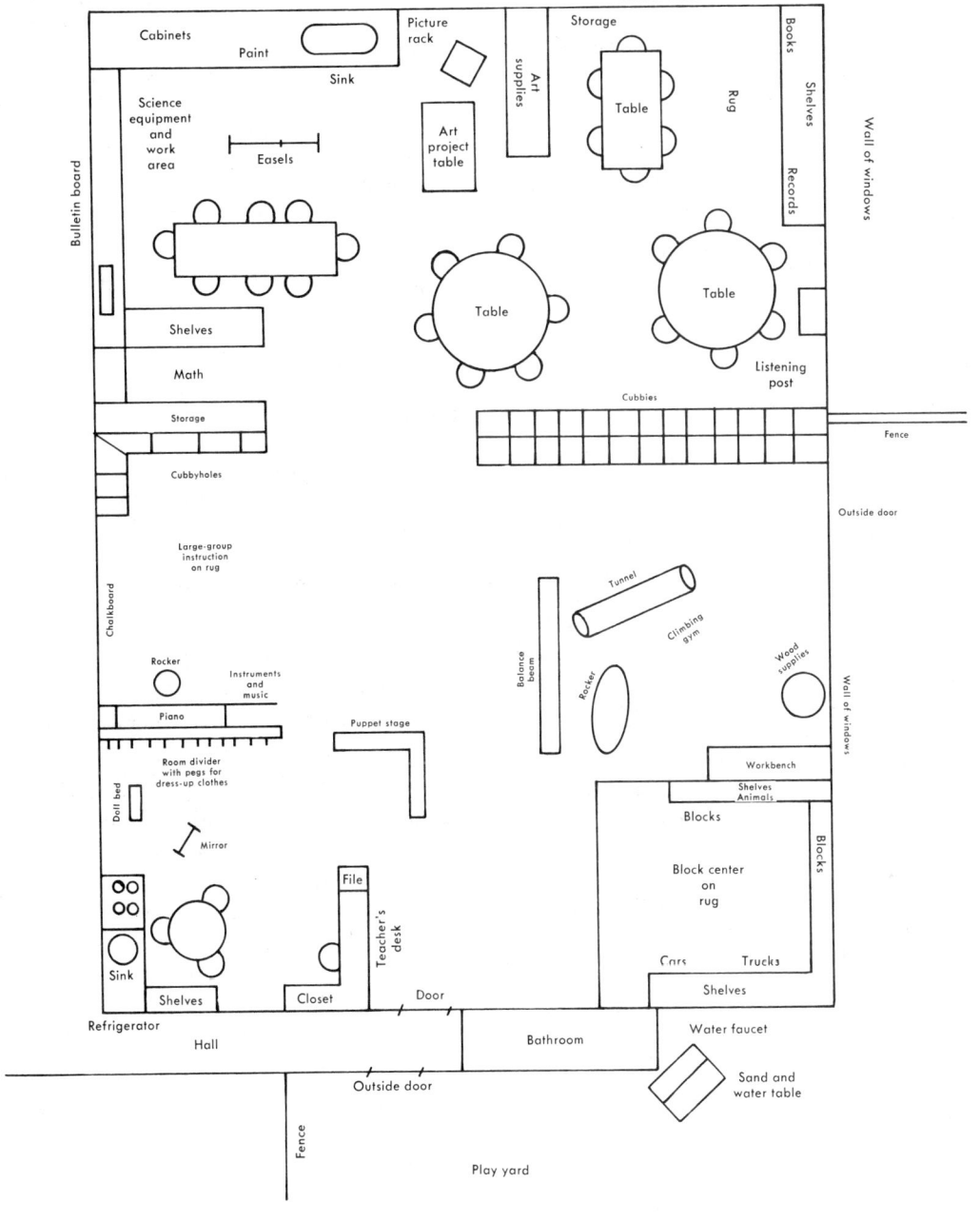

Fig. 4-1. Kindergarten room of Ann Masters.

Masters. Ann gives the following rationale for the placement of equipment and materials in her room:

Blocks: The block corner includes large and small blocks, trucks, cars, animals, people, traffic signs, etc. Blocks help children understand and deal with their world by bringing it down to a size that they can control. Blocks lead to learning in math, social science, and science by allowing children to explore. Blocks also lead to group cooperation and give movement to restless bodies. Their use helps develop the large and small muscles.

Woodworking: Working with wood, nails, and tools gives young children a sense of accomplishment and sensory pleasure. Woodworking helps develop the fine motor muscles.

Large play equipment: Climbing, crawling, rocking, and balancing improve coordination and control. This equipment is portable.

Cubbies: Cubbies give children a place to put their own belongings and projects. They help give each child a sense of personal pride and belonging.

Listening center: A listening center helps provide for quiet time. Attentive listening is a necessary skill. Earphones help cut down possible distractions and make it possible for each child to hear a lesson on tape or record. This helps free the teacher to work with other children.

Book center: Books are the child's window to other worlds. Books read by the teacher and later placed in the book center are especially valuable. This entire corner can be used as a language arts center, with games to develop sounds, the alphabet, etc. Storage is available.

Art center: The art center should be placed near the sink. Children need ample time to express themselves through the use of art materials. The art corner needs drying rack easels, project tables, and supplies with good storage.

Science center: A place where children can observe and explore. A display area is necessary for many "hands on" activities.

Math center: This area has storage for its games and supplies. It is used to help children develop the ability to work with numbers and their relationships.

Music center: Placement in this part of the room allows the materials to be used with large and small groups. Movement of large, but portable, play equipment leaves room for rhythms and movement. The piano and other instruments can be placed in this area.

Puppet stage: (Can be used for other dramatic play, such as store.) The stage allows children to express themselves as a protected "someone else."

Homemaking center: This area allows children to participate in dramatic play.

Fig. 4-2 represents the kindergarten room of Pat Balazs. Pat has described her room also.

Green rug: We all gather here at the beginning of class.*

Listening center: This is where we listen to records and tapes with our headsets.

Orange rug: We choose games here at free-choice time and gather here for story time.

Art center: We paint, draw, and cut and paste here.

Science/math center: We work here every day.

Game table: At this table we work puzzles and play learning games.

Snack center: Each day a boy or girl from each group is host or hostess at snack time.

Housekeeping corner: This is our housekeeping corner, with dolls, dress-up clothes, and a miniature kitchen.

After school begins and the children have become well acquainted with their room, ask yourself these questions:

1. Does the room look as if it belongs to the children?
2. Did the children have a part in planning it—placing some of the equipment and materials, putting up their own drawings, etc.?

---

*There are four groups in each class, who go to four or more activity centers each day. The activity centers listed are only representative of activities that might be available on a given day. During the year the activity centers change according to the interest of the children and teacher plans.

Organizing for instruction 35

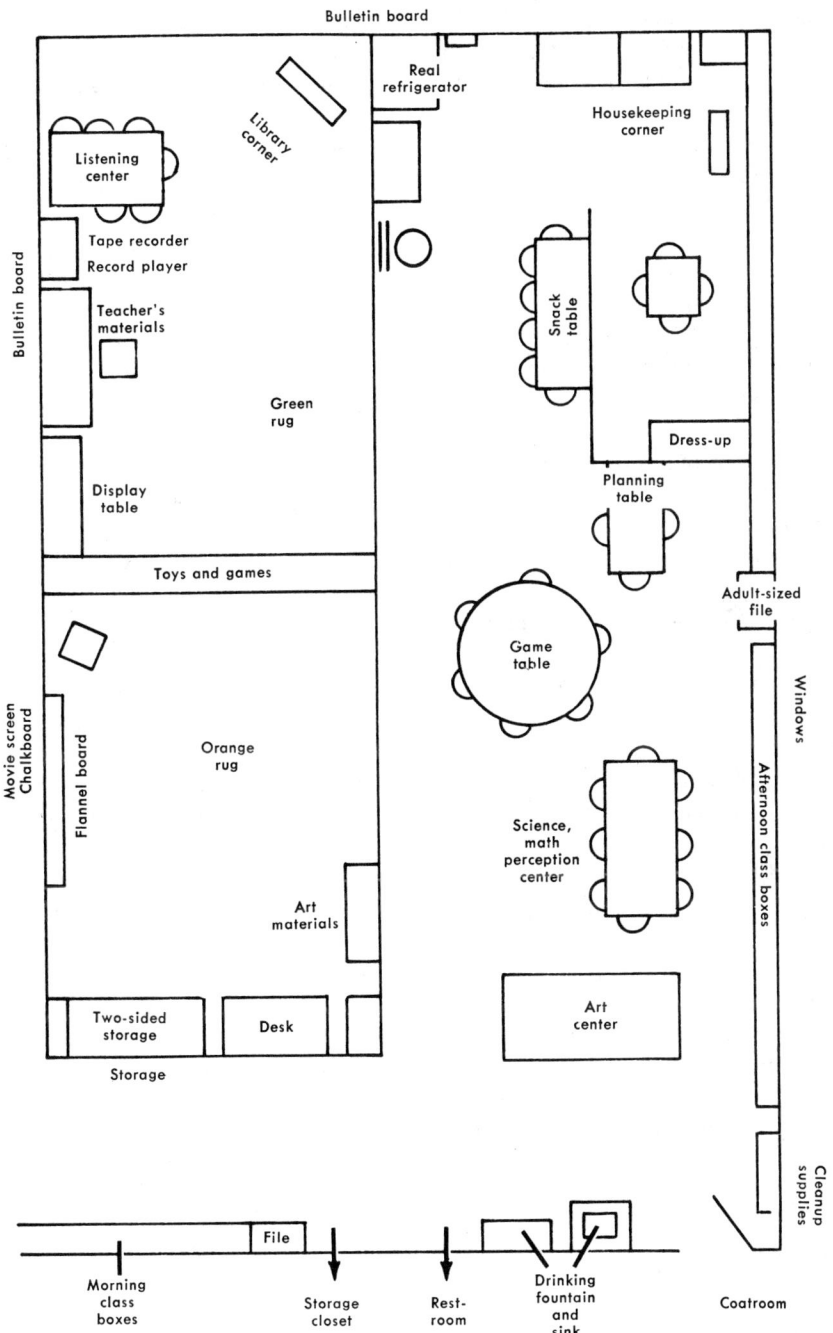

Fig. 4-2. Kindergarten room of Pat Balazs.

3. Does each child have a picture or some type of work on display?
4. How much of the artwork or displays are the children's? How much is yours?
5. Is the room cheerful and inviting—conducive to learning?
6. Are the children surrounded by beauty? Are objects of nature displayed in the room?
7. Are there colored, attractive cloths covering display tables? (In England and Europe this is often seen.)
8. Have you provided for a quiet place, such as a library corner with books attractively arranged on a table or in a bookcase?
9. Does the room look cluttered or overstimulating? Is movement from place to place facilitated?
10. Are learning centers clearly labeled so that children can locate them quickly? Do the centers invite participation?
11. How long have you left up some of the displays and work? Are materials in the centers varied from time to time?
12. Do you feel that each piece of equipment serves a functional purpose?
13. Does room arrangement facilitate groups of various sizes?

Successful kindergarten teachers spend a considerable amount of time preparing and organizing their classrooms. They know that a well-designed and equipped room is paramount to helping kindergarten children learn and manage themselves.

The film *Room to Learn* (see Appendix D) shows many excellent ways to design, set up, and manage a classroom for young children.

OUTDOOR ENVIRONMENTS

Outdoor kindergarten environments throughout the country differ widely in the possibilities they have to offer for optimal play and learning. Certain sections of the country (particularly in the warmer climates) are more conducive for outdoor activity periods than others. Unfortunately most outdoor areas have been designed solely for play purposes without any attention having been given to the multitude of possibilities the out-of-doors has for learning experiences.

When weather permits, children need the opportunity to be outside sometime during the kindergarten session. Out-of-doors activities contribute greatly to their physical and mental health. In colder climates parents need to be reminded to dress their children properly for outdoor, cold-weather activities. We often hear kindergarten teachers lament the fact that so much time is spent in putting on and taking off boots and coats. Many teachers take care of that problem by scheduling outdoor activities to take place immediately after the children arrive at school or just before they depart for home.

In *Guide to an Effective Kindergarten Program*, David and Mary Mindess (1972) have an excellent chapter entitled "Utilizing the Outdoor Environment," in which they present many ideas on how to use the outdoor environment as a valuable educational learning experience for children. For example, they show how shadow play can be used to help children expand their powers of observation and problem solving. They also show how a map-drawing project might be developed using an asphalt area.

According to the Ohio Ad Hoc Kindergartens Guideline Committee (1978):

For outside play there should be between 75 and 200 square feet of ground surface for each child using the space during a single time period. The play area would benefit the children greatly if it were designed not only with a variety of surfaces (sand, grass, woodchips, and asphalt) but also with a compatible variety in landscaping (hills, tunnels, slopes, and level areas). Scheduling of outdoor play space should respect the young child's need to be active without constantly competing with older children for space and/or equipment. Recognizing the limitations of school building design wherever possible, it is recommended that the kindergarten have convenient access to rest rooms, the multipurpose room, and the out-of-doors.

When new school buildings are designed, having provisions made for a covered patio is highly recommended. Some schools have designed small garden plots for growing flowers and vegetables. Valuable learning experiences grow out of such motivating and real-life activities. Whatever your circumstances, be sure to ask yourself if you are taking full advantage of what the out-of-doors has to offer your kindergarten group.

SCHEDULING FOR THE KINDERGARTEN DAY

Teachers and administrators plan daily kindergarten schedules that meet the needs of the children in their groups, that fit into the overall pattern of the school program, and that meet state minimum requirements. Today, kindergarten scheduling is an important school issue. For some time, the majority of kindergarten programs have operated on half-day sessions. With the constantly growing number of working mothers who must provide child care arrangements while their children are not at school, however, schools are experiencing more pressure to provide full-day programs. In many school districts where tax levies have failed, school boards have become deeply concerned about meeting budgets and are looking closely at ways to economize. Partly because of the heavy cost of busing, some boards have decided to operate their kindergarten programs on full-day schedules on alternating days. (See Chapter 11 for research on alternating days.) There are also some districts that provide full-day or extended-day kindergarten programs every day. These are districts that are trying to provide a more enriching program for their five-year-olds.

Those who specialize and work in the area of child development know that kindergarten children who attend an all-day session require a different kind of scheduling than those attending a half-day session. Children on full-day schedules need a program that is very carefully structured. Morning sessions usually give more attention to the academic areas. It is imperative that the afternoon program provide time for relaxation, experiences with the expressive arts, play, and a "trying out" or assimilation of concepts already presented. The pacing of activities needs to be carefully taken into consideration.

Since many different types of schedules are possible, each teacher needs to experiment with various time blocks in order to arrive at the best possible arrangement. In working out any program schedule, one must

38 *Kindergarten: programs and practices*

keep in mind that it must be child oriented, flexible, and carefully paced. As the year progresses, teachers should be alert to making scheduling changes that may become necessary.

The three sample plans presented here can be adapted to meet the needs of each kindergarten program.

Half-day schedule — 2½-hour morning session

8:00-8:45*	Teacher planning. Preparation time. Meetings and special conferences.
8:45-9:00	Arrival of children. Greetings of friends and teacher. Care of wraps. Browsing time and quiet activities until school begins.
9:00-9:15	Opening. Attendance. Sharing and discussion. Planning for work period—children select activities.
9:15-10:00	Work period—children work individually or in small groups. Children's choice plus teacher-planned activities (teacher may clude work at learning centers (involving language arts, math activities, cooking experiences, etc.).
10:00-10:15	Cleanup.
10:15-10:30	Outdoor activities (when weather permits).
10:30-10:45	Toileting, hand washing, juice and snack.
10:45-11:00	Music—group singing, playing of instruments, creative rhythms.
11:00-11:20	Story time, dramatization, films, social studies, etc.
11:20-11:30	Evaluation. Preparation for departure.

Half-day schedule — 3-hour morning session

8:00-8:45	Teacher planning. Preparation time. Meetings and special conferences.
8:45-9:00	Arrival of children. Greetings of friends and teacher. Care of wraps. Browsing time and quiet activities until school begins.
9:00-9:15	Opening. Attendance. Sharing and discussion. Planning for work period—children select activities—teacher may assign.
9:15-10:15	Work time—small-group activities, learning centers (involving language arts, math activities, cooking experiences, etc.) Emphasis may be on developing skills and subject matter activities. Cleanup.
10:15-10:30	Outdoor play.
10:30-10:45	Toileting, handwashing, juice and snack.
10:45-11:00	Story time, dramatization, films, social studies.
11:00-11:15	Music activities.
11:15-11:50	Creative art activities, woodworking, blocks, housekeeping, other free-choice activities. Cleanup.
11:50-12:00	Evaluation. Preparation for departure.

The full-day, everyday kindergarten schedule that follows was developed on an experimental basis by a kindergarten teacher (Catherine Rose) who wanted a quality program that provided for expanded opportunities in the expressive and communication arts. The schedule is flexible and is based on the children's interests and developmental levels and needs, as well as the program goals. Films, listening post experiences, finger plays, programs for parents and classmates, field trips, and arts and crafts are integrated throughout the program.

Full-day, everyday, enriched kindergarten

8:30-8:45	*Arrival.* Children enter informally; they talk with each other and the teacher. The teacher

---

*Afternoon schedules may use same time blocks.

Organizing for instruction 39

	greets each child. Personal needs, such as getting on clothes for physical education, care of wraps, and buying bus tickets, are taken care of. Children begin choosing time when ready and/or work individually with the teacher.
8:45-9:05	*Choosing time.* Children choose active play, dramatizations, creative activities, and other learning experiences from a variety of manipulative and instructional games, materials, and equipment. Children are given opportunities for the development of creativity through self-expression in art, block play, dramatic play, carpentry, and language experiences.
8:45-9:45 F	*Art.* Art is taught by the art teacher on alternate Fridays.
9:05-9:15	*Opening.* The teacher and children meet together to discuss plans for the day and any special event, such as a field trip, holiday, or a child's birthday. Children share topics of interest. Recognition is given for individual accomplishments.
9:15-9:45 T,W 1:45-2:15 F	*Physical education.* Class is directed by the elementary physical education teacher, who utilizes indoor and/or outdoor facilities.
9:15-9:30 M, Th, F 10:10-10:30 T, W	*Language arts.* Children receive an introduction to and individual help with learning the alphabet, letter sounds, handwriting, vocabulary and oral language development, reading, and composition. Children participate individually and in groups in teacher-directed language experiences, such as writing group stories, having discussions, dictating stories, making books, and developing creative and original compositions. Children are encouraged and given opportunities to read books. The teacher and fifth-grade tutors work with children who are interested in learning to read.
9:30-9:45 M, Th, F 10:30-10:45 W	*Music, rhythms, and games.* Children are actively involved in music through singing, rhythm instruments, and Dalcroze eurhythmics. Children participate in group games and/or outdoor activities.
9:45-10:00	*Rest and snack.* Children rest informally at tables, socialize, and have a snack.
10:00-10:30 M 10:30-10:45 T, W 10:00-10:15 Th, F	*Science and/or social studies.* Children's natural curiosity and interests, as well as selected key concepts of kindergarten curriculum, form the basis for discussions, group projects, field trips, art work, and related educational activities.
10:15-10:45 Th	*Art and art appreciation.* A creative approach in art is developed and/or art appreciation is encouraged through discussing famous paintings, artists, and their styles.
10:15-10:30 F	*Sharing.* Children discuss or share items of special personal interest.
10:30-11:05	*Library.* Children go to the school library to select books to take home and to listen to a story told by the librarian.
10:45-11:05 T, W, Th	*Thinking story.* The teacher reads a story intended to teach a concept and/or develop thinking skills, questioning techniques, listening skills, and decision-making skills.
11:05	Children get ready to go home.
11:15	*Dismissal.* All children leave for lunch. The teacher says good-bye to each child.
12:30-12:45	*Arrival.* Children return to school, visit informally, and take care of personal needs.

12:45-1:10 M, T, W, F	*Choosing time.* Children select activities of their choice and/or work individually with the teacher. (See notes for morning choosing time.)	
12:45-2:00 Th	*Swimming.* Children go by school bus to the local YWCA for swimming instruction.	
1:10-2:00 M	*Creative dramatics.* The teacher guides children in various forms of creative dramatics, such as storybook dramatizations and improvisations. Children have opportunities to develop creative expression through movement and "thinking" games.	
1:10-1:45 T	*Problem solving.* The teacher reads a story, shows a film, and/or leads a discussion to prepare for creative problem-solving work that follows later in the day. The teacher and children clear the classroom of furniture for Dalcroze eurhythmics.	
1:10-1:45 W	*Cooking.* The teacher and children cook together. Parents and first graders sometimes work with the kindergartners. Good health habits, nutrition, and the use of natural foods are stressed.	
1:10-1:45 F	*Group discussion.* The teacher leads a discussion of the *Scholastic Weekly* Reader Surprise, which is followed by a related craft and/or social studies project.	
2:00-2:15 M, W, Th 1:45-2:00 T 2:15-2:30 F	*Rest.* Children rest on rugs.	
2:15-2:45 M	*Outdoor play.* Children use the outdoor playground, weather permitting.	
2:00-3:00 T	*Dalcroze and/or creative problem solving.* Group 1 has Dalcroze eurhythmics with the Dalcroze teacher. The classroom teacher works with Group 2 on creative problem-solving techniques. After 30 minutes, the groups change places.	
2:15-2:30 T, Th	*Math.* Children use Cuisenaire rods to develop their math foundation. Math concepts and skills are developed informally throughout the program (e.g. in cooking, when serving snacks, and in discussing the calendar).	
2:45-3:05 M, W, Th 2:30-3:05 F	*Literature and evaluation.* The teacher reads or tells a story or poem, and/or does finger plays. The teacher leads a discussion, encourages comments and questions concerning the story, and fosters esthetic appreciation of literature, authors, and illustrators. The teacher and children comment on and evaluate the day's activities.	
3:15	*Dismissal.* The teacher gives a friendly and warm goodbye as children leave.	

A kindergarten teacher soon discovers that schedules sometimes need to be adjusted or altered and that they need to be flexible. There will be times when certain activities require more or less time on a particular day. Good judgment should be used in the stretching or shortening of time blocks. There may be a day when a project might consume a large block of time, thus eliminating music or a story. This can be made up for on another day, when more time can be devoted to these subjects. The important thing to remember is to be sure a *balance* is maintained over a period of time.

PROGRAM PLANNING

One of the most challenging tasks for the kindergarten teacher involves writing, developing, and implementing long- and short-

term goals and objectives for the kindergarten program. Teachers must develop plans on a daily, weekly, monthly, and yearly basis. As the kindergarten teacher gains experience, outlining a year's program becomes easier. Even the experienced teacher who has a tentative program outlined will have to design a program to meet the particular needs and interests of each group of incoming children. Each year, children come to school with varied experiences. Some enter with two or three years of preschool education; others with none. Some children enter the kindergarten speaking little or no English; others speak fluent English and perhaps have command of another language. Then there are youngsters with emotional or physical problems that need special attention. Setting goals and objectives are important, but the most effective ones are decided on only after the children in the class have been carefully observed and evaluated.

Books and materials, as well as curriculum guides, are available with complete lesson plans, including numerous activities, poems, songs and rhythms, games, experiments, and the like, for use by the kindergarten teacher. Generally these lessons are blocked out by weeks and months, sometimes for an entire year. While these preplanned lessons can be used as resource materials, it is unwise to use them as a basis for daily planning. Good planning takes into account the strengths and weaknesses of the particular group of children involved. Teachers often remark that they cannot even use the same exact plan for both morning and afternoon kindergarten sessions, since differences in the two groups warrant modifying the plans.

Curriculum guides

Some school districts develop curriculum guides with a separate section on kindergarten or have a separate curriculum guide for kindergarten. Usually these guides contain a philosophy, a list of long- and short-term goals; objectives for the program; separate sections on different areas of the curriculum; lists of books, films, and other resources; and many additional aids to help the teacher. Most systems revise and update their curriculum guides periodically. Guides developed in larger school systems are often available to others at minimal cost (see Appendix H).

Long- and short-term goal planning

Based on sound principles of child growth and development, long-term goals are generally determined by the philosophy of the school and by discussions among curriculum directors, early childhood specialists, administrators, and often parents. Long-term goals give direction to the ongoing kindergarten program. Periodically, plans need to be made to reach these long-term goals. These plans are usually made on a daily, weekly, monthly, or other designated basis.

Plans help the teacher develop a progression or continuity of learning, so that what the child learns on one day is related to the next. (This aspect is often neglected at the kindergarten level.) The day-to-day activities should be related and built on. Within a day's activities, often different areas of the curriculum can be correlated to one another.

Lesson planning in the kindergarten

When planning a program for the kindergarten child, one should take the following factors into consideration:
1. The varying needs, interests, and abilities of the five-year-old
2. Problems and situations that the child must deal with in the world about him
3. The expectations of the kindergarten program within the community
4. Cooperative planning between child and teacher in working toward accessible goals and objectives
5. Provision of experiences and situations that will help child and teacher achieve these goals
6. Consideration of the materials, space, and equipment that will be needed for these experiences
7. Provision for the proper balance of time for the various activities within the program

Since groups of children vary widely in their abilities and interests, curriculum content needs to be flexible. When the above considerations are taken into account, one may formulate a tentative selection of beginning activities. During the year, additional activities should be planned to give impetus and proper balance to the kindergarten program.

These activities may center around units of experiences. In the kindergarten, these experiences often spring from the immediate environment of the children. Thus, subject matter is best learned through firsthand experience. Curricular areas are not blocks of subject matter to be learned. Curriculum should be a sequence of desirable life experiences.

The plan should answer three basic questions for the teacher:
1. *What* am I going to teach?
2. *Why* am I going to teach it?
3. *How* am I going to teach it?

Before planning for the next day's work, one needs to evaluate what has gone on before:
1. How far did the group move ahead?
2. What objectives were they able to reach?
3. What problems did they encounter?
4. What happened today that ought to be included in the planning for tomorrow?
5. What materials will be needed and what procedures should be used to present this material?

Writing good lesson plans is important and helps organize thoughts and ideas. A format for an activity for one day's lesson is given on the opposite page.

In most school systems the kindergarten teacher takes the primary responsibility for developing the program and providing for a wide range of activities. It is important, as

Activity: _____ Date: _____

Objectives	Materials	Procedures	Evaluation
Motivation			

curriculum is developed and activities are formulated, that teacher and children plan together. All too often kindergarten children have been told *what* to do and have not had the opportunity to be included in the planning process.

Equally important to the planning process is communication with first-grade and other primary-level teachers. Knowing something of the local nursery schools as well as day care facilities and programs can be of help in the developing of a rich learning environment for the five-year-old.

Work time-activity period

When kindergarten children are asked what they like best about the kindergarten day, they will invariably say "work time." This period of the day can be the heart or core of an effective kindergarten program. Work time is generally a large block of time, from 45 to 60 minutes, including cleanup and evaluation. During this time, children have the opportunity to choose and work with one or more activities, including block building, woodworking, dramatic play, work with puzzles and games, cooking, using language and math materials, and the like. These activities may be arranged in interest or learning centers. They may be activities centering around a theme or unit that lasts for a day or they may be ongoing and extend over several days.

Children should be encouraged to remain with an activity to completion and not flit from one activity to another. The teacher may suggest which activity or activities a child might engage in during the work time period. This might occur when a child through self-choice has elected one particular activity over an extended period of time and the teacher wants to redirect the child into work with another activity. Or, the teacher might assign a child or group of children to a particular activity to introduce a new concept or skill or perhaps improve on some concept or skill already introduced. The teacher can also use this period profitably to observe and record behavior of children and to check and test them in certain areas. It is also one of

the best times of the day to individualize instruction and guide children in choice making or to redirect when necessary.

When five-year-olds have the opportunity to self-select activities at their own level of development and at their own particular rate of speed, interest and commitment build. It is an exciting way for children to work with the many different kinds of materials and media. It is one of the best ways for children to learn how to solve problems, to work cooperatively with others, and to share materials. Classroom management problems almost always decrease.

Certain limits and guidelines must be established and discussed by the teacher with the children before work time periods are implemented. When possible, the teacher and children together determine certain guidelines. Considerations might be the number of children engaged in a particular activity, expectations or standards, where completed work is placed, or how many choices may be selected. It is wise to set up these expectations as each activity is introduced.

Work time choices are generally made immediately preceding the work time period. There are several ways of recording the particular activities children choose. The teacher might say, "Who would like to work with the large blocks?" or "Who would like to work at the science center?" The response is then placed in a record book or kept on a clipboard.

Some teachers like the "ticket system," whereby children select a "ticket" from a board or rack placed in a center, such as woodworking. The ticket is then placed in a box. The card is returned to the rack when a child is finished working at that center, and another child may then select the ticket. Usually a numeral, designating the number of children who can work in a particular center, is placed at eye level, where children can readily see the number of boys and girls at work. They can then decide for themselves if there is sufficient room to join the group.

One teacher used an easel sign-up sheet system, and another created an apron with many pockets. Each colorful pocket contained cards with activities for selection. Kindergarten teachers are creative!

The following point of view is by an expert in the area of designing kindergarten work time.

Kindergarten work time — a view from the sidelines

Ethelouise Carpenter*

To many beginning teachers and to people unfamiliar with kindergarten practices, the "work time" is a vague part of the program—vague in that it is so big, so all-inclusive, and so varied in content. This name is given to it on the basis of our beliefs that a child's play is his work and also that during this time when he is working with many materials, results seem to be a little more tangible. However, this is a part of the child's day that calls for and develops social and mental skills as well as physical ones. It is the most relaxed and fruitful time for him to learn to live with his world of other people, with materials, with ideas. The extent to which this part of his kindergarten day is successful will be a measure of his entire kindergarten experience. It is most important that it be rewarding.

*Formerly Associate Professor of Education, Kent State University, Kent, Ohio.

Continued.

Kindergarten work time — a view from the sidelines, cont'd

From the sidelines you should see these characteristics:
1. Small groups or individuals working at many things simultaneously.
2. An atmosphere of informality.
3. Evidence of good organization.
4. Calm voices, happy, serious conversation.
5. Children working independently, with the teacher moving from group to group, giving special help where needed.
6. Freedom from clutter and confusion.
7. Emphasis on the activity, the manipulation of the total environment.
8. Evidence of freedom of choices, recognition of individual differences.
9. Quiet areas and active areas.

You may expect to find children showing these signs of good group relationships:
1. Asking and giving help of and to each other.
2. Making decisions as they work.
3. Commenting on each other's ways of doing.
4. Asserting leadership; being willing to follow as well.
5. Withdrawing from the leader who becomes dictatorial.
6. Awaiting turns to use materials.
7. Helping another child finish in order to proceed as a total group.
8. Taking responsibility for assigned duties and those unassigned.
9. Shifting interests, thereby making wider use of a variety of groups.
10. Self-selecting activities that are alternately restful and more active.
11. Engaging in spontaneous laughter.
12. Discriminating against undesirable behavior rather than persons themselves.

You may see the teacher step in when:
1. An argument persists and is becoming destructive to children or things.
2. A child needs help in getting "over a hump." (This is not the same as doing it for him.)
3. The teacher foresees physical danger (blocks piled precariously).
4. A child's stage of development indicates readiness for new suggestions, a needed skill.
5. A child needs a friend, needs comfort, needs a distraction.
6. A child does not finish what he starts before going on to something else.
7. A comment, a word of encouragement, an enthusiastic suggestion may raise an imaginative inkling to a wellborn idea. (Catching the little things, the comments, the interesting concepts that might bear fruit.)
8. Sharing of materials and equipment is not working out.
9. It seems best to draw the work time to a close, by either an established signal or other means.
10. Children are not doing their share of work or are interfering with others.
11. It seems necessary to call together a small group to help rechannel ideas and energies.
12. Children need to be reminded of the activity chosen.
13. Children cannot reach materials that are not readily available.

Learning centers

Centers are generally described as interest or learning centers. Some teachers use the terms interchangeably. According to Kaplan (1973, p. 21), a learning center is "an area in the classroom which contains a collection of activities and material to teach, reinforce and/or enrich a skill or concept."

Learning centers are sometimes classified as either skill, activity, or interest centers. The activities in a skill center are organized to help teach or reinforce one or more skills. Skills or concepts should be first introduced by the teacher. Students work at their own rate of speed. Usually, a child or a small group of children work at one particular center at a time. Kaplan (p. 27) further states:

> The make-up of a learning center changes according to the purpose and type of the center. Each center will have a different variety and quantity of activities. . . . The placement of a center changes according to its use. Some centers are displayed on tables while others can be stored in boxes and brought out periodically.

Children do not always have to stay in a particular center to use some of the materials. When appropriate, an activity or a game may be taken from the center and brought to a table or used on the floor.

Interest centers have been used for years by kindergarten teachers as part of the ongoing program. They center around topics of current interest to the five-year-old, or they may attempt to stimulate new interests. Woodworking, housekeeping, science, blocks, music, art, and other such interest centers are still favorites of kindergarten children. Most kindergarten programs begin the year by involving children in various activities using the interest center approach. A small number of centers are used in the beginning so as not to confuse the child. More centers can be added as the year goes on.

Learning centers have been found to be valuable at the kindergarten level if the teacher thoroughly understands how to design and use them. Examples of learning centers are given in subsequent chapters.

When planning any kind of interest or learning center, one should keep in mind the following guidelines:

1. Design the center according to the needs and interests of the children who will be using it.
2. Make sure activities and materials are related to the objectives, have enough variety to appeal to a wide range of pupil interests and abilities, and range from simple to difficult and from concrete to abstract.
3. Choose an appropriate area in the classroom for the center.
4. Identify the center with a name or symbol.
5. Gather and make appropriate materials.
6. Develop guidelines for use of the center. Be sure children know how to use them. This may be done by oral explanation or through use of printed words or symbols that the children can understand.
7. Make evaluation of center activities an ongoing process by you and the children.

Claire Cherry has developed two curriculum charts: *Motivational Curriculum Chart No. 1 for Early Childhood* and *Learning Centers for Early Childhood (Motivational Curriculum Chart 2)*. Both charts give valuable information in helping teachers develop a curriculum. These are distributed by CATEC Consultants, 2754 San Gabriel St., San Bernardino, Calif. 92404.

Whether separate activities, interest centers, learning centers, or a combination of all these are used, it is important that the classroom environment be designed in a way that provides optimal learning possibilities.

Grouping

Individualization of instruction at any level implies grouping. With the diversity of needs and experiential background of children in the typical kindergarten, grouping is essential. Grouping provides for ample participation from each child, allows for pacing according to learning styles, allows children with similar interests or abilities to work together, and also promotes social interaction.

Several types of groups are possible:
1. Interest group—children who want to work on construction or share the same book
2. Skill group—children working on the same math concept or doing a sequence story together
3. Friendship group—two or more children who are "pals" at play
4. Buddy group—an older child helping a younger one with a skill or reading a story; or one kindergarten child helping another

Groups may be temporary—for a day or two—or they may be extended depending on purpose.

Groups may be informal—sometimes 5 minutes or maybe 20.

Groups should be flexible, with children moving from group to group when appropriate, as in the "open" model.

Aides or parent volunteers could assist with one group as the teacher works with another.

The teacher may work with groups on alternate days.

A 60-minute work period could have three groups of 20 minutes each. (Columbus Public Schools, 1974)

Teaching responsively to the individual child implies grouping of various types. The teacher must experiment with differing arrangements to suit the particular class and learning needs of the group. Careful supervision of children in each group is, of course, necessary. However, grouping is beneficial and productive.

SUMMARY

Eliason and Jenkins (1977, p. 31) remind us that "the curriculum is everything that takes place in the classroom, including the determination of goals, the scheduling of the program, the planning of unit and lesson plans, and the continual evaluation of each of these areas."

Organizing for instruction is often the key factor in the success or failure of the kindergarten teacher. To the extent that the total environment meets the needs of all involved, growth in learning, a sense of achievement, and self-respect are fostered.

REFERENCES AND SUGGESTED READINGS

Ad Hoc Kindergarten Guidelines Committee. *Recommended kindergarten guidelines, state of Ohio.* Columbus, Ohio, 1978.

Association for Childhood Education International. *Selecting educational equipment and materials for school and home.* Washington, D.C.: The Association, 1976.

Broman, Betty L. *The early years in childhood education.* Chicago: Rand McNally & Co., 1978.

Coble, Charles R., and Hounshell, Paul B. Science learning centers. *Science and Children,* September 1978, p. 13.

Cohen, Monroe D. (Ed.). *Selecting educational equipment and materials for school and home.* Washington, D.C.: Association for Childhood Education International, 1976.

Columbus Public Schools (Division of Instruction). *Grouping.* April, 1974.

Eliason, Claudia Fuhriman, and Jenkins, Loa Thomson. *A practical guide to early childhood curriculum.* St. Louis: The C. V. Mosby Co., 1977.

Hildebrand, Verna. *Introduction to early childhood education* (2nd ed.). New York: Macmillan Publishing Co., Inc., 1976.

Kaplan, Sandra Nina, Kaplan, JoAnn Butom, Madsen, Sheila Kunishima, and Taylor, Bette K. *Change for children.* Santa Monica, Calif.: Goodyear Publishing Co., Inc., 1973.

Mindess, David, and Mindess, Mary. *Guide to an effective kindergarten program.* Englewood Cliffs, N.J.: Parker Publishing Co., 1972.

Spodek, Bernard. *Teaching in the early years.* Englewood Cliffs, N.Y.: Prentice-Hall, Inc., 1972.

Voight, Ralph Claude. *Invitation to learning: the learning center handbook.* Washington, D.C.: Acropolis Books Ltd., 1973.

CHAPTER 5

The well-being of the five-year-old

Play

We can explore the properties of play as we examine the many facets of this phenomena. But the kernel of its meaning to the child will always remain one of the mysteries of human existence. (Riley, 1974, p. 141)

Today, one of the most controversial and misunderstood issues at the kindergarten level revolves around play and its place in the education of the five-year-old. Throughout history, people have held different attitudes toward play. There have at times been people who regarded it as sinful or a waste of time. Even now, we still find critics who question the rightful use of play in the kindergarten program. In order to justify its very existence, teachers are often forced to define play in academic terms.

There has been a tendency among parents and some educators to rely on what children can demonstrate as a result of their experience in the classroom rather than consider the intangible aspects of the child's developing personality and intellectual functioning. The crux of the impatience with play and play-associated activity really lies in the lack of understanding of what play is all about in the life of the five-year-old.

Play to young children has always been as much a part of them as eating or sleeping. Play appears early in the life of the child, and many authorities believe that if one attempts to prevent a youngster from playing, the social and cognitive aspects of the child's life can be seriously disturbed. Observe children as they play almost from the time they get up until they go to sleep at night. Just try to deny them this human right! It is almost impossible to do so. No matter what the conditions might be, children find ways to play. Even when toys and equipment are nonexistent, they will devise and invent their own.

WHAT IS PLAY?

One of the most difficult tasks for today's educators has been to define play. Play has as many definitions as there are authors who attempt to define it. As discussed by Spodek (1974, p. 13), "We tend to see activities as being either all work or all play, and to think that if something is work it cannot be play and if it is play it cannot be work."

There are many people who feel that play is essential to childhood and should not be interfered with. Critics of this position often question whether any kind of meaningful learning takes place under such conditions. According to them, children's play should be structured and used for the purpose of developing concepts at the cognitive and affective levels.

Some kindergarten teachers believe that play is an activity to be engaged in after children have completed teacher-assigned activities. Putting together a puzzle, for example, might be termed "play" by some educators if the child selected the activity. This activity would not be termed "play" but "planned learning," however, if the puzzles were selected by the teacher as a means of teaching concepts such as shape and size discrimination. As one can understand, there is a fine line between "play" and "planned learning."

CONTRIBUTORS TO PLAY

Throughout history, educators, philosophers, psychologists, craftsmen, and others have written about play and its importance in the lives of young children. History tells us that the ancient Greeks were the first exponents of play in education. As many teachers and parents also believe today, Plato felt that much could be learned about young children by watching them at their play. Even Comenius used puzzles and pictures in his lower schools to motivate the play interests of children. Froebel, "father" of the kindergarten, "looked upon play as the cornerstone of his system and planned his materials for the 'self-employment' of little children" (Caplan and Caplan, 1974, p. 261).

Milton Bradley, who organized the Milton Bradley Company in 1863 (which still exists today), produced many suitable pieces of play equipment and materials for young children. Bradley was a strong proponent of teaching children to learn through play and strongly supported the kindergarten movement in the United States.

Karl Groos was the first person to question why the various forms of play exist. He saw play as a means of helping children release and work out their negative feelings.

One of the most prominent educators and makers of toys was Caroline Pratt. She believed that children learned "not only by doing, but also by thinking and planning the doing. . . . [Miss Pratt] grasped the concept of embodying in play material physical activity and learning opportunities about shape, size, scale, community, interdependence, and aesthetics" (Caplan and Caplan, 1974, pp. 268-269).

Many contributions regarding play have been made by child psychoanalysts and psychologists. Among these contributors have been Anna Freud, Susan Isaacs, and Lawrence Frank. Anna Freud, for example, has believed strongly in the values of play both in and out of the therapeutic setting and has lectured widely on the subject.

According to Gesell and Ilg, pediatricians who did research at Yale University, a child will often put forth his most strenuous energies as he plays. Through his complete concentration, he can acquire emotional satisfactions that he cannot acquire from other types of activity.

From Jean Piaget, the noted Swiss psychologist, we learn that play has a strong cognitive dimension. "Play", according to Piaget, "is a way of taking the outside world and manipulating it so that it fits the person's present organizational scheme" (Spodek, 1972, p. 204). Piaget has outlined three stages in the development of children's play: sensorimotor, symbolic, and playing games that have rules.

Millie Almy and Barbara Biber, authorities in early childhood education, have written and spoken widely on the intellectual benefits and outcomes in children's spontaneous play.

Sara Smilansky has elaborated on the original Piaget play categories and has labeled them functional play, constructive play, dramatic play, and games with rules (Rubin, 1977, p. 17). Smilansky's findings and written work on the sociodramatic play of young children have been highly significant. Her research on sociodramatic play was done with children in Israel. The results of this carefully designed study reveal that sociodramatic play is a vital learning tool for young children. Smilansky's (1968) book, *The Effects of Sociodramatic Play on Disadvantaged Preschool Children*, has made an excellent contribution to the study and understanding of sociodramatic play. It has come to the attention of educators that there is a correlation between a child's ability to engage in sociodramatic play before he is six years of age and his later intellectual achievement in elementary school (Riley, 1974, pp. 143-144). Those who would eliminate sociodramatic play from the curriculum of young children or give it low priority should read and study the research in this area. Brian Sutton-Smith has written widely on the role of play in cognitive development and is a known authority on children's play. Smilansky and Sutton-Smith, through their careful and intensive investigations of children's play, have made outstanding contributions in this field.

VALUES AND PURPOSES OF PLAY

Play holds countless values for the five-year-old. Since play is often a controversial subject at this level, teachers need to be well versed as to the values and purposes of play, and to be able to defend their position that play activities are necessary and important at this age.

Play promotes physical growth

Children learn body control through active physical play. The ability to throw and catch a ball, for example, is generally improved as youngsters grow and repeat their efforts. Children need many opportunities to run, skip, climb, slide, and the like. These types of activities are necessary to promote development of the large and small muscles.

Play provides children with a sense of power

Children are masters of their environment, and they engage in activities that are meaningful and realistic. As children experience success through play, their confidence, feelings of power, and initiative are enhanced. Have you ever noticed the facial expression on a child who has just swam the length of the pool for the very first time? It has been said that as children acquire good physical skills, their self-confidence seems to improve. Confidence gained in this way is apt to carry over into the classroom and often motivates children to work harder in other areas of learning.

Play nurtures problem solving

Through play, children learn to discriminate, to make judgments, to analyze, to synthesize, and to solve problems. One bright-eyed child (Susan) had just returned to kindergarten after having her tonsils removed at a local hospital. She and two other boys were playing hospital (one of the favorite games of children this age). Susan had been telling them that her hospital bed went up and down when the nurses or her parents used the crank connected to her bed. The children asked the teacher if they could use a long table at the side of the room for their hospital bed. "Why do you want the long table?" the teacher asked. "Because we want a hospital bed long enough so I can lie on it," Susan explained. The teacher then helped the children carry the table to their play area. Noting that the table couldn't be lowered, the children figured that if they used several of the hollow blocks they could make their own steps for Susan to get out of bed. Getting into and out of the hospital bed was tried by all of the children.

Play fosters emotional growth

Play provides children with a way to deal with their emotions. Fear, anxiety, joy, and hope can all be re-created in play experiences. By acting out a happening, a child can often bring frustrations out into the open, and even unpleasant experiences can be reduced to controllable size. Five-year-old John had been misbehaving in the classroom. Mrs. Jones (the kindergarten teacher) and Mr. Talbot (the principal) had had several discussions about John's problem. Mr. Talbot had told John that if things didn't improve, it would be necessary for him to call his mother. "Things" did not improve. One day soon after, a visitor to the classroom found John sitting all alone in the dramatic play corner. He was talking on the telephone to his mother and pretending that he was Mr. Talbot. Not seeing the visitor in the doorway, he said, "Hello. Is this John's mother? This is Mr. Talbot. As you know, John has been getting into trouble in Mrs. Jones's room. He's been naughty and has been hitting other children. I want you to talk to him about this, but I don't want you to spank him or anything like that." The conversation went on and on until another child entered the room. John was playing out his anxiety and hoping that his mother wouldn't be too hard on him.

Play provides an opportunity to acquire concepts

Self-activity and experiencing are still a young child's best means of learning and acquiring facts and concepts. Facts and concepts are best understood and maintained when they are used. A child, for example, is shown how to water the flowers with a sprinkling can. In watering the flowers over a period of time, the child learns how much water to give them without giving them a complete soaking.

Play provides a means for playing out roles and encourages self-expression

In their play world, children are often free of adult interference. They can pretend and role play any adult or animal character, any real or imagined thing or situation. Play and fantasy are a vital need of children, for which opportunities need to be provided.

On one occasion some of the children in a kindergarten were playing "family." The "mother" directed the "father" to take the "dog" out for a walk until supper was ready. The "mother" continued to iron. When the "father" and "dog" returned, the meal was still not complete, so the "dog" promptly went to a corner of the kitchen, curled up on a rug, and dozed! (The legs of one of the students was blocking the path, so the "dog" walked between the student's legs.)

One afternoon a kindergarten class was presenting a rather long puppet show. The puppeteers stood behind the piano, and the audience sat on the floor in front. At the completion of the play the kindergarten narrator, assuming the role of teacher, announced to the audience, "And now, we will *evaluate!*" Our words come back to haunt us.

KINDS OF PLAY

In many kindergartens one can generally find the following kinds of valued play experiences:

1. Physical play (large-muscle play activities, both indoors and outdoors)
2. Manipulative play (such as puzzles, unit blocks, interlocking toys, Cuisenaire rods)
3. Dramatic play (playing out roles, parts of stories, and the like)
4. Games (structured play activities including rules)

Several authorities, including Spodek, relate that games have often been excluded from early childhood programs because they were considered inappropriate for this age level. "Actually children at the four- and five-year-old level are beginning to move into a stage where game playing is possible. Simple games or musical activity containing elements of games are quite appropriate for children" (Spodek, 1972, pp. 206-207).

GROUP GAMES

Even though a good portion of time is to be allowed for children's free-play activities, games of low-level organization have a special place in the kindergarten program and can strengthen all aspects of a child's growth and development. At five, children are beginning to enjoy simple group games. Rules and directions for games must be kept simple and few. At this age, games should be chosen according to the children's interests, abilities, and cultural backgrounds.

As children enter the late preoperational stage (between five and seven years of age), games having a *minor* element of competition may be used. "Games in which a child who is caught may become 'it' without losing the game work well if the adult is cognizant of the game-playing experience of the group and minimizes this competitive part of the game-playing situation for players who do not yet understand it . . ." (Bogdanoff and Dolch, 1979, p. 43). Most children accept being "caught" matter of factly. In no way should a child who is caught be made to feel left out, inferior, or embarrassed.

Within the last few years, articles on children's play have revealed that educators are looking more favorably on using group games of low organization with kindergarten children. It is believed that children need to have more opportunities in which to develop group cooperation and group spirit. Group games also give children the opportunity to sharpen their perceptual skills and to think quickly as decisions and choices need to be made.

When children participate and cooperate spontaneously without being coerced into the group, simple games can provide rich potential for growth and development.

(Games involving singing are of special delight to young children and are discussed along with movement and rhythm in Chapter 7.)

Following are a few of the favorite kindergarten games.

Follow the Leader
FORMATION: With the leader at the head, the children form a single line.

DIRECTIONS: As the leader makes different movements, such as jumping, waving arms in the air, etc., the children imitate them. On a given signal, the leader goes to the back of the line. The next child becomes leader.

Simon Says
FORMATION: The children line across the room with the leader in front.

DIRECTIONS: Each time the leader precedes an activity with the words, "Simon says, 'Do this,'" the children do what the leader does. If the leader says, "Do this," not mentioning the words "Simon says," the children are not to do the action. A child who does the action when he is not supposed to, then takes the leader's place.

Duck, Duck, Goose*
FORMATION: The children form a large circle. One child is chosen to be the leader.

DIRECTIONS: The leader walks around the circle and taps each child on the head, saying, "Duck, duck, duck." The one he taps while saying, "Duck, duck, goose," chases him around the circle to the place the tapped one occupied. If he is caught before getting there, the leader goes into the center and sits. The new leader (the one who was tapped) continues the game by finding a new "goose." (Caution children to run around the circle just once. In order that each child has a turn, have children sit down in place after they have run around the circle, and the "goose" taps only those standing.

Beckoning
FORMATION: The children form a circle. One child is in the center.

DIRECTIONS: The child in the center beckons to a child forming part of the circle. The child beckoned to comes into the circle and shakes hands with the first child. The first child goes

---
*One of the very favorite games of five-year-olds.

56 Kindergarten: programs and practices

back to become part of the circle and sits down, and the second child repeats the action of the first child. The game continues until each child has been beckoned to.

Hot Ball

FORMATION: Forming a circle, the children sit cross-legged on the floor.
DIRECTIONS: The children pretend to put on gloves to protect their hands from the "hot" ball. A ball is rolled into the circle toward some child. He must not hold it but must bat it away from himself as quickly as it comes near enough for him to reach it. He must not let it touch him except on his hands. (Keep encouraging the children to get the ball away from them as quickly as possible without reaching in front of their neighbors for it.)

Quiet Ball*

FORMATION: Forming a circle, the children sit cross-legged on the floor.
DIRECTIONS: A ball is given to one child, who rolls it on the floor to another child. This child rolls it to another, and the game continues in this manner. (Encourage children to roll the ball straight and not bounce it.)

THE TEACHER'S ROLE

The role of the teacher in guiding children's play *cannot* be overemphasized. Unfortunately, there are some teachers who do not thoroughly understand the play of children with all of its ramifications. They provide the equipment, the time, and the space and then release the five-year-olds to play without guidance or intervention of any sort during the play period.

There are numerous ways in which teachers can facilitate and guide play:
1. Set up the play environment but not the play process. Children need time, space, materials, and equipment. They also need freedom to choose activities

---
*Similar to "Hot Ball," but no one must talk during the game.

and freedom to move within their environment.
2. Keep "tuned in" to children's play situations. When warranted, add a suggestion or ask a question that will enhance the play. On occasion, children may ask you to take part in the play situation. Children are pleased when teachers take on an assigned role or "come to visit" in the playhouse.
3. If necessary, stop the play if danger is involved. Safety should hold top priority.
4. Redirect the play if a certain play episode has been exhausted or is about to run down.
5. Encourage divergent thinking and make it possible for children to try out their own original ideas. Allow them to use materials and equipment in differ-

ent ways. For example, instead of using the large blocks for building, one child wanted to use the blocks for making an expressway. He laid them in a long line. Then he asked for some long, narrow boards. When the teacher inquired why he wanted the boards, he remarked, "I'm going to make a ramp so my truck can get off the expressway. Don't you understand?"

AN ADDED THOUGHT

One of the most difficult problems facing kindergarten teachers today concerns children who enter kindergarten with such varied experiences, including play. Some children have had narrow, unrewarding experiences with play; other children have had rich play experiences in the home and in the preschool. How does the kindergarten teacher plan for this discrepancy? Teachers must individualize and adjust their programs to accommodate children with such varied experiences. Another difficult problem kindergarten teachers face is knowing how to provide the proper balance between spontaneous and structured play. Additional empirical research is needed to guide teachers in providing this balance and to help implement the best play environments possible.

From infancy to adulthood, play in some form is essential to human survival. It deserves a place in all of our lives and can be justified for its own sake. Many educators and parents alike now accept play as a vital learning force. University courses in early childhood education, developed solely on the aspect of play, are becoming more abundant in number and are in great demand by students. Riley (1974, pp. 139-140) says it so well:

> Whatever it is called, or for whatever reasons, some educators feel disinclined to use the term; the fact remains that play is the very essence of childhood. It is the activity that enables him to discover and understand himself, his feelings, his ideas; it is the process for him of developing his concepts, sorting out his ideas, his relationships to his peers, his family and the universe. It is his way of integrating his perceptions and his ideas into his individual growth pattern. Without this process of integration, random learnings or experiences remain just that—isolated and never coming together. A child who does not play—if we can imagine such a being—is in serious trouble.

Health

By sharing and comparing observations and viewpoints, parents and teachers can work well together in guarding the health of children as they grow and develop. (Metropolitan Life Insurance Co., undated, p. 2)

The well-being of the child is of utmost importance to the kindergarten teacher. When goals are being set up to ensure the children's well-being, emphasis should be on programs and practices that will help youngsters internalize that their lives are very important and that they need to learn how to keep themselves and others healthy and safe. Individuals cannot be prepared for effective living unless they have well-functioning bodies and can make reasonably successful adjustments to the many problems they will face in their lifetimes. Health and safety become increasingly important aspects as automation, changing moral standards and values, leisure time, environmental concerns, mounting pressures, and other changes in our society create or intensify health and safety problems.

Five-year-olds will be off to a good start in kindergarten if they enter as healthy, happy youngsters. Children cannot do their best work if they are hungry, do not feel well, or have learning deficits. Many health problems, such as hearing loss, speech impediments, skin problems, and defective vision can frequently be corrected or im-

58   Kindergarten: programs and practices

proved if noticed and given proper treatment. Infections, impetigo, conjunctivitis (pink eye), and even head lice can occur in the best of homes and need immediate attention. It is truly an art to look *at* and listen to children—to really see and hear them and be responsive to their individual needs. A teacher can often acquire and refine this art through daily association with many children. By being keenly aware, one can gain valuable insights concerning a child's physical and emotional health.

HEALTH EXAMINATIONS AND FORMS

Some school districts require, and others strongly suggest, that entering kindergarten children have a thorough examination by their family doctor, eye doctor, and dentist before entering school. In some states the following immunizations are required: diphtheria, whooping cough, tetanus, polio, and measles—both 3-day and 10-day. A tuberculin test is recommended. Smallpox immunization is determined at the discretion of the family physician. The school must also have information from parents on allergies, special prescription medicines that the child might be taking at school, etc. School authorities and teachers should strongly urge parents to carefully fill out health forms on their child at the time of registration. Withholding information concerning a child's health can cause serious trouble, as in the following case.

Two kindergarten teachers took their classes on a field trip to see a recently born baby colt. Both classes rode the bus to a farm outside the city. After getting off the bus, the classes walked through a meadow of tall grass to the place where the baby colt and mother were resting. Suddenly one of the teachers (Mrs. Monty) noticed that John's face was beginning to swell. Within minutes, his face was swollen like a balloon and his eyes were nearly drawn shut. Being an experienced teacher, Mrs. Monty suspected that John was having an allergic reaction. (She had no previous knowledge of John's allergy problem.) Sensing the seriousness of the situation, the teacher gathered the children together and ask them to return to the bus. Both teachers worked quickly without frightening the children. Mrs. Monty knew that a relative of John's lived on a street the bus would be taking back into the city. She asked the driver to stop at the relative's house. Fortunately, the relative was home and knew the name of John's doctor. The relative called John's mother; and by the time the bus arrived at the doctor's office, she was there to assist. The doctor was able to take care of the allergic reaction by giving prompt medical treatment. This situation would not have occurred, however, if John's mother had been careful to include this information on his kindergarten health form. Mrs. Monty never found out why John's mother had failed to do so.

Chart of communicable diseases of childhood

Even though most teachers take courses in school health and have a background of information on health and safety of young children, they often ask for a chart on communicable diseases of childhood for quick reference. Such a chart is provided in Table 2. Any suspected disease should be referred to the school nurse.

DETECTING HEALTH PROBLEMS

Parents are usually in the best position to note signs of illnesses or health problems in their children; however, in supervising a child for several hours a day, the kindergarten teacher may be in an even better position than a parent to observe a child's health and to notice significant changes. A few health problems develop so gradually that early signs may escape notice. By observing each child day by day, individually and within the group, a teacher may detect indications of defects in vision, hearing, orthopedic problems, and allergies, as well as learning difficulties with a physical or emotional cause. A teacher can then discuss these observations with the school nurse and the child's parents.

Vision

The following experience with my own (K.B.) five-year-old son, Kim, and his vision impairment illustrates how perceptive a kindergarten teacher can be to children's health problems.

One day Kim's teacher stopped me in the hall (I was teaching in the school). "Kay," she said, "Kim seems to be having trouble with his eyes." "That's strange," I said, "he had his eyes checked by a specialist before school began in the fall; and the doctor said Kim's eyes were normal, but that he would like to see him in another year." Just then, someone interrupted our conversation. About a month later, Kim's teacher approached me again and said, "Kay, I'm sorry to keep bugging you, but Kim is having real problems with his eyes. When I read a story to the children, Kim's eyes cross immediately." My immediate reply was, "We will make an appointment with another doctor as soon as possible."

On examining Kim, the second specialist found that Kim had strabismus (cross-eye). After being fitted with glasses (on the very first day), Kim did not want to take his glasses off even to go to bed. The glasses had made a world of difference to this little boy.

As Kim's mother, and as a teacher, I felt guilty at first, thinking I should have been more observant. I had relied totally on the first specialist's findings. Later, I discovered the reason my husband and I had not observed Kim's eyes crossing was that, when we read to him, Kim was either on our laps or sitting beside us. Had this vision defect been allowed to persist, not only might some vision have been lost, but also Kim's ability to read would probably have been impaired.

Amblyopia (lazy eye) is another problem often not detected until learning difficulties arise. Some schools now have specific clinics to discover this eye defect.

Hearing and speech

Usually, screening tests for hearing acuity are given routinely in schools. They are valuable in that they may detect hearing loss that was not evident to either the parents or the teacher. In addition to testing done on a routine basis, teachers should report to the parents when they suspect a child's hearing is not normal. Indications of a suspected hearing loss may be evident in a

Text continued on p. 66.

Table 2. Communicable disease chart for schools*

Incubation and symptoms	Methods of spread
Chicken pox (varicella) *Incubation:* 2-3 weeks, usually 13-17 days. *Symptoms:* skin rash often consisting of small blisters which leave a scab. Eruption comes in crops. There may be pimples, blisters and scabs all present at the same time.	Direct contact, droplet, or airborne spread of secretions of respiratory tract of an infected person or indirectly with articles freshly soiled with discharges from such persons.
Common cold *Incubation:* 12-72 hours, usually 24 hours. *Symptoms:* irritated throat, watery discharge from nose and eyes, sneezing, chilliness and general body discomfort.	Direct contact with an infected person or indirectly by contact with articles freshly soiled by discharges of nose and throat of the infected person.
Flu (influenza) *Incubation:* usually 1-3 days. *Symptoms:* abrupt onset of fever, chills, headache and sore muscles. Runny nose, sore throat, and cough are common.	Direct contact with an infected person or indirectly by contact with articles freshly soiled by discharges of nose and throat of the infected person. Possibly airborne in crowded areas.
German measles (rubella) (three-day measles) *Incubation:* 14-21 days, usually 16-18 days. *Symptoms:* skin rash and mild fever. Glands at back of head, behind ear, and along back of neck are often enlarged. Some infections may occur without evident rash.	Direct contact with an infected person or indirectly by contact with articles freshly soiled by discharges of nose and throat of the infected person.
Hepatitis A (infectious) *Incubation:* 10-50 days; average 25-30 days. *Symptoms:* usually abrupt onset with loss of appetite, fever, abdominal discomfort, nausea and fatigue. Jaundice may follow in a few days.	Person to person contact, presumably in the majority of cases by fecal contamination. May be spread by ingestion of fecally contaminated water and food.
Hepatitis B (serum) *Incubation:* 45-160 days, average 60-90 days. *Symptoms:* usually inapparent onset with loss of appetite, vague abdominal discomfort, nausea, vomiting; often progresses to jaundice. Fever may be absent.	Chiefly through blood or blood products by inoculation or ingestion of blood from an infected person. Contaminated needles and syringes are important vehicles of spread. Also may be spread through contamination of wounds or lacerations.

References: American Academy of Pediatrics. *Report on the committee on infectious diseases* (18th ed.). Evanston, Berenson, Abram S., Ed.: *Control of communicable diseases in man* (12th ed.). Washington, D.C.: American
*Courtesy of the Ohio Department of Health, Bureau of Preventive Medicine, Columbus, Ohio.

Minimum control measures	Other information
Period of communicability: communicable at least 5 days before blisters appear and until all scabs are crusted. *Control:* exclude from school until all scabs are crusted.	Children with certain chronic diseases, like leukemia, are at extreme high risk for complications.
Period of communicability: 24 hours before onset of symptoms until 5 days after onset. (However, period may vary.) *Control:* exclude from school until symptoms are gone.	
Period of communicability: probably shortly before onset of symptoms and at least 3 days after onset of symptoms. *Control:* exclude from school until symptoms are gone.	Routine immunization is not recommended for children.
Period of communicability: most highly communicable from 7 days before and at least 4 days after the onset of rash. *Control:* exclude from school for at least four days after the onset of symptoms.	Immunization of all children entering school is required by law. The disease, while mild in children, is very serious for unborn babies if it is contracted by a pregnant woman.
Period of communicability: most highly communicable during the last half of the incubation period and continuing for approximately one week after jaundice. *Control:* exclude from school until at least 7 days after onset of jaundice. Student should be under physician's care.	Consult the local health department for help in controlling the disease within the school. Adequate sanitation facilities are necessary in reducing the spread of this disease. An adequate supply of soap and paper towels is essential. Students should wash their hands after each toilet use and before meals. Observe cafeteria personnel for symptoms of the disease and give particular attention to handwashing practices of all food handlers. Gamma globulin is usually *not* recommended for classroom contacts.
Period of communicability: most highly communicable during latter part of incubation period and during acute illness. *Control:* exclude from school until symptoms are gone. Students should be under a physician's care.	Notify your local health department.

Ill., 1977.
Public Health Association, 1975.

Table 2. Communicable disease chart for schools—cont'd

Incubation and symptoms	Methods of spread
Impetigo *Incubation:* 2-5 days, occasionally longer. *Symptoms:* Blister-like lesions which later develop into crusted pus-like sores which are irregular in outline.	Direct contact with draining sores.
Head lice (pediculosis) *Incubation:* the eggs of lice may hatch in one week and sexual maturity is reached in approximately two weeks. *Symptoms:* irritation and itching of scalp or body; presence of small light gray insects and/or their eggs (nits) which are attached to the base of hairs.	Direct contact with an infested person and indirectly by contact with their *personal* belongings, especially clothing and headgear.
Measles (rubeola) *Incubation:* 8-13 days; usually 10 days. *Symptoms:* acute highly communicable disease with fever, runny eyes and nose, cough, and followed by a dark red elevated rash that occurs in patches.	Direct contact with secretions of nose, throat and urine of infected persons; indirectly airborne and by articles freshly soiled with secretions of nose and throat.
Meningitis (bacterial) *Incubation:* 1-7 days. *Symptoms:* acute disease with sudden onset of fever, intense headache. Behavioral changes may occur including irritability or sluggishness.	Direct contact with secretions of nose and throat of infected persons or carriers.
Meningitis (aseptic-viral) *Incubation:* varies with causative agent. *Symptoms:* acute disease with sudden onset of fever, intense headache, nausea, forceful vomiting, and stiff neck. Behavioral changes may occur including irritability and sluggishness.	Varies with causative agent.
Mononucleosis *Incubation:* 2-8 weeks. *Symptoms:* fever, sore throat, swollen lymph glands.	Direct contact with saliva of infected person.
Mumps *Incubation:* 12-26 days, commonly 18 days. *Symptoms:* usually fever followed by painful swelling under the jaw or in front of the ear.	Direct contact with saliva of infected person, or indirectly by contact with articles freshly soiled with discharges of such persons.

The well-being of the five-year-old 63

Minimum control measures	Other information
Period of communicability: from onset of symptoms until sores are healed. *Control:* exclude from school until adequately treated and sores are no longer draining.	Early detection and adequate treatment are important in preventing spread. Infected individual should use separate towels and wash cloths. All persons with lesions should avoid contact with newborn babies.
Period of communicability: while lice remain alive on the infested person or in his clothing and until eggs (nits) have been destroyed. *Control:* exclude from school until disinfestation is accomplished.	The local health department should be notified of any occurrence of lice. When a student is found with head lice, all family members should be inspected and those infested should be treated.
Period of communicability: from onset of symptoms until a few days after rash appears. *Control:* exclude from school until at least 4 days after the rash appears.	Immunization of all children entering school is required by law. Notify the local health department if a case occurs in the school. One of the most readily transmitted communicable diseases.
Period of communicability: no longer than 24 hours after initiation of antibiotic therapy. *Control:* exclude from school until adequately treated. Student must be under a physician's care.	Notify the local health department if a case occurs in the school. Antibiotic therapy may be necessary for intimate contacts. Classroom contacts are usually *not* candidates for antibiotic therapy.
Period of communicability: varies with causative agent. *Control:* exclude from school during fever period. Student must be under a physician's care.	It is important to determine whether meningitis is aseptic or bacterial since the symptoms are essentially the same. Aseptic meningitis is a much less serious disease.
Need not be excluded from school under ordinary circumstances.	Not highly communicable.
Period of communicability: 48 hours before onset of swelling and up to 9 days after swelling occurs. *Control:* exclude from school for at least 9 days after swelling occurs.	Immunization against mumps is available. The disease may have serious complications in adults.

Continued.

Table 2. Communicable disease chart for schools—cont'd

Incubation and symptoms	Methods of spread
Ringworm (scalp, skin, and feet)	
Incubation: unknown. *Symptoms:* *Scalp:* scaly patches of temporary baldness. Infected hairs are brittle and break easily. *Skin:* flat, inflamed ringlike sores that may itch or burn. *Feet:* scaling or cracking of the skin, especially between the toes, or blisters containing a thin watery fluid.	Directly by contact with infected persons or animals or indirectly by contact with articles and surfaces contaminated by such infected persons or animals.
Scabies (itch)	
Incubation: first infestation in 4-6 weeks; reinfestation symptoms may occur in a few days. *Symptoms:* small raised areas of skin containing fluid or tiny burrows under the skin resembling a line which appear frequently on finger webs, under side of wrists, elbows, armpits, thighs, and belt line. Itching is intense, especially at night.	Direct contact with sores and, to a limited extent, from undergarments or bedding freshly contaminated by infected persons.
Scarlet fever and strep throat (streptococcal)	
Incubation: 1-3 days, but may be longer. *Symptoms:* *Strep throat:* fever, sore and red throat, pus spots on the back or the throat, tender and swollen glands of the neck. *Scarlet fever:* all symptoms that occur with strep throat as well as strawberry tongue and rash of the skin and inside of mouth. High fever, nausea and vomiting may occur.	Direct or intimate contact with infected person or carrier; rarely by indirect contact through transfer by objects or hands. Casual contact rarely leads to infection. Explosive outbreaks of strep throat may follow drinking of contaminated milk or eating contaminated food.
Venereal diseases (gonorrhea, syphilis, herpes simplex)	
Incubation: *Gonorrhea:* 3-9 days. *Syphilis:* 10-90 days. *Herpes simplex:* up to 2 weeks. *Symptoms:* *Gonorrhea:* early symptoms in the male are a thick yellow discharge from the sex organs appearing 3-9 days after exposure, and a painful burning sensation during urination. The same symptoms may also appear in the female, but often are so mild that they are unnoticed.	*Gonorrhea:* direct personal contact—usually through sexual intercourse. *Syphilis:* direct personal contact—usually through sexual intercourse. *Herpes simplex II:* direct personal contact—usually through sexual intercourse.

Minimum control measures	Other information
Period of communicability: as long as sores are present. *Control:* exclusion from school is necessary for ringworm of the scalp and skin until treatment has begun.	Preventive measures are largely hygienic. All household contacts, pets, and farm animals should be examined and treated if infected. Scalp ringworm is seldom if ever found in adults.
Period of communicability: until student and household contacts have been adequately treated (usually requires one treatment). *Control:* exclude from school until student and household contacts have been treated adequately. (Single infection in a family is uncommon.)	Disinfection of the general environment is not necessary. After treatment of student and family *no* waiting period for re-entry is necessary.
Period of communicability: with adequate treatment, communicability is eliminated within 24 hours. *Control:* exclude from school until 24 hours after treatment is started.	Early diagnosis and medical treatment are essential in the care of the student and in the prevention of serious complications.
Period of communicability: *Gonorrhea:* communicable until treated. (Up to 8 months.) *Syphilis:* as long as early symptoms are present (up to 3 years). *Herpes simplex II:* most contagious when blisters are moist, however, may remain communicable for several weeks. *Control:* Herpes, Gonorrhea and Syphilis—there is no reason for restricting attendance except in the specific recommendation of the health department or family physician.	The control of the veneral diseases is the responsibility of the physician and the health department. Information must be held to the utmost confidence in order to successfully control these diseases. Pelvic Inflammatory Diseases (PID) is a serious complication of Gonorrhea and requires medical treatment.

Continued.

Table 2. Communicable disease chart for schools—cont'd

Incubation and symptoms	Methods of spread
Venereal diseases—cont'd	
Syphilis: may include a sore which develops at the site the organism enters the body; a rash, unexplained and prolonged sore throat, fever and headache.	
Herpes simplex II: very painful sores or blisters on or around the sex organs.	
Whooping cough (pertussis)	
Incubation: 7-21 days, usually 10 days.	Direct contact with discharges of an infected person, or indirectly by contact with articles freshly soiled by discharges of infected persons.
Symptoms: begins with cough which is worse at night. Symptoms may at first be very mild. Characteristic "whooping" develops in about two weeks and spells of coughing sometimes end with vomiting.	

Tuberculosis

Very few students have been found to be infected with tuberculosis.
Skin testing policies for tuberculosis testing in students are determined by local health departments.

Animal bites

1. The community should be made aware of the potential dangers of animal bites.
2. Preventive vaccination of owned dogs and control of all stray dogs should be encouraged.
3. All biting animals should be confined for a ten-day observation period.
4. All unprovoked attacks by wildlife should be considered as potential exposures to rabies.
5. All animal bites should be reported to the local health department so that an investigation of the case may be made.

---

child's behavior or appearance. For example, the child may be inattentive, may not respond to questions when the head is turned in another direction, may have to have things repeated, may show a tilting of the head, may do poor schoolwork, and/or may have behavior problems.

Since imitation is the chief way of learning speech, many speech problems are related to hearing difficulties. Sometimes speech problems are due to errors in articulation. Often these can be corrected by special training. It is also not unusual to have a child in a kindergarten class who stutters

The well-being of the five-year-old 67

Minimum control measures	Other information
Period of communicability: from 7 days after exposure to 3 weeks after onset of "whooping" in untreated children, or 5-7 days after treatment is started.	Immunization is required by law for entrance into school.

Recommendations to schools

If an animal bite occurs:
1. Confine biting animal if possible.
2. Try to obtain as complete a description as possible if the animal escapes.
3. Give first-aid immediately by copious flushing of wound with water or soap or detergent with water.
4. Refer for medical treatment by or under direction of physician.
5. Report all animal bites to the local health department serving the area where the bite occurred.
6. Work with animal control officials to keep dogs off school grounds as much as possible.

In health instruction classes:
1. Teach the proper conduct toward animals to avoid being bitten.
2. Emphasize the dangers in handling stray dogs, cats and wild animals.
3. Stress the necessity of students reporting bites of all animals, especially bats.
4. Encourage immunization of pets.

and stammers. This sometimes is due to an emotional cause, or it can occur when children think faster than they can express themselves. When in doubt, one should refer the parents and child to a speech specialist immediately. Early detection may lead to improvement or correction of the problem.

Other perceptual problems

Often when a child has a perceptual problem, it is not clear whether the problem relates to vision, hearing, or speech, or to something else. At first, a teacher may notice only that there is something unusual about behavior and performance. . . . Children of normal, even excep-

68 *Kindergarten: programs and practices*

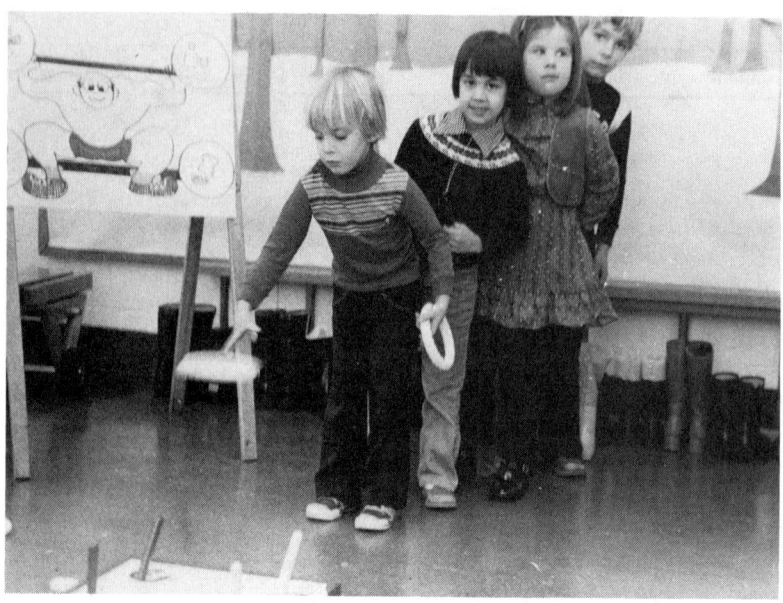

tional intelligence, who have good vision and hearing may nevertheless have perceptual problems which cause them to print upside down and backwards, copy symbols in reverse, or be unable to read and spell even the simplest words. Such disorders are sometimes called "minimal cerebral dysfunction," "minimal brain damage," or "dyslexia." Clues to perceptual problems show up in schoolwork as well as in behavior which may be strangely hyperactive, distractible, awkward, and noisy. . . . Perceptual problems can be improved and even corrected with special educational and psychological techniques. But first of all, it takes awareness to note the need for diagnosis. (Metropolitan Life Insurance Co., 1969, p. 17)

Again, kindergarten teachers who are keen observers can often spot possible perceptual difficulties in children and can make the needed referrals before the problems become compounded.

Activities to aid motor learning, visual motor integration, and visual discrimination are provided on pp. 74 to 87.

Special problems

Some children who enter kindergarten have diabetes, epilepsy, cancer, heart disease, kidney problems, etc. Children with diabetes can lead normal lives when the condition is managed through medication, proper diet, and adequate exercise. Proper medication can also help children with epilepsy lead normal lives. Teachers need to know which children in their classes have diabetes or epilepsy so that they can be aware of any adverse symptoms as well as the kinds of reactions that might be expected while a child is under the influence of prescribed medication.

Children with special handicaps may spend part of their school time outside the regular classroom with specialists, paid aides, or parent volunteers. Whatever the scheduling pattern, it is imperative that kindergarten teachers and specialists consult regularly with each other to provide the child with the best possible program.

Children with handicaps need to be

treated in as nearly the same manner as the other children in the class as possible. Extra attention may be needed, however, to meet their particular needs, to help them progress along with the class, and to help them be accepted within the group. Within reason, and whenever possible, boys and girls with handicaps need to take part in school activities just as their peers do. A kindergarten teacher's attitude of respect and acceptance is vitally necessary in helping other children in the class model the same. In cases where this is not done, children have been known to be outright cruel to a handicapped child. Even five-year-olds, with the proper guidance and understanding, can be very accepting of children with handicaps and can help them in ways that adults often cannot.

Allergies

Many children in the United States suffer from a major allergy, while still others experience some relatively less severe allergic problems. Teachers are becoming increasingly aware, through research and new findings, that allergies in school-age children can cause problems of major proportions. Children with allergies often experience social as well as academic difficulties and, in some cases, have severe learning disabilities. If children are allergic to certain foods, these foods must not be included in their snacks. Children forget easily and will need to be reminded which foods they cannot eat. Since most screening programs do not check for allergies, it is important that kindergarten teachers learn some of the common symptoms of allergies to help detect and refer cases unreported by parents. Within the last ten years there have been many helpful articles written on children's allergies. When allergies are properly diagnosed and treated, the health of the child can be greatly improved, and learning difficulties can often be decreased or eliminated.

Hyperactivity or hyperkinesis

Hyperactive children probably represent one end of a normal spectrum of personality types.... They are more active than the average child, especially in situations—like the classroom—where a great deal of activity is considered inappropriate. They are also more impulsive, excitable, impatient, and distractible.

Hyperactive youngsters are likely to be of normal or above-average intelligence. Yet they have trouble with their schoolwork because they can't concentrate and can't show what they do know. (Papalia and Olds, 1979, p. 456)

One of the most effective means for helping hyperactive children is to break up their work into small, manageable segments and to include physical activity between these segments. It is also a good idea to permit these children to choose a variety of ways in reporting what they have learned. This might include individual conferences and using the tape recorder. Other ways for the child to express himself might be through painting and drawing. In *Introduction to Clinical Allergy*, Feingold (1973) discusses the possibility of helping hyperactive children by placing them on diets free of artificial food colorings and flavorings.

Sometimes drugs are prescribed for a hyperactive child. These drugs apparently help the children to focus their attention on the tasks at hand and thus to concentrate better. The drugs do not help all hyperactive children do better in school, though. And even when they appear to bring about an improvement in school performance, it is important to consider the long-range effects of giving drugs to solve a nonmedical problem.... Because we don't yet know the answer to this and other equally important questions about the administration of stimulant drugs to children, it is best to consider these drugs only as a last resort, after more conservative ways of handling the problem have been tried. (Papalia and Olds, 1979, p. 457)

Teachers should keep in mind that it is not their job to diagnose any suspected ailment. Instead, they need to share and discuss their observations with the other members of the health services and with parents.

PROPER FOOD AND NUTRITION

A proper diet is crucial to children's health during their growing years and in the years to come. For health and vitality, young children need to eat the right foods. Since they are so active, their diet needs to be planned with special care. Children's diets should contain meat, eggs, fish, or cheese; a wide variety of vegetables, both raw and cooked; fruit; and whole-grain cereals and bread. Milk certainly is important but should not be served to the exclusion of other foods. (Remember, some children are allergic to milk.) Some food containing vitamin C should be served every day.

Teachers can help by planning lessons that offer education for good nutrition and by teaching children to choose wisely from a great variety of foods. Kindergarten children delight in helping choose, prepare, and serve healthful foods such as vegetable soup, ice cream, flavored gelatin, and the like.

KINDERGARTEN SNACK TIME

Snack time provides for a good change of activity and for a time to be sociable. Energy snacks are often advisable during the kindergarten session, especially for those children who may not eat enough at mealtime to fill their total needs or for those few children who arrive at school without breakfast or lunch. Milk, fruit, fruit juice, a wedge of cheese, whole-grain crackers, and raw carrots or celery are good examples of snack foods. Snack time can be educational as well as provide a relaxing time for teacher and children to talk informally. It gives children an opportunity to set tables, serve food, and gain added experience in learning good table manners. Children should take turns setting the table, serving the food, and making certain that all of the others clear their places properly as they leave the table. Some teachers choose a host or hostess who is responsible for each table. Sometimes helpers work as a team to prepare and serve the food. This can be a valuable group experience in learning how to work together. Snack time should not immediately precede or follow vigorous activity.

A small fee is generally collected from parents to pay for snacks that are served during the kindergarten day. Some snacks and meals are provided through federally funded programs. In other localities, parents donate the food. Before setting up a fee structure for snacks, teachers need to check with their building principals regarding policy.

REST

Conditions and circumstances often determine whether kindergarten children should have a scheduled rest period. For years it was thought that kindergarten children should rest (lie on rugs) for 15 or 20 minutes per day, about halfway through the session. It is now thought that with careful, balanced program planning that alternates quiet and active periods, most kindergarten children do not need scheduled rest periods each day. In the beginning of the fall term, after much vigorous activity, on hot days, or after long holidays, however, children may need a short rest period. Naturally, special consideration should be given to rest for individual children who require it. Some teachers ask that youngsters rest their heads on tables for rather long periods of time. This is a very uncomfortable position and should be used sparingly, if at all.

When rest time seems advisable (for example, in extended-day or full-day kindergarten programs), children may lie down on small rugs, or better still, on towels that can be laundered. The teacher may read a quiet story or play some soothing music to help them relax. In instances where the teacher can sit in a rocker during rest time and relax too, the children are more apt to settle down and be quiet. Gently rubbing the backs of restless children will often soothe and help them relax. A darkened, quiet room is conducive to rest.

EMOTIONAL HEALTH

An emotionally healthy kindergarten teacher and a stable classroom environment are conducive to the emotional health of five-year-olds. Teachers need to be constantly aware of their own values, feelings, and frustrations, and to work on developing positive strategies for coping with them so that these do not interfere with their teaching and relationships with children. Often kindergarten teachers have been heard to make remarks such as, "The moment I walk into my kindergarten room in the morning and have those 25 eager faces looking up at me, my own problems seem to fade away. I become so engrossed with the many things the children have to tell me and the immediate requests they expect me to meet that I smile and feel truly blessed for the challenge they present."

Because of the physical and emotional demands placed on them, kindergarten teachers must take the time to care for their own physical and emotional health. It is easy to become so absorbed in the everyday teaching of five-year-olds that one's own health can be impaired.

Specialists tell us that approximately one out of ten people will need treatment sometime during their life for emotional problems. Many, if not most, of these problems are thought to have originated during the early childhood years. It therefore behooves teachers, parents, and concerned citizens to work together in trying to discover what problems young children have and their causes, and to plan remediation before it is too late. "Approximately three percent of all children have severe emotional problems, and another eight percent are unable to function normally. Emotional problems include extreme hyperactivity, childhood schizophrenia, autism, and general destructive or aggressive behavior" (Engs and Wantz, 1978, p. 148).

Some children find it difficult to learn and to solve problems because of overprotective parents. Sometimes they are afraid to try things for themselves; for example, to climb equipment, to run an errand for fear of getting lost, to ask another child for a turn on the swing, to try a harder puzzle, and the like. Children need many experiences on how to solve problems on their own. A wise teacher is there at the right moment to give the encouragement and emotional support that is needed. If children are not introduced to a variety of learning experiences geared to their comprehension and ability, the result may be low motivation, insecurity, lack of self-confidence, and poor emotional health.

As illustrated in the following example, there are times when children cannot tell an adult what is bothering them.

Tim attended the morning kindergarten session. During the lunch hour, his mother would take him to a sitter who lived near the school. The sitter had a two-and-a-half-year-old son. Each day, Tim's mother would pack some books, an apple, perhaps a piece of candy, and some toys for Tim to play with in the afternoon while he was at the sitter's house. On occasion, the little boy would take the apple or candy out of the bag and eat it. Tim would tell the sitter, but she rarely did anything about it. Tim's mother mentioned the problem to the sitter and thought that she had taken care of it.

One evening when Tim was a junior in high school, his mother came home from the college where she taught and found that he was ill. She went to his room and they talked for a while about many things. He asked her what class she had taught that evening. She remarked that it was a class in kindergarten education. He said, "What kinds of things do you discuss in that class?" She told him many of the areas that were covered; then, all of a sudden, he said, "Mother, all I ever remember about kindergarten was that you made me go to that awful lady's house." Can you imagine how she felt? "Tim, why didn't you tell me what was troubling you?" she asked. "Mother," he replied, "I didn't know how to say it."

So often, children (and adults) cannot express in words how they really feel inside. Teachers and parents alike must ever be on the alert for signs of things that are troubling youngsters. Fortunately for Tim, he was able to handle the situation concerning the sitter. Another child might not have been so fortunate.

According to Engs and Wantz (p. 148), "Mental health can mean a happy and productive life, and the lack of mental health can mean a miserable existence fraught with anxieties, insecurities, and the inability to achieve even a modicum of happiness or success."

PHYSICAL FITNESS AND ACTIVITY

Child development authorities and medical specialists tell us that young children need plenty of exercise to help build strong bodies. Both large and small muscles are developing at this time, and children seem to delight in learning how to control them as they go about their play.

Several European countries and the U.S.S.R. place great emphasis on helping young children develop strong, healthy bodies through exercise, both planned and unplanned. In 1961, after the late President John F. Kennedy insisted on giving more attention to improving the physical fitness of Americans, more emphasis was placed on planned fitness programs for school-age children. Additional physical education teachers were hired to set up programs in the elementary schools. Physical education teachers began to work more with kindergarten-age children on a broader scale and developed some excellent programs emphasizing physical fitness, movement experiences, and rhythmic activities. It is sad to note, however, that there are some kindergarten children, yet today, who are never permitted to play or exercise outdoors (during the kindergarten session) throughout the school year. Often kindergarten children are excluded if "gym time" becomes the prerogative of older children in the school. Whether activities for physical fitness are scheduled indoors or outdoors, however, they should be included in every kindergarten day.

It is advisable that kindergarten children have their own playground and equipment. This is not always possible, since many times they must share the playground with other elementary classes. Suggested playground equipment for kindergarten children include the following: jungle gyms, monkey bars, climbing towers, individual swings with canvas seats, slides (with safety guards), suspended tires, horizontal bars, walking boards, sliding poles, trapezes within easy reach of the children, low basketball hoops, balls of various sizes, large wheel toys, and the like. The Adventure Playgrounds of Europe offer us many ideas concerning play possibilities for children.

A large space should be provided for children to walk, run, skip, hop, and play informally. At times, activities ought to be planned to help develop certain physical skills. Kindergarten and physical education teachers, working together, can develop excellent health and fitness programs—they need to work more closely than they have in the past.

The following activities are designed to aid in motor learning, visual motor integration, and visual discrimination.

Text continued on p. 88.

Motor learning, visual-motor integration, and visual discrimination

Robert Robinson

MOTOR LEARNING
Body localization

DEFINITION: The ability to locate and identify body parts.

PSYCHOEDUCATIONAL RATIONALE: Before children can develop and express an adequate self-image, they need to be able to name and locate body parts.

BEHAVIORAL OBJECTIVES: The child will identify his own body parts as basic body parts are called out. The child will be able to draw body detail.

ACTIVITIES
1. Select six body parts. Have the child face a full-length mirror. As each body part is called out, the child places both hands on it. After the child has mastered the first six, begin with another set of six, interspersing them with the original set. Concentrate on difficult locations. Areas to be included: head, knees, ears, hips, eyes, fingers, elbows, mouth, feet, nose, ankles, toes, shoulders, seat, chest, back, stomach, wrist, waist, palms, knuckles, chin.
2. Read verbal instructions to the child from a list.*
    a. Using two body parts at the same time:
        (1) Put your chin on your knees.
        (2) Put your hands on your hips.
        (3) Put your heels together.
    b. Touching body parts to surroundings:
        (1) Put your hands on the wall.
        (2) Put your back to the wall.
        (3) Put your head on the desk.
    c. Imitating instructor movements:
        (1) Nod your head.
        (2) Close your eyes.
        (3) Click your fingers.
    d. Stating the usage of body parts (the child provides names):
        (1) I see with my _____.
        (2) I smell with my _____.
        (3) I shrug my _____.
        (4) I write with my _____.
3. Give the child a large, full-body photograph. On instruction, he points to body parts (eyes, nose, hands, mouth, feet, ears, eyebrows, eyelashes, knees, etc.)
4. Draw (or have another child draw) around the child on large brown wrapping paper. The child fills in details to make a life-sized self-puzzle. Cut apart to make a puzzle—head, neck, arms, legs, feet, etc.
5. Use a photo of the child. Cut up as parts of a puzzle. Have the child assemble it.
6. Use body parts to locate surroundings. (Touch table with nose, wall with back, floor with knees.)

*These are done as separate activities. For increased difficulty, combine two or more areas.

Continued.

Motor learning, visual-motor integration, and visual discrimination, cont'd

7. Have the child touch one body part with other body parts. (Ear on shoulder.)
8. Draw an incomplete man on the chalkboard or on paper and ask the child to supply the missing part.
9. Cut out a picture of a part of the body. Give it to the child and ask him to complete the person around the part.
10. Cut up a paper doll and put the pieces in an envelope. Give it to the child and ask him to reassemble the person.
11. Set up an obstacle course including something to crawl through, go under, go over, and squeeze through.
12. Encourage creative movement using the whole room. Use your own imagination! Suggestions:
    a. Show me how small you can be.
    b. Show me how tall you can be.
    c. Show me how wide you can be.
    d. Show me how tall and thin you can be.
    e. Show me how long and thin you can be.
    f. Standing in your own place, make your feet move slowly.
    g. Standing in your own place, make your feet move fast.

Body balance

DEFINITION: The ability to maintain gross and fine balance.
PSYCHOEDUCATIONAL RATIONALE: The maintenance of body balance is fundamental to readiness for more advanced perceptual-motor experiences.
BEHAVIORAL OBJECTIVES: The child will be able to increase the time static balance can be maintained and maintain balanced body movements during difficult movement patterns.
ACTIVITIES

1. Have the child stand on floor marks with shoes off. The child walks forward on toes six steps, backward on toes six steps, and sideways to the right (left) on toes six steps. Have the child repeat these procedures, walking on heels.
2. Place several tiles or textured squares on the floor in a curved-line pattern. Have the child remove shoes and stay on tiles as he walks the pattern from beginning to end. Tell the child that this is a river with stepping stones in it.
3. Use tape to make a Z on the floor (parallel lines 8 feet long, diagonal line 10 feet long). Have the child skip forward on the Z and backward to the starting point.
4. Basic balance: The child stands on one foot for a period of 20 to 25 seconds. He repeats with the other foot. Variation: The child closes his eyes.
5. Blind man's stand: The child sits on the floor, crosses his arms, closes his eyes, and stands up.
6. Blind man's rise: The child lies on the floor, crosses his arms, closes his eyes, and stands up.
7. Tiptoe stand: The child stands on tiptoes and closes his eyes (20 to 25 seconds). Variation: The child repeats on one foot at a time.
8. Knee walk: The child walks on his knees, hands in the air. Variation: The child varies speed and stops on command.

9. Ankle-grasp walk: The child holds his hands on his ankles and walks. Variation: The child walks backward, sideways, and varies speed.
10. Rocking horse: The child stands with hands on hips, legs astride. He rocks forward, lifting his heels from the floor. He rocks back, lifting his toes.
11. Rooster walk: The child holds his head and chest high and walks forward with his knees straight and his hands at the side of his chest.
12. Elephant walk: The child bends forward at the waist and allows his arms to hang limp; he clasps his hands. Big lumbering steps should sway the child from side to side.
13. Duck walk: From the deep–knee bend position, the child places his hands behind his back to represent a duck's tail and walks forward.
14. Bunny hop: The child places his hands at the side of his head for ears and hops forward on both feet.
15. Crab walk: The child sits on the floor and places his hands palm down behind his back. He walks on his hands and feet in a backward direction.
16. Frog hop: After doing a deep knee bend, the child places his hands on his hips. He extends one leg to the side and returns.

Walking

DEFINITION: The ability to walk erect in a coordinated fashion without support.

PSYCHOEDUCATIONAL RATIONALE: Walking is a muscular act requiring balance and coordination. Children should be given an opportunity to develop this skill since it is an aid in developing more advanced coordination.

BEHAVIORAL OBJECTIVE: The child will be able to walk in a coordinated fashion without support or being awkward.

ACTIVITIES
1. Shoeless walk.
    a. (Have children remove shoes for all walking beam activities; line up and walk the beam one at a time.)
    b. (Place the tip of a pointer—3 or 4 feet long—on the beam about 6 feet ahead of the child; direct the child to watch the tip of the pointer, which is moved across the floor until the child reaches the end of the beam.)
    c. Step onto the beam. Look down at the tip of the pointer. Walk Indian fashion, heel to toe, keeping eyes on the tip of the pointer.
    d. (Attach a piece of string from the end of the beam in a straight line to the wall. Put a red X or other object of interest on the wall at the far end of the string as a visual fixation target. Remind children to watch the target.)
    e. This time as you walk, look at the red X.
2. Butterflies.
    a. Walk as in shoeless walk. Look at the red X.
    b. This time, spread your arms out at the sides like a tightrope walker or the wings of a butterfly; move them slowly up and down.
    c. Have your arms just far enough forward that you can look at your target and still see your hands moving up and down out of the corners of your eyes.

Continued.

Motor learning, visual-motor integration, and visual discrimination, cont'd

3. Backward walk.
   a. Walk backward, heel to toe (actually, toe to heel). Eyes always on target. Judge where the end will be.
   b. This time, walk backward, waving your arms up and down slowly at your sides like a butterfly and "see" them out of the corners of your eyes.
4. Forward and backward walk.
   a. Walk forward on the beam until I say "reverse"; then backward until I tell you "forward" again, etc.
   b. (After children develop some mastery, change directions to front—back; forward—backward, etc.)
   c. Keep your eyes on the target.
   d. (Repeat using normal-sized, giant, baby steps, etc.)
   e. (Good place for children to play "Captain, May I.")
5. Stepping off distances.
   a. (Divide the beam into fractions—halves, quarters. You may use different-colored lines, such as red in the middle, green at the quarter mark, etc. You can use these divisions to emphasize multiples, etc., after the mechanics of starting, stopping, and reversing are mastered.)
   b. This time, using normal steps, I want you to walk to the red line, stop, and go backward to the green line, stop, and then go forward to the end.
   c. (Turn the beam over so that markings are on the bottom side. Repeat stepping-off routines with no guidelines. Stress fractional parts of the board as well as other addition and subtraction problems in arithmetic.)
   d. I have turned the beam over so you cannot see the markings. This time, walk to the middle and stop when you think your *toe* is exactly in the middle of the beam. We will then look down and check before you go on to the end.
   e. (Continue on above routines until it is easy for children to walk the beam while watching a fixation target. They should get to the point where they can walk forward and backward, making simple judgments of their stopping positions.)
6. Peripheral targets.
   a. Notice the red circle on the chalkboard next to the halfway point on the beam. Walk the board, keeping your eyes on the target. When you think you are next to the circle—without looking at it—put your finger on the circle. Now look and see how close your fingers came to the center of the circle. Lower your arms and continue walking.
   b. The beam is at an angle to the chalkboard (or well). An X is at both ends of the beam. Begin at the *far away* end of the beam; keep your eyes on the target. When you think you are just close enough to reach out and touch the chalkboard with your fingertips, *stop* and try, without looking. While your arm is trying, turn your head and look to see how close your fingers came. Then continue walking to the end of the beam.
7. Walking beam activities. (Select appropriate activity.)
   a. Walk backward, arms out at sides.

b. Walk sideways, weight on balls of feet, arms out at sides. Walk right to left, and left to right.
c. Walk forward with your right foot always in front.
d. Walk forward with your left foot always in front.
e. Walk backward with your right foot always in front.
f. Walk backward with your left foot always in front.
g. Walk forward with your hands clasped behind your body.
h. Walk backward with your hands clasped behind your body.
i. Walk forward with your arms folded on your chest.
j. Walk forward with your arms held straight over your head.
k. Walk backward with your arms held straight over your head.
l. Walk forward with your arms held straight out in front.
m. Walk forward with an eraser on top of your head.
n. Walk backward with an eraser on top of your head.
o. Walk to the middle, kneel, and pick up the eraser; place it on your head, rise, and continue.
p. Walk sideways, crossing your right foot over your left foot. Repeat with your left foot over your right foot.
q. Walk the board after putting a book under one end so that it slants up.

Jumping

DEFINITION: The ability to jump single obstacles without falling.
PSYCHOEDUCATIONAL RATIONALE: Children should be able to coordinate themselves in simple jumping tasks. Jumping is a prerequisite to the development of other motoric skills.
BEHAVIORAL OBJECTIVE: The child will be able to jump without difficulty or awkwardness.
ACTIVITIES

1. Jumping together: Face the child and hold hands. Jump together while counting to ten.
2. One-foot jump: The child jumps back and forth over a line, four times on the right foot, four times on the left foot, and repeats.
3. Snake jump: The child crouches in a squatting position and then jumps up with the hands outstretched like the body of a snake.
4. Rabbit jump: The child squats low on his heels. Place the child's hands palm down, fingers pointing toward the floor behind him. The child moves his hands forward and brings his feet forward between the hands with a little jump. The child repeats, simulating a rabbit.
5. The child jumps on both feet—up and down.
6. The child jumps on one foot—up and down.
7. The child jumps on both feet—eyes closed—up and down.
8. The child jumps on one foot—eyes closed—up and down.
9. The child jumps forward.
10. The child jumps backward.
11. The child jumps sidewise—left and right.
12. The child jumps and turns one quarter, one half, and all the way around.
13. The child jumps forward three steps with his eyes closed.

Continued.

Motor learning, visual-motor integration, and visual discrimination, cont'd

Body coordination

DEFINITION: The ability to move one's body in coordinated movement.

PSYCHOEDUCATIONAL RATIONALE: Children need to be taught the enjoyment of free movement.

BEHAVIORAL OBJECTIVES: The child will be able to execute coordinated body movements and progress to more intricate exercises in time.

ACTIVITIES
1. Swaying: Stand, arms overhead, and lean to the left, right, back, and front, keeping your feet flat on the floor.
2. High-stepping horse: Walk by bringing your knees very high in the air and coming down toes first.
3. Butterflies: Extend your arms and move them up and down in a graceful movement while tiptoeing around the room.
4. Frog leaping: Squat, hands on floor in front of feet, and leap forward.
5. Bend and stretch: Stand, arms raised over your head. Bend and touch your toes. Raise your arms and stretch up, keeping your arms and legs straight.
6. Bunny bounce: Hands at the side of your head, hop forward by flexing your knees.
7. Swinging: Face your partner, hold hands with your arms slightly extended, and swing your arms from side to side.
8. Pony ride: Squat and extend your hands to the front, as if holding reins; flexing your knees, bounce up and down.
9. Rag doll: Bend forward, allowing your arms to hang limp. Bounce your upper body from the waist. Your legs remain stiff.
10. Rope jumping.
    a. Forward—feet together.
    b. Forward—alternating feet.
    c. Forward—one foot at a time.
    d. Backward—feet together.
    e. Backward—alternating feet.
    f. Backward—one foot at a time.
    g. Hot pepper forward.
    h. Hot pepper backward.
11. (Have children lie on their backs and slide their arms slowly overhead until they touch; return.)
12. (Have children lie on their backs, slide their legs apart, and slowly return.)
13. Angels in the snow: Lie on your back with your legs straight, arms at sides. Without lifting your arms or legs from the floor, at the same time slide both arms toward your head and both legs outward; return.
14. (Have children lie on their backs, legs straight and arms at sides.) Slide your right arm up and your left leg out. Reverse—slide your left arm up and your right leg out. Slowly!
15. (Have children lie on the floor and try to make circles in the air with their feet.)

Imitating

ACTIVITIES
1. Throwing.
    a. Overhand.
    b. Underhand.
    c. Both hands (vary type of throw).
    d. Throw from knees.
2. Kicking.
    a. Pretend you are kicking a football.
    b. Kick backward—alternate feet.

Sensory-motor integration

DEFINITION: The psychophysical integration of fine and gross motor activities.
PSYCHOEDUCATIONAL RATIONALE: The ability to perform both fine and gross motor activities is a prerequisite to the development of good body coordination.
BEHAVIORAL OBJECTIVE: The child will be able to move the body in an integrated way through a number of specific exercises.
ACTIVITIES
1. Balls.
    a. Bounce and catch.
    b. Bounce and bounce.
    c. Bounce the ball with both hands continuously.
    d. Bounce the ball with one hand.
    e. Alternate hands while bouncing the ball.
    f. Throw the ball up and down, catching it.
    g. (Person in center of circle. Calls a number; bounces; the child with the number steps forward to catch it.)
    h. (Two lines. Toss [or bounce] the ball from one line to the other, to each child in turn, and back across the line again. Variations: One step back each time line finishes.)
2. Balloon batting. (Children attempt to keep an inflated balloon in the air by batting it with open hands.)
3. Whiffle ball. (Hang a whiffle ball from string; direct children to keep the ball moving by batting it with their palms. Use four children in a circle.)
4. Bean bag toss. (Have children toss bean bags into a bucket or container with a similarly sized opening.)
5. Clothespin drop. (From a standing position, the child drops a clothespin into a large-mouthed bottle.)
6. Clothesline walk. (Lay a clothesline in a loopy pattern and have children step in loops without touching the rope.)
7. Close your hand in a tight fist. Open your hand very wide. Repeat.
8. Finger touches: Holding your hands in the air, tap your pointer finger against your thumb. Repeat and tap your middle finger against your thumb. Continue with your ring and little fingers.

Continued.

Motor learning, visual-motor integration, and visual discrimination, cont'd

9. Snapping fingers: Use one hand at a time, then both.
10. Tapping fingers: Place your palm on the table and tap one finger at a time against the table. Use both hands alternately.
11. Paper crumple: Holding a sheet of paper in each hand, start crumpling the paper into a ball. Do not touch your body with your hands and do not put your hands together.
12. Finger plays: Pick up small objects such as pennies, marbles, beans, etc.

VISUAL-MOTOR INTEGRATION
DEFINITION: The ability to coordinate fine muscles such as those required in tracing, copying, and other eye-hand tasks.
PSYCHOEDUCATIONAL RATIONALE: The coordination of visual stimuli with fine motor responses is necessary before the child can be able to write legibly.
BEHAVIORAL OBJECTIVES: The child will be able to trace and copy forms, letters, and numerals without difficulty or gross errors.
ACTIVITIES
1. Draw a vertical line, circle, square, triangle, and diamond on the chalkboard. Have children come to the board and trace the forms with fingers. Children then draw the forms on the chalkboard and chalk in the designs, after which they trace the perimeters, first with a finger and then again with chalk.
2. Children then copy the forms on drawing paper using felt-tipped pens or crayons; they fill in the designs and again trace the perimeters. They cut out the forms and place them on the paper, trace again, and cut out for practice.
3. Provide open stencils of forms for precise tracing followed by coloring and cutting. Use hardboard forms for precise perimeter tracing, coloring, and cutting.
4. Have the child cut out sandpaper forms and sort them.
5. Have the child complete paint-by-number pictures.
6. Have the child make finger painting pictures.
7. Use templates. The child traces inside first, then outside.

 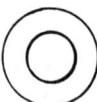

8. Use drawing roads and stencil letters (1/2 inch wide at first, then narrower).

9. Fold paper into squares, rectangles, and triangles. The child traces on the folds with his finger and then a pencil.
10. Use acetate to cover a sheet with lines, patterns, or letters. The child traces over them with a crayon.

11. Use dot-to-dot puzzles of letters.

12. Project letters onto an easel to trace.
13. Use dots to mark where to start to make a form or letter.
14. Use dots as markers to indicate where letter parts should be joined.

15. Prepare a series of pictures with the first picture complete. Others in the row must be completed to look like the first one. Later do not present the initial model.

16. Give the child a single design (circle, square, etc.). Have him add lines to make it into an object. Use similar activities for letter completion.

VISUAL DISCRIMINATION

DEFINITION: The ability to see differences between visual stimuli that vary in shape, size, and color.

PSYCHOEDUCATIONAL RATIONALE: The ability to see likenesses and differences in one's environment is a prerequisite to symbolic differentiation and interpretation as required in reading.

BEHAVIORAL OBJECTIVES: On instruction, the child will be able to recognize and differentiate among various letters, sizes, configurations, and shapes.

ACTIVITIES

1. Present a series of different-sized and colored buttons; present a duplicate and have the child point out the match.
2. Lay out four identical books—three facing in one direction and the fourth reversed; have the child point out and comment on the difference. Extend directional exercises with papers, pencils, or other objects.
3. Arrange four checker patterns—three identical and one slightly different; have the child point out the difference.
4. Use design cards for visual matching—teach matching and differentiation of design cards.

Continued.

Motor learning, visual-motor integration, and visual discrimination, cont'd

5. On instruction, the child will pick out a letter from an array of letters. The child is given a sheet with 15 lines of letters. Tell the child to listen carefully and circle a certain letter. Give the child a sample strip with five letters (c d f h p) and say, "Circle d".
6. Make cards of similar letters for visual discrimination. Use the following sets: b d p g, h u v n, c e u s, y h k t, m n w r, x z v w, f l t h, a r e s, i j y l. Next, show the card and ask which of the letters below is the same as the letter on top:

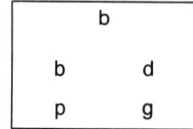

7. What is missing?
   a. Materials: Group of objects.
   b. Procedure: Lay objects on the table. Have the child look at them and then close his eyes. Remove an object. The child must tell what is missing.
8. Shape hunt.
   a. Materials: Two sets of tagboard shapes.
   b. Procedure: Hide one shape per child in the room. Tell children "They look like these." Give one shape to each child. Each must find his own shape. If he sees another one, he must walk right by it and say nothing. Hide and pass out shapes again.
9. Feel the shape.
   a. Materials: Geometric shapes.
   b. Procedure: Place a shape in the child's hands (behind his back). The child feels it and tells what shape he thinks it is.
10. Matching.
    a. Materials: Prepare sheets of paper with colored shapes on each side (slide them into a plastic slipcover so that they can be reused); crayon to connect the matching shapes.

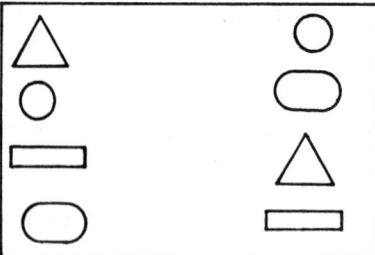

    b. Procedure: Have the child draw lines to connect the matching shapes.

11. Watch the spinning wheel.
    a. Materials: Large cardboard wheel with spinner; separate cards with shapes, pictures, etc., each one different; and small cover pieces.

 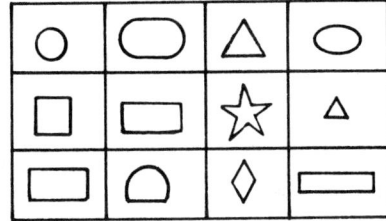

    b. Procedure: (Similar to bingo.) You or a child spins the arrow. When it stops, children use squares of paper to cover the same picture if it appears on their card. The child who covers his card first becomes the next spinner.
12. Camera.
    a. Materials: Chalkboard, or paper and pencil.
    b. Procedure: Tell children, "We are going to play a game called "Camera." I want you to shut your eyes while I draw a shape on the chalkboard. When I say "click" you may open your eyes and "take a picture" of the word on the board. You will need to take the picture very quickly, because I will erase the word [or remove the paper] as soon as you open your eyes. Then I will ask someone to develop his film." This person will then come and draw the picture he saw on the chalkboard.
13. What has changed?
    a. Materials: Blocks, flannel board shapes, or construction paper shapes.
    b. Procedure: Place several objects in a row. The child closes his eyes while you either remove one article or change the position of one or two articles. The child opens his eyes and must tell what has changed. (Make this more complicated as the child improves.)
14. Change-O.
    a. Materials: Paper and marker, or chalkboard.
    b. Procedure: Draw a circle on the paper. Let children look at it. Have children close their eyes while you change the circle (add another line or shape, etc.) Ask, "Who can tell us how the circle is changed?" The child who describes the change correctly may make the next change. (Use other shapes or designs. Make designs more complex as children advance.)
15. Popsicle sticks.
    a. Materials: Popsicle sticks or tongue depressors.
    b. Procedure: Create a pattern for the child; have him repeat it.

 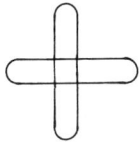

Continued.

Motor learning, visual-motor integration, and visual discrimination, cont'd

16. Train sticks.
    a. Materials: Ten Popsicle sticks or tongue depressors colored at each end (different colors on one stick).
    b. Procedure: Children match colored ends of sticks to form geometric shapes. End colors must match before the stick can be used. This can be done with a time limit.
17. Pegboard copy game.
    a. Materials: Two pegboards, colored pegs, and string.
    b. Procedure: Make a design on one pegboard with pegs. Then outline the design with string, letting the child see the design as a whole. Discuss the design with the child and remove the string. The child then duplicates the design on his own board. (When the child gets better at this, original board can be removed.) Check the design by referring to the model. (Use string again.)

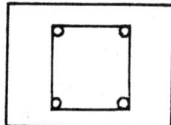

18. Fish.
    a. Materials: Oak tag cards in pairs with one geometrical figure on each card—square, circle, triangle, oval, star, diamond, rectangle. Use different colors for large variety.
    b. Procedure: Cards are dealt one at a time, each player holding five cards. The remainder of the pack is placed in the center of the table, face down. The object of the game is to get as many pairs of cards as possible. The player on the dealer's left starts by asking any child he wishes for a card that matches one that he has in his hand (e.g., purple triangle). If the child has this card, he gives it to the first player. If he does not have it, he tells the first player to go fish. The first player then takes the top card from the pack. If it is the card he asked for, he takes another turn. If not, the next player takes a turn. (Play with two or more children.)
19. Tinkertoys.
    a. Materials: Tinkertoys
    b. Procedure: The teacher makes a three-dimensional object with tinkertoys. The child reproduces the object. Increase complexity as the child gains proficiency.
20. Fit the pieces.
    a. Materials: Oak tag or cardboard shapes (circle, diamond, etc.), and envelopes.
    b. Procedure: Cut each shape into various segments, place in an envelope, and draw the shape on the envelope. The child tries to fit the segments into the outline of the shape on the envelope to make a whole.

21. Card game.
    a. Materials: Sixty 2-inch square cards with ten simple shapes or designs (six cards for each design).

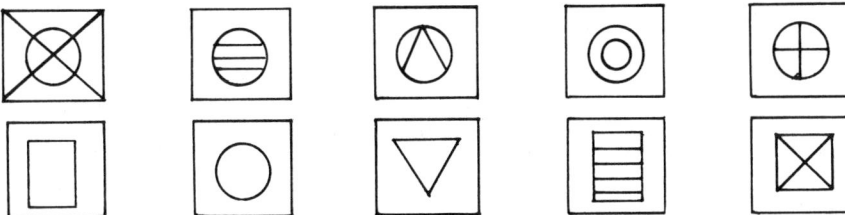

    b. Procedure: Four children (or less). Deal cards (each child gets 15). Each child places his cards in a pile in front of him, face down. Each child then turns over the top card at the same time to show the others. If he sees a card like his, the child calls "match." The child who has the matching card gives it to the caller. If there is no match, each child turns over the next card. When the pile has been gone through, it is shuffled, and children repeat the procedure. The child with the most matched pairs wins.
22. Bead patterns.
    a. Materials: Cards with bead patterns and string with beads.
    b. Procedure: String variously colored and shaped beads on a string in a pattern. Have the child copy the pattern. After practice the child can copy the pattern from a card rather than the model.

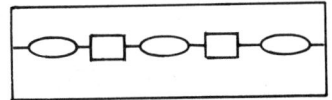

23. Cube block designs.
    a. Materials: One-inch cube blocks in various colors; for more advanced stages, cards with block patterns printed on them.
    b. Procedure: Construct a pattern using blocks (first use one color, then use several colors). Have the child repeat the design with other blocks. If he is unsuccessful, he may place his blocks on top of yours. When the child can copy complex models of one or two colors, introduce other colors. When the child can copy models, introduce pattern cards to copy.
24. Parquetry block designs.
    a. Materials: Parquetry blocks; design cards for blocks.
    b. Procedure: Same as for cube block designs except now there is a variation of shapes.

Continued.

Motor learning, visual-motor integration, and visual discrimination, cont'd

25. Dominoes.
    a. Materials: Cards with shapes rather than dots.
    b. Procedure: Same as for dominoes. Each child is dealt six cards. One child begins by putting down one of his cards. The next child matches one of his cards to the first, as shown below. The winner is the child who uses up all of his cards first.

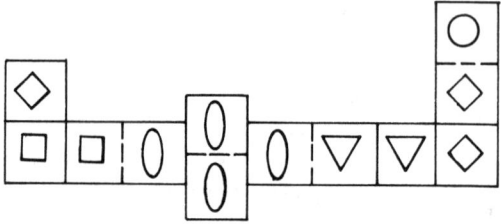

26. Design boards.
    a. Materials: Two pegboards (10 inches × 10 inches) with screws and bolts to form a pattern; rubber bands.

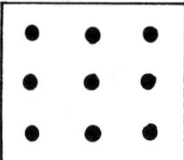 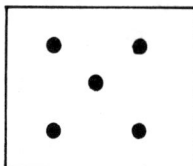 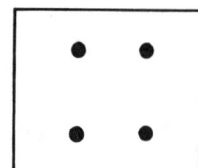

    b. Procedure: Create a pattern with rubber bands on the first board. The child repeats the pattern on his board.
27. Washers with design boards.
    a. Materials: Two boards as for design boards; metal washers (can be painted several colors).

b. Procedure: Place washers on the first board in a pattern. The child repeats the pattern on his board.

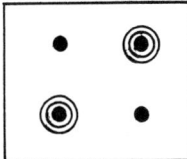

28. Use Frostig materials.
29. Use parquetry blocks and designs.
30. Use cube designs and blocks.
31. Make matching boards with yarn ties and fasteners.

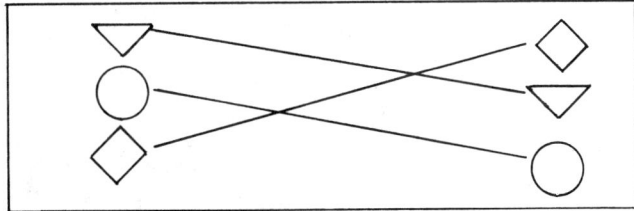

32. Use pictures of objects wherein all but one (and later more) belong to the set. Have the child identify the one that does not belong (Example: curved vs. straight lines).
33. Use pictures in which shapes are hidden.
34. Use puzzles.
35. Classify objects according to color, size, and shape.
36. Make a board with nails evenly spaced for making designs with rubber bands.
37. Prepare dittoed sheets wherein the child must find objects in varying spatial positions.
38. Dominoes: Have the child match various designs.
39. Have the child match playing cards.
40. Have the child match and sort letters, numbers, and words.
41. Have the child find the missing part in a magazine picture that has had a piece cut out.
42. Use a dittoed sheet with numerals or letters in a column on the left side. Have these same symbols with variations typed in a horizontal row. Ask the child to circle each symbol that is just like the one in the left column.

d   c b d e f g b e d k h d e f h l p d b

Safety

As a child learns safety rules, he takes a big step in growing up. He shows by his behavior that he can be trusted to do many things without constant supervision. Along with this greater freedom comes a sense of achievement and perhaps special rewards. (Metropolitan Life Insurance Co., 1970, p. 13)

Thousands of children in the United States are either permanently crippled or die by accidents each year. It is the responsibility of parents, teachers, and the community to work together in providing safe environments for children. Kindergarten teachers have a unique opportunity to help the five-year-old develop a better understanding of safety, whether it be in the home or school, on the playground, on the street, on the bus, or in the car. Children of this age are not too young to learn how to protect themselves from traffic, fire, water, poisons, harmful drugs, and other dangers. A goal of highest priority in the kindergarten would be to help children live and learn in an environment that is supportive of high standards of health and safety. Certainly children can and should participate in the formulation of rules and standards that are simple and clear-cut, and that will help them achieve a greater respect for safety.

During the summer, many communities are now involving interested groups in conducting "Safety Town" programs or similar safety programs for preschool children. Attendance is on a voluntary basis. These programs are usually very well organized and give children concentrated and thorough training in traffic safety.

MAINTAINING A SAFE SCHOOL ENVIRONMENT

Teachers and other school personnel share the responsibility of setting up and maintaining a safe school environment. Periodically,

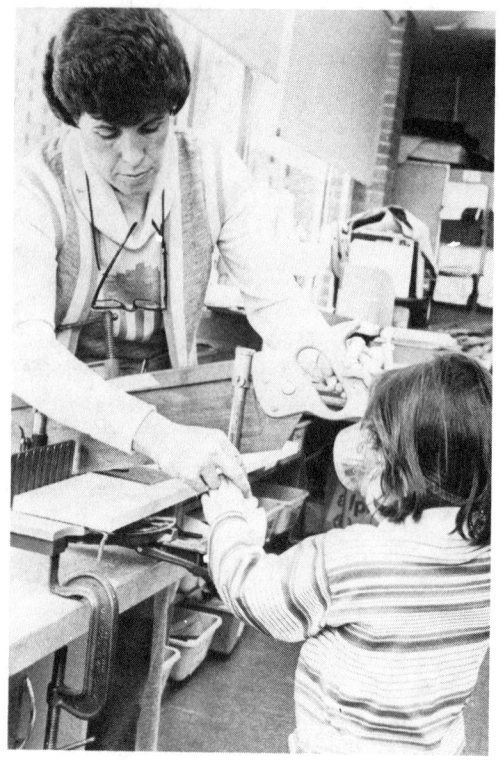

materials and equipment should be given safety checks. It is not uncommon to find poorly anchored playground equipment and equipment with sharp edges or splintered wood surfaces. Unsafe equipment needs to be reported immediately to the principal or custodian in charge.

Young children need specific instruction in the proper use of tools, scissors, and pointed objects. Some activities, such as woodworking, require close supervision. Children should never be left unsupervised. It is a good practice to show children how to carry their chairs safely from one area of the room to another, and to teach them to pick up objects from the floor to prevent stumbling and to wipe up water from the floor. Children can be taught to be more aware of any existing danger to themselves and to others.

Safety to and from school

It is imperative that children be able to give their names, addresses, and telephone numbers. Some children wear a necklace or bracelet or carry a card bearing this information. Early in the year, safety rules concerning crossing streets and riding the bus need to be discussed. These rules should be reviewed periodically, since children tend to forget. Having bus drivers, school guards, firemen, and policemen come to the kindergarten room and talk to the class gives a more personal touch and helps children identify more readily with these community helpers. It is important that teachers impress on children—and reinforce parents' warnings—that they must not talk to, ride with, or take anything from a stranger. Hopefully, children would trust their teachers enough to inform them of any stranger who approached them under such conditions.

Emergencies

The teacher new to a district should ask the principal for information and procedures concerning fire drills, tornado and hurricane drills, and any other safety procedures. As indicated in Chapter 3, it is important to rehearse safety drills early in the school year. Local fire and safety departments make periodic checks with schools to see that fire drills are conducted and carried out properly. In preparing children for emergency situations, teachers need to establish a definite signal that means, "Stop what you are doing, *now!* Listen carefully!" The children should be informed as to what they are to do. Time must not be wasted. (Procedures should be discussed thoroughly with the children and practiced prior to drills.) Being careful not to frighten the children, one must act quickly.

It is also very important that teachers be aware of what type of emergency is being signaled from the principal's office. A college supervisor was observing a student teacher in a kindergarten. The children were busily engaged in work time activities. Much talking was taking place. An alarm rang, and the supervising teacher signaled the children to stop their work immediately. They did. She informed them all to stand against one side of the room with their hands on the wall above their heads. It wasn't long before the principal appeared and said, "Folks, you've all been burned up!" He had given the alarm of a fire drill, and the teacher had misinterpreted it for an air raid drill!

No matter how careful teachers try to be to ensure children's safety, accidents will occur. Most accidents are simple bruises, slight falls, skinned arms and legs, and the like. In the case of more serious accidents, one should follow emergency measures as outlined by the school. Telephone numbers of parents and doctors should be readily available. Names and telephone numbers of nearby neighbors also need to be on file with the teacher and in the school office in case of an emergency wherein the parents cannot be reached. It is important to be well informed on first aid measures and on what type of aid can or cannot be administered by a teacher. When in doubt, one should check with the principal and school nurse. Checking a child's individual records will also reveal procedures specified by the parents. Some schools require teachers to take a first aid course. In some areas these courses are free.

Special hazards

It is necessary that teachers as well as parents help children understand the danger of playing with matches and cigarette lighters and of engaging in other dangerous activities. Some drug education should also be included at the kindergarten level.

SAFETY: A PRIORITY

Safety must be a priority at the kindergarten level, and both spontaneous and planned lessons concerning safety should be a part of the ongoing curriculum.

We need to give children of five more responsibility for their own safety. Since children develop and mature at different speeds, some fives will be ready for more responsibility than other fives. But all need help from family, school, and community in learning more about their own safety and that of others.

The following episodes are examples of problems and accidents that have been reported by kindergarten teachers. These examples provide a good opportunity to think through what one might do in each case.

What would you do if?

1. You have just taken your class of kindergarten children to the playground. You are the only teacher present. As you look toward the slide, you see Linda topple over the side from the very top. She lands on the blacktop surface of the playground and lies there motionless.
2. Your kindergarten class is housed in the basement of a church directly across the street from the elementary school building. You have no telephone in your room, but there is one in the church office. Mary, one of the children in the class, suddenly develops a severe nosebleed.
3. It is February, and there are 9 inches of snow on the ground. Your kindergarten class is engaged in work time activities. You, another teacher, an aide, and another adult are present. Three children are walking about the room in their stocking feet as they go about their activities. These children had worn snow boots to school and had complained about their feet being too hot. You have permitted the children to take off their snow boots. The fire alarm rings. You have had no previous warning.
4. Billy, a lively five-year-old, suddenly picks up and swallows a pill intended for Julie.

SAFETY ACTIVITIES

The following activities relating to fire safety and traffic safety are designed to further develop safety concepts in children:

Fire safety

PROBLEM 1: HOW CAN FIRE BE PREVENTED?

CONCEPTS
    1. With care, fires can be prevented.
    2. Fire drills are important.
    3. Safety measures are taken in case of fire.

ACTIVITIES
    1. Approach the problem by:
        a. Taking a walk to the nearest fire alarm box.
        b. Showing a filmstrip.
        c. Reading a story about a fire engine.
        d. Visiting a fire station.
    2. Discuss with the children how fires can best be prevented.
        a. Never *use or play* with matches
        b. Keep them in a safe place out of reach of very young children.
        c. Help father rake the leaves, but do not burn them for him. Let father handle the matches.
        d. Give old papers and magazines to the school paper drive instead of letting them accumulate in the attic or basement.

e. Keep oily cleaning rags in cans or keep them washed.
   f. Stress the importance of thoroughly putting out a campfire by using water, dirt, or wet leaves.
   g. Make a chart on campfires.
   h. Do not leave a fire. Put it out with wet leaves, sand, dirt, or water.
3. Make a small fire in a pan. Put an asbestos plate under the pan. Extinguish the fire by covering it with sand or dirt. This will prove that fire needs air to make it burn.
4. Take the group around the building to find safety provisions: fire extinguisher, fire exits, fire bell.
5. Stress the importance of using a flashlight instead of a candle in a jack-o-lantern.
6. To culminate activities on the prevention of fires, make an activity booklet by folding a long narrow strip of brown wrapping paper into sections. Leave one section for the title and have the children use the others to illustrate the rules for preventing fires. Have each child make an activity book.

PROBLEM 2: HOW CAN WE MAKE OUR FIRE DRILLS VITAL?

ACTIVITIES
1. Discuss with the group the following important rules:
   a. When the fire alarm rings, walk quietly to the nearest exit.
   b. Keep hands at sides and walk quickly, but do not run.
   c. Be alert and ready to listen at all times in case a change in direction is made.
2. Close the door of the classroom after everyone has left. Stress the importance of fire drills to *each* child. Fire drills may keep *him* from getting hurt in case of a real fire.
3. Make a chart on fire drill rules.
   a. Walk—do not run.
   b. Do not push.
   c. Do not talk.
4. Have the children make a border of flames (use red paper) to paste around the edge of the chart.
5. Have several practice fire drills.
6. Make a mural. Have each child draw himself walking in a straight line.
7. Discuss the proper procedure to observe when a child's clothing catches on fire. Pretend to smother the fire with a blanket or coat, or by rolling the child on the floor. Also have the children dramatize this.
8. Cover a lighted candle with a glass jar. Help the group realize that the fire of the candle goes out when it has no air.
9. Discuss what a child should do if he discovers a fire himself. Ask him to notify an older person immediately and ask this older person to turn in the alarm or call the fire station. Have the children dramatize this procedure.
10. Make a simple fire truck out of an egg carton. Use silver buttons for headlights and black buttons for wheels. Paint the truck with red powdered paint.
11. Make a table model of a burning house (flames of red paper), using pipe-cleaner people, an egg carton fire truck, etc. Use dramatic play to show the procedure that should be used in asking an adult to turn in an alarm, or in smothering a fire in case of burning clothing. Let the children manipulate the pipe-cleaner figures to show all this.

Continued.

Fire safety, cont'd

BOOKS TO BE READ TO THE CHILDREN

Book	Author	Publisher
Firemen (Unit Study Book No. 103)	Eleanor Johnson	Educational Printing House, Inc.
Fireman Fred	Jene Barr	Albert Whitman & Co.
The Little Fire Engine	Lois Lenski	Oxford University Press
True Book of Policemen and Firemen	Irene Miner	Children's Press

Traffic safety

Charlene Redmond

RATIONALE

The purpose of this center is to make children aware of the many signs that they should be familiar with in their travels to and from school. The idea is not for kindergarten children to learn to read every traffic sign or signal; but through various activities, they will be introduced to them and will realize how important traffic safety is.

OBJECTIVES

The children will (1) match words with the correct sign picture, (2) recognize signs in a picture and circle them, (3) associate names of various signs by viewing them and reciting their names orally, (4) associate signs and their usual color, (5) physically be able to hold and handle various signs to become aware of their shape and form, and (6) listen to a recording and actually set up a situation involving signs that they may use.

ACTIVITIES

1. Find the signs: Make duplicate sets of cards with safety signals. The children match the safety signs that are alike.
2. Match 'em up: The children look at a row of signs and then find the one that corresponds with the word given. It is not necessary for them to know how to read the words; they match the printed word within the sign to the word on the card.
3. Color signs: The children associate signs with their identifying colors. For example: a stop sign would be red and white; a yield sign would be yellow; and a "go" light would be green, etc. Make duplicate signs—one set with the appropriate color; the other without the identifying color but with the appropriate words. The children match the signs.
4. Setting up for safety: The children listen to a recording and follow the directions given. The purpose is to have them set up a flannel board using various signs and props. For example: "Find the ice cream truck and place it on the board. Now find the little boy in the yellow sweater and blue pants standing by his bike. What sign should be put in between the truck and the boy?" Another situation might be: "Find the two automobiles

and place them on the board. What sign would be placed in the air that the people in the cars might be looking up at?" Several different situations are described on the recording so that the children have an opportunity to associate the signs with their descriptions and then locate them and place them on the board.

CULMINATING ACTIVITY

One suggestion for an activity that the entire class could do together would be to go on a walking field trip around the community and identify all of the signs that are seen on the trip. On returning to the classroom, class could use cardboard or paper signs to act out the trip as it actually happened.

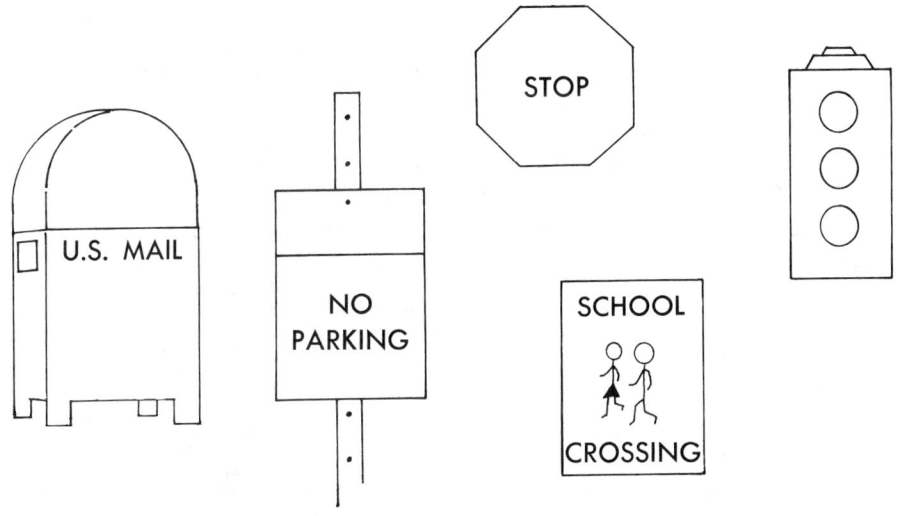

Child abuse and neglect

Child abuse and neglect is a cycle that must be broken by people who care. (Wolfe, 1979, p. 6)

Because of the high statistics of child abuse and neglect, the child abuse movement has developed rapidly. It is imperative for teachers to be able to detect child abuse, to know the correct procedures for reporting such cases, and to be able to lend support to abused children under their care.

The U.S. Department of Health, Education, and Welfare reports that approximately 1 million children are abused or neglected annually, 100,000 to 200,000 are physically attacked, and 60,000 to 100,000 are sexually abused (Brenton, 1977, p. 51). It has been found that 85% of the children abused are under six years of age, 75% are under four years of age, 25% are under one year, and 16% are under six months (Sanders et al, 1975, p. 335).

CHILD ABUSE AND NEGLECT DEFINED

It is a most difficult task to define child abuse and neglect, because it is so multifaceted. Christina Wolfe, longtime advocate and friend of young children, says that "child abuse can be defined as any physical injury, sexual abuse or mental injury inflicted upon a child other than by an accidental means" (Wolfe, 1979, p. 1).

The National Committee for Prevention of Child Abuse (1976, p. 1) defines child abuse as "an injury or pattern of injuries to a child that is nonaccidental . . . damage to a child for which there is no reasonable explanation . . . includes non-accidental physical injury, sexual molestation, neglect, and emotional abuse."

The following types of child abuse and neglect are thoroughly discussed by Schmitt (1975). His article in *Childhood Education* ("What Teachers Need to Know about Child Abuse and Neglect") is one of the most informative ones written on this subject.

1. Physical abuse
2. Drug abuse
3. Medical care neglect
4. Sexual abuse
5. Emotional abuse
6. Severe hygiene neglect
7. Educational neglect

CHILD ABUSE AND NEGLECT REPORTING

It has only been recently that child abuse and neglect have been identified and recognized as major problems in our society, requiring both state and federal legislation. In 1962 Kempe and his colleagues wrote an article on the battered child syndrome that appeared in the *Journal of the American Medical Association*. The information contained in the article drew considerable public attention. Authorities began to realize that many children were needless victims of neglect and abuse. An effort was initiated to locate these children. In time, this led to the development of a system of reporting child abuse and neglect to the proper authorities (Newberger, 1977, p. 374).

In 1974 the President of the United States signed into law legislation that required the establishment of a National Center on Child Abuse and Neglect (NCCAN). NCCAN, under the sponsorship of the Department of Health, Education, and Welfare's Children's Bureau, undertakes studies and authorizes grants to states and social agencies for work in reducing the child abuse problem.

Even though we now have evidence that child abuse and neglect are becoming quite widespread throughout our society, many people are still under the illusion that these are problems occurring exclusively with children of poor people. Children of more affluent families also suffer from child abuse and neglect; but at times, when treated, their injuries are termed "accidents." It is becoming increasingly evident that child abuse occurs among families from all racial, social, and economic backgrounds.

CAUSES OF ABUSE AND NEGLECT

Poor housing, unemployment, mental illness, alcoholism, husband and wife discord, hyperactive youngsters, and many other circumstances often trigger parents to lash out at their children. Sometimes stress and frustration produce intense anger that needs an outlet; the child may then become the recipient of that anger. It has been discovered that a large number of abusive parents were abused themselves as children. These parents may have little or no recollections of ever being loved by their parents. Most of them grew up with a very poor self-image. In order to escape punishment, they had to please their parents. Sometimes their parents swore and yelled at them. Sometimes they were physically abused. Rarely were their needs for love and affection met.

Kempe found that aggressive behavior was displayed by the parent when demands for performance were not met by the child (Pollock and Steele, 1972). Children raised under these conditions usually develop fearful and anxious behaviors. Abused children may dislike physical contact and will tend to isolate themselves or shy away from others. In some cases mental and social development may be retarded or speech development slowed down. It is possible that if these children are not identified and given extensive treatment under protected care, they could well become parents who will abuse their own children in the years to come (Sanders et al, 1975, p. 335).

THE TEACHER'S ROLE

As a teacher, you may come in contact with children who are neglected or abused. These children may:
1. Have bruises, abrasions, burns, belt marks, missing teeth, or untreated injuries
2. Be abnormally afraid of their parents, show evidence of poor home care, lack strength, or be in need of medical care
3. Exhibit signs of emotional neglect (be aggressive one moment and passive the next, etc.)

Teachers can play an important role in detecting and helping abused and neglected children. Since teachers see children on a regular basis, they are in prime positions to not only detect signs of abuse, but also to report them to the proper authorities. Early referral of families at risk is crucial for early intervention and remediation.

Experts in the field of child abuse caution teachers against questioning abused children too closely about their injuries. However, children may openly disclose to a teacher how they acquired their injuries. These disclosures and any noticeable appearance of suspected abuse should be recorded and dated. It is important for teachers to look for a pattern of repeated incidences in which these signs occur. Teachers should refrain from making derogatory statements about parents of abused children and should not take the initiative to contact the parents themselves. It is *vital*, however, that suspected cases be reported to the proper authorities (Brenton, 1977).

The method of reporting child abuse differs from state to state. Some cases are channeled to a local department of social services, some to county welfare agencies, some to police departments, etc. Since 1967 all 50 states have enacted laws on child abuse reporting.

Teachers are urged to consult their building principals and other school authorities regarding proper procedures in channeling information on suspected cases of abuse and neglect.

To report a suspected (you do not need proof) incident of child abuse or neglect, telephone, in most states, the local office of the Department of Child Welfare, part of the Department of Public Welfare. (Telephone that office and ask.) Usually, you will be required to give your home address and name so investigators can contact you for more information if necessary. This information will be kept confidential, and no one will know that you made the report. An investigation of the family situation will be made. Any person can report child abuse or neglect, and some states have made it illegal not to report when an incident is suspected (Pizzo, 1974, p. 3)

Once cases are reported, child protective services, the county welfare agency, or other designated agencies carry on the task of rehabilitating abusing families. Many children's agencies are revamping their programs and retraining their workers to deal with this complex issue. Workers need to learn new and effective skills in dealing with family intervention involving interpersonal relationships.

The teacher needs to find out from the county agency what will happen to the family and child once the case is reported and what sources of help will be available to them. Most communities have resources such as Parents Anonymous and family counseling. The social worker is a good resource for advice about the child even before a case is reported and can make the decision of how to approach the parents (Wolfe, 1979, p. 5).

In the classroom, teachers can provide a caring, stable, and supporting environment for the neglected or abused child. They can serve as adult models in a nonthreatening way and can deal positively with the child's feelings. The teacher may be the child's only support system.

Often, child abuse is predictable and preventable. Abused children need to be protected. Causes of child abuse and neglect can be detected and treated. In many cases abusive parents can be counseled by experts in the field and helped to make changes in their family life. *We must care enough to act.*

Behavior

As adults working with very young human beings, you need an endless supply of understanding and energy to help children develop self-control. (Stone, 1978, p. 30)

One of the highest goals for a kindergarten teacher is to help children develop a respect for themselves and other people and be able to demonstrate this respect. The ultimate goal is to hope that all children, having internalized this respect and control over their own actions, can learn to gradually take over control of their own lives. This places an almost awesome kind of responsibility on the kindergarten teacher, who is in a key position to help this transformation take place.

In order to know what to expect from five-year-olds, it is important to have a background of information on what children of this age are like and what they can do. This can best be accomplished by studying child development and observing the fives very carefully as they go about their work and play. When teachers are aware and knowledgeable about the behavioral characteristics of kindergarten children, they are in a better position to plan and carry out a program that will help children develop appropriate behavior and inner self-control.

When children enter the kindergarten situation, they come from families with wide, divergent practices regarding discipline and child-rearing methods. This knowledge must be considered when one is establishing specific rules and expectations for the classroom. It should also be kept in mind that it is almost impossible for five-year-olds to be in school together without encountering some confrontations with each other or rebelling at times against school rules. No matter how children have been reared, they will have boundless energy; they will be curious, explosive, and by nature self-centered.

TEACHERS WHO CARE AND ARE IN CONTROL

There are innumerable strategies and methods for controlling the behavior of children. Most teachers earnestly try to find effective, humanistic, and democratic ways of managing children. Children need teachers who are caring and warm, and who believe in good control. We well know that young children are not experienced enough to be in charge of themselves over long periods of time. They need the skillful guidance of the teacher or caregiver who knows and understands how *long* it takes for children to grow and develop appropriate behavior and inner controls (Stone, 1978, p. 2). Good teachers are ones who are firm without being harsh, and ones who will give children those little reminders that are so often necessary.

If you, as a teacher, are poorly prepared for the day, feel rushed or tired, or are in disharmony with your family or school personnel, beware of trouble! Plan to arrive at school in plenty of time to set up your room and to greet each child as he steps through the door. Be on the lookout for the child with a new pair of shoes, the child who wants to tell you something very special, or the youngster who appears unhappy and is about to break into tears.

Carefully organized rooms that are colorful, warm, tidy, and rearranged (on occasion) promote cooperative behavior. Materials and equipment should be stored in their proper places. Traffic patterns should be planned so that children will have designated areas to work and play in without continuously bumping into each other.

Some kindergarten teachers and parents expect too much, too soon, from five-year-olds. One thing is certain. We can count on children to act their age. The fives are going to "misbehave" if we ask them to sit at tables for long periods of time, or if we make them stand in lines beyond reasonable time limits. Children like to be able to move about the room and get involved with materials and equipment that are right for their age.

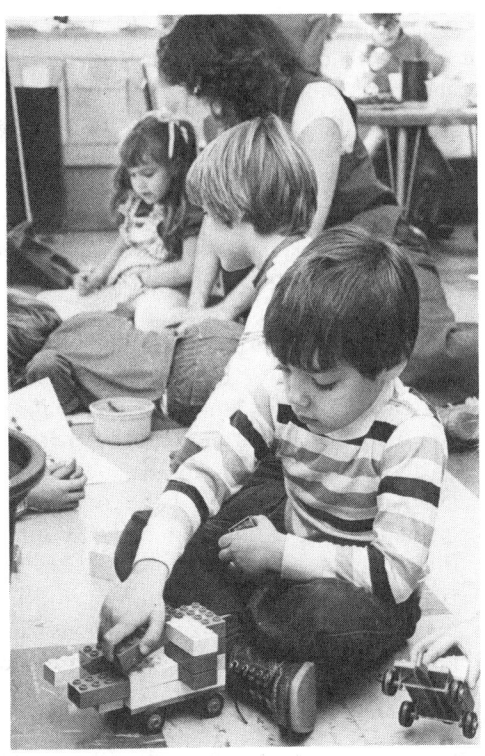

Today, with more emphasis being placed on the so-called "basics," some kindergarten teachers are eliminating or greatly reducing the time their fives can spend working with clay or blocks, engaging in water play, listening to stories, and spending time out-of-doors. All children, and particularly those with special behavior problems, will feel more cooperative and relaxed if they are permitted to engage in activities such as the above sometime during the kindergarten session. One of the basic principles in planning a curriculum for kindergarten children is to provide a balance of activities that are quiet and active. When this balance is not maintained, children are likely to become involved in aimless behavior and "trouble" usually evolves. Likewise, a program that is *overdemanding* will push children to the point where they become overanxious and whiny; yet a too-easy program, or a program that is too much the same, may cause misbehavior and disinterest. Quality kindergarten programs that meet the needs of individual children take much time and preparation. Children in this type of program are generally highly motivated and want to learn. They simply do not have the time to misbehave.

SETTING LIMITS

In order to feel really secure in the classroom, children need limits that establish what behavior is expected. If children do not respect these limits and nothing happens, they will often develop insecurities about themselves that may lead to more major problems in the future. When children cross limits that have been set, some form of discipline is needed. "Some rules are genuinely necessary, and their enforcement is desirable not only because research shows that establishing firm limits, coupled with warmth and a simple explanation of the reason behind the rule, enhances the child's self-esteem . . . but also because it increases his ability to establish inner controls" (Hendrick, 1980, p. 91).

Punishment, of any kind, is not to be used until an expected form of behavior has been explained (expectations set) and adequately taught. This may require an extended period of time and training before the "correct" behavior becomes a part of the personality.

WHEN CHILDREN MISBEHAVE

There is no one way to handle behavior problems. Children differ in how they will respond to the teacher's request. Experienced teachers can usually discover rather quickly what ways and means are most effective in getting each child to respond in positive ways. Some children who are quite sensitive will respond favorably to a disapproving glance or a shake of the head. Use of nonverbal cues can often help teachers maintain good classroom control. They reduce the amount of unnecessary words used to control behavior and sometimes are even more effective than words in conveying messages. Bolder or more aggressive children may need a stronger type of treatment. The following suggestions may be helpful in guiding behavior problems.

Denial of the activity

It is sometimes necessary to remove children from an activity until they can control their behavior. They should then be invited back to the activity, *provided* that they can control the undesired behavior; or they may be directed to another activity.

Conferences

When two children are involved in a dispute, they should be asked to sit down and talk the problem over. Many times children can settle their own disputes in this manner.

Sometimes it is necessary for the teacher to call one or more children aside to discuss a particular problem. Often, disruptive behavior can be redirected by careful guidance on the part of the teacher. For example: Some of the boys had finished work at their tables. Others were still putting finishing touches on their work. Several of the boys began to run around the room. The teacher approached the boys calmly and remarked, "What are you playing?" "We're just running," the boys answered back. "Why don't you run around the edge of the large rug and pretend it's a racetrack?" suggested the teacher. And so they did. In this way, the boys worked off some pent-up energy but did so within a restricted area where they were not disturbing the other children.

Ethelouise Carpenter, formerly an associate professor of early childhood education and much respected kindergarten teacher, sometimes used the "meeting time" conference method. When the total class needed to be involved to discuss a problem, she would ask a child to pick up the "meeting time" sign (which was child-made). That child would call the other children together on the rug to discuss the problem at hand. Many problems were resolved in this manner. The "meeting time" method can also be used when two children are having a problem. It can be suggested that they find a quiet corner, talk over their problem, and see if they can resolve it between the two of them.

High degree of expectancy

Having a high degree of expectancy in each child can be effective. When a teacher says, "I'm really disappointed in your behavior," and the child truly senses it, the child will generally comply. It is well to remember that a high degree of trust must be built up between teacher and child.

Isolation

The isolation method should be used with care. Some authorities believe that isolation may be used in cases where children are secure, but this method could be detrimental to children who are already loners or isolates. Isolation should not mean placing a child in another room or in the hall (Vannier, 1974, p. 94). The child should be placed within sight of the teacher, on a "thinking chair," for example.

Redirection

For the child who insists on running around the room, teachers can put out their hands, look the child in the eye, and say, "Please stop your running until we go outside for recess." The child should then be guided to another activity. If possible, the teacher should stay long enough to see that the child becomes interested in the new activity. Redirecting a child to another activity is an effective method in many instances.

Positive reinforcement

Much has been written about the use of positive reinforcement and praise for appropriate behavior. Praise must be honest and well earned. It should not be overused. Words and expressions used to convey praise ought to be varied, such as "beautiful!" "I like that," "Keep up the good work," etc. Teachers should comment favorably when children do what is expected of them. They should let children know when they are pleased about their good behavior.

Teacher's voice and remarks

Teachers' voices and the ways they use them are perhaps their most effective tools for controlling behavior and maintaining a comfortable classroom climate. For the most part, a teacher can maintain a well-modulated speaking voice throughout the day.

When there seems to be a need for more control, the voice ought to become firmer and carry a tone of conviction. Some teachers become masters at using tone control and inflection as an aid in guiding behavior. Children will many times respond positively when teachers make statements or give reminders in nonthreatening ways. The following examples are ways in which kindergarten teachers have spoken to a particular child or group of children to help them respond in more productive ways.

- I'm afraid you won't be able to report on what we're talking about, Tommy. Do you know why?
- Mary, I don't believe you are comfortable in that spot. Can you find another space?
- John, whose turn is it?
- Let's all give our attention to Pam.
- Donna, are you forgetting today?
- Do you know why I had to stop right in the middle of giving this direction?
- Terri, can you manage yourself, or do we have to help you?
- I see people who are ready today.
- This group will have to come back. They forgot how they were asked to get their coats.
- John, why couldn't you hear what I asked you to do?
- Your hammer is making enough noise. You don't need to shout.
- Jack, can you save your conversation until later?
- There are three sixth-grade boys waiting for us to get ready so they can begin to show the movie.
- Sharon, we need your help. You showed us yesterday that you knew exactly the way in which the blocks are to be put away.
- What good workers you are! Now let's see how quickly we can clean up our room before Mr. Taylor pays us a visit.
- Wasn't that kind of Patty to make room for Susan?
- Let me see everyone's eyes.
- I have a whole room of Elizabeths. I'm sorry, Elizabeth, now you may tell us about your kitten.
- Thank you for helping Mary pick up her books. That was very kind of you.

It is important to keep in mind that these are only examples of what some kindergarten teachers have used successfully with their children. As a teacher, you should try to develop your own way of communicating with children. You will find it rewarding and challenging.

• • •

When dealing with children's misbehavior, one must be constantly aware that misbehavior can be caused by many reasons. Indeed, the misbehavior must be dealt with, but causes should be probed and analyzed. Children who are fearful, angry, ill, mistreated, etc., are likely candidates for displaying troubled behavior.

As Caldwell (1977, p. 13) puts it, "Vigilance by and extended contact with adults who model nonaggressive behavior is indeed one necessary precondition for the development of children who can cooperate with one another and with adults—and be happy in the process."

Summary

The well-being of the five-year-old is the paramount concern of all who serve the "caring" function. All activities planned and directed by the teacher will hopefully enhance the possibilities for learning for each kindergarten child. As we have said, the child learns as a whole, integrated being within the environment. One should thus consider carefully all factors that impinge on the well-being of each child.

REFERENCES AND SUGGESTED READINGS
Play

Ad Hoc Kindergarten Guidelines Committee. *Recommended kindergarten guidelines, state of Ohio.* Columbus, Ohio, 1978.

Almy, Millie. Spontaneous play: an avenue for intellectual development. *Young Children,* 1967, 22(5), 265-277.

Apline, Virginia M. *Play therapy* (6th ed.). New York: Ballantine Books, Inc., 1971.

Bogdanoff, Ruth F., and Dolch, Elaine T. Old games for young children: a link to our heritage. *Young Children,* 1979, 34(1), 43.

Bruner, Jerome S., Jolly, Alison, and Sylva, Kathy. *Play: its role in development and evolution.* New York: Basic Books, Inc., Publishers, 1976.

Caplan, Frank, and Caplan, Theresa. *The power of play.* New York: Anchor Books, 1974.

Curry, Nancy E. Consideration of current basic issues on play. In Georgianna Engstrom (Ed.), *Play: the child strives toward self-realization.* Washington, D.C.: National Association for the Education of Young Children, 1971.

Ellis, M. J. *Why people play.* Englewood Cliffs, N.J.: Prentice-Hall, Inc., 1973.

Frank, L. Play is valid. *Childhood Education,* 1968, 44(7), 433-440.

Freud, Anna. *Normality and pathology in childhood: assessments of development.* New York: International Universities Press, 1968.

Friedberg, M. Paul. *Playgrounds for city children.* Washington, D.C.: Association for Childhood Education International.

Gilmore, J. Barnard. Play: a special behavior. In R. N. Haber (Ed.), *Current research in motivation.* New York: Holt, Rinehart & Winston, 1965.

Hanson, Margie R. *Moving learning action pack.* Washington, D.C.: American Alliance for Health, Physical Education, and Recreation, 1979.

Hartley, Ruth E., Frank, Laurence K., and Goldenson, Robert M. *Understanding children's play.* New York: Columbia University Press, 1952.

Herron, R. E., and Sutton-Smith, Brian (Eds.). *Child's play.* New York: John Wiley & Sons, Inc., 1971.

Hirsch, Elizabeth S. (Ed.). *The block book.* Washington, D.C.: National Association for the Education of Young Children, 1974.

Isaacs, Susan. *Intellectual growth in young children.* New York: Schocken Books, Inc., 1968.

Kamii, C. An application of Piaget's theory to the conceptualization of preschool curriculum. In Ronald K. Parker (Ed.), *The preschool in action: exploring early childhood programs,* Boston: Allyn & Bacon, Inc., 1972.

Kritchevsky, Sybil, and Prescott, Elizabeth, with Walling, Lee. *Planning environments for young children: physical space.* Washington, D.C.: National Association for the Education of Young Children, 1969.

Marzollo, Jean, and Lloyd, Janice. *Learning through play.* New York: Harper & Row, Publishers, Inc.,1972.

McClinton, Barbara Sweany, and Garner Meier, Blanche. *Beginnings: psychology of early childhood.* St. Louis: The C. V. Mosby Co., 1978.

Mills, Behen Collantes. Play: a child's avenue for learning. In *Understanding the young child and his curriculum.* New York: Macmillan Publishing Co., Inc., 1972.

Mitchell, Elmer, and Mason, Bernard S. *The theory of play.* (Rev. ed.). New York: A. S. Barnes & Co., Inc., 1948.

Montessori, Maria. *Dr. Montessori's own handbook.* New York: Schocken Books, Inc., 1965.

Morrison, George S. *Early childhood education today.* Columbus, Ohio: Charles E. Merrill Publishing Co., 1976.

Osmon, Fred Linn. *Patterns for designing children's centers.* New York: Educational Facilities Laboratories, Inc., 1971.

Phillips, John L. *The origins of intellect: Piaget's theory.* San Francisco: W. H. Freeman & Co. Publishers, 1969.

Piaget, J. *Play, dreams, and imitation.* New York: W. W. Norton & Co., Inc., 1962.

Rasmus, Carolyn, and Fowler, John. *Movement activities for places and spaces.* Washington, D.C.: American Alliance for Health, Physical Education, and Recreation, 1977.

Riley, Sue Spayth. Some reflections on the value of children's play. In Jan McCarthy and Charles R. May (Eds.), *Providing the best for young children.* Washington, D.C.: National Association for the Education of Young Children, 1974.

Robinson, Helen F. The decline of play in urban kindergartens. *Young Children,* 1971, 26, 333-341.

Singer, Jerome L. *The child's world of make-believe: experimental studies of imaginative play.* New York: Academic Press, Inc., 1973.

Smilansky, Sara. *The effects of sociodramatic play on disadvantaged preschool children.* New York: John Wiley & Sons, Inc., 1968.

Spodek, Bernard. *Teaching in the early years.* Englewood Cliffs, N.J.: Prentice-Hall, Inc., 1972.

Spodek, Bernard. The problem of play: education or recreational? In Doris Sponseller (Ed.), *Play as a learning medium.* Washington, D.C.: National Association for the Education of Young Children, 1974, p. 13.

Stone, Jeanette Galambos. *Play and playgrounds.* Wash-

ington, D.C.: National Association for the Education of Young Children, 1970.
Sutton-Smith, B. The role of play in cognitive development. *Young Children*, 1967, *22*(6), 361-370.
Wolfgang, Charles H. An exploration of the relationship between the cognitive area of reading and selected developmental aspects of children's play. *Psychology in the Schools*, July 1974, pp. 338-343.
Wolfgang, Charles H. *Helping aggressive and passive preschoolers through play.* Columbus, Ohio: Charles E. Merrill Publishing Co., 1977.

Health

Bedworth, David A., and Bedworth, Albert E. *Health education: a process for human effectiveness.* New York: Harper & Row, Publishers, Inc., 1978.
Birch, Herbert E., and Gussou, Joan Dye. *Disadvantaged children: health, nutrition and school failure.* New York: Harcourt Brace Jovanovich, Inc., 1970.
Cornacchia, Harold J., and Staton, Wesley M. *Health in elementary schools* (5th ed.). St. Louis: The C. V. Mosby Co., 1979.
Engs, Ruth, and Wantz, Molly. *Teaching health education in the elementary school.* Boston: Houghton Mifflin Co., 1978.
Feingold, B. F. *Introduction to clinical allergy.* Springfield, Ill.: Charles C Thomas, Publisher, 1973.
Feingold, B. F. *Why your child is hyperactive.* New York: Random House, Inc., 1975.
Metropolitan Life Insurance Co. *Looking for health.* New York: The Company, 1969.
Metropolitan Life Insurance Co. *Watching your child's health*, New York: The Company, undated.
Papalia, Diane E., and Olds, Sally Wendkos. *A child's world: infancy through adolescence* (2nd ed.). New York: McGraw-Hill Book Co., 1979.
Rubin, Kenneth A. Play behaviors for young children. *Young Children*, 1977, *32*(6), 16-23.
Scott, Gwendolyn D. and Carlo, Mona W. *Learning, feeling, doing.* Englewood Cliffs, N.J.: Prentice-Hall, Inc., 1978.
Thin Edge Series. *Anxiety, depression.* National Association for Mental Health, 1975.
Vannier, Maryhelen. *Teaching health in elementary schools* (2nd ed.). Philadelphia: Lea & Febiger, 1974.
Wanamaku, Nancy, Hearn, Kristin, and Richarz, Sherrill. *More than graham crackers:* nutrition, education, and food preparation with young children. Washington, D.C.: National Association for the Education of Young Children, 1979.

Safety

American Automobile Association. *10 Traffic safety guides, 1974-1975.* Washington, D.C.: The Association, 1974.
Anderson, C. L., and Creswell, William H. *School health practice* (6th ed.). St. Louis: The C. V. Mosby Co., 1976.
Cornacchia, Harold J., and Staton, Wesley M. *Health in elementary schools* (5th ed.). St. Louis: The C. V. Mosby Co., 1979.
Metropolitan Life Insurance Co. *Your child's safety.* New York: The Company, 1970.
National Safety Council. *Accident facts.* Chicago: The Council, 1975.
Raman, S. Pattabi. Role of nutrition in the actualization of the potentialities of the child: an Arriso perspective. *Young Children*, 1975, *31*(1), pp. 24-32.
Vannier, Maryhelen. *Teaching health in elementary schools* (2nd ed.). Philadelphia: Lea & Febiger, 1974.

Child abuse and neglect

Brenton, Myron. What can be done about child abuse? *Today's Children*, September-October 1977, 66, 51-52.
Chase, Naomi Feigelson. *A child is being beaten.* New York: Holt, Rinehart & Winston, 1975.
Delany, J. J. The battered child and the law. In C. Henry Kempe and Ray E. Helfer (Eds.), *Helping the battered child and his family.* Philadelphia: J. B. Lippincott Co., 1972.
Derdeyn, Andre P. Child abuse and neglect: the rights of parents and the needs of their children. *American Journal of Orthopsychiatry*, 1977, *47*(3), 377-387.
Drews, Kay. The child and his school. In C. Henry Kempe and Ray E. Helfer (Eds.), *Helping the battered child and his family.* Philadelphia: J. B. Lippincott Co., 1972, pp. 115-123.
Education Commission of the States; Child Abuse and Neglect Project. *Education policies and practices regarding child abuse and neglect and recommendations for policy development.* Report No. 85. Denver, April 1976.
Fontana, V. *Somewhere a child is crying.* New York: Mentor Books, 1976.
Halperin, Michael. Annotated bibliography of books, pamphlets, and films. In *Helping maltreated children.* St. Louis, The C. V. Mosby Co., 1979, pp. 174-184.
Heisner Report. What are you going to do about *your* abused child? *Instructor*, February 1978, 87, 22-23.
Helfer, Ray E., and Kempe, C. Henry. (Eds.). *The battered child* (2nd ed.). Chicago: University of Chicago Press, 1974.
Katz, Sanford, Howe, Ruth-Arlene, and McGrath, Melba. Child neglect laws in America. *Family Law Quarterly*, 1975, *9*(1), 1-362.
Kempe, C., et al. The battered-child syndrome. *Journal of the American Medical Association*, 1962, *181*(1), 17-24.

Kline, Donald, and Christiansen, James. *Educational and psychological problems of abused children.* Logan, Utah: Utah State University, Department of Special Education, 1975.

Metropolitan Life Insurance Co. *Your child's safety,* New York: The Company, 1970, p. 13.

Murdock, G. G. The abused child and the school system. *American Journal of Public Health,* 1970, 60, 105.

National Committee for Prevention of Child Abuse. *Prevent child abuse.* Chicago: The Committee, 1976.

Newberger, Eli H. Child abuse and neglect: toward a firmer foundation for practice and policy. *American Journal of Orthopsychiatry,* 1977, 47(3), 374-375.

Pizzo, P. D., et al. Child abuse and day care. *Voice for Children,* 1974, 7(1), 1-7.

Pollack, C., and Steele, B. A therapeutic approach to parents. In C. Henry Kempe and Ray E. Helfer (Eds.), *Helping the battered child and his family.* Philadelphia: J. B. Lippincott Co., 1972, pp. 3-21.

Sanders, Lola, Kibby, Robert W., Creaghan, Sidney, and Tyrrel, Eva. Child abuse: detection and prevention. *Young Children,* 1975, 30(5), 332-337.

Schmitt, Barton. What teachers need to know about child abuse and neglect. *Childhood Education,* November-December 1975, 52, 58-62.

U.S. Department of Health, Education, and Welfare, Office of Human Development, Office of Child Development, Children's Bureau, National Center on Child Abuse and Neglect. The teacher and the school: the role of the teacher; the role of the school. In *Child abuse and neglect: the problem and its management.* Vol. 2. *The roles and responsibilities of professionals.* DHEW Publication No. (OHD) 75-30074. Washington, D.C., pp. 67-79.

Wolfe, Christina (child advocate—Junior League of Akron, Ohio, Inc.). Unpublished report, February 1979.

Wooden, Kenneth. *Weeping in the playtime of others: America's incarcerated children.* New York: McGraw-Hill Book Co., 1976.

Behavior

Broman, Betty L. Behavior and parent education. In *The early years.* Chicago: Rand McNally & Co., 1978.

Caldwell, Bettye. Aggression and hostility in young children. *Young Children,* 1977, 32(2).

Hendrick, Joanne. Helping young children establish self-discipline and self-control. In *The whole child* (2nd ed.). St. Louis: The C. V. Mosby Co., 1980, pp. 84-97.

Sears, R. R., Maccoby, E. E., and Levin, H. *Patterns of child rearing.* Evanston, Ill.: Row Peterson, and Co., 1957.

Stone, Jeannette Galambos. *A guide to discipline* (Rev. ed.). Washington, D.C.: National Association for the Education of Young Children, 1978.

Vannier, Maryhelen. Children: their growth, development, and characteristics. In *Teaching health in elementary schools* (2nd ed.). Philadelphia: Lea & Febiger, 1974, pp. 84-99.

OTHER RESOURCES

Health: sources of information

American Dental Association
211 East Chicago Ave.
Chicago, Ill. 60611

American Home Economics Association
2010 Massachusetts Ave., N.W.
Washington, D.C. 20036

American Medical Association
535 North Dearborn St.
Chicago, Ill. 60610

U.S. Department of Health, Education, and Welfare
Public Health Service
Federal Drug Administrtion
Rockville, Md. 20852

Safety: sources of information

Aetna Life Insurance Co.
151 Farmington Ave.
Hartford, Conn. 06105

American Automobile Association
Pennsylvania Ave. at Seventeenth St., N.W.
Washington, D.C. 20006

National Safety Council
425 North Michigan Ave.
Chicago, Ill. 60611

Child abuse and neglect: sources of information

American Humane Association
Children's Division
P.O. Box 1266
Denver, Colo. 80220

Child Abuse Project
Education Commission of the States
1860 Lincoln St.
Denver, Colo. 80203

National Center on Child Abuse and Neglect
U.S. Children's Bureau
P.O. Box 1182
Washington, D.C. 20013

A POINT OF VIEW—THE INTEGRATED DAY

We believe in the integrated day for the five-year-old. The day should provide alternatives, balance, relevance, continuity, and sequence—a melding of ideas and spaces, encounters and interactions.

To plan for the integrated day, we suggest that you, the reader, review the "Statement of Beliefs" at the beginning of the text, the characteristics of the kindergarten child, your earlier study of child growth and development, and your own philosophy of teaching.

Consider carefully the levels of development as outlined by Jean Piaget, the Swiss psychologist who has impacted so intensely on our work with children. (These levels are presented on the following page for your immediate reference.)

Then observe each child carefully. What needs are evident? What strengths and weaknesses do you see? Can you detect specific learning styles? What interests are expressed?

Remember, for convenience and to avoid confusion, the areas of the kindergarten curriculum are discussed separately. However, throughout, we have suggested ways of combining and building on learnings from many areas in relation to what "makes sense" for the child. Wholeness and unification are the goals.

Learning centers offer rich opportunities to coordinate skills; themes or units can cut across subject lines. Instruction in many subjects can be related to a common theme; for example, the theme "Man Travels" could be used to develop language, social studies, mathematics, creative projects, and even music skills. Social skills and language skills are foundational to virtually every area. Music undergirds many activities. Curriculum building for the five-year-old demands thoughtful preparation, extensive resources, a knowledge of each child and the group, and the flexibility to draw on a strong data base from research, practical experience, and the academic disciplines.

A resourceful teacher will find innumerable ways to achieve a unified program. As you study the chapters that follow, consider the possibilities for integrating ideas and experiences to make learning "real" to the kindergartner.

PIAGET'S MODEL OF THE STAGES OF DEVELOPMENT

    Stage 1. Sensorimotor (0 to 24 months of age)
    Stage 2. Preoperational (2 to 7 years of age)
    Stage 3. Concrete operations (7 to 11 years of age)
    Stage 4. Formal operations (11 years of age on)

Children are in the preoperational stage during their kindergarten experience; therefore, one should consider the following growth patterns when planning a kindergarten curriculum. *During this stage:*

1. Children are quite egocentric and self-centered.
2. Their learning requires many experiences with concrete objects.
3. Children's language growth is very rapid.
4. Their cognitive development centers largely around newly acquired words and concepts.
5. Tasks involving sorting and classifying engage the children's interests and attention. Their ability to categorize becomes much more refined as their intellectual development continues.
6. Children are active in learning about things that are equivalent, or the idea of one-to-one correspondence.
7. Much of children's judgments are based on what they can see. They usually center on one variable only. It is difficult for children to understand that an object can have more than one property.
8. Explanation for phenomena are artificial, often magical.
9. Problems are often solved by trial and error.

CHAPTER 6

Learning to live together: the social studies

Ambrose A. Clegg, Jr.*

> The basic goal of social studies education is to prepare young people to be humane, rational, participating citizens in a world that is becoming increasingly interdependent. . . . A commitment to foster human dignity and rational process are keys to the structure of the social studies curriculum. . . . But without action, neither knowledge nor rational process are of much consequence. . . . Commitment to human dignity must put the power of knowledge to use in the service of humanity. Whatever students of the social studies learn should impel them to apply their knowledge, abilities, and commitments toward the improvement of the human condition."
> (NCSS, 1979, p. 261)

The statement quoted above, drawn from a current position statement of the National Council for the Social Studies (NCSS), reflects three key elements in the social studies curriculum. It involves a commitment to prepare young people to become citizens who (1) are humane individuals, (2) evidence rational thought process, and (3) are willing to act on their informed judgments and their carefully examined convictions in determining decisions that affect public policy. This broad goal is accomplished through four major domains of learning:

1. *Knowledge* about human beings and the social and physical environment in which they live. This knowledge must be selected and organized to provide information and insights into the enduring and pervasive problem of society.
2. *Abilities and skills* in developing various intellectual thought patterns, including the processing and evaluation of data, and in developing effective human relations and interpersonal communication skills.
3. *Valuing*, or the systematic examination of the attitudes, beliefs, and basic values that underlie the various cultures of the world. The study of beliefs and values is important because it helps us understand what individuals and groups consider important in a society. Moreover, they are often guides to action and strongly influence the course and direction of major social institutions.
4. *Social participation* in a democracy implies the commitment of individuals

---
*Assistant Dean for Teacher Education, Kent State University, Kent, Ohio.

and groups to the resolution of important problems confronting society. This action is guided by the values of human dignity and rational thought processes. It implies the application of knowledge, thinking, and commitment to one's values in the social arena at local, state, national, and international levels. Social studies programs ought to develop young people who are able to identify and analyze both local and global problems and who are willing to participate actively in the political process to develop alternative approaches and well-thought-out solutions for them.

Each of these four domains, or curriculum components, must be viewed as equally important. To ignore any one of them weakens the entire social studies program. "The relationship among knowledge, abilities, valuing, and social participation is tight and dynamic. Each interacts with the others. Each nourishes the others" (NCSS, 1979, p. 266).

In the following pages, we shall discuss each of these four domains of learning of the social studies curriculum. While they are intended to provide a broad kindergarten through grade 12 (K-12) framework, their essential outline begins at the kindergarten level. Throughout the chapter we shall make specific illustrations and applications of these guidelines to situations at the kindergarten level.

THE DOMAIN OF KNOWLEDGE

The task of the social studies curriculum is to identify and select the most useful and powerful facts, concepts, and ideas that will provide children with a sound basis of knowledge about themselves as human beings and about the social and physical environment in which they live. The long-range goal is to provide a background of knowledge that will allow students to deal with the most enduring and pervasive problems of our society. This knowledge must include a wide input from the various social sciences and also reflect a global perspective in the knowledge of varying cultural groups throughout the world.

While these represent long-range goals for the entire school curriculum, K-12, a sound beginning for them starts in the kindergarten. Kindergarten teachers have a remarkable opportunity to help develop children along the path to such goals. The kindergarten teacher is often the child's first teacher and has an opportunity to set patterns of intellectual curiosity and to develop certain touchstones for our common American values—touchstones that are essential to the education of citizens in a democratic environment. Moreover, kindergarten teachers can help children become aware of the importance of knowledge, simple reasoning processes, and a commitment to human dignity. There are also many opportunities in which children can participate actively in day-to-day decision-making processes within the community of their own classroom and school.

Most kindergarten programs focus on children as individual human beings, on their participation in small social groups, and on the physical world about them. Using such important concepts as home, neighborhood, work, and occupations, many programs also help develop a sense of the cultural context of the community. Five-year-olds also learn to recognize elements of their culture by participating in seasonal or patriotic holidays—such as Halloween and Christmas, Martin Luther King's and George Washington's birthdays, Valentine's Day, and Memorial Day.

Fig. 6-1 provides a useful way of looking at the purposes of social studies and relating it to the four major domains described at the beginning of this chapter. It also provides a useful guideline for selecting content that is

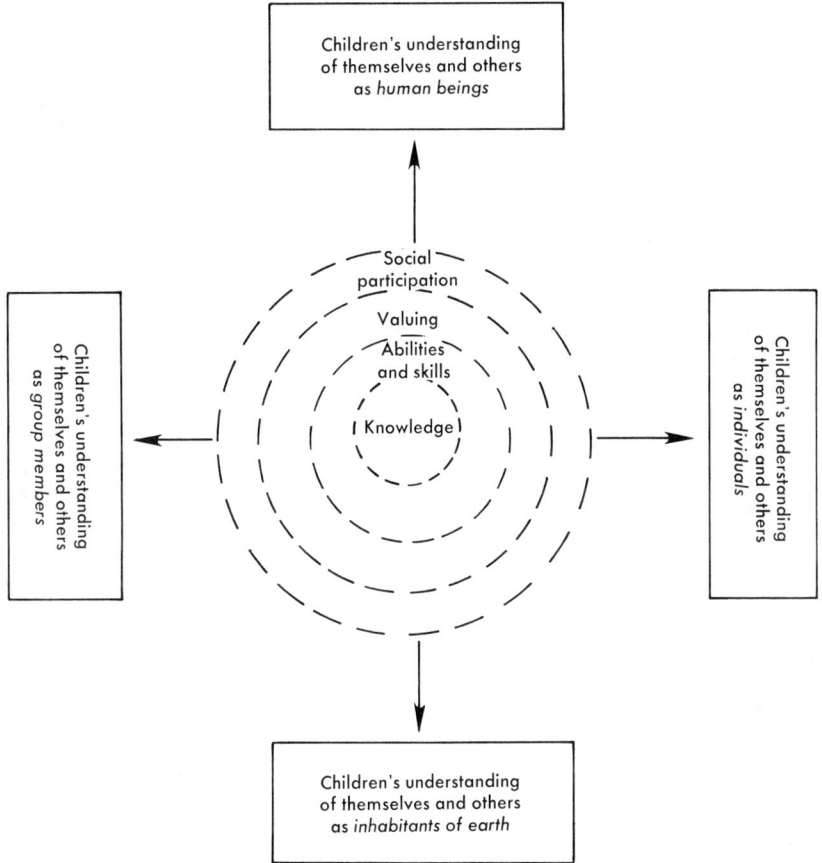

Fig. 6-1. Purposes and domains of learning in social studies. (Adapted from Anderson, Lee F. A guide to thinking about social studies in elementary schools. Technical paper for *Windows on Our World*, Houghton Mifflin social studies program. Boston: Houghton Mifflin Co., 1978.)

appropriate and for eliminating that which is not. Following this conceptualization serves to develop children's understandings of themselves and others as individuals, as human beings, as members of groups, and as inhabitants of the earth and of our solar system.

This conceptualization is especially useful because it also helps bridge the gap between three major traditions in kindergarten education that have served useful but somewhat incomplete purposes in the past. The first of these emphasized the importance of social growth and development and placed heavy emphasis on social learning. The second tradition emphasized content knowledge of the world around us or a simplified version of the expanding environment concept in which kindergarten children would study the home, the family, and their immediate neighborhood. Children in the upper grades would progress through studies of their community and state, to studies of the nation, and finally to studies of the world. The third and most recent approach has been to select key concepts from each of the major social

110   Kindergarten: programs and practices

science disciplines, particularly sociology, psychology, and history and geography. It includes the study of such concepts as personal identity and self-concept; family; work; national or cultural traditions; and time, place, and space. Each of these three traditions has had an important place in the growth of kindergarten social studies curriculum, and each has been reflected in commercially published teaching materials for kindergarten. The approach suggested in Fig. 6-1 provides an opportunity to draw from each of these approaches to form a newer, more integrated approach to the study of human beings, using the four major domains of social studies learning.

Knowledge about individuals

At the kindergarten level, children's knowledge of individuals includes a growing awareness of basic physical characteristics of people—their similarities and differences, and how they grow and change. Five-year-olds can begin to notice such characteristics as the color of their hair and eyes, how tall they are, how much they weigh, and when they get a new tooth (or more often, when they lose one!). They can recognize, too, that they have feelings and attitudes as individuals. There are days when they are happy and other days when they are sad. Many look forward eagerly to favored activities at school recess or to milk-and-cookie time. They can laugh at broadly humorous, slapstick comedy, and they can also cry when they are hurt physically or disturbed emotionally—or even shed tears of empathy at a sad part in a story. They know that there are days when they are healthy and feeling fine and other days when they are sick and feeling awful. They find their place among their friends by identifying their birthdays and being able to tell how soon theirs will come. They can relate to members of their family and know whether they are the oldest or youngest of the children or somewhere in between. They know that they are young people and that some day they will grow up to be adults like their parents, but they have no idea of how long it takes to become an adult; nor do they have any real conception of the age difference between themselves and their parents. Social studies lessons or units of study on this topic are usually entitled "Learning about Me," "Who Am I?," "All about Me," etc.

Knowledge about groups

In addition to studying about themselves as individuals, youngsters in kindergarten also study about themselves as members of groups. Much of their personal and social life revolves around participation and membership in small groups within the family, the school, and the neighborhood. Such groups usually include no more than two, three, or four members, are close and intimate in their daily contact, and provide an important basis for many everyday functions.

Human beings are not only individual, but they are also social beings. Unless we choose to live as hermits, almost all of human life occurs in a context with other people, both adults and children. It is important that children learn something about how these groups form and about the rules for membership in them. Children should learn not only leadership roles but also follower or participant roles in groups. They can also learn how quickly groups change in membership patterns.

Group membership

Children should come to understand ways in which group members depend on one another. Thus, children should have opportunities to cooperate with one another, and from time to time, as members of the group, to teach and learn from one another. They must also learn the need to assume responsibilities within groups if group goals are to be achieved. Not only do children learn leadership roles, but they must also have the opportunity to learn membership or participatory roles. Kindergarten teachers must ensure that many children have the opportunity to learn to be leaders, rather than allow the role to be usurped by the naturally talented leaders, the big and the powerful, or the noisy and boisterous ones.

Some key elements for learning about groups in the kindergarten include learning how conflict arises, how differences are openly discussed, how conflicts are settled, and the need for rules in any group or society. Experienced teachers know that the fewer rules there are, the better a group can get along. Yet, many five-year-olds want to have a rule for everything as a means of enforcing and regulating group conduct. For these children, it is a time of pushing and shoving, a time of testing out boundaries, a time of identifying growing roles and new friendship relations, and a time of searching for personal identity within a group. While teen-age adolescents will quickly conform to the norms and pressure of a group, young four-, five-, and six-year olds will more easily walk away from a group or simply not participate. Small friendship groups form quickly as children walk to school or play on the playground. Yet, other work groups may just as easily be established (or fall apart!) as children move from one learning center to another corner of the classroom or curl up alone in a rocking chair.

Democratic values

Children can easily learn democratic values of group membership in the kindergarten. The notion of *fair play* is already well developed by the time children are five years old. Schools reinforce this many times over in providing opportunities for taking turns and for sharing equipment and materials. Similarly, children learn respect for property, both that which is private, such as other children's sweaters, rubbers, raincoats, toys, and books, and that which is public in nature, to be shared by all for the common good. Children can learn to take care of playground equipment, balls, and jump ropes, as well as to conserve (or not waste) classroom supplies, paper, paint, or clay. Even such fundamental concepts as *one person, one vote* can be introduced early as children choose classmates for various housekeeping tasks, such as watering the plants, distributing materials, logging in the day's temperature, or distributing milk and cookies.

While most five-year-olds need a well-defined social world with some fairly clear rules and boundaries, they can sense immediately teachers and children who are unfair in their dealings with others or who abuse their authority. While children themselves may not always be fair—they may hog the ball or monopolize the playground equipment—they also can recognize the lack of fairness in a bully or in a teacher whose attitude is very arbitrary; and they will protest against it. Sometimes that protest takes the form of loud shouting, crying, or striking out physically. The task of the teacher is to help children learn to verbalize their protests and to find constructive and positive ways of dealing with misbehavior among the group members.

Knowledge about human beings

In the two preceding sections we focused on the kindergartner as an individual and as a member of a group. We turn now to developing children's understandings of their place within the human race. This is the beginning of the study of human culture and of how human beings differ from all other living things. In the kindergarten, youngsters can begin to learn the similarities and differences between themselves as human beings and the many other living but nonhuman creatures of their world. Children are fascinated by their pets, whether dogs or cats, or turtles or goldfish, or gerbils. The classroom can supply a counterpart to the home by keeping guinea pigs in a cage in the corner and watching them run about, grow, and reproduce. What family doesn't feel proud when its turn comes to play host to the class pet over the weekend or during the Christmas holidays! Children quickly develop attitudes of affection and tenderness for living things and learn to develop patterns of responsibility for feeding pets, watering plants, or arranging flowers. They can experience a sensitivity to life when they bury a favorite pet.

There are many similarities between the human being and other living things, such as the birth, life, and death cycle and the ability to "learn" certain behaviors (for example, doing tricks or finding a way through a maze). The skillful teacher, however, will begin to raise questions about how we, as human beings, differ distinctly from animals in our ability to think about complex ideas, to make decisions, to communicate with others, to invent and use tools, and to perform other uniquely human functions. When children bring up the examples of the highly complex behaviors exhibited by chimpanzees and dolphins that they have seen in person or on television, teachers should help children realize that the explanation and understanding of such phenomena is on the cutting edge of science. These animals have abilities to perform highly complex tasks, and there is much we do not know and need to learn about their behavior and its relationship to human behavior.

It is important for the teacher to recognize both the religious and ethical implications of some of these topics. The question of evolution versus divine creation has, in some areas, become once again a controversial issue. While the Stokes trial of 1927 assured the right of schools to teach scientific knowledge about the theory of animal evolution, advocates for other points of view have as-

Learning to live together: the social studies 113

serted in recent years the obligation of the school to teach the religious theory of divine creation as a unique and direct act. It is important that teachers recognize this as a potentially controversial issue and be aware of the sensitivities of young children. The classroom is not a place for indoctrination in particular views. Indeed, it must be open to the presentation of many alternative views and to discussion of the value implication held in each.

What is of concern here is that children begin to examine the world about them and other living things within it, and learn to identify those characteristics that make them uniquely human. This is also the school's first opportunity to help children understand something about the *range* of human behavior, from its most noble and sublime achievements to instances of cruel, evil, or depraved behavior that some humans have inflicted on others at various times in our history. It is also the school's first opportunity to help children learn that, unlike animals, human beings must accept moral responsibility for their decisions and their actions.

Knowledge about human culture

Another aspect related to learning about what makes people human is understanding more about the nature of human culture. While there are many definitions of culture, the task of the elementary school is to acquaint students with four elements that are common throughout the world. These involve human beings' use of technology, institutions, language, and beliefs.

Technology

The technology of a culture refers to its use of tools as well as to the skill involved in making those tools. It suggests the creative and inventive abilities of human beings to use materials about them in new ways to help them meet life's basic needs of food, clothing, and shelter, and also of recreation and leisure activities. Kindergarten children can quickly see a whole host of tools used in our everyday culture from knives, forks, and spoons; to shovels and rakes; to hammers and saws; to bulldozers and lawn mowers. They can easily see how each of these tools has simplified life. Children can also become aware of how our changing technology has produced more highly efficient tools that have made our work easier and that have produced more leisure time. Tractor lawn mowers have greatly simplified the task of mowing grass. Elevators have eliminated the need to climb stairs. Bulldozers move great mounds of earth that once took people many days to move with shovels. Derricks and cranes lift large pipes and even whole sections of buildings high into the sky.

As we indicated earlier, five- and six-year-olds have little sense of time or chronology and so could hardly appreciate the advance that the automobile is over the bicycle or the horse-drawn carriage. Teachers, however, can show pictures of those "old fashioned" ways that people used long, long ago. Some of the children's parents may have no living memory of the horse-drawn ice truck or grocery wagon, or of the delivery boy who delivered groceries from the neighborhood store on a bicycle. Nevertheless, it is important for kindergarten youngsters to realize that our culture is filled with tools and implements that human beings have made and that have changed drastically over time. And although astronauts first walked on the moon only a few years ago, the youngsters in today's kindergartens will probably see interplanetary travel as an everyday reality in their lifetime.

It is important that kindergartners begin to understand that there are other cultures with different levels of technology throughout the world. These cultures have made different adaptations to their environment, to the resources available to them, and to their level of knowledge. To build such understandings of other cultures, it is important that the teacher take advantage of a number of occasions to bring to the class such things as a Chinese abacus, chopsticks, and musical instruments from other cultures. The kindergarten child needs to see that other cultures may not have the same industrial technology—and that they may use wood and grass for making houses, and clay for pottery. The teacher should also be alert and sensitive to present these tools and articles of other cultures as normal—not strange, weird, or curiosities. Such attitudes tend to reinforce a feeling of smugness and self-centeredness (or ethnocentrism) about our own culture. It is important that even in the kindergarten, the foundations be laid for developing a respect and understanding for various cultural differences as well as similarities throughout the world. What is important is that children learn that other cultures have different ways of meeting needs. Children must learn to respect these differences, rather than develop a feeling of superiority about the technical advances that our American culture has produced.

Institutions

Every society makes use of institutions as a way of dealing with basic and recurring social needs. The five most basic types of institutions include the family, schools, and government, as well as economic and religious institutions. A coordinated K-12 social studies program will provide a comprehensive examination of these five major types of cultural institutions. The kindergarten is an appropriate place for children to learn some basic understandings about several of these institutions.

FAMILY. Typically, kindergartners can begin to study the role and function of a family as a human organization that is found in all cultures. This grouping of human beings provides for the common basic needs of food, shelter, clothing, love, nurturance, and life support. It is important that children see the family, whatever its structure might be, as an institution of our culture that provides these elements of support. Some families are large and have many children, whereas some are small and have only one or two children. Many families have both a mother and father. In others, there is only a mother or grandmother to provide all of these vital functions. Less frequently, a father alone provides these services to young children.

In the past, when many families lived on farms, it was common for grandparents to remain with their children and play an essential role in the care and nurturance of their grandchildren. This is much less common today. While the terms *extended family* and *nuclear family* are too complicated for kindergarten children, these concepts can be talked about in terms of big families and little families, and children can draw pictures or bring in snapshots of their families. Family gatherings—when children, parents, grandparents, and perhaps nieces and nephews may take part in important joyful occasions, such as school graduations or wedding anniversaries, or in the sadness of funerals—also offer an opportunity for discussion about the extended family. The kindergarten teacher, however, should be quick to recognize that familial concepts of *grandparent, uncle, aunt, cousin, niece, nephew,* or *in-law* are hopelessly beyond the understanding of most four-, five-, and six-year-olds. Indeed, many adults have trouble understanding complex relationships such as second cousins, half brothers or sisters, or stepchildren. Kindergartners simply use these familial concepts as if they were the personal names of people. At best, children will know that there is a vague family relationship between themselves and these other members of the extended family.

The kindergarten teacher must have a marked sensitivity when dealing with the study of the family. In past years, school textbooks all too often presented a false stereotype of the ideal family as a white, middle-class family with mother and father and two or three children living happily in a suburb.

Within the past several years, textbook publishers have become very responsive in recognizing such stereotypes and have increasingly shown families with a single parent in a variety of settings including inner-city as well as suburban and rural areas, and representing different cultural and ethnic groups.

The social studies program also offers an excellent opportunity for kindergarten youngsters to become aware that families are a world-wide institution and that families exist in every culture. Through the use of stories, filmstrips, and large display picture cards, teachers can begin to help children recognize that the family is a universal institution, even though there may be many local differences. Primary-grade children need to see pictures and hear stories about families that exist and live together in oriental cultures and about migratory peoples, such as those in the African Sahara or those in the Equatorial Forests. They also need to learn about families in many of the island cultures of the Pacific, where fishing and the life of the sea is a primary focus. While five-year-olds are too young to appreciate fully the differences of place and widely separated space throughout the world, they can begin an awareness that varying cultures have many similarities and that the family unit, despite some differences, is a common cultural institution of all humans.

SCHOOLS. To a lesser extent, kindergartners can begin to see the school as an institution for transmitting the culture and as an organized way of helping young people learn what they need to know in order to become adults. Five-year-olds can also begin to see something of the differences between what they learn at school and what they learn at home, as well as how the school is an organized extention of the teaching that began in the family.

Children can begin to understand, too, that many adults work and earn salaries as staff members of this institution: teachers, principal, custodian, cafeteria workers, and secretary. Each has a different and specialized role or task to perform.

CHURCHES. Kindergartners may also be able to begin to understand that churches, temples, and synagogues provide an organized place for religious activities. In many communities they can see the diversities of these churches, at least in outward forms of building and names. It is certainly beyond the ken of five-year-olds to understand much about religious beliefs or sectarian differences, and kindergarten teachers should be very careful to show respect and understanding for the religious differences among children. It is equally important that teachers be sensitive to children from families where no formal religion is practiced and where the custom of going to church on Sunday may not be a common practice at all.

In many urban areas, the kindergarten teacher may be able to illustrate that Jewish children observe the Sabbath on Saturday and that their families anticipate the Sabbath with Friday evening services at a temple or synagogue. Once again, it is important that the teacher show a *variety* of cultural observations of religion, but in a way that encourages mutual respect and understanding for these differences.

Kindergarten teachers should be very sensitive not to promote a stereotype that would suggest that one religious preference or practice is accepted by everyone. In this respect, teachers should be especially aware of the tradition of separation of church and state in American public education and should be particularly wary about introducing religious hymns or prayers as part of the opening of the school day or as moments of thanksgiving before or after milk and cookies. It is not at all uncommon for a kindergarten teacher to ask children to join hands and bow their heads while the teacher recites a sectarian grace or prayer of thanksgiving, or for a teacher to ask children to join in unison in a choral recitation of such a hymn or prayer.

All of this is not to suggest that within the home and the family such worship should not be carried out. Rather, it is to say that five-year-olds are very compliant and that they willingly accept the authority of the teacher, who must not encourage them to participate in a religious activity that might violate their constitutional right to freedom of, and freedom from, religion. Teachers must be very sensitive to children's religious outlooks and views, particularly those of minority students, when planning classroom activities during religious holiday times. To ask Jewish children to sing "For Christ Our Savior Is Born Today" shows little respect for the cultural traditions of these children, particularly if Hanukkah has not been observed in the classroom.

Occasionally, with somewhat older children, it may be appropriate to introduce some material about religion in other cultures. Once again, the teacher must be sure to remember not to foster the impression that other religious practices, customs, and ideas are weird, strange, or funny. Rather, these cultural differences must be approached with sensitivity and with the recognition that each society, in its own unique way, pays reverence to its awareness of a divinity or spiritual force.

Language

A third element of culture is the use of language. This includes not only oral words or sounds but also the use of signs and symbols that human beings make and use to communicate ideas, information, and feelings. Kindergartners should be helped to recognize that language is more than the spoken word or printed communication. Very often the most intense and expressive forms of education, music, dance, and art are equally important as forms of human language. Inner-city children are aware of graffiti on the walls of buildings, sidewalks, and subway cars. Posters, murals, and paintings convey quickly other types of communication. Opera, ballet, and drama often convey intense emotion and feeling in ways that can hold audiences spellbound, move them to tears, or bring them to their feet with rousing cries of "hurray!" or "bravo!"

In the social studies curriculum, students can begin to learn that different societies have dealt with language and communication in varying ways. The influence of transportation and communication has both enhanced and inhibited the development of language and other forms of communication. What is important in the area of social studies is to examine the vehicles of communication, both personal and public, and to look at the free flow of information for citizens in a democracy. In an era of mass communication, it is important that children begin to recognize the role of television as a central element of communication in their lives. Far more than newspapers, radio, books, or other forms of communication, television is a central force in the lives of five-year-olds. At a very simple level, they can begin to identify what people learn from various sources and how much authority or credence they should place in these sources. Is knowledge from television more or less reliable and accurate than what they may learn from their friends or their parents? Has television replaced communication between family members in the home? Have cartoons and children's programs replaced the parent or grandparent as the spinner of tall tales, humorous stories, and "once-upon-a-time" bedtime stories?

A sophisticated analysis of the management of news, the influence of propaganda, and the absence of critical or unpopular views on television and in the newspapers is too difficult for kindergarten children and should be reserved for those in the upper grades. It is important, however, that five- and six-year-olds become aware of the nature of language in their culture, its importance as a primary means of learning, and the central place it plays in their lives. Teachers can help children get a sense of this by listing the number of programs that are watched regularly and by helping them to understand how much time they spend watching television. Even though their sense of time is very incomplete and distorted, children can usually list, with assistance, those programs that they watch before dinner and before going to bed in the evening, and on Saturdays or Sundays. The teacher can then help the children understand how much time they actually spend watching television. Children will exaggerate, of course, and some will say that they watch everything. But this type of activity provides a good chance for getting other data from parents, for involving parents in the classroom effort, and for inviting parents to the classroom to discuss the impact of television on their children's lives.

This simple form of data gathering provides an early introduction to the skill of observing human behavior and of gathering objective data about some activity. It may also point up the need of the school to encourage children to explore other forms of communication, such as can be provided by the school or public library. Browsing through picture books or coming to a story hour is to young children what their older brothers and sisters may call doing research. Wherever possible, kindergarten teachers should organize field trips to the public library. If the library is within walking distance, the class might take a trip there perhaps several times during the year. If they have to take a school bus, then this requires more advanced planning with the principal and perhaps some allocation of funds. Nevertheless, the school library and the community library can begin to provide additional sources of communication beyond the exclusive use of television within the home.

Involving children in dramatic play, role playing, dance, poetry, singing, individual art projects, and perhaps group murals is discussed elsewhere in this book. All of these represent expressive forms of communication, however, that should be included as integral parts of the social studies program. It is important that these approaches be developed early and that they be valued in the school program. Unfortunately the arts become less important as a student moves to the upper grades, where reliance on the oral voice of the teacher and the printed textbook are so predominant.

Beliefs and values

The fourth element of culture about which kindergarten children should have some initial knowledge is the beliefs and values of people. Children should come to understand that beliefs are ideas that people have about what is true and what is false, about what is good and what is bad, and about what is right and what is wrong. This element also includes ideas or beliefs about what is beautiful or ugly, attractive or unattractive. Perhaps it includes, as well, what people believe about themselves and how they relate to the forces outside of themselves that they are unable to control. These beliefs may include well-thought-out theologies about the nature of man and God, or they may be less complex and sophisticated and combine elements of folklore, mythology, magic, witchcraft, or superstition as ways of explaining the forces of and beyond nature that affect us. Many of these beliefs are organized into complex codes or structures that affect our daily activities. While the sophisticated understanding of the belief systems of various cultures is reserved to the social studies of the upper grades, youngsters in kindergarten can certainly begin to think about what they do believe.

As we indicated previously, children begin to learn early the importance of fairness and fair play and thus can begin to talk about their belief in what happens when one practices fair play. They can talk about the values of honesty, truthfulness, helpfulness, and friendliness. They can also begin to explore the world of reality and fantasy and talk about what they believe to be real and true. They can talk about ghosts and goblins at Halloween time and try to decide whether they really believe in such creatures. The line between reality and fantasy is often a

blurred one for kindergartners, and sometimes the stories of "once upon a time" and "long, long ago" are as real and true to them as any actual event in their daily lives. Four- and five-year-old youngsters have a highly developed sense of imaginary friends and acquaintances and are willing to give ready belief to such adult inventions as the Tooth Fairy, Santa Claus, and Superman. By the time children are six or seven years old, they are usually willing to give up a firm belief in their fantasies, but they will continue to act out the exploits of Superman or react happily to the gifts of the Tooth Fairy or Santa Claus.

Beliefs indicate our state of mind or willingness to act with a ready sense of trust, confidence, and assurance about something. The sources of these beliefs are varied, but chief among them are authority and the reliance on sensory evidence. Whatever his mother or father says is often accepted without question by the child who has not yet come to school. Parents represent a supreme source of knowledge and authority. In the kindergarten, however, parental knowledge and authority may be supplanted by the authority of the teacher who now commands a new arena of the child's life. "My teacher says . . . !" is probably the most authoritative statement a young child can make. Teachers need to be alert to this transfer of supreme authority. It is important that as early as kindergarten, children are encouraged to use all of their senses—eyes, ears, nose, etc.—to gather reliable information that can be used along with that supplied by the teacher. Or perhaps it might even be used to challenge the teacher's observations and source of knowledge. This healthy skepticism is important if the child is to grow and is to learn to be a resourceful individual rather than a compliant one who accepts docily and blindly every statement of authority.

It should also be noted that there are sources of knowledge outside of us as human beings and that statements based on faith in divine inspiration and counsel have been important guides for mankind in many cultures. This source of knowledge, although based on authority much like that of parent or teacher, finds its verification entirely outside of man's observable experience and knowledge. Thus, the kindergarten teacher must be aware of the statement "God says so!" or its equivalent with some groups, "The Bible [or the Koran] says so!"

In short, every culture has a way of summing up the major statements about itself. These become known as the central beliefs of the society. They often express the relationships people have to one another as individuals and the relationships they have to the unknown and often incomprehensible forces outside of themselves. While these beliefs may not always be rational or subject to careful proof by observation or empirical methods, they represent, nevertheless, the important touchstones of a society. Although it is difficult for kindergartners to verbally express these statements, because they often involve abstract language, five-year-olds can make good approximations of belief statements that are meaningful to them. Here is what one group of kindergartners wrote:

I believe that:
1. Friends are important.
2. You should be nice to your pets.
3. You should be nice and not fight with people.
4. Teachers and parents know a lot of stuff.
5. Superman isn't real, but he's fun to watch on TV.

Variation and change in human culture

An important task of the social studies program is to have students examine the geographical variations and historical changes in human culture and recognize that while all cultures have common elements of technology, institutions, language, and beliefs, there are many differences as well as similarities.

GEOGRAPHIC VARIATIONS. As we suggested earlier, children need to see that in other parts of the world, families may be organized differently and that parents or grandparents may play different roles. The availability of resources directly affects advances or limitations in the growth of technology and in the use of tools. Language patterns differ markedly throughout the world. Some languages are highly expressive, almost poetic in their statements. Oriental written languages were originally based on symbolic pictures. English has many words to describe the same things. For example, *house, home, castle, cave, hut, apartment,* and *flat* all indicate some form of shelter. Institutions also vary widely throughout the world, and the kindergarten teacher can help set the tone, as children recognize in later years, that not everything must imitate the American pattern. Social and political institutions particularly take varying forms and reflect the history, beliefs, and values of a culture.

What is important is that children begin to recognize the diversity in the world about them and try to identify the values and beliefs that have given rise to various institutions. In the kindergarten, teachers should see to it that the illustrations of institutions reflect this geographic diversity. Large color story prints are readily available from most textbook companies. In addition, the teacher who has traveled or who can reproduce color pictures from the *National Geographic* or similar magazines can develop a wide repertoire of 35-mm slides that can easily be made into an attractive slide-and-tape show with a carousel projector. The pictures can show that in other cultures throughout the world, institutions that may have different characteristics have been formed as organized ways of taking care of basic social needs.

HISTORICAL CHANGE. Closely related to geographic variations is the importance of historical change in the human culture. Cultural institutions are not static but grow and change over time, albeit quite slowly. The very fact that such institutions represent organized approaches within a culture to deal with basic needs suggests that they preserve or conserve the best elements of the society while at the same time they meet the changing needs of daily life. It is important that older children begin to understand the concepts of *cultural invention* and *cultural diffusion,* which help explain the changes in human culture over time. Even kindergartners, however, whose concepts of time are not well developed at all, should at least know that things have changed and that there is an increasingly rapid tempo of change in our lives today. As we noted previously, the teacher can provide pictures and can talk about the changes from horse-drawn vehicles and bicycles, to automobiles, to airplanes, to space ships. Children can also recognize the change in technology from radio to television, which took place in their parents' lifetime.

In summary, it is important that the kindergarten teacher begin to teach simple understandings of the concepts of geographic variation and historical change in human culture.

Cultural heritage

An important aspect of understanding oneself and others as members of the human race is to have a good understanding of one's own cultural heritage. Students should know something of their own roots in order to gain a perspective of their cultural identity. They should know about the great events and persons that have influenced or changed their culture. Thus, history has an important place in giving depth and dimension to the study of the four aspects of culture discussed previously; the invention and development of tools and technology; the growth, change, and decline of institutions; the development of language and its usage; and the formation of ideas, beliefs, and values that have greatly affected the culture.

This perspective of geography and history avoids the mindless memorization of states and their capitals, and lists of exports and imports. It avoids having children learn a useless catalog of dates, kings and wars, congressional acts, and birthdates of presidents. Instead, geography plays its proper role as the study of the distribution and variation of things across place and space. History records and interprets significant events and studies the concept of change over time. Four- and five-year-olds have little sense of historical time and have great difficulty establishing meaning for events and places that are distant from them. Nevertheless, kindergartners can take part in the annual cycle of public holidays, such as Labor Day, Veterans Day, Armistice Day, and Memorial Day. Kindergartners can share in these celebrations when older students visit the kindergarten and read stories about the events they commemorate.

Similarly, many schools celebrate the birthdays of important figures, such as Christopher Columbus, Martin Luther King, George Washington, and Abraham Lincoln. Kindergarten children can take part in school assemblies or can participate in celebrations in their own classrooms. It is important, however, that these celebrations of parts of our national heritage be genuine and meaningful. Teachers should avoid such legends and half-truths as Washington and the cherry tree or Lincoln and the rail fence, which would build up mythologies of national heroes who appear to children to be larger than life and free of all human faults. While every culture needs its heroes, we should not make them into gods incapable of any wrong. Such myths come back to haunt teachers and breed cynicism in adolescents when they discover that the "facts" they learned in kindergarten are not true.

The kindergarten teacher must also be especially careful to provide a multicultural and global emphasis in selecting events of our national and cultural heritage. Minority groups, both racial and ethnic, have largely been underrepresented or omitted entirely in the school curriculum. It is important that teachers provide appropriate recognition to great leaders, both men and women, from all ethnic and cultural groups in America. Thus, time must be found to commemorate such leaders as Harriet Tubman, Susan Anthony, and Clara Barton, as well as the more familiar ones mentioned previously. If our educational program is to be truly multicultural, it must start in the kindergarten. It is also important that young children begin to identify with events outside of themselves. Not only should they be aware of American patriotic holidays, but they should also know about United Nations Day and UNICEF (United Nations International Children's Emergency Fund), the campaign to aid needy people throughout the world, usually conducted at Halloween time.

Lastly, the school should give an appropriate place to the seasonal, cultural, and religious holidays of the year. Halloween and Thanksgiving are two that are frequently celebrated. The first is purely seasonal and closely related to the old agricultural traditions at the end of harvest. It also offers exciting possibilities for fantasy and imagination. Thanksgiving, a holiday that all Americans celebrate, provides a good opportunity to touch base with the meaning of this day and its historical origin with the pilgrims in New England. Kindergartners can celebrate with a small mini-Thanksgiving Day luncheon at school by helping prepare cranberry jelly, bread stuffing for a turkey, or similar tasks. They can also draw Thanksgiving scenes on place mats or create table decorations using the holiday motifs.

The cycle of religious holidays also offers many opportunities for youngsters to develop a closer awareness of their culture. The kindergarten teacher should approach the celebration of Christmas by giving attention to the cultural, ethnic, and religious heritage of the children in the class. For Christians, who celebrate the birth of Christ, Christmas is a religious festival of great spiritual importance. For others, it is little more than a secular holiday of Yuletide, in which Santa Claus, Rudolph the Red-nosed Reindeer, holly leaves, and the exchange of presents are outward symbols. For still other groups, such as Jewish people or Oriental people who may be Buddhist or Shintoist, Christmas has no immediate religious meaning. Yet, often schools celebrate Christmas with all the pageantry and solemnity of a Christian Sunday school. Children participate in plays in the roles of winged angels, Joseph and Mary, or perhaps camels or donkeys. They sing, "For Jesus Christ is born today" or "Oh, come let us adore Him, Christ, the Lord!"

This is not to suggest that the classroom be sterile and avoid the public recognition of important cultural and religious holidays and festivals. Not at all! It is, rather, to suggest that the teacher must relate to our legal traditions regarding separation of church and state and also to the need for a respect and understanding of the beliefs of all groups of children. Young children in the kindergarten are willing and eager participants in all school activities. They are also docile and uncritical, and completely unaware of the subtle influences of religious teaching that may be occurring through the unwitting actions of the teacher.

Kindergarten teachers should plan cooperatively with principals, parents, and members of the community, where appropriate, to provide a soundly conceived and balanced approach to varying viewpoints within the community. The kindergarten is the place where children begin to develop an awareness of cultural traditions outside of themselves and begin to develop respect and understanding for the differences as well as the similarities in religious traditions. While Hanukkah does not have the religious significance or importance of Christmas, the fact that it occurs close in time to the Christmas season provides a good opportunity to tell the biblical story of the Maccabees and explain the meaning of the menorah, the symbolic seven-branch candlestick.

Similarly, schools typically take note of Easter time, and kindergartners frequently draw, color, or cut out rabbits as part of the

Easter season activity. While the symbolism of the rabbit and fertility associated with the Christian meaning of resurrection and new life is far too complex for kindergartners, some sense of the religious importance of the event should be conveyed. But it is important also to help children be aware of the Jewish festival of Passover, which occurs almost at the same time and commemorates the flight of the ancient Jews out of Egyptian captivity into the promised land of Israel.

Where there are children from other ethnic and cultural groups in the school, parents can be encouraged to come to the class to talk about the meaning of important cultural celebrations. The frequent involvement of parents can do much to strengthen the program and develop effective rapport with members of the community. More important, it gives positive support to a multicultural and global approach to the curriculum, even at the kindergarten level.

In summary, children in the kindergarten classroom can participate in the celebration of many cultural holidays that are seasonal, patriotic, and religious in nature. By doing so, their learnings are directed toward establishing some understanding of their cultural and national heritage. What must be avoided, however, is spending large amounts of time on symbols (e.g., cutting out identical tri-cornered hats, silhouettes of Lincoln, or valentine hearts) and putting little or no emphasis on the meaning of these external symbols and stereotypes. It should also be noted that while good kindergarten programs may combine many creative aspects into an appropriate culminating activity, it is important that the "tail not wag the dog." Specifically, little valid social studies learning occurs when inordinate amounts of time are spent rehearsing and preparing for a Thanksgiving pageant that involves a lavish production, memorized speeches, and exquisite costumes rather than knowledge about the Pilgrims, the meaning of Thanksgiving, or the many variations in the way the holiday is celebrated among different ethnic or cultural groups in America.

ABILITIES AND SKILLS IN SOCIAL STUDIES LEARNING

Earlier in this chapter, we talked about abilities and skills as the second important domain of learning in social studies. We defined abilities and skills as the development of intellectual thinking processes, including the ability to handle new data, to integrate it with existing factual knowledge, and to evaluate that new knowledge in terms of its validity and reliability. We also identified the importance of effective human relation skills and the ability to communicate well in an interpersonal manner.

Gathering information

Throughout the previous section on the domain of knowledge, we considered the importance of observing and learning many kinds of information and factual knowledge. Since most kindergarten children are just beginning to learn to read, teachers must depend on a variety of other sources from which children can gain information. Perhaps the most frequently used methods are oral conversation, directed classroom discussion, observation of large study prints, discussions with classroom visitors, and movie, slide, and tape presentations. All of these are basic methods of gathering information.

Forming concepts

We also stressed the importance of identifying similarities and differences in a variety of settings. While this process is more complex than gathering information that can be recalled by rote, the kindergarten provides an important place for beginning this more abstract task, which leads toward the ability

to categorize and ultimately form abstract verbal concepts.

There are many reading readiness tasks that provide necessary backgrounds for social studies learnings. These exercises focus on identifying things that are the same and things that are different in geometric figures, colors, sounds, and textures. Children can differentiate among colors and can name them; they can find the geometric shape or the drawing that is dissimilar in a set. The ability to discriminate is important as children observe study prints and begin to note similarities and differences in such things as structures of houses, types of clothing, food utensils, and patterns of family life. Many young children will have difficulty verbalizing some of these differences. It may be sufficient in the early part of the year for them to say simply, "They are different!"

Later the teacher can help them discriminate and then verbalize characteristics that are different as well as those that are the same.

As children learn to identify characteristics that are similar and those that are different, they must also begin to discern features that are *essential* and shared in common by all the items in the category. For example, a *roof* can be flat or sloped; it can have gables or dormers; it can be rounded and dome shaped; or it can be angular and steepled. Nevertheless, all of these kinds of roofs share the common characteristic that they cover and enclose a building. As children become more assured in their learning of the essential elements of the concept *roof*, this concept can be extended to include the billowy top of a large circus tent, the covering of an open porch, or possibly the roof that covers an outdoor walkway between buildings. These latter examples all have variations of the definition that a roof covers and encloses a building; nevertheless, we still call each a roof.

Another important step in concept development is to identify nonexemplars to be certain that children really can identify the essential element. Pictures of a floor, (which might be thought to cover a basement), a wall, or a door might all be used to test whether they have the correct concept of a roof.

Defining concepts

Lastly, the experienced kindergarten teacher will recognize quickly that children have great difficulty summarizing and explaining the definition of a concept. This requires some considerable degree of generalizing using abstract terms. More important, the definition must be so worded that it involves the essential characteristics of the concept and applies equally to all elements. Young children need carefully directed experience in this activity, and it is quite appropriate in the beginning stages to prompt wording that they can agree expresses their idea but that they would have had difficulty forming themselves. Teachers should also accept approximations in children's language that conveys the essential meaning. For example "A roof is something that goes over the top of the house and hooks the sides together." This expresses, in children's language, the notion of covering and enclosing and is a good working definition for five-year-olds.

A more difficult task of concept formation is explaining and summarizing how several different types of buildings in a community differ. Kindergartners would find it quite difficult to express in words how a church differs from their own home or from a store. While they will be able to observe and say that all the buildings have walls, a roof, and windows, it is difficult for them to distinguish and verbalize that the functions in each of these three buildings are quite different. Few, if any, children at this age would be able to sum up the characteristics of a church or synagogue and be able to define it as "A church is where you go to pray." Even more difficult would be a generalization such as "The shape and arrangement of a building depends on what you use it for."

Complex concepts

In the foregoing paragraphs we discussed a number of specific skills and abilities to be learned and practiced in relation to concept formation and the development of generalizations. Our example of the concept *roof* was deliberately very simple. The social studies curriculum, however, abounds with a variety of concepts that are much more complex and abstract and for which concrete visual symbols are difficult to present. Such terms as *group, society, family, law, rule, leader,* and *responsibility* are important for children to begin to learn at the kindergarten level.

These concepts will be revisited again and again as most social studies curricula spiral through grades 1 through 12.

Ideally, children should see the concept of *law* expanded in complexity and sophistication as it ranges from family and classroom rules, to local traffic regulations and zoning ordinances, to statewide driving laws, to a whole range of federal laws governing minimum wages, health insurance, military service, and regulation and control of interstate commerce. At its most abstract level, they will see the concept expanded to include international law, made up of treaties and conventions mutually agreed to by several nations and enforced by world courts and/or international peacekeeping military forces.

While this range of concepts is far beyond the needs of kindergarten children, teachers should be aware that they are laying foundations for important conceptual learning. Thus, what they teach should be accurate and not have to be unlearned at some later point. For the same reason, the tasks of observation, differentiation, and the formation of definitions are critical learning tasks that will be continuously used by students throughout their lives.

Relational concepts

One class of concepts that is especially difficult for kindergarten children is relational concepts. These are usually concepts of time, space, or association. They are quite abstract, yet it is important for children to learn them early. Try asking a four- or five-year-old, "When is *tomorrow*?" The child will probably reply "Tomorrow is kind of like today except it hasn't come yet." The kindergarten teacher should work consistently throughout the year to try to develop the notions of past, present, and future time through constant reference to days in the week, months and seasons of the year, birthdays, holidays, etc. Even learning to tell

time is a complex task for many children because they have not grasped the idea of how long a minute or an hour may be. As we noted earlier, the concept of chronological time is simply too abstract for most five-year-olds. Such phrases as "long, long ago" or "in the olden days" are usually satisfactory.

Similarly, young children need considerable experience in talking and thinking about family or generational associations such as parents and grandparents. Family pictures showing mothers and grandmothers as children or as young adults help children begin to understand that these family relatives were once children themselves. It is equally important for kindergartners to learn that teachers also were once children; most five-year-olds believe that their teachers were always old and were always teachers.

Other relational concepts that are difficult for kindergarten children to conceptualize are *under, above, beyond, far, near* and *between,* as well as serial or rank order words, such as *first, second,* and *third.* Each of these involves a relationship between people or things in terms of space, time, or place. Such concepts can only be developed by having children constantly experience them by pointing out relationships of near and far, putting things in place order, rearranging furniture and books, or doing similar activities in the day-to-day classroom life.

These examples give some indication of the complexity of concept development as an intellectual task. While some of these thinking processes may be beyond the capability of kindergarten children, we call to the attention of teachers here so that teachers can anticipate the importance of concept formation and the steps leading toward the development of generalizations or principles. Yet, it is in the kindergarten that this level of thinking process can and should be developed through simple examples that are common in children's everyday experience or that can be supplied by photographs, study prints, or films. What is important is the intellectual task of leading children from the singular and concrete to the general and abstract.

Other thinking skills

In addition to comparing, contrasting, classifying, and conceptualizing, other thinking skills that can be developed with five-year-olds are inferring, hypothesizing, imagining, and evaluating. While each of these is a complex, intellectual function, they can be introduced in elementary form through simple, everyday materials. What is important is that the thought processes be started at simplified levels and not be left to the upper grades on the assumption that young children are not capable of such intellectual functions.

Inferring

At the simplest level, children can make inferences by making observations or examining data and asking what does this mean or what does this suggest might be true. With practice and help from the teacher, they can distinguish these inferences from observed facts. For example, a factual statment is: "The temperature outside is 20 degrees, and the sky is cloudy." An inference statement would be: "It will snow soon." Thus, the children conclude or draw an implication from observed data and/or previous life experience about what might be true. That it might snow is a reasonable inference drawn from factual data. Simple exercises like these can help children begin to discriminate fact from inference and move toward higher order intellectual processes.

Hypothesizing

Another intellectual task is hypothesizing. Kindergarten children can quickly grasp the notion of conditional statements, the truth of which is to be tested by observation or experimentation. The simplest form of hypothetical thinking is to consider, "What would happen if. . . ?" Using the example of inferential thinking above, the teacher might ask, "What would happen to the water in a stream or a pond if the temperature were to be very cold for several days?" Assuming that students have had experience with winter life, they would probably be able to hypothesize that the water would stand still, or that it would turn to snow or ice. Each of these would be acceptable formulations in children's language of possible results. Many kinds of similar "What would happen if. . . ?" questions could be posed by teachers, and observational data could be gathered to provide possible answers.

When children have had enough firsthand observation or experience, it may be possible for them to formulate statements in the conditional "If . . . then . . ." form. For example, "*If* it gets very cold, *then* water will turn to ice." Similarly, other daily observations could be cast into the hypothetical form: "*If* it gets very cloudy and the weather is warm, *then* it will rain." Five-and six-year-olds can have fun with these kinds of statements, especially if they formulate them early in the day and then see if they can collect evidence to support or to reject them. While the content level is simple, the task is complex; for the hypothesis must be a reasonable one supported by some prior evidence or logical deductions, and then it must be proved or disproved on the basis of observed evidence. Despite the simplicity of the content, training in the intellectual task provides children with experience in a high-order thinking process.

Imagining

Quite a different thought process is imagining. Children develop this ability when they are asked to create a reality that might be, but that does not actually exist. Imagining can take many forms, from creating ideas of how things might be in the future if existing things were to change, to examining alternatives to past historical events or even to present events as part of a decision-making task. When children look at alternatives, they can also begin to imagine consequences of such alternatives. At the kindergarten level, for instance. children could begin to look at any of the institutions we have mentioned and imagine how they might change in the years to come. Children can imagine how our life might change if our present tools were to disappear. They might also be asked, "If we were to have interplanetary travel, would we need to have schools and homes on these planets? What might they look like?" Another task might be to imagine what a school building would look like if there were no rules. Each of these tasks require children to hypothesize and then create a new reality through verbal description, drawings, or a model in a sand table that displays their creative idea as a reality that might be.

Many young children are good at imaginative thinking, since they live very much in a world that is both reality and fantasy. This type of thinking is extremely important if we are to prize creativity in children. All too often, however, teachers ask students to be conformists by providing the one right answer that is verified in the textbook. Yet, in real life the person who is imaginative and who can find many alternative solutions to problems is the one who usually gets ahead.

Evaluating

A final type of intellectual skill is the ability to evaluate or make judgments about the worth of something. This implies that children develop criteria for making these judgments and are then able to supply data focused on one or more of these criteria. An evaluation is not pure whimsy or personal opinion. Rather, it reflects carefully thought out and reasoned judgment about the merit or worth of an idea, story, or drawing. At the simplest level, children can attempt to evaluate their own painting or dramatic play. For instance. having done three paintings of themselves or members of their families over the past week, the children can decide which one they like best. It is very common for five-year-olds, when asked why they like a particular choice, to simply say, "because ___." On further probing, they may come back and say only, "I just do." Such responses suggest that children have not had experience in using criteria and data to support their judgments. Thus, teachers should deliberately suggest criteria such as the use of color, imaginative form, or arrangement of space. Teachers might have to prompt youngsters quite a bit with questions such as, "What did you like about the color?" The children might then talk about brightness or intensity or the use of various colors. Similarly, a teacher might ask, "What did you like about what the people were doing in the picture?" or "Does this painting tell us something about yourself?" Teachers will have to continue to suggest criteria and help children supply relevant data for quite a while until they learn to develop the skill of evaluating.

Many of these intellectual skills and abilities are dealt with in other sources. The reader is referred to *Teaching Strategies for the Social Studies* by Banks and Clegg (1977) for more detailed suggestions. Two excellent social studies textbook series developed by commercial publishers have incorporated many of these thinking skills and abilities as an important part of their curriculum programs. These are the Houghton Mifflin social studies series, *Windows on Our World*, edited by Anderson (1978), and the McGraw-Hill social studies series, edited by Cherryholmes and associates (1978). The teacher's guide material for both of these series is excellent and reflects heavily the NCSS guidelines that have formed the basis for this chapter.

VALUING

At the outset of this chapter, we talked about the process of valuing as the systematic examination of attitudes, beliefs, and basic values that underlie various cultures of the world. We noted that the study of values is important because it helps children understand what groups and individuals consider important in a society. We take the position here that the study of values and beliefs should be a conscious and deliberate part of the social studies program. It is critically important that children learn to identify the values that guide them in their daily lives and that are operating in the groups and institutions of which they are a part.

Basic values

At the simplest level, values are those principles or ideas that we consider very important, that we hold dear, or that we cherish. Some values are basic or of enduring worth and are maintained steadfastly throughout life. One such set of values is personal and social in nature. It includes respect for self (sometimes called self-awareness or self-concept), respect and understanding for others (sometimes called human dignity), and a more general value, respect for life in its many forms.

Another set of basic values is political and includes certain commitments that the school should evidence toward our democratic way of life. These involve the values of openness and fair play, freedom of speech, participation in public decision making (government), and the concept of one person, one vote.

We believe that these are basic values to which the school in the American society must be dedicated. They represent basic commitments to human dignity and the common frame of our American way of life. We believe that these basic values and commitments can and should be taught, not only by word but, more importantly, by action throughout the entire school day and should be evidenced by teachers as well as by pupils. We hold that schools cannot be neutral on such important basic values as these (see Banks and Clegg, 1977, 481-485).

Other values

Many value considerations are embedded within the enduring and pervasive issues selected for study in the K-12 social studies curriculum. Some of these include patriotism, loyalty to one's friends and nation, the right of self-determination among nations, free enterprise, conservation of land and resources, limited local government, and a strong centralized government or national control of resources, industry, and the distribution of goods.

Many values such as these, however, are not nearly as central or as pervasive as the basic and enduring political values defined above. While the value of local government control, for example, may be strongly held by some, it may be disdained or rejected by others in favor of a greatly centralized authority. A person's commitment to either may be influenced or changed entirely by events, the views of others, personal experiences, or the experience and tradition of one's culture.

What is important is that these values are not viewed as polarized along a continuum of truth and falsity or good and evil, as some critics have suggested. Instead, they represent competing values for which appropriate and legitimate rationales can be developed. It is the task of the social studies curriculum to help children identify the values embedded in various social studies issues, analyze their sources, and consider the consequences of actions that are likely to flow when these values are held.

None of the foregoing is intended to suggest any notion of moral or ethical relativism; that is, that one value is as good as another or that it makes no difference which values are held. The touchstones against which all of our value analyses must be made are the two

Table 3. Kohlberg's six stages of moral judgment*

Level and stage	Content of stage		Social perspective of stage
	What is right	Reasons for doing right	
Level I: Preconventional			
Stage 1: Heteronomous morality	Sticking to rules backed by punishment; obedience for its own sake; avoiding physical damage to persons and property.	Avoidance of punishment, superior power of authorities.	Egocentric point of view. Doesn't consider the interests of others or recognize that they differ from the actor's; doesn't relate two points of view. Actions considered physically rather than in terms of psychological interests of others. Confusion of authority's perspective with one's own.
Stage 2: Individualism Instrumental purpose and exchange	Following rules only when in one's immediate interest; acting to meet one's own interests and needs and letting others do the same. Right is also what is fair or what is an equal exchange, deal, agreement.	To serve one's own needs or interests in a world where one has to recognize that other people also have interests.	Concrete individualistic perspective. Aware that everybody has interests to pursue and that these can conflict; right is relative (in the concrete individualistic sense).
Level II: Conventional			
Stage 3: Mutual interpersonal expectations Relationships and interpersonal conformity	Living up to what is expected by people close to you or what people generally expect of a good son, brother, friend, etc. "Being good" is important and means having good motives, showing concern for others. It also means keeping mutual relationships such as trust, loyalty, respect, and gratitude.	The need to be a good person in your own eyes and those of others; caring for others; belief in the Golden Rule; desire to maintain rules and authority that support sterotypical good behavior.	Perspective of the individual in relationships with other individuals. Aware of shared feelings, agreements, and expectations which take primacy over individual interests. Relates points of view through the concrete Golden Rule, putting oneself in the other guy's shoes. Does not yet consider generalized system perspective.
Stage 4: Social system and conscience	Fulfilling duties to which you have agreed; laws to be upheld except in extreme cases where they conflict with other	To keep the institution going as a whole and avoid a breakdown in the system "if every-	Differentiates societal point of view from interpersonal agreement or motives. Takes the point of view of the system that

*From *PROMOTING MORAL GROWTH: From Piaget to Kohlberg* by Richard Hersh, Diana Pritchard Paolitto and Joseph Reimer. Copyright © 1979 by Longman Inc. Reprinted with permission of Longman Inc., New York.

Table 3. Kohlberg's six stages of moral judgment—cont'd

Level and stage	Content of stage		Social perspective of stage
	What is right	Reasons for doing right	
	fixed social duties. Right is also contributing to the society, group, or institution.	one did it"; imperative of conscience to meet one's defined obligations. (Easily confused with stage 3 belief in rules and authority.)	defines roles and rules; considers individual relations in terms of place in the system.
Level III: Postconventional; or principled			
Stage 5: Social contract or utility and individual-rights	Being aware that people hold a variety of values and opinions and that most of their values and rules are relative to their group. Relative rules usually upheld in the interest of impartiality and because they are the social contract. Some nonrelative values and rights (e.g., life and liberty) must be upheld in any society and regardless of majority opinion.	A sense of obligation to law because of one's social contract to make and abide by laws for the welfare of all and for the protection of all people's rights. A feeling of contractual commitment, freely entered upon, to family, friendship, trust, and work obligations. Concern that laws and duties be based on rational calculation of overall utility, "the greatest good for the greatest number."	Prior-to-society perspective. Rational individual aware of values and rights prior to social attachments and contracts. Integrates perspectives by formal mechanisms of agreement, contract, objective impartiality, and due process. Considers moral and legal points of view; recognizes that they sometimes conflict and finds it difficult to integrate them.
Stage 6: Universal ethical principles	Following self-chosen ethical principles. Particular laws or social agreements usually valid because they rest on such principles; when laws violate these principles, one acts in accordance with principle. Principles are universal principles of justice; equality of human rights and respect for the dignity of human beings as individuals.	The belief as a rational person in the validity of universal moral principles and a sense of personal commitment to them.	Perspective of a moral point of view from which social arrangements derive. Perspective is that of a rational individual recognizing the nature of morality or the fact that persons are ends in themselves and must be treated as such.

132 Kindergarten: programs and practices

most basic and enduring of all values, those of human dignity and freedom of expression. Values that may be liberal or conservative, or appropriate in one culture and not in another, must be judged as worthwhile or good by the extent to which they enhance or diminish these two basic values.

Moral education

A more complete analysis of determining what is morally good or right is beyond the scope of this chapter. In the past decade Lawrence Kohlberg developed an extensive theory of moral education with a well-defined set of six stages of moral judgment based on Piaget's work in cognitive development (Table 3). Kohlberg, moreover, proposed that an essential role of the teacher is that of moral educator. For an excellent summary of Kohlberg's theories and their application to moral education, the reader is referred to *Promoting Moral Growth: From Piaget to Kohlberg* by Hersh and associates (1979).

The kindergarten provides an excellent opportunity to introduce children to the study of values. The teacher can begin to consciously consider such values as patriotism, loyalty, respect for self and others, and cooperation. For the most part, the kindergarten will focus on the development of the basic personal values that deal with children's growing sense of personal identity and self-awareness, and with their participation in the class as a social group. The school represents an entirely new experience, different from the home and the neighborhood play groups, and often larger and more complex than the nursery school or day care center in which some children may have had earlier experiences. Thus, the kindergarten has a primary concern for the values associated with the development of a strong and healthy self-concept and awareness of one's own identity, and for the values involved in the process of socialization (or of becoming a member of the kindergarten and school groups).

A unique combination of these values was developed more than 20 years ago by Miel and Brogan (1957). In *More Than Social Studies: A View of Social Learning in the Elementary School,* they identify a number of

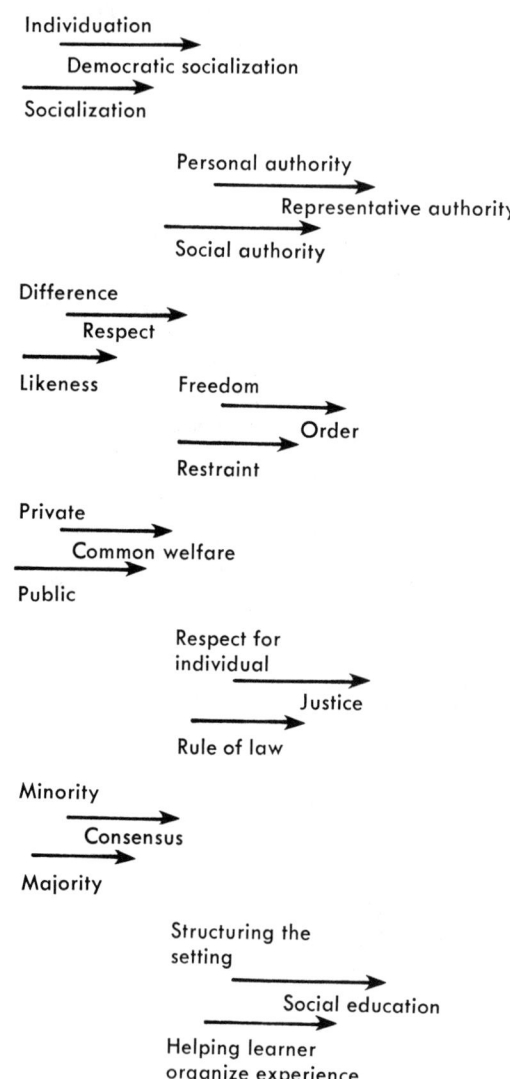

Fig. 6-2. Value concepts of a democratic society. (Adapted from Miel, Alice, and Brogan, Peggy. *More than social studies: a view of social learning in the elementary school.* Englewood Cliffs, N.J.: Prentice-Hall, Inc., 1957.)

basic concepts important to a democratic society, including socialization, respect for people, human welfare, decision making, authority, order, and justice (Fig. 6-2). What is unique is that they identify elements that are often in tension with one another but that when taken together form the essential components of a much larger concept essential to a democratic way of life. For example, the concept *society* is seen as being composed of the elements *individual* and *group*. Similarly, the value of respect for people is made up of the elements *difference* and *likeness*. Miel and Brogan take care to point out that these concepts are not either-or choices, nor are they "middle-of-the-road positions, something halfway between falsely conceived opposites—in short . . . no position at all." They view these concepts or values as

creative ways for working out relationships within the factors that are operating when people try to live together in organized groups. These new creations, which are more than and different from the elements making up the relationships, are disciplining concepts. They contain their own guides to correcting violations of the core idea. If either element in the relationship is given undue emphasis, the consequences in human relationships will show that the integrity of the concept is being destroyed. (Miel and Brogan, 1957, p. 5)

Democratic behavior

Closely related to the concepts of a democratic society are those that relate to basic values inherent in our social behavior. While basic concepts such as order and justice are very abstract for kindergartners to deal with, there are many practical ways of dealing with external behaviors that reflect growing awareness of the respect for basic human dignity. Miel and Brogan have identified the following behaviors: sharing, communicating, participating, cooperating, demonstrating loyalty, and exercising citizenship. These are shown with their corresponding elements

in Fig. 6-3. Each of these democratic behaviors represents an important component in developing and demonstrating respect for oneself and for others. They also imply membership in a social group, whether a small work or play group or the larger classroom or school groups. In each case, needs of the individual are balanced with needs of the group and vice versa.

In this way children can begin to establish effective working relationships that demonstrate an acceptance of the basic value

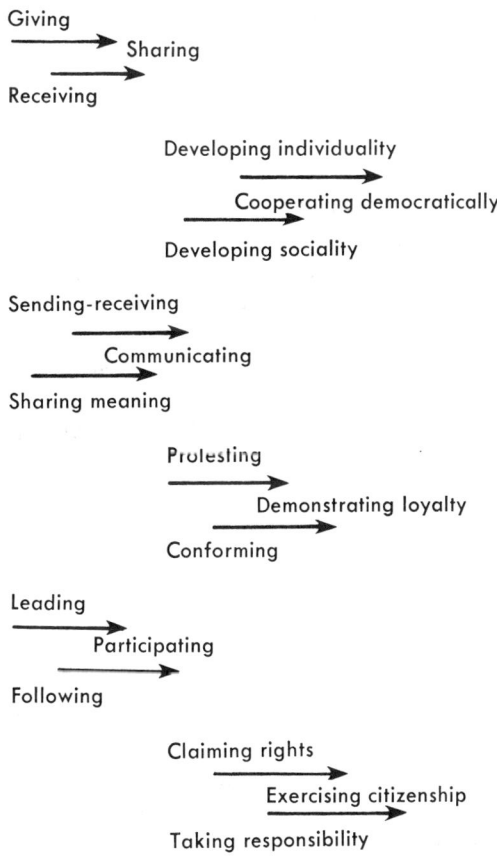

Fig. 6-3. Value elements of democratic behavior. (Adapted from Miel, Alice, and Brogan, Peggy. *More than social studies: a view of social learning in the elementary school.* Englewood Cliffs, N.J.: Prentice-Hall, Inc., 1957.)

of human dignity. Note that the behavior *sharing* implies both giving and receiving. The value of sharing emphasizes a mutual function and a balance between the needs and rights of an individual with those of a larger group. This is not at all to say that all activities must be on a shared basis. Indeed, there will be times when an individual can expect to receive support, assistance, and affection from the groups in which he participates. The concept of sharing sums up the give-and-take that is essential to democratic human relationships. People willingly take turns, share goods and services, and assume part of the support for the institutions, groups, or agencies to which they belong. They also share in the ideas of others and assume responsibility both individually and as a group when things go wrong.

What is important is that both elements of the value—giving and receiving—operate in a mutually interdependent way. As Miel and Brogan have pointed out, if either is given undue emphasis or is carried to an extreme, the consequence in terms of human relationships is a diminishing of human dignity. To overemphasize the importance of giving is to diminish the value of individuality. To exaggerate the concept of receiving is to encourage selfishness and lessen one's sense of respect for the group and its members.

Similarly, each of the other behaviors shown on the chart emphasizes a mutual interdependence of the elements of the particular behavior. One element may receive more emphasis than another at varying times. What is important, though, is that both be recognized as wholesome and important and that a judicious balance be achieved in the classroom in order to assure the continued growth of a healthy self-concept and personal self-awareness, as well as the development of effective skills in group membership and human relations.

Thus, *participating* reflects the elements of leading and following as membership within a group changes and as roles and responsibilities of group membership change.

Cooperating reflects the need of individuals to work with others to achieve what the individual could not accomplish alone. It also reflects the need to develop cooperation as a norm of operation for a healthy group. All too often we have emphasized competition when, in fact, cooperation is far more effective in accomplishing both individual and group goals and purposes. This is not to deny the place of competition as an important value in our society. But with young children, teachers must see that they have the opportunity to compete in the classroom or on the playground on bases that are fair and with the same privileges and opportunities as adults, namely selecting the events, choosing the competitors, and setting the time limits or conditions for the competition. All too often, schools promote competition, particularly in athletic events, to such an exaggerated degree that it becomes detrimental to other values for which the school claims to stand. Competition becomes unhealthy when it results in an elite group of players and consigns all others to the permanent role of spectator. Competition becomes destructive of human dignity when it forces children to compete on an unfair basis beyond their level of competence or skill. This does not simulate the real world, where, in actuality, adults have the opportunity to freely choose to participate or not in competitive situations and to withdraw from them readily if they find the consequences to be unacceptable. To the extent that cooperation is more productive of positive human interrelationships and thus human dignity, it is a more powerful value than competition, which can easily become destructive of human dignity.

Demonstrating *loyalty* is another example of balancing the element of conforming (ac-

Learning to live together: the social studies

cepting the decisions and traditions of a group) with the element of protesting when the needs or rights of individuals are restricted or violated. Individuals owe allegiance to and willing compliance with group decisions that have been cooperatively arrived at. They also have an obligation to provide cooperation and support when the group is in need or in trouble. This also suggests a willing conformance to group-established rules, norms of behavior, and long-standing traditions and customs. On the other hand, individuals also demonstrate loyalty by being willing to take unpopular positions or to stand out against the crowd when they feel compelled to voice disagreement or reservations with decisions of the group. This becomes especially important when individuals see their own rights being infringed on in favor of group desires. It is important that young children in kindergarten recognize that while majority rule is a useful concept in American democracy, it cannot be permitted to override the substantial rights of the minority. When this occurs, members of the majority must be willing to hear the protests of those in the minority and be willing to reconsider decisions that may do harm to the ultimate value of human dignity.

It is equally important that young children learn that there is nothing wrong with voicing objection to the "establishment" so long as the manner of that objection is itself consistent with the democratic process. In too many schools, however, there is a covert set of values of obedience, conformity, and passivity that the school teaches quite explicitly in its expectations and in its actions. Coupled with this is the notion that it is improper and perhaps un-American to challenge the established views or rulings of authority. In recent years some people have curiously branded the right of protest as un-American, even though the right to petition the government for redress of grievances is one of the basic freedoms protected by the Bill of Rights. What is important about this element of loyalty is that as young children grow older, they must learn to distinguish between carping criticism and principled dissent. To know the difference between the two and to choose the right time to act accordingly is to understand the concept of loyalty in its fullest dimensions.

Teaching strategies

In the preceding paragraphs we identified content material in the general domain of values that is appropriate for kindergarten children. Three teaching strategies are presented in Tables 4 to 6 that are appropriate for dealing with values. The series of questions in the tables are carefully designed to elicit responses that will help children identify and explore their feelings, engage in interpersonal problem solving, and analyze values based on observations, feelings, or reactions to events that they have studied or observed. Extensive classroom testing has demonstrated that these are fruitful strategies that encourage thoughtful and provocative discussions. They can be used easily by kindergarten teachers with the simple content examples about self and relations with others that we have discussed previously.

A word of caution is in order. While young children may be very talkative and open with many of their feelings, teachers should exercise discretion about questions or class discussions that may lead to undue invasions

Table 4. Exploring feelings*

Teacher	Student	Teacher follow-through
What happened?	Restates facts.	Sees that all facts are given and agreed upon. If students make inferences, ask that they be set aside temporarily.
How do you think . . . felt?†	Makes inference as to feelings.	Accepts inference.
Why do you think he would feel that way?	Explains.	Seeks clarification, if necessary.
Who has a different idea about how he felt?	Makes alternative inferences and explanation.	Seeks variety, if necessary. Asks for reasons, if necessary.
How did . . . (other persons in the situation) feel?	States inference about the feelings of additional persons.	Seeks clarification, if necessary. Encourages students to consider how other people in the situation felt.
Have you ever had something like this happen to you?‡	Describes similar event in his own life.	Ensures description of event.
How did you feel?†	Describes his feelings, may re-experience emotions.	Seeks clarification, if necessary. Provides support if necessary.
Why do you think you felt that way?	Offers explanation. Attempts to relate his feelings to events he has recalled.	Asks additional questions, if necessary, to get beyond stereotyped or superficial explanation.

*From *People in Families* Teacher's Edition by Mary J. Shindelus and Mary C. Durkin in *The Taba Program in Social Science.* Copyright © 1972 by Addison-Wesley Publishing Company, Inc. Reprinted by permission.
†These questions are repeated in sequence several times in order to obtain a variety of inferences and personal experiences.
‡If students have difficulty responding, you may wish to ask, "If this should happen to you, how do you think you would feel?" or "Has something like this happened to someone you know?" Another useful device may be for the teacher to describe such an event in his own life.

of a child's or family's privacy. Frequently, five-year-olds will be very open about their feelings of love and warmth or anger and hostility toward classmates or members of their family. While it is important for the child to voice such feelings and for the teacher to help the child begin to deal with them, teachers must remember that they are teachers and not therapists, psychologists, or social workers. Children should be encouraged to participate in discussions such as these on an entirely voluntary basis, and no child should be forced to voice a feeling that he himself does not own and willingly share. When children are reluctant to participate, teachers should simply overlook this reluctance and encourage the children to participate at some later date. Also, if teachers are to build a

Table 5. Interpersonal problem solving*

Teacher	Student	Teacher follow-through
What happened? or What did . . . do?	Describes events.	Sees that all events are given. Tries to get agreement or, if not possible, a clear statement of differences in perception of what occurred.
What do you think . . . (a protagonist) should do? Why?	Gives response.	Accepts response; seeks clarification where necessary.
How do you think . . . (others) would react if he did that? Why?	Makes inference and explains.	Accepts. Seeks clarification, if necessary.
Has something like that ever happened to you?†	Relates similar event in his life.	Provides support, if necessary.
What did you do?‡	Relates recalled behavior.	Seeks clarification, if necessary.
As you think back now, do you think that was a good or bad thing to do?	Judges past actions.	Encourages student to judge his own past actions. The teacher may need to prevent others from entering the discussion at this point.
Why do you think so?	States reasons.	Accepts reasons. If necessary, asks additional questions to make clear the criteria or values which the student is using in judging his actions.
Is there anything you could have done differently?	Offers alternative behavior.	Accepts. Asks additional questions to point up inconsistencies where they occur, e.g., "How does that agree with reasons you gave earlier?"

*From *People in Families* Teacher's Edition by Mary J. Shindelus and Mary C. Durkin in *The Taba Program in Social Science.* Copyright © 1972 by Addison-Wesley Publishing Company, Inc. Reprinted by permission.
†If students have difficulty responding, you may wish to ask, "If this should happen to you, how do you think you would feel?" or "Has something like this happened to someone you know?" Another useful device is for the teacher to describe such an event in his own life.
‡These questions are repeated in sequence several times in order to obtain a variety of responses.

Table 6. Analyzing values*

Teacher	Student	Teacher follow-through
What did they do . . . (with reference to some matter)?	Describes behavior.	Sees that description is complete and accurate.
What do you think were their reasons for doing/saying what they did?	States inferences.	Accepts. Seeks clarification, if necessary.
What do these reasons tell you about what is important to them?†	States inferences regarding values.	Restates or asks additional questions to ensure focus on values.
If you . . . (teacher specifies similar situations directly related to student, e.g., "If you accidentally tore a page in someone else's book") what would you do? Why?‡	States behavior and gives explanation.	Accepts, may seek clarification.
What does this show about what you think is important?	States inferences about his own values.	Accepts. Seeks clarification, if necessary.
What differences do you see in what all these people think is important?	Makes comparisons.	Ensures that all values identified are compared.

*From *People in Families* Teacher's Edition by Mary J. Shindelus and Mary C. Durkin in *The Taba Program in Social Science*. Copyright © 1972 by Addison-Wesley Publishing Company, Inc. Reprinted by permission.
†This sequence is repeated for each group or person whose values are to be analyzed. Each group is specified by the teacher and has been previously studied.
‡This sequence is repeated in order to get reactions from several students.

sense of trust with children, they must treat many of these discussions with a sense of confidentiality. Information about family backgrounds should not be the topic for gossip among teachers in the faculty lounge. Only in the event that a teacher obtains data about serious violations of law, such as child abuse, should this information be brought to the attention of the school counselor or principal. Even then, this should be done in an ethical way, with the teacher and others aware of the many legal issues surrounding such matters.

In summary, the study of values is an important part of the social studies curriculum, especially in the kindergarten, where the program deals with the basic values of human dignity and the right of self-expression, as well as with values related to self-awareness, self-concept, and relationships with others.

SOCIAL PARTICIPATION

We stated at the outset of this chapter that knowledge, skills, and values by themselves are incomplete as prerequisites for citizenship. Students must have opportunities to try out their knowledge and abilities by participating in some way in the public decision-making process. We deliberately use the phrase *decision-making process* rather than *governmental process* to suggest that there are many activities in the classroom, school, playground, and neighborhood in which kindergarten children can become involved. The word *government* suggests a more distant, adult activity, such as voting in

federal or local elections or serving as an elected official.

While schools have always claimed that education serves the goal of enlightened citizenship, the reality is that few schools give students actual experience in working out problems that are within their abilities to solve. Student government and student newspapers have generally had a very limited focus within schools and are usually reserved to upper elementary grades and high schools. Despite this rather poor record of translating citizenship education into reality, or of using the schools as a laboratory for citizenship training, we propose that kindergarten teachers find every opportunity to have children become effectively involved in decision-making processes within the classroom. There are many issues that lend themselves to involving students in seeking ways to solve them. These include discussions on such matters as sharing equipment and materials, learning to take turns, and deciding who will handle various classroom jobs, such as watering the plants or distributing milk and cookies. Behavior problems also offer many opportunities for examining some of the values of cooperation and sharing (e.g., dealing with the bully on the playground, sharing limited equipment and space, or setting standards for good manners in the lunchroom). Other activities might include planning for a Halloween or Christmas party, planning for a cookie-making session after which the cookies would be shared with another class, planning the class's participation in a school assembly program, a UNICEF drive, or even the familiar litter cleanup campaign.

At this simple level, the kindergarten's function is to give children an opportunity to become involved in determining their own affairs. To have input into such simple decisions as "Shall we participate? If so, how?" is itself an important gain in social participation. In some of the problem situations mentioned above, it may be the teacher or perhaps several of the children who suggest that there is an issue to be solved. If, however, there is indeed to be democratic participation, the teacher must be prepared to encourage the children to participate in discussions of the issues and alternative solutions and not handle the matter entirely alone.

A critical element in social participation in the classroom is that children genuinely have an opportunity to make decisions. While teachers can and should identify the areas in which children are able to participate, they should also be prepared to accept decisions that the children have made and then help the children live with the consequences of those actions. For example, it is false and hypocritical for a teacher to ask children whether they wish to participate in a school assembly program when the teacher knows ahead of time that their participation is clearly expected by the principal. If the class decides "no," the teacher must then manipulate or force them into a "yes" decision. Similarly, children should not be extended an opportunity to participate in making rules or planning activities that may violate school policies or that cannot realistically be carried out. Thus, it is important for kindergarten teachers to decide well in advance which decisions they alone must make because of their professional competence and maturity as adults and which decisions can be cooperatively made with the input of five-year-old children. Frankly, the issue is more one of the teacher's own need for authority and control than it is one of health, safety, or school policies. There are many activities in the daily kindergarten life that are clearly within the teacher's authority. When teachers are able to share some of this authority, though not lose final responsibility, children's practice and experience in social participation can be enhanced.

A frequently neglected aspect of social participation is evaluation of student involvement. After a Valentine's Day or Halloween party, children can easily ask themselves, "How well did we plan for the party? How much fun did we have? Did anything go wrong? What could or should we have done about it?" When it comes time to select new people for jobs, the children might ask, "How well have Christopher and Maria done their tasks? Are there some things that Robert and Cynthia need to bear in mind when they take over the new jobs next week?" Learning to identify and evaluate the quality of performance of office holders is just as important for kindergartners as it is for voters electing public officials. It is vital, however, that when such evaluations are made, the teacher set a model for positive, supportive, and constructive evaluation rather than permit the picky, negative, or personal criticisms that children sometimes make.

The freedom to make mistakes is another critically important aspect of social participation. No society is perfect, and adults know that they too make mistakes or faulty decisions on matters of public policy and government. What is essential, however, is that children have genuine opportunities to learn from their own mistakes. They need to realize that they have made errors and that they can find appropriate ways of correcting them. For example, a group of children may work cooperatively for several days to plan a model town using blocks and a sandbox. If the entire edifice collapses as a result of poor planning or lack of follow-through by various members of the group, no serious harm will result. On the other hand, children should not be free to decide to take a class walk along a busy intersection or along unguarded railroad tracks simply because they have not been there before. Much learning can occur by evaluating what went wrong at the sand table; but the risk of serious injury or accident is too great to permit in the example of the class walk.

In summary, kindergarten children can

participate in a number of decision-making experiences in the classroom and in the school. The key point is that the kindergarten teacher must create a variety of realistic and viable opportunities for genuine decision making that is within the ability of five- and six-year-olds. Children must be able to perceive that the choices they make are real ones and that they have the opportunity to say "no" to suggestions from the teacher. Children should also have the opportunity to participate in evaluating the performance of students who hold varying duties within the classroom. What is most important is that teachers set an atmosphere of freedom in which children can learn the process of democracy in making choices and living with the results of those choices.

SUMMARY

In this chapter we have reviewed four domains of social studies learning: knowledge, skills and abilities, valuing, and social participation. We have identified appropriate curricular materials in the knowledge area for kindergarten, stressing the simplest levels of knowledge of self, others, and various aspects of culture, including one's own cultural heritage. In the area of skills and abilities, we have identified a variety of intellectual skills, with particular emphasis on concept formation. In the area of values, we have discussed the importance of basic values, such as human dignity and the right of self-expression (to which the school should be committed). We have also considered a number of specific behaviors appropriate to the democratic way of life that support the value of human dignity in our daily activities. We have regarded social participation as the direct outgrowth of knowledge, abilities, and values. As we have shown, the input of students into the decision-making process of the classroom is analogous to the later tasks of the adult citizen who acts responsibly and participates actively in helping make decisions on important public issues.

We believe that social studies is a vital element in the school curriculum. If it is taught well and if sufficient time is allocated during the school day to the social studies curriculum, kindergarten children will make an important start in the development of their subsequent knowledge and skills as effective citizens.

REFERENCES AND SUGGESTED READINGS

Anderson, Lee F. A guide to thinking about social studies in elementary school. Technical paper for *Windows on Our World*, Houghton Mifflin social studies program. Boston: Houghton Mifflin Co., 1978.

Banks, James A., and Clegg, Ambrose A., Jr. *Teaching strategies for the social studies* (2nd ed.). Reading, Mass.: Addison-Wesley Publishing Co., Inc., 1977.

Cherryholmes, C., Manson, G., and Martorella, P. *Looking at me.* Teacher's manual. McGraw-Hill social studies series. New York: McGraw-Hill Book Co., 1979.

Hersh, R., Paolitto, D., and Reimer, J. *Promoting moral growth: from Piaget to Kohlberg*. New York: Longman, Inc., 1979.

Miel, Alice, and Brogan, Peggy. *More than social studies: a view of social learning in the elementary school*. Englewood Cliffs, N.J.: Prentice-Hall, Inc., 1957.

National Council for the Social Studies. Social studies curriculum guidelines. Revised position statement. *Social Education*, 1979, *43* (4), 261-278.

Shindelus, Mary J., and Durkin, Mary C. *People in families*. Teachers edition. In The Taba Program in Social Science. Reading, Mass.: Addison-Wesley Publishing Co., Inc., 1972.

CHAPTER 7

The expressive arts

The expressive arts have long been considered a vital component of quality early childhood programs. The inclusion of the expressive arts in the kindergarten curriculum provides the teachers and parents with a powerful medium for extending the total development of the five-year-old. There is much evidence in the literature concerning its values and contributions. The expressive arts include music, dance, story telling, dramatics, puppetry, poetry, art, and other forms of self-expression. They are a heritage not to be denied to any of our children.

Goals of the expressive arts include the following:

1. To foster self-expression in all children
2. To enable children to use their imaginations and become more creative persons
3. To build positive self-concepts
4. To problem solve and promote critical thinking
5. To provide opportunities for children to try out their ideas and to encourage divergent thinking
6. To help clarify understandings of the social and physical world
7. To express feelings and emotions
8. To release energy in constructive ways and to promote relaxation
9. To appreciate esthetics and beauty in life
10. To use the expressive arts as a springboard or entry into other areas of the curriculum
11. To appreciate and better understand other people and their contributions
12. To tap potentials of children that cannot be reached in any other way
13. To introduce children to the many different kinds of media that are available to them

Music and movement

MUSIC

To make words sing
Is a wonderful thing—
Because in a song
Words last so long. (Hughes, 1954, p. 36)

Have you ever observed the expression on young children's faces when they are completely absorbed in playing a singing game, moving to a rhythm record, or playing an instrument? They seem to be off in another world, unaware of outside interference. As they hear distinct beats, they clap their hands or rock and sway to the music. Just watch their eyes light up as they sing words to such catchy tunes as "I'm a Little Teapot," "Bingo," "Six Little Ducks," "Wheels on the Bus," or "My Dog Rags"!

Music is a vital part of daily living for the

five-year-old. It is one of the most important areas of development for children of this age. One of its greatest values is that it provides children with many experiences for expressing themselves openly without fear of ridicule or embarrassment. Music becomes a part of children's lives as opportunities are provided for singing, responding physically to different rhythms, participating in creative expressions, playing instruments, and listening quietly. Musical experiences should foster a love and appreciation of music through listening as well as through active participation. A well-organized music program provides for a wide range of musical activities and experiences that are geared for kindergarten-age children and that meet their various needs and interests. All areas of the curriculum, such as language and math, can be strengthened and made part of a unified experience through a well-coordinated music program. One of the best ways of helping children understand other people and their cultures is through music.

Children who find it difficult to express themselves verbally often respond readily to music by clapping or moving to it. This mode provides a way of communication for these youngsters so that they feel a part of the total group. Musical experiences need to provide children with a feeling of fun and joy, esthetic enrichment, and a release from tensions and fears. Through music, children can voice their feelings in a nonthreatening environment. Teachers and parents need to be cognizant of children who seem to display talent in music; even at age five, boys and girls gifted in this area can often be identified and should be encouraged to develop their musical talent through careful training and self-discipline. The kindergarten year is an excellent time to begin the development of musical taste and the motivation of an ever-growing appreciation of music.

The old adage, music is better "caught than taught," is sound philosophy for enriching children's lives through music at the kindergarten level. In a music program for five-year-olds, there needs to be a minimum amount of verbalizing. One should avoid presenting musical concepts beyond children's capabilities or forcing music on them. The teacher who has an interest and respect for music will communicate this to children. Youngsters will reject what is too complex for them. McCall (1971, p. 7) reminds us that "chronological age, previous musical experiences, and cultural background are determining factors in a child's acceptance or rejection" of music.

Music is one fine art that has a direct line to the soul and spirit. The angry or frustrated child unconsciously stamps out a warlike rhythm, pounding with feet, fists, and occasionally, head! A happy, excited youngster bounces and skips, twirls and twists in a merry outburst of joy. The pensive, perhaps apprehensive child retreats to a corner and finds solace in gentle humming or in humming to a teddy bear. In a child's world, music doesn't walk alone. It is always accompanied by dolls, bears, cowboys, Indians, snowflakes, spaceships, butterflies, dragons, and monsters! Music, you see, is one of the best fields for a child to learn from his or her own experience. It is not an experience which is always directed at or planned for him or her nor an experience that demands the help of others but one that can be carried out by himself or herself for his or her own particular enjoyment. (Austin, 1959, pp. 53-61)

Kindergarten children should have the opportunity of exploring many different kinds of music. Popular and contemporary music should be included in the curriculum along with the rich cross-cultural music of people throughout the world. Opportunities can also be provided for children to compare their own verses to songs they already know. Tape recorders are helpful in recording children's creative efforts.

The expressive arts

To provide meaningful musical experiences for children of this age, a number of goals need to be recognized and programmed toward achievement:

1. To have a variety of musical experiences that will bring pleasure and enjoyment to children
2. To recognize and plan for well-balanced musical experiences for all children, regardless of physical, social, emotional, or intellectual limitations
3. To offer opportunities for listening, creating, singing, moving rhythmically, and experimenting with sound
4. To allow the fives to engage in musical experiences that are based on an action art, not a performing art (to place emphasis on the child's enjoyment of the musical experience rather than on an expected outcome)
5. To introduce musical concepts and understandings that are appropriate to this age level
6. To encourage and help children who show evidence of talent in music to increase their musical skills
7. To provide musical activities that will enhance other learning, such as acquisition of language, listening skills, auditory discrimination, and social understanding
8. To arrange an environment in which children feel free to explore and engage in a variety of musical experiences representative of contributions from ethnic groups and other cultures
9. To allow children to express themselves musically in an atmosphere of freedom and trust, where divergent and creative interpretation is encouraged (Bayless and Ramsey, 1978, p. vii)

The teacher's role

Teachers who have a background in music and who can play the piano or guitar or sing with ease have an edge over teachers who cannot. But teachers who have little or no formal background in music can provide

profitable and happy musical experiences for children if they realize and appreciate the importance of music in the lives of young children and then go about searching for ideas and resources that will build meaningful activities. During my (K.B.) supervision of early childhood teachers, one of the best examples of good musical experiences for young children was provided by a teacher who could neither carry a tune nor play an instrument. Realizing how much her class enjoyed and profited from music, she was determined to provide them with a variety of musical experiences. She searched for good records, brought to the class many resource visitors, attended workshops and read widely, allowed children who could sing and carry a tune to lead songs, and created innumerable ways to include music in her program. The children danced and painted to music and embraced music in classroom activities throughout the entire day. This teacher was a confident person and would not allow her lack of formal training to stand in the way of providing what she knew was "right" for children.

It is important for teachers to use music in many informal situations as well as in planned ones during the school day. Children should have opportunities to sing often, to listen to a variety of musical selections, and to respond rhythmically in a happy, relaxed environment in a setting with plenty of space to move.

Listening

Listening is considered the foundation and beginning of all musical experiences. In a six-year study ending in 1969, Petzold (pp. 82-87) reported that children's musical development will be seriously limited if they do not acquire an aural (listening) understanding of the elements of music while they are young. "Children must be exposed to listening with intent to identify sounds, rhythms, intensities, pitch. . . . It is one aspect of the child's musical development to hear sounds; it is quite another to know how to identify them within some sort of conceptual framework related to a subject matter area" (Margolin, 1976, p. 267).

A high level of listening skill cannot be developed unless attentive listening is stressed and expected. In planning listening activities, one needs to give careful attention to arranging the environment in a way that will maximize conditions for developing good listening habits. Articles such as small toys in children's hands, which might distract them from listening, should be put away. The children should be seated where they can hear well. Other unnecessary sounds that might interfere with their ability to hear should be screened out. Since listening is involved in developing all musical skills, teachers need to plan a variety of carefully chosen activities to improve the five-year-old's listening ability.

Suggested activities to develop listening skills

1. Field trips offer endless ways for children to hear sounds firsthand. For example, if a train whistle blows, have the children match the sound with their voices.
2. Make a tape of the different kinds of environmental sounds, both those of nature and those that are man-made. Have the children identify these sounds. Discuss their various tone qualities. As the children gain more experience, they can begin to classify and categorize the sounds (e.g., those that belong to trains, airplanes, sirens, animals, etc.).
3. Read stories to the children about sounds. Many stories invite participation in which children can produce the sound asked for in the story by either using their voices, parts of their bodies, or instruments that lend the desired sound effects.
4. Use a set of step bells or the piano and show the children how high and low tones are produced. After the children have had many opportunities to hear the differences between high and low sounds in this manner, remove the instrument from sight. See if the children are still able to tell which tones are high or low without seeing someone play the instrument. (This should be accompanied by reaching the hands high in the air when referring to high notes and stooping low with the body when referring to low notes.)
5. Take containers of the same size and place materials such as beans in two, corn in two, etc. After rearranging the containers, have the children shake them and "match" the two that sound exactly alike.
6. Encourage the children to stop their work at different times of the day to listen for sounds and noises that are in the classroom as well as outside.
7. After hearing a song, ask the children to describe the story behind the song's words.

McCall (1971, p. 9) reminds us "that listening begins with a vague impression of the whole. Details of the structure gradually emerge by focusing on one element at a time." All too often we, as teachers, do not focus on just one musical element at a time, nor do we provide enough listening exposure and active involvement for the children to refine this element. Repetition of listening activities with careful teacher guidance will help children develop their perceptions and understanding of music and will enable them to start to formulate concepts of and about music (McCall, p. 9). For example, if we are trying to help children distinguish the difference between high and low sounds, we must provide many listening experiences that incorporate sounds of high and low pitches and then give the children the opportunity to distinguish between the sounds.

For listening purposes, music should be

carefully selected. Is the purpose to help children relax, to discover the difference between fast and slow tempos, or to identify a certain instrument? While they are listening to specific types of music, children might be asked questions such as the following:
- Is the music loud or soft, high or low, happy or sad?
- Does the music move fast or slow?
- Is it walking, running, skipping, or galloping music?
- Can you name any of the instruments you hear?
- Does the music sound like it is a march or lullaby?
- Do some parts of the music (phrases) sound alike?
- How does the music make you feel?

Other suggestions for enhancing listening experiences

1. Listen for rhythmic patterns.
   - In children's names.
   - In nursery rhymes, such as "Deedle, Deedle, Dumpling."
   - In various types of music—running, walking, skipping, galloping.
2. Listen for melody patterns.*
   - In singing songs. Does the melody go up or down (e.g., "I'm a Little Teapot")?
   - In listening to recordings, When does the melody go up? When does it go down?
3. Listen for various sounds of instruments in music.
   - Identify instruments such as the triangle, piano, organ, violin, or drum.
   - Permit the children to choose instruments and play rhythmic patterns that sound like tiptoeing, walking, etc.
   - Provide opportunties for the children to hear instruments of the orchestra by playing recordings such as "Instruments of the Orchestra," by having resource visitors play band and orchestral instruments, and through use of a motion picture film.
4. Listen and move.
   - What does the music tell you to do?
   - Can you make a marching sound with your feet?
   - Can you make a tiptoeing sound with your feet?
   - Can you make a skipping sound with your feet?

Developing musical appreciation

A balance of good listening activities is important for growth in musical appreciation. Children need to be exposed, to listen, and to try out different types of music so they can begin to develop musical tastes and preferences. Youngsters become acquainted and aware of some kinds of music through informal exposure as they go about their daily activities, such as listening to TV and hearing music from the car radio. If their appreciation for music is to grow and develop, children need to be introduced to music of enduring quality. Naturally the music selected must be appropriate for their level of experience and understanding, (Bayless and Ramsey, 1978, p. 31)

Children who are introduced to good musical literature through carefully selected and planned activities will begin to develop improved listening skills and a receptive, appreciative attitude toward many types of music (Smith, 1970, pp. 120-121).

Singing

A song can lift spirits and feet. (Landreth, 1972, p. 108)

Singing comprises the most favorite aspect of the music program. There are very few kindergarten children who do not like to sing. Some do not sing on pitch, and some may lag a half measure or so behind the

---

*Body movements may be used to show how the music goes up and down.

others; but, in general, children of this age seem to thoroughly enjoy singing their favorite songs and learning new ones. Songs often heard on television or taught by the teacher in a group situation are often sung by children as they work or play. In an accepting environment, children will create little songs as they build with blocks, paint pictures, or put away materials. They like to sing songs about animals, holidays, and experiences they have had at the circus or at the park. They like to sing "Good Morning," "Happy Birthday," and about personal things, such as their new shoes or the loss of a tooth.

Call-and-response singing

Call-and-response singing, wherein the teacher sings a question, such as "What did you have for breakfast?" and the child sings the answer by matching the teacher's tones, are fun-type activities and help the teacher determine which children can match tones.

At first, many children will not be able to match tones with accuracy, but continued use of conversational singing without drill often produces excellent results. Many kindergarten teachers use conversational singing to give directions or ask questions. It has been said that if parents and teachers would use conversational singing (with discretion), most children (excluding those with physical impairment of the vocal chords) would be able to carry a tune. Kindergarten children can and should learn to distinguish the difference between their speaking and singing voices. This can be accomplished by hearing the same words sung and spoken—first by the teacher and then by the children.

"An-drew, what did you have for break-fast?" "Orange juice."

Through repetition, the fives can learn to control the volume of their singing voices by singing songs having contrasts of soft and loud.

Scalewise songs

Scalewise songs such as the following are excellent ones to use in helping children match their singing voice to the tones of the scale.

Five Little Monkeys

(Start at top of scale and sing downward. Substitute "puppies," "elephants," etc., for "monkeys.")

Five little	C
monkeys	B
jumping on a	A
bed,	G
One fell	F
off and	E
bumped his	D
head.	C

(Repeat the scale.)

Mama called the	C
doctor, the	B
doctor	A
said,	G
"No more	F
monkeys	E
jumping on the	D
bed."	C

(Repeat using "four little monkeys," etc.)

The Snowman

(Begin at top of scale on C, above middle C, and sing downward.)

A chubby little	C
snowman	B
Had a carrot	A
nose. A-	G
long came a	F
bunny, And	E
What do you sup-	D
pose?	C

(Sing second verse using same pitches as first verse.)

That hungry little	C
bunny,	B
Looking for his	A
lunch,	G
Ate that little	F
snowman's nose,	E,
Nibble, nibble,	D
crunch.	C

(Now start up the scale. Begin on middle C.)

Nibble (C), Nibble (D), Nibble (E), Nibble (F), Nibble (G), Nibble (A), Nibble (B), Crunch!!! (C)

(Clap hands loudly on last crunch.)

PEARL H. WATTS
(SOURCE UNKNOWN)

Selecting songs

Kindergarten children particularly like songs about themselves, about animals, and about pets, nature, space, machines, toys, holidays, and seasons. Humorous and nonsense songs such as the "Peanut Song" (Bayless and Ramsey, 1978, p. 60) are very appealing to this age group.

When selecting a good song for kindergarten children, consider the following. The song should:

1. Have an easy-to-sing melody
2. Have an appropriate voice range (a good range is from middle C to eight tones above middle C)
3. Use repetition (words and rhythm)
4. Have a distinct rhythm
5. Have content and subject matter that children can understand
6. Be written in such as way as to help children learn musical concepts
7. Have repeated musical phrases (longer songs) even if the words are different
8. Have melody lines with pleasing progressions and simple intervals (seconds, thirds, and fifths, etc.)
9. Not have *unusual* syncopation

Sources for songs

We should not overlook the fact that children themselves are a source of songs (Nye, 1975, p. 99). Children bring to school their favorites: songs sung in their homes; ones they have heard on radio or television or from records; and those learned from sisters, brothers, and friends. Television programs have produced many songs that children enjoy hearing and learning.

Five-year-olds should have many opportunities to sing the delightful nursery rhymes, Mother Goose rhymes, and other chants of early childhood. According to Scott (1968, p. 140), "The memorable language of the Mother Goose or nursery rhyme has its appeal in rhythm, imagination, humor, surprise, and nonsense. Children derive untold pleasure from the primitive repetition, chanting, and suggestions for body action which these rhymes afford. The musical quality, cadence, and acceleration of these classics have prompted many musicians to write tunes for them." Ella Jenkins, famous contemporary musician and folk singer, has shown thousands of children and adults how to use and enjoy nursery rhymes to the fullest.

Perhaps the best source of songs for young children can be found in the many well-known folk songs. They are beautiful in nature and often easy to learn. One of the best and most complete American folk song collections was written by Ruth Crawford Seeger (1948). In *American Folk Songs for Children,* Seeger (p. 21) reminds us:

> This kind of traditional or folk music is thoroughly identified with the kind of people who made America as we know it. It is a music they liked and still like. They made it and are still making it. Some of it came with them from other countries and has been little changed. Some of it grew here. All of it has partaken of the making of America. Our children have a right to be brought up with it.

It is one of the aims of education to induct the child into the realities of the culture in which he will live; may we not say that this traditional music and language and ideology, which has not only grown out of but has in turn influenced that culture—and is still influencing and being used by it—should occupy a familiar place in the child's daily life, even though it may not be current in the particular neighborhood in which he happens to be living. . . .

Sensing the great need for suitable song material for the fives, we wrote *Music: A Way of Life for the Young Child* (1978). The book contains a wealth of songs for young children and includes a complete chapter on music for the preschool and kindergarten-age child. Much of the song material in the book is geared for the five-year-old. Other songbooks are listed at the end of this chapter.

Presenting new songs

1. New songs can be introduced at spontaneous times when the situation seems just right, or at a planned group time.
2. They may be introduced to a small group of children who are informally gathered together, or to the entire class.
3. It is best to introduce a new song without any accompaniment (provided the teacher's voice is accurate). (It is easier for children to match tones with the human voice than to a melody played on an instrument.)
4. Playing simple chords on the piano, autoharp, or guitar to accompany songs adds variety and pleasure to the singing.
5. Some songs need a short verbal introduction; others will not.
6. Occasionally, songs may be introduced by using a picture, diorama, or poem.

Teaching the song

1. Sing the song slowly (not too slowly) and distinctly. Keep the rhythm flowing.
2. Smile as you sing. Make the music come alive.
3. Sing the song through several times—on the same day if possible.
4. Encourage the children to join in naturally.
5. It is not good practice to teach a song line by line. (This method, if used repeatedly, can often destroy the entire effect of a song, lose meaning, and cause children to dread learning a new song. *Note:* This does not mean that difficult musical phrases and words are left neglected. Without drilling, work on difficult musical phrases and hard-to-pronounce words.
6. Do not be disturbed if some children have difficulty reproducing the pitch or melody of songs. It takes time, practice, and patience to help children "find" their singing voices.
7. Constantly keep in mind that enjoyment of the music is the highest priority and goal.

Children enjoy both spontaneous and planned singing. These are happy, natural experiences for the five-year-old and should be a part of every child's day.

Selected favorites

Action songs

The Bus Song
Eensy, Weensy Spider
Follow, Follow*
I Wiggle
Jack in the Box
Hokey Pokey
Hop Si Hi†
Make a Little Motion
The Old Gray Cat
Pitter Patter
Skip So Merrily

---

*A favorite.
†Excellent for introduction to skipping.

152 *Kindergarten: programs and practices*

Animals

Barnyard Family
I Am Mama Kangaroo
Little White Duck
My Dog Rags
My Farmer Friends
One Elephant
Six Little Ducks

Counting songs

Johnny Works with One Hammer
This Old Man
One Elephant
Pairs
Ten Little Frogs
Three Blue Pigeons
Tres Pajarillos

Feelings

Happy Birthday
Hello, Hello, and How Are You
If You're Happy
Theodore

Folk songs; singing games; songs of other countries

Ah-Shav! (Jewish)
Bingo (Scottish)
Bow Belinda
Chiapanecas (Mexican)
Chiu, Chiu, Chiu (Uruguayan folk song)
Clap Your Hands
Frog Went a-Courtin'
Hawaiian Rainbows
Hush, Little Baby
Japanese Rain Song
Jim-Along, Josie
Oh, John, the Rabbit
London Bridge (English)
Looby Loo (English)
The Muffin Man (English)
Les Petites Marionettes (French)
Sandy Maloney (English)
Six Little Ducklings (German)
Stodola Pumpa (Czech)
The Train Is a-Coming
Twinkle, Twinkle Little Star (French)

Holidays and seasons

Boo! Boo!
Candles of Hanukkah
Dancing around the Christmas Tree
The Easter Bunny Is Coming Soon
Hiyah, Hiyah (Indian)
Jack-o'-lantern
Love Somebody
Mary Had a Baby
Mr. Turkey
My Dreidl
Santa's Helpers
Up on the Housetop
Valentine
We Wish You a Merry Christmas

Home-community

The Diary
Fire Song
Fun with Daddy
Helping Mother
If You Were a Farmer
A Policeman
Riding On a Train
Singing Postman
When I Grow Up

Nonsense songs

Miss Polly
The Peanut Song

Patriotic

America, We Love You
Battle Hymn of the Republic (chorus)
Flag Song

Science and nature

Beauty in the World
Color Game
Come Walk with Me
Mister Wind
The North Wind
Sky Bears

Spirituals

All Night, All Day
Shout for Joy
There's a Little Wheel

Instruments

Children are fascinated by the sounds of musical instruments. Have you ever watched the face of a young child who, for the first time, has just produced music by pressing down the keys of a piano? You will see youngsters time and again crawling back onto the piano bench to make those sounds that are so pleasing and enjoyable.

The fives should be encouraged to use their bodies as instruments to make sounds. They can experiment in many different ways by clapping their hands, snapping their fingers, and shuffling and stamping their feet to music. After much experimentation with various kinds of body percussion, introduction of sound-producing objects and instruments can follow. Children should be allowed to sort out and classify objects and devices according to the sounds they make. For example, all instruments and objects with belllike tones should be placed together. Collecting and experimenting with sound-making devices is a very important step in introducing instruments to children.

Introducing instruments

As soon as children show evidence of responding to the beat and tempo of music, they can begin learning how to use and play percussion instruments. Both commercial and homemade instruments may be introduced at this time. Following is a listing of a typical commercial set of rhythm instruments. The makeups of these sets differ according to the manufacturer. They can be ordered in different sizes, such as 16-pupil set, 22-pupil set, 30-pupil set, and so forth, including individual sets. Companies take great care to ensure that each set contains the proper balance of instruments for the number of students involved.

30-pupil set
1 hand drum
1 bongo drum
6 pairs rhythm sticks
1 pair of wood blocks
2 tone blocks with mallets
2 sand blocks
2 tambourines
2 wrist bells
2 jingle bells mounted on wooden handles
2 triangles with holders
2 castanets
2 maracas
2 pairs of finger cymbals
1 pair of cymbals

Commercial sets usually come with a baton and instructor's book. These are considered a part of the rhythm instrument set.

Complete instructions for making instruments can be found in Chapter 3 of *Music: A Way of Life for the Young Child* (Bayless and Ramsey, 1978).

Experimenting with the instruments in order to explore the sounds they make, and ways in which to produce these sounds, is a vital learning experience for children. Many teachers have become discouraged from using instruments with kindergartners because of initial, unpleasant experiences. This has usually occurred when instruments were handed out to every child without previous explanation and the children were allowed to bang away. Introduced in this manner, discrimination of beats and sounds is virtually impossible. When careful thought is given to introducing instruments, before children are allowed to play them, much enjoyment and learning can take place.

As children develop sensitivity to music, the teacher must guide them into experiences with instruments of good quality, such as resonator bells, tone blocks, tambourines, and the like. The children should have an opportunity to listen to someone play the instrument, talk about it, and show how the sound is produced on it. As different instruments are explored, the teacher can then ask questions that might include: "Does it play loudly?" "Does it 'sing' a little song?"

"What does it sound like?" Often one can find songs or recordings with selected passages that highlight the sound of the instrument, such as "Tubby the Tuba" or Peter and the Wolf."

It is wise at this time to establish a few basic, simple rules for handling the instruments. For example, until it is time to play the instruments, the children might place them on the floor in front of or behind their chairs. Also, instruments should be placed —not thrown—into a box or container.

Orchestrating with instruments

The teacher should establish situations in which the child can select the instrument he believes to be the most appropriate for certain music or to accompany certain songs, poems, and stories. The formalities of the rhythm band of past years, with its required conformity, have resulted in its virtual absence from the modern school. This dictatorial type of instrumental performance is in opposition to sound theories of learning and to the creative approach wherein children are involved in exploring, questioning, designing, and performing music. (Nye, 1975, p. 82)

One can find many songs, rhythms, and stories in which instruments can be used to add sound effects or for accompaniment (e.g., bells to accompany the song "Jingle Bells" and the wood block to simulate the ticking of the clock in the song "Hickory, Dickory Dock"). If teachers and children plan and make choices like this together, the children themselves will begin to see that some of the sound-making articles that they collected will also fit a particular part of the music. They will begin to evaluate, to listen, and to make choices and decisions concerning what sound or combinations of sounds go well together. This then becomes their music making. If instruments are introduced in this way, the children will better understand what each instrument's tone is like and how it can be played and used, and they will soon be using instruments to accompany their songs and movements. Thus, basic elements of orchestrating are begun.

It is helpful if the teacher can play the piano to accompany children as they play their instruments. There are also many good recordings available that are excellent to use with instruments. Some of these recordings introduce and explain the instruments; others tell children exactly what instruments to use and where to play them. Others encourage creativity on the part of the teacher and children. Then there comes the time when the entire class plays instruments together. Hopefully, by this time, the instruments will have all been introduced, one at a time, to the children so that they know the sound each instrument makes and how that sound is produced. At this point, children can help orchestrate the musical selections by suggesting which instruments would go well with particular phrases or parts of the music. The total-group experience should be the result of many individual and small-group explorations.

Musical value in using instruments

A great deal of learning about music can be secured from the use of instruments if teachers guide children in sound exploration, including dynamics (loud-soft), pitches (high-low) tempos (fast-slow), and many other facets that are basic to the understanding of music. It is surprising how quickly children of this age can begin to differentiate between these musical terms and put them into actual practice.

The fives are at an age when they ought to have many pleasurable experiences with instruments. Along with playing the instruments, resource visitors (both older school-age children and adults) may be invited to come to the classroom and share their expertise with different instruments. The children may also be taken to the music room to hear the orchestra or to the football field to hear and see the band play. Such experiences can hardly be matched. Building an appreciation for instruments with kindergartners can be a most satisfying experience for both teacher and children provided careful planning is carried out. When this is done, one can then feel that a good foundation for appreciating musical instruments has been established.

MOVEMENT

It is hardly necessary for educators to remind us that movement is as natural to young children as eating and breathing. It is synonymous with the growing child, and it would be most difficult to estimate the amount of learning that takes place through psychomotor activities. According to Chenfeld (1976, p. 261), movement is such a natural way of life that, as people grow up in our society, they have to be taught *not* to move. People are often required to sit for long periods of time, which can become stressful.

Movement exploration is, as the term implies, discovering how the body can move and what great movement potential the body has. It makes the child aware of his own abilities. It gives him the opportunity to understand and accept his body, to lose his self-consciousness, and to learn the joy of free movement. . . . Many times, movement exploration may lead directly into a creative dance experience or may form the basis for a folk dance. As such, it is the process, the solving of a problem, and the discovering of a new way, rather than an end product, that are important. (Clark, 1969, p. 12)

Movement activities for kindergarten children vary greatly from one program to another. It is not uncommon to see 5 or 10 minutes a day of marching to music or playing rhythm instruments as the total movement program. When this occurs, it is generally due to the teacher's lack of knowledge and experience in initiating and carrying out movement activities. With a little imagination and courage, teachers can develop appropriate movement activities that are right for the child of this age.

Kindergarten children should have many opportunities to explore their own natural body movements before they are asked or required to respond to the steady beats of music. These movements would include the locomotor movements (those that propel the body through space, such as walking, hopping, jumping, running, and leaping). The nonlocomotor movements would include bending, swaying, rocking, and the like. As children's muscle coordination shows signs of improvement, they can then begin to coordinate the rhythmic movements of their bodies to the beat of a drum or other outside stimulus.

Teachers who are imaginative and willing to experiment can develop a strong creative rhythmic program for five-year-olds. A sound movement program is developed and implemented by the teacher paying close attention to the children as they move—as they sway from one foot to another, as they skip on the playground, pound with hammers, or rock their bodies back and forth. There is no set way to begin movement. Children are inventive, and one of the best ways to begin movement is to start with the children's own good ideas. Many times the entire class will pick up on one child's idea and extend it. Trying out the ideas of other children often gives the more timid children courage to try out their own. Then, once the children begin to share their ideas freely with each other, the teacher can play a vital role in expanding those ideas. The following is an example.

Tommy was telling the class that his grandfather, who had broken his leg, had just returned home from the hospital. His leg had been put in a walking cast. Tommy tried to explain to the class what a walking cast was like and seemed frustrated when the children didn't understand. At that point the teacher said, "Tommy, show us how your grandpa walks with his cast on. Without any hesitation, Tommy got up from the floor and showed the class how his grandpa walked on his return from the hospital. Then the teacher encouraged the rest of the class to pretend that they too had on walking casts; soon the entire class was clomping about the room in unified movements and in steady rhythm with each other.

The imaginative teacher uses "word pictures" or descriptive phrases to help create a feeling or mood and to stimulate children's thinking and moving. For example, the teacher might say, "Let's walk as if we were pulling a heavy load in our wagons," or "Let's push up our stomachs like a rising cake in the oven." When appropriate, a few chords on the piano or a few drum taps may be added to pick up the tempo of the children's natural movements.

Materials to enhance movement

In *Creative Movement for the Developing Child*, Cherry (1971) lists many different types of movement that young children enjoy and experience. With the introduction of each body movement, such as crawling, Cherry presents a thorough description of the movement and then gives suggestions and varied activities to help develop skill in the movement. She believes that music motivates children to respond rhythmically and suggests using familiar melodies, such as "Twinkle, Twinkle, Little Star," substituting appropriate words of the original to help describe particular body movements.

There are also many excellent recordings (some with illustrated storybooks) that provide children with plenty of ideas for creative movement. Anne Lief Barlin's *Dance-a-Story* recordings with illustrated storybooks have been used successfully with kindergarten-age children. Many companies are producing individual story and movement records of excellent quality. Hap Palmer's records have become all-time favorites. His captivating melodies and rhythms seem to make up the kind of music children respond to. They literally are caught up in the spirit of the words, melody, and rhythm. Selected classical recordings provide a great resource for enhancing movement. *The Nutcracker Suite*, *Peer Gynt Suite*, *The Snow is Dancing*, and other favorites provide a basis for creative movement and an appreciation for the classics. The more contemporary *Autumn Leaves* and *The Syncopated Clock* are often used as background music to help children initiate movement.

Folk songs and singing games also provide opportunities for children to move freely. These are excellent to use with young children, since most of the songs are within their singing range and invite movement and participation. As mentioned previously, Seeger's *American Folk Songs for Children* is perhaps the best known collection of folk songs in America. Because of their nature, most of the songs invite participation and improvisation. Three fourths of the tunes in Seeger's collection "are accustomed to action, to being danced to, clapped to, worked to. Children listening often start clapping of their own accord, or skipping, or jumping, or kicking their feet, or trying some new motion" (Seeger, 1948, p. 24).

At times the use of props such as scarves, long feathers, strips of crepe paper fastened onto small paper towel rolls, balloons, and rhythm and melody instruments enhance movement. Props also aid in making children less inhibited. The opportunity to hold something in their hands often gives balance to their bodies and lends variety.

Tips for promoting movement exploration

1. Provide the children with ample space for movement activities.
2. Establish boundary lines.
3. Tell the children ahead of time what the signals are for "starting" and "stopping."
4. Help the children develop the ability to learn how to use their own space.
5. When possible, avoid demonstrating movements.
6. Be accepting of the children's movements and their interpretations to music.
7. Be sensitive to the timid child or one who does not enter freely into movement activities. Be patient. Go slowly. Do not force the child to participate.
8. An imaginary trip to the zoo or circus may be a "starter" for children who are hesitant to express their own ideas. (*Remember:* Children cannot create in a vacuum).
9. Encourage the children to listen, think and move.

Summary

Growing children need to keep moving. This is very much a part of their learning process that continues throughout their lifetime. Remember that movements expressed by children are often accompanied by their innermost feelings and ideas. The sensitive teacher will find ways in which these thoughts and feelings can be expressed in a trusting environment.

The dramatic arts

STORIES
Choosing and using books with five-year-olds

It is not by chance that children develop a love and understanding of good literature. Hopefully, over the years, positive attitudes and feelings about books will evolve and be nurtured as children have many pleasant experiences with them. Teachers share an awesome responsibility in convincing children that much pleasure and enjoyment can come from books, that they can be great sources of information, and that they can help satisfy one's own quest for knowledge.

There should be many opportunities for children to listen to stories and verse, whether they be read or told. Books appealing to various interests and abilities should be freely accessible. Thus, children begin to acquire a lifetime interest in books and in reading.

Since parents and teachers are generally the ones who select children's books, and through whom children gain a love for good literature, understanding the needs and interests of children is paramount. Too many times, adults are guilty of merely picking up a book and using it with children just to have a story to read or to fill a time gap; they have no special reason for choosing that particular book. Care should be taken to select a book that is right for a particular child or a particular group of children. Youngsters are constantly giving out clues and sending messages if adults will only take the time to tune in, listen, and respond. Too many children are forced to exist on an impoverished literary diet. We need to enrich this diet.

It is never too early to introduce children to the joy of sturdy, boldly illustrated books or to the special appeal of miniature books. The fives are attracted by brightly colored pictures of simple objects. There is a great difference between gaudy pictures and simple, bold illustrations. One should shop for quality, seeking the best instead of the mediocre. This does not necessarily mean that the most expensive books are the best ones. A beautifully designed, well-illustrated picture book with an intriguing story line can be enjoyed time and time again. Such is the case with *The Color Kittens*, by Margaret Wise Brown, and Maurice Sendak's *Where the Wild Things Are*. Books better known as the classics will be enjoyed by some children; for others, a contemporary book might be more appealing and meaningful. A child's book needs to say something, and say it well.

Young children have difficulty distinguishing between fact and fantasy. Story material should be realistic so as not to confuse them. There has been much misunderstanding and controversy over the use of fairy tales with kindergartners; in general, fairy tales deal with rather complicated concepts and for some children produce fear and anxiety. They are better introduced and used with older children. Most children like Mother Goose rhymes and nursery rhymes, but these should be used with discretion. Old English wording often needs to be explained in terms that can be understood. If children cannot understand the language of a particular story, it will not be enjoyed. Careful selection of first stories is essential for children facing language difficulties.

The illustrations in a book should closely represent the text. Illustrations and text should support each other in a way that will make the entire meaning more clear. Colored illustrations are not always necessary, and too many unnecessary details can be distracting. Recall the beauty of *The Egg Tree*, by Katherine Milhous. *Dandelion* and *Mop Top*, by Don Freeman, are also excellent choices. In Dare Wright's *Gift from the Lonely Doll*, one will find beautifully captured photographs used for illustration.

The plot of the story should be simple and well developed. Unnecessary details can destroy continuity and understanding. Children will often lose interest with a more complicated plot. Characters should be few in number, well described, and unforgettable.

Children need to be able to identify with at least one main character.

Many teachers are beginning to take clues from children and write and illustrate original stories. The above-mentioned criteria should also apply. Such stories are generally tailor-made around a specific concept or idea and for a particular child or group of children.

With people traveling to all parts of the world today, there is much opportunity for discovering some of the beautiful children's books of other lands. Many have been translated into English. These books should be shared with our children with the hope of bringing about better understanding and appreciation of other cultures. For example, Ladushki's *Russian Folk Rhymes and Tales for Little Ones* can be secured from Progress Publishers in Moscow and is a beautiful example of the foreign touch.

There is also an increasing supply of books dealing with different ethnic backgrounds, so that the needs of many children can be met.

Presenting stories

Most will agree that story time should occur every day, although not necessarily in the same time slot. Not only is it one of the most enjoyable times of the day, but it is a time when children can gain a wealth of information about people and the world around them. It is also a time when children and teacher (or child and parent) can develop a closeness with each other, trust, and better understanding. A variety of stories and verse should be used and presented in different ways. All too often, teachers just read to children without exploring the unlimited ways in which stories and verse can be introduced or used.

Constructing a diorama—taking a scene or idea from a book and reproducing it dimensionally by placing objects and figures in front of a background—is an excellent way to introduce a story or verse. Dioramas can be made by using shoe boxes or other suitable containers of various sizes and shapes. Children's interest can often be aroused or enhanced by the use of a carefully constructed diorama. (Watch the children's eyes light up when they look into a diorama in which the Three Bears are staring at Goldilocks, who is asleep in Little Bear's bed!) After the diorama is used to whet the children's appetite, it should be placed where they can readily see it, but not so close as to cause distraction from the story being read or told. Some teachers like to present a story by using a series of dioramas, each made separately and depicting different parts of the story. A lazy Susan makes an excellent base for dioramas made into parts or sections. Robert McCloskey's *Make Way for Ducklings* and Edna Miller's *Mousekin's Christmas Eve* are stories that lend themselves well for use with a diorama.

Another of children's favorite ways for having stories and verse presented is through the use of a flannel or felt board. Teacher-designed figures and objects made from flannel, felt, Pellon, Styrofoam, and other similar materials are generally much more suitable and of better quality than those commerically made. Figures and objects should contain only enough detail to help tell the story; otherwise they will be a distraction. After the teacher has presented the story or verse, the children can use the figures and felt board to retell the story in their own way. This approach is an excellent means for improving, promoting, and developing language facility and power.

Puppets are perhaps the young child's favorite means by which stories can be introduced or enhanced. Children relate well to the character or animal depicted in the story and almost become a living part of it. Again, after the teacher has told the story with puppets, the children can relive the story by playing it out through manipulation of the same puppets. From this point they will often depart and make up their own stories.

Real objects or props relevant to the story or verse are often overlooked as a means of helping to convey an idea, clarify a concept, or help maintain interest. One should not include too many, however, and should choose only those that would lend understanding and interest.

Another way of presenting a story is by the "chalk talk" method. While telling the story, the teacher uses chalk or crayon to draw pictures of the characters and scenery on a flip chart close to the children. The pictures need to be few in number, drawn quickly, and they must add meaning and interest to the story. While sketching, the teacher should maintain eye contact with the children. This is a very old method of story telling and much beloved by children.

Perhaps the most satisfying and intimate way of presenting a story is just to tell it. Having complete, direct eye contact with the children helps build that closeness and warmth so necessary in making the story come alive. Children are usually more attentive and apt to stretch their own imaginative powers when stories are told. There was a time when it was considered inappropriate for the storyteller to use hand and facial gestures. Today it is not only considered appropriate but sometimes necessary in helping to convey meaning, just as long as it is not overdone and does not become too overpowering. Sometimes it takes a bit of doing to get up the courage to become a good storyteller. *The Art of the Storyteller*, by Marie L. Shedlock (1941) is perhaps the clearest and most readable material about storytelling as an art. *The Way of the Storyteller*, by Ruth

Sawyer (1951) combines the philosophy and the rich experience of one of the best modern storytellers. Teachers often say, once they have made the plunge, that nothing compares with telling a story to children.

The storyteller must know and enjoy the story so well that it lives for the listener. One should work on building up a repertoire of appropriate stories that can be told. When the time is right, the one that best suits a particular child or group of children, or that fits a certain occasion, time, or place, can be selected. Whether read or told, the length of stories ought to be kept within the limits of the children's attention span. If interest begins to wane, stories need to be shortened or finished at another time. A good rule to remember is to bring the story to a close while interest and attention are at high points. Many people fail to do this (better known as "milking a good thing dry"), and results are disastrous.

Sometimes stories are spoiled because the presenter interrupts the story line too often to clarify a concept or word meaning, or to reprimand a disruptive child. Before beginning the story, the teacher should see that the children are comfortably spaced on the floor and seated near enough, if pictures are used, to see the illustration clearly. Easels or equipment that might be distracting should be moved away from the group. Teachers seldom need to interrupt a story to discipline a child. Interruptions may indicate a poor choice of story or lackluster presentation.

Additional suggestions for telling a story include the following:

1. Know the story. Read it aloud several times. Make it a part of you.
2. Record the story on tape. Check your rate of speech, enunciation, etc.
3. Will you have an introduction? If so, write it out or think it through carefully.
4. Retell the story on tape or sit in front of a mirror and tell the story.
5. Ask some friends to listen to your story and give you their reactions.
6. Develop your voice: pitch, inflection, and rate of speed.
7. Use continual eye contact with the children.
8. Display a sincere, expressive face. Be warm and friendly.
9. Be sensitive to timing, not only in relation to the length of the story but also in making necessary pauses during the story for reaction or emphasis.
10. Speak to the child who is farthest away. Those in between will hear you.
11. Seat the children so that all can see you. Make sure they are comfortable.
12. Learn the story incident by incident or in a picture outline.
13. Do not try to alter the essential story line.
14. Avoid unfamiliar words that are not in the children's experiences.
15. Allow for imagination. Do not over explain.
16. If at all possible, do not stop the story sequence to answer questions.
17. If, on occasion, you might leave out a part, try to weave it in if it is necessary to the understanding of the ending.
18. Avoid asking the children at the end of the story, "Did you like it?" The looks on their faces or hearty claps will give you the answer.

Introduction and follow-up

Some teachers give little thought as to how they introduce or follow up a story. Props, motivation, leading questions, or follow-up are not always necessary. Perhaps moving directly into the story is the best approach. At other times, props or leading questions would be most appropriate. When asking leading questions, one should be specific;

otherwise, the children will be apt to become confused. Questions should be worded carefully so as to build up a sense of wonder and suspense. If leading questions or statements are to be used at all, they should (for the most part) be well thought out before the story is presented. Children's and teacher's comments and questions can then be woven in as the occasion presents itself. The teacher may want to assess comprehension informally and might ask the children to listen for answers to a few well-chosen questions. Following the story, the children can then provide the answers. At other times, comprehension and carry-over can be assessed without asking the children to listen for specifics ahead of time.

If a story has been introduced through use of a felt board or diorama, the children can, as mentioned previously, retell or dramatize the story. Characters and events can be put in sequence. For example, if a series of dioramas are used for one particular story, the children can put these in the order they appeared and tell about that part of the story. When dramatization is used as a follow-up device, it is fun to let children do some of the actions of the story together. After listening to *The Little Rabbit Who Wanted Red Wings*, by Sherwin Bailey, the children could look into the Wishing Pond, turn around three times, and "sprout wings." It is a freeing kind of way to participate and get involved. Sometimes entire stories can be enjoyed in this manner. If stories are dramatized, great care should be taken so that the children do not become frightened or threatened by the experience. At times, just acting out favorite parts of a story is sufficient.

Bibliotherapy

According to the Dictionary of Education (1973), "Bibliotherapy is the assignment of books to be read on various subjects to help a child or a parent to understand a problem or to help him see the problem in a different way."

There are several good bibliotherapy books for young children. One such book is Don Freeman's *Mop Top*. A little boy, later to be called Mop Top, refused to have his hair cut. One day he accompanied his mother to the grocery store. After a while, he decided to hide amongst the cleaning mops. Soon a customer came by and grabbed the little boy's hair, thinking it was a cleaning mop. This action really shook the little boy and finally convinced him that he had better get his hair cut.

Books: the lifetime investment

For young children, books are a source of enjoyment and a vehicle for furthering language and personality development. The following are suggestions for increasing children's pleasure in books: Enlist the help of the librarian in bringing the best and latest literature to the children. Encourage parents to buy good books for their children and encourage children and parents to begin a personal library or a special bookshelf for special books. Provide parents with book lists, brief reviews, and book club information. Suggest that parents give books as gifts to their children; by doing so the parents will demonstrate an attitude of caring about fine literature. Perhaps the best way to gain skill in recognizing quality in children's books is to make a thorough study of some of the finest that have been published (Caldecott and Newberry award winners) and use them as a basis for judging others.

Sharing books with the fives is an enjoyable and worthy privilege. Children's books are really something very special!

• • •

The following storytelling activities incorporate most of the expressive arts discussed in this chapter:

Kindergarten storytelling activities

Julie Piccione

OBJECTIVES

Children will develop skills in:
1. Describing pictures orally
2. Recalling
3. Sequencing, summarizing, and remembering details and main ideas of stories
4. Interpretation, visual memory, and reasoning skills
5. Appreciation of story telling through listening
6. Appreciation of story telling through dramatics
7. Better understanding of our language
8. Use of language in daily conversation with the teacher and peers for development of skills in speaking in complete sentences
9. Appreciation of music by singing about a story or by making up their own songs
10. Manipulative skills through use of puppets

ACTIVITIES

1. The teacher can be the storyteller. Children should have the opportunity to have stories read to them.
2. The teacher can start a story and have the children finish it the way they think it should end.
3. The children can give descriptions of the story and illustrate their ideas on either a felt board, a chalkboard, or by making pictures out of construction paper.
4. Using episodic pictures: Comic strips tell children many things. The children are not using just one picture to tell a story, but a strip to tell each incident that happens.
5. Narrating without the help of a picture: The teacher can read a story (e.g., *Three Billy Goats Gruff*) and then have a child retell the story in his own version.
6. Field trips: Field trips can also be a part of story telling. The children have the opportunity to tell about their trip and are able to express their feelings, likes, and dislikes.
7. Filmstrips: Children like visual slides. Movies and filmstrips can be very beneficial to children. When the movie is over, the children have the opportunity to tell about the story—what they saw—and can also ask questions.

DRAMATIC PLAY

McCaslin (1974 p. 5) says that dramatic play

is the free play of the very young child in which he explores his universe, imitating the actions and character traits of those around him. It is his earliest expression in dramatic form but must not be confused with drama or interpreted as performance. Dramatic play is fragmentary in nature, existing only for the moment. It may last for a few minutes or go on for some time. It may even be played repeatedly, if the interest is sufficiently strong, but when this occurs, the repetition is in no sense a rehearsal. It is, rather, the repeating of a creative experience for the pure joy of doing it. It has no beginning and no end, and no development in the dramatic sense.

8. Poetry: Children love poetry. They can dramatize an experience, mood, or even a thought by poetry. They can do this by dressing up, using puppets, or using some type of motion.
9. Drama: Children also love to act out stories. They can do this by using puppets or even dressing in costumes to tell their stories.
10. Picture books: These books are very helpful when it comes to storytelling. Children are able to look at the pictures and make up their own stories from beginning to end.
11. Books: Nursery rhyme books and books with words are amusing to children. They like to learn nursery rhymes. When children learn a particular rhyme, they like to find the book the rhyme is in and point to each word (or words) as they read.
12. Recipe book: A different approach to storytelling is having children think of their favorite foods. Each one will tell the teacher how to make it as the teacher writes the recipe on a ditto. After all recipes are written down, the teacher will ditto them off and make a recipe booklet for each child. This makes a great Mother's Day gift.
13. Narrating with pictures: Each child can tell about one picture. Record the children as they tell their stories. Then let them hear themselves as you play their stories back to them.
14. Magic: When magic tricks are performed, children's imaginations are extended. Get an overhead projector and turn it on. Take a clear glass pie dish and fill it half way with water. Put a few drops of food coloring in the water and gently turn the dish. Magic shapes will appear. Have the children tell what they think the shape is.
15. Music. Before storytelling takes place, the children may want to make up a song about their day (getting up or going to bed or anything that may happen in between).

MATERIALS

Records	Picture books	Overhead projector
Books	Flannel boards	Piano
Filmstrips	Finger plays	Costumes
Movies	Poems	Puppets*
Large picture cards	Nursery rhymes	

---

*Puppets can be made by using socks, gloves, paper bags, tongue depressors, or Popsicle sticks. Construction paper makes very good finger puppets. Commercially produced puppets are also very nice but may be expensive.

Dramatic play is a means of assimilating things that children have experienced in some way. It also helps them release unacceptable feelings, reverse roles, and solve problems. At this age there is a wide panorama of dramatic play. Children like to act out real-life adult roles, such as nurse, doctor, teacher, and fireman. They also like to role play folk heroes, such as cowboys, spacemen, kings, queens, and the like. The sociodramatic play of children is quite real, and attempts are often made to imitate actions and behavior of adults. One often sees five-year-olds enacting bride-and-groom scenes with veils, high heels, and black coats and ties. Gradually children's play becomes

164 *Kindergarten: programs and practices*

more concrete and realistic. Money is made for the grocery store or ice cream stand. Play or clay dough is used to represent the pies and cakes.

Kindergarten teachers need to supply some of the props and materials for children's dramatic play. Some of these materials should be accessible to the children on an everyday basis. Other props can be added as play themes change. Teachers also need plenty of space for storage of materials. One often-heard definition of a kindergarten teacher is a person who has a two-car garage and the cars are sitting outside! In general, however, children are better off with a few basic items. From basic materials, they can use their imaginations and improvise almost anything they need. In some cases teachers supply too many ready-made articles and thereby limit the resourcefulness and flexibility in play.

Besides supplying props, teachers need to observe and guide dramatic play. By watching attentively, they can often learn what is meaningful and urgent in the lives of their children. Perceptive teachers may help youngsters through troublesome feelings and help them understand events and things that are puzzling to them. During observation, however, one must be careful not to interpret children's sociodramatic play too literally, or leap to premature conclusions regarding what is seen and heard. Rather, one should keep studying the children as they play. Often patterns will emerge that will provide a deeper understanding of five-year-olds' personalities and problems. A word of caution should be heeded: Much of the dramatic play of children requires no adult intervention. Left to their own, dramatic play is a natural way for children to grow and develop.

Creative dramatics

Although Creative Dramatics has come into comparatively recent use in the classroom as a method, it is not a panacea for all the social and educational ills, nor is it something new or "faddy." . . . Always children have "played out" their experiences—testing, proving, trying out, relating themselves to their world and their society. Froebel has given us many insights into the significance of child play, which is akin to Creative Dramatics and in which Creative Dramatics finds its base.

It is unique and different from formal drama in that it is always improvised and is not designated for an audience. It is "sharing with" rather than "acting to." (Henry, 1967, p. 53)

The following guidelines may be helpful:
1. Creative dramatics is the playing out of ideas, experiences, and stories with improvised dialogue and action. It is never

the same twice. A stage is unnecessary; an audience, incidental.
2. This form of dramatic play is primarily for the children who participate. There is usually no audience except that part of the group not playing at the moment.
3. Acting as guides, teachers draw out children's ideas rather than imposing their own. Children plan, play, and evaluate under guidance.
4. Perfection is not sought, although children are encouraged to do the best creative work of which they are capable.

Through participation in creative dramatics, children can acquire a certain amount of poise and confidence. Such participation also helps them develop a sense of responsibility and independence. As children have the opportunity to become involved in creative dramatics, creative ability usually increases. It is a great chance for children to grow in understanding of people and their ability to work and play together.

Creative dramatics makes an excellent contribution to quality living in the kindergarten. It has therapeutic as well as artistic value and should hold a rightful place in every kindergarten classroom.

Stories that the fives like to dramatize include favorites such as *The Three Bears, Caps For Sale, The Tortoise and the Hare, Ask Mr. Bear,* and many more.

Pantomime

Pantomime is a means by which ideas can be conveyed without words. The fives seem to thoroughly enjoy pantomime activities, and it is an excellent way to begin work in creative dramatics.

Since many of his thoughts are spoken entirely through the body, the five-or six-year-old finds pantomime a natural means of expression. . . . In kindergarten such basic movements as walking, running, skipping and galloping prepare for the creative use of rhythm. Music can set the mood for people marching in a parade, horses galloping on the plains. . . . rhythmic movement becomes dramatic when the participant makes use of it to become someone or something other than himself. (McCaslin, 1974, p. 36)

Children should be encouraged to pantomime activities and people that are familiar to them. If it is a guessing game type of activity, teachers may want to have children whisper into their ears what they plan to pantomime. Sometimes those little actors, who want to stay on stage as long as possible, will say "no" to every guess the other children give them. This method keeps the little performer honest and gives the other children a chance to participate. If a few children cannot think of something to pantomime, a whispered suggestion will often get them participating. Another way would be

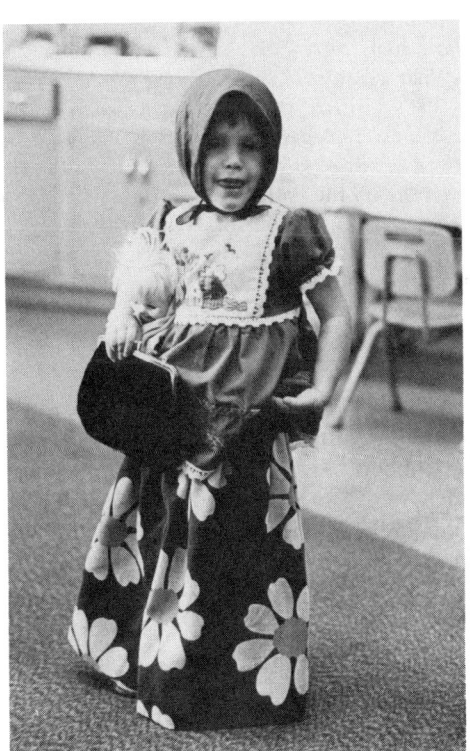

for teacher and child to pantomime something together. It's great fun this way.

The following story in movement is a favorite activity among children.

The Bear Hunt

PROCEDURE: Leader tells everyone to repeat exactly what is said and done. Hands beat alternately on the knees. This represents walking down a path looking for a bear. This motion is repeated throughout the hunt. (Use your imagination. More objects and motions may be added.)

THE ACTUAL HUNT: Each time the group repeats what the leader says and does. (Try to keep the rhythm consistent).
Leader says: Do you want to go on a bear hunt?
Group repeats: Do you want to go on a bear hunt?
Leader: Let's go!
(Group repeats, etc.)
Leader: Oh, look!
What's that?
That's a river.
Can't go under it.
Can't go over it.
Gotta go through it.
All right.
Let's go! (Leader moves as if swimming. Swims eight strokes. Then goes back to beating hands on knees.)
Oh, Look!
What's that?
That's a bridge.
Can't go under it.
Can't go through it.
Gotta go over it.
All right.
Let's go! (Leader pounds chest to make a noise of walking over a bridge. Then goes back to beating hands on knees.)
Oh look!
What's that?
That's a swamp.
Can't go under it.
Can't go over it.
Gotta go through it.
All right.
Let's go! (Leader makes a movement with hands as if the grass were very high—makes big sweeping movements to push it away. Then goes back to beating hands on knees.)
Oh look!
What's that?
That's mud.
Can't go under it.
Can't go over it.
Gotta go through it.
All right.
Let's go! (Leader makes upward movement with hands as if it were hard to pull feet out of the mud. Then goes back to beating hands on knees.)
Oh, look!
What's that?
That's a tree.
Can't go under it.
Can't go over it.
Gotta go up it.
All right.
Let's go! (Leader makes movement as if climbing a tree. All of a sudden, the leader looks up.)
Oh, look!
What's that?
That's a *BEAR!* (Leader screams, then reverses steps. Repeats movements previously made very fast—no words are said: down the tree, back on the path; through the mud, back on the path; through the swamp, back on the path; over the bridge, back on the path; across the river, back on the path. Leader then gives a sigh of relief and wipes brow.)

Puppetry

Puppetry is an excellent means of expression and communication. Many good books have been written on puppetry to help teachers better understand and use this valuable dramatic arts medium. It has long been known that children can often respond through puppets when they cannot respond in other ways. "Puppets have therapeutic power. The timid or withdrawn child can find release through the puppet, whereas the aggressive child must learn to subordinate himself to the personality of the character he is presenting" (McCaslin, 1974, p. 71).

Hand puppets are probably the most valuable for kindergarten children to use. Cloth, sock, or paper bag puppets are very popular. Stick puppets are also easy for children to make and manipulate. These types can be made quickly and give almost instant satisfaction.

When constructing paper bag puppets, one should be sure that the bags are of a size that children can manipulate easily. To keep the bottoms of the paper bag from tearing, the edges may be folded up a couple of times. A good point to remember in decorating puppets is to accentuate the puppet's features. Large buttons or dimensional objects may be used for eyes, etc. Slippers make excellent puppets. (Did you ever think of taking a bedroom slipper, folding it in half, and decorating it to become a dog?) In most cases, puppets can be made very inexpensively and bring great joy and satisfaction to five-year-olds.

In his article in *Young Children*, Smith (1979) speaks extensively on the interactional approach of using puppets to help children clarify their values and develop sound problem-solving skills. We recommend that the article ("Puppetry and Problem-solving Skills") be read and studied in its entirety.

Another method that we have found successful in using puppets with kindergarten children is for the teacher to allow the child to select one puppet while the teacher takes another. Situations that interest children of this age are used to stimulate the dialogue. The following is an example. The scene takes place at an ice cream stand. The teacher takes the part of the clerk, and the child (through the mask of the puppet) comes to the ice cream stand to buy an ice cream cone. A long dialogue takes place over the different flavors of ice cream and the prices of the cones depending on size.

Once children discover how this kind of interaction can occur between puppets, they can take the teacher's place and carry out the second puppet's role.

Puppets are very popular with young children. They are useful aids in helping children express themselves in a way that no other medium can.

POETRY

Poetry and the five-year-old belong together. "There is no better way to bring about sensitivity to beauty, feeling for rhythm and appreciation of the humorous than through enjoyment of poetry in the classroom." (Henry, 1967, p. 67)

Poetry, nonesense verse, jingles, limericks, rhymes, and finger plays offer sheer delight to the kindergarten child. Who has not overheard the young child chanting a well-loved verse? Yet this area of literature is often overlooked or neglected.

Sensory experiences, memory, language development, and appreciation are fostered through careful selection and presentation of poetic and rhythmic materials. What child could forget Sendak's (1962) *Chicken Soup with Rice* or "If You Ever Meet a Whale" from Bisset's (1967) *Poems and Verses about Animals?*

Most young children like the plays on words, alliterations, and catchy rhythms that rhymes provide. (Encourage word play but be forewarned that young children can become avid punsters.) There are several good books of rhymes on the market today. (Remember your own enjoyment of De Angeli's [1954] *Book of Nursery and Mother Goose Rhymes?*)

All of us are familiar with poems that have such strong appeal or rhythm that it is difficult for children to sit still. Mother Goose rhymes have pleased children for generations because of their strong rhythmic quality. (Recall "Hippity Hop" or "Ride a Cockhorse" or "Higgeldy, Piggeldy.") "Poems with strong rhythmic appeal, like Stevenson's 'My Shadow' or 'The Swing,' create a feeling of freedom of movement that releases the inhibited child" (Henry, 1967, p. 68).

As teachers, we need to choose poems that we ourselves enjoy—and then learn to read them well or share them extemporaneously. Poems with humor, poems that tell a story, theme poems, or poems about children or our families are appealing. Suggestions for selecting and presenting poetry are provided in the following paragraphs.

Keep several collections of poetry near your desk or easily available. You will find that more and more, the children will ask for their favorites.

Several unusual collections of poems should be part of your collection. Wyndham and Young's (1968) *Chinese Mother Goose Rhymes* offers unusual versions of rhymes that appeal to children. Lawrence's (1967) *A Beginning Book of Poems* contains several categories of poems to suit most classrooms. Particularly popular is Ciardi's (1961) *I Met a Man* for its many humorous poems and riddles. *Miracles* by Lewis (1966) is a collection from around the world that would enhance social studies discussions and perhaps even prompt the beginning collector of poems. Inexpensive books from Dover Publications delight the ear—*Peter Piper* (1970), *Mother Goose Melodies* 1970, *Eenie, Meenie, Minie, Mo* (1970), and *Counting Out Rhymes* (1970) are but a few that are obtainable in most bookstores.

As you go about selecting poems, keep in mind their appropriateness for the age of the child and how they will be used. Let children know you appreciate poetry and share poetry often with them.

Try an old favorite such as:

Old King Cole

I:	Old King Cole was a merry old soul.
II:	And a merry old soul was he.
I:	He called for his pipe
II:	And he called for his bowl,
Unison:	And he called for his fiddlers three.
I:	And every fiddler he had a fine fiddle
II:	And a very fine fiddle had he.
I:	"Twee Tweedle dee, Tweedle dee" went the fiddles.
II:	And the fiddles went "Twee Tweedle dee."
Unison:	Oh, there's none so rare As can compare With King Cole and his fiddlers three.

OLD RHYME

From the French comes:

A Goblin Lives in Our House

High:	A goblin lives in *our* house
Medium:	in *our* house
Low:	in *our* house.
Unison:	A goblin lives in *our* house all the year around.
Solo I:	He bumps
Solo II:	And he jumps
Solo III:	And he thumps
Solo IV:	And he stumps.
Low:	He knocks
Medium:	And he rocks
High:	And he rocks
Medium:	And he rattles at the locks.
High:	A goblin lives in *our* house
Low:	in *our* house
Medium:	in *our* house.
Unison:	A goblin lives in *our* house all the year around!

Ideas dictated by kindergarten children and chanted include:

Unison:	I like big things.
Solos:	As big as a *big* cloud
	As big as a *giant*
	As big as a *mountain*
	As big as a *mom*
	As big as a *rocket*
	As big as a big *tree*
	As big as a *skyscraper*
	As big as the *sun*
	As big as the *sky*

As big as the whole *school*
As big as a *planet*
As big as a *bus*
Unison: I like *big* things!

Or try this version:

Unison: I like things that are cold.
Solos: Cold as *ice*
Cold as *snow*
Cold as *a Popsicle*
Cold as *winter wind*
Cold as a *Frigidaire*
Cold as *hands without mittens*
Cold as a *puppy's nose*
Cold as *lemonade* in summer
Unison: I like *cold* things!

A song or a chant may spur poetry writing:

Wiggles

I can wiggle my fingers.
I can wiggle my toes.
I can wiggle my elbows.
I can wiggle my bones.
I can wiggle my tummy.
I can wiggle my head.
But, oh, I would much rather
Wiggle my nose instead.

M. RAMSEY

Theodore

I have a fuzzy teddy bear
As cuddly as can be—
I call my teddy Theodore
He means a lot to me.
I take my teddy bear to bed
Each and every night—
I put my arms around him
Then everything's all right.

M. RAMSEY

Guess Who

Hello, listen, tell us please
Who's lost a front tooth?
Let us see—

Hello, listen, tell us please
Who's lost a front tooth?
Deedle, deedle, dee.

K. BAYLESS

Children enjoy saying things aloud. They take pleasure in combinations of sounds that feel good to the mouth and tongue. Choric interpretation will give every child in the class the satisfaction of making poetry come alive (Henry, 1967, p. 16).

Forced memorization of poems has no place with the five-year-old. Some children appear to have an affinity for poetry and enjoy sounds and the feel of words on the tongue. Many have been read to since infancy and, on entering school, may have an extensive repertoire of finger plays and verse.

You may find that choral verse or speaking in unison is enjoyable and promotes interest in rhymes—many of the Mother Goose rhymes lend themselves easily to choral sharing.

Kean and Personke (1976, pp. 125-126) suggest the following guidelines for choral reading:

1. Choral verse should be fun.
2. Choral reading should occur often and for its own sake.
3. Choral reader requires a leader, not a teacher.
4. Selection of poetry should be by children.
5. Interpretation is the province of the children.

Although of little literary value, finger plays are enjoyable to the kindergartner and provide another way of playing with words, appreciating rhyme, and sharing with others.

Steiner and Pond's (1970) *Finger Play Fun* offers a wide variety of fingerplays, both old and new.

Certainly everyone remembers:

One, two, buckle my shoe,
Three, four, shut the door—

and

This little pig went to market.

and

Eenie, meenie, minie mo—

or

>   One for the money—

or

>   Here are the beehives—

and

>   Here are mother's knives and forks—

Finger plays are a legitimate learning experience and not an educational gimmick. Always keep in mind the element of humor. Often children's subtle humor is not the kind that is appreciated or fully understood by adults.

Humor is one of the striking elements in Chukovsky's (1968) *From Two to Five*. No one working with the young child should miss this book. Chukovsky, a Russian poet and an observer of children, their speech, and their patterns of learning, enhances our appreciation and understanding of the "linguistic genius" of the young child.

What has Chukovsky (p. viii) to say about the early years?

- That the thought processes of children do not change, only the symbols of their interpretation are adapted to the social structures of their day.
- That the young child uses fantasy as a means of learning, and adjusts it to reality in the exact amounts his needs demand.
- That poetry is the natural language of little children, and nonsense serves as a handle to the proportion of logic in an illogical world.
- That the fetish of practicality is a blight upon the literature of childhood.

Children delight in rhymed monologues, as all of us know!

We are reminded that to become a poet, the youngster must be full of animal spirits—and, we might add, open to the world and its many opportunities—guided by an adult who is also open to experience and who is a lover of words and good literature.

We need to read haiku; try with children the possibilities of word arrangement; read poems of many lands; listen to sounds about us; and try limericks, rhymes, and verses. We need to catch the rhythm of music and roll sounds around on our tongues. We need to stimulate the imagination.

Black

Black as the sky at night
Black as licorice candy
Black as a crow
Black as the spider who frightened Miss Muffet
Black as the inside of a closet
Black as the dark of night
Black as firemen's boots
Black as my mother's hair.

Blue

Blue is water in the sea.
Blue as the feathers on a jay
Blue is the sky in spring.
Blue are the blueberries so good to eat.
Blue are eyes that look at me!

Quiet

I like quiet things
    Stars at night
    A bunny rabbit
    You when you're asleep
    Combing your hair
    Street at night
    Lobster, sand, a cloud
    Snow falling.
I like quiet things.

Remember to listen as students talk about their ideas and their feelings before they start to write. This may be the most important thing you can do. So few people listen to children. Often teachers do not listen. Many parents do not listen, and some (children) do not even have a friend who listens to them or considers their responses significant. The poems that they write will be ways in which they can be heard. (Hassett and Whisnant, 1973, p. 1G)

Anything that children do can be used as the theme of a poem. Both cinquain and simple haiku can be used with kindergartners in a group led by the teacher.

Cinquain:
   Line 1—noun
   Line 2—two adjectives that describe the noun
   Line 3—three verbs that tell what the noun does
   Line 4—a phrase that tells something about the noun
   Line 5—the noun again, or a synonym or related word

Haiku, a Japanese form, consists of only three lines having 5, 7, 5 syllables—or 17 in all. It is usually about nature or feelings and emotions. A group haiku is a good beginning, or two children may compose together at first; then perhaps children might make individual oral offerings. It is not necessary to stress the "syllable" aspect. Children working together will often produce delightful word images.

We are pleased to share with you the work of several young poets of the Kent State University School. The poets, Adam Elman, Christopher Higgins, Chad Dostal, Elia Freedman, Charles Cooney, April Keller, and Julie Lewis obviously enjoyed this adventure into poetry!

Brontosaurus
Big, reptile
Walking, hiding, laying
Lives in the water.
Dinosaur.
ADAM

Dinosaur
Large, long
Fight, dying, bringing
He is bringing food.
Enormous.
CHRIS

Wriggley
Small, colorful
Hunting, playing, running
He plays with Dad.
Happy.
CHAD

Lucktra
White, furry
Jumping, barking, running
He loves to play (with me).
Sad.
ELIA

Dime, dime
I had a dime,
I want to buy a timer.
Penny, penny
I had a penny.
I bought it for Kenny.
CHARLES

A cat in a hat
Sat on a bat.
APRIL

Once upon a time
There was a cat and dog.
Who were always curious
About the logs.
And about the hog.
JULIE

You, too, can spur creativity, imagination, and feeling as you explore the delights of poetry with the five-year-old.

Art and woodworking

ART

In quality kindergarten programs, ample time is provided for art experiences. Art activities are a natural and satisfying means of expression for the five-year-old. At this level, few children are self-conscious about their artwork. They often enjoy sharing their thoughts and ideas with friends and adults. Most children of this age enjoy art and take it seriously. Not all children of this age, however, paint or enter into art activities freely. There will be those few who are reluctant to use easel paints or get their hands messy working with finger paints or mold-

ing materials. Given time, however, a sensitive and understanding teacher can often help these youngsters thoroughly enjoy and profit from such experiences.

The purposes of art education are described in the following paragraphs.

Art helps children develop a sensory awareness and esthetic sense—it helps them become aware of things, people, and events in their environment. Art can be a way in which children perceive their everyday world.

Art can contribute to self-knowledge. Five-year-olds discover their own abilities, thoughts, and ideas as they see them visually. For example, "This is my train. I drew it. It has two engines and ten box cars. See how the track curves?"

Art enhances and motivates children to use their imagination. "As a child is given materials to express an idea, the images that go through his mind and become transformed on paper through his own planning permit him to materialize what has occurred internally" (Margolin, 1976, pp. 232).

Art experiences can help children discover their own uniqueness and sense of well-being. A sensitive teacher can help kindergarten children appreciate the uniqueness in their own works of art. "Uniqueness supports self-appreciation. Self-appreciation builds a healthy self-concept which in turn permits an appreciation of others and their abilities as well" (Margolin, 1976, p. 234).

Through good art experiences in education, children can come to understand and make use of artistic terminology such as intensity, balance, light, dark, shape, etc.

Kindergarten children should be exposed to art (including photographs and illustrations) and art materials of high quality. This includes the appreciation of artistic works of other cultures and countries.

Most children five years of age are in the preschematic drawing stage. There are some important differences between drawings of four- and five-year-olds. Some of these differences are:

Objects do not seem to float in space quite as much.

Now there is a right-side-up; we begin to see a line that stands for the sky, and a line that stands for the ground.

This base for the objects to rest on grows stronger as the youngster grows older.

With a greater feeling for order in the drawings by five-year-olds there comes a greater understanding of the relative sizes of objects portrayed. Perhaps the greatest change comes about in representing the human figure. At this age, children begin to draw a body with arms and legs.

The greatest change seems to come in the representation of the human figure. The head-feet representation no longer suffices. There is now a body, usually with arms coming from it rather than from the head and with fingers, though not always the right number. There are legs, usually drawn with double lines to suggest volume, with some indication of feet, shoes, or even toes shown. (Brittain, 1979, pp. 40-41)

Recent observations and studies of preschool and kindergarten children have revealed the following:

A youngster draws what he is interested in, and whatever is important to him at that time. The art of drawing seems to be an occasion in itself, and the child is engaged in the process rather than in producing a product recognizable to an adult. Sometimes he is eager to talk about what he is doing, or painting seems just a way of passing time. Each child is unique in what he brings to the activity—his complex understandings, his purpose, his reactions in the process of self-expression. (Brittain, 1979, p. 21)

The teacher's role

The most important factor in any art experience is the teacher. Teachers need to be sensitive, perceptive, and aware that children's joys, hopes, and ideas are the basis for their art expression.

Brittain (1979, p. 160) brings out an important point by stating that "children need adult support to be creative, spontaneous thinkers to face and deal with problems at their own level of competence." Brittain also tells us that the teacher should help children find solutions to problems of their own making.

This point reminds us of an incident that occurred in a kindergarten where the children were studying safety. They had made traffic lights from empty, washed Clorox bottles and had glued colored construction paper lights on the bottles to represent the colored lights on a regular traffic light. The gluing process had taken place on Friday, and by Monday morning about half of the construction paper lights had fallen off. At first, both the supervising teacher and the student teacher were depressed by the situation. Then they decided to turn it into a problem-solving lesson. They discussed the problem with the children and asked them if they had any ideas about why the construction paper lights had fallen off the bottles. The teachers then asked the children to discuss the problem with their parents at home and bring in (with their parents' permission) different types of adhesives. When the different adhesives were brought into the classroom from home, the class experimented with the different kinds. They found that one type of adhesive used on plastic was far superior to the others. The class then proceeded to repair their traffic lights.

Teachers should also develop problems for the children to solve. For example, "This sawdust mixture is cracking. It's too dry. What shall we do with it so it will stick together better?"

Guidance from teachers also gives five-year-olds needed encouragement to experiment with different media to see what will happen when: a brush and paint meet the paper; sawdust, wheat paste, and water are mixed together; green paint is mixed with yellow paint; water is added to soap flakes, which are then whipped with a beater. The list of possibilities goes on and on.

When children appreciate their own art-

work, they are more apt to respect the work of their peers. Teachers can certainly be models in helping children respect their own works of art and those of others.

Teachers' continued guidance and help is necessary as children progress with their drawing, painting, and other art activities. On one occasion, a kindergarten teacher was teaching a lesson on homes, in particular, bedrooms. The teacher and children were deeply involved in discussing what things were in each child's bedroom. After the discussion, the teacher asked the children to draw a picture of their bedroom with everything in it. Five minutes went by. Timmy got up from his table and took his drawing to the teacher. "I'm finished, Mrs. Thomas!" he said. "Tell me all about your picture, Timmy," she responded. "There's a bed and a chair over there in the corner," he said. "Is that all you have in your bedroom?" she asked. "Oh, no," he answered, "I have a lamp, a table, a dresser, lots of toys..." and on and on he went, describing his bedroom. "My, you have lots of things yet to draw on your picture, don't you?" the teacher suggested. Timmy smiled at Mrs. Thomas, wheeled around, and went to his table and began drawing. He was still working on his picture when the class period ended.

Avoid the use of patterns and dittoed outline pages. Children enjoy experiences with art materials and media and should have the opportunity to use the raw materials in unstructured ways. "Structured" art works against young children's opportunities to develop their creative powers.

One should constantly be concerned about safety. It should be made clear to children that they are not to use art materials for touching or hitting other children. Safety techniques in using woodworking tools is important. When necessary, children's clothing can be protected by using smocks or other protective coverings.

Establishing an art center

The art center may be located in a permanent area in the classroom or may be changed on occasion, depending on the types of activities planned. Certain points should be followed when setting up the art center.

The art center should:
1. Be close to a sink
2. Be out of the flow of classroom traffic
3. Have ample room to accommodate each child
4. Not be placed near equipment and surfaces that are hard to clean
5. Have an out-of-way space to place paintings and other completed artwork
6. Be so arranged that it is easy to supervise
7. Be a warm, inviting place in which to work—uncluttered

Art materials and media*

Brushes (different types and sizes)
Chalk (assorted colors)
Clay (as well as garbage can, plastic liner for clay) and other modeling materials, including objects that can be flattened into clay
Cloth of different types (burlap, felt, etc.)
Clothes hangers
Collage materials
Colored papers (assorted colors and sizes—construction paper, tissue, rice, etc.)
Cornstarch
Crayons (assorted sizes)
Easels and easel clips
Felt-tipped pens, markers
Flour
Glue
Liquid starch
Muffin tins (or egg cartons) for paints and sorting

Paints (tempera, finger, water color, spray, poster)
Paper (newspaper and newsprint, manila, white drawing paper of assorted sizes, tagboard, cardboard, wallpaper, wrapping paper, rolls of mural paper, waste computer paper, print shop end rolls, etc.)
Paper clips
Paper bags, plates, cups, straws (assorted sizes)
Paper cutter
Paper punch
Papier-mâché
Paste
Pencils (variety of shapes and sizes, also colored)
Plaster of paris or substitute
Plasticine
Pipe cleaners
Printing materials
Q-tips, cotton balls, etc.
Rubber bands
Salt
Sandpaper
Sawdust
Scissors (right and left handed), pinking shears (for the teacher)
Screening
Seeds
Sponges
Stapler
String
Tape (marking and other)
Teacher's picture file (an important item)
Wire
Yarn

Description of selected art materials: paper, paint, crayons, and adhesives

A. Paper.*
   1. Newsprint (unprinted newspaper): Lightweight, absorbent, available in large sizes

---

*This list of art materials and media for use with kindergarten children is only a beginning. Use your imagination to expand it.

*Other types of paper will be found useful, but the ones described here are the ones used most commonly and satisfactorily with young children. Often printing offices, paper companies, and other businesses contribute odds and ends of paper that will meet many teachers' and children's needs. The sizes in which they come as "scraps" often suggest possibilities to children. The backs of old mimeographed materials from school offices are fine for experimental tearing and pasting.

(18 × 24 inches) (24 × 36 inches); desirable for children's painting.
2. Cream manila: Rough surface, firm; used for crayon application and construction.
3. Finger paint paper: Glazed surface; white; used with finger paint; size of sheet—approximately 16 × 22 inches.
4. Construction paper: Heavy; rather rough surface; folds smoothly in only one direction; assorted colors or one-color packages. Usually used in mounting (as base for pasting thinner papers) or in construction. Available in sizes 9 × 12 inches to 24 × 36 inches.
5. Poster paper: Lightweight; variety of colors and white.

B. Paint.
1. Tempera (also called poster, showcard, and easel paint).
   a. Powder form: Mix with enough water for good application of paint to newsprint. In some instances paint may need to be thicker or thinner than usual, depending on use. Also colors available. Washable.
   b. Thick liquid form: Thin with enough water to use easily (about 1 tablespoon in a small jar or frozen juice can); fill can half full of water. All colors available. Easier to use; colors richer.
2. Finger paint.
   a. Commercial kinds: Powdered—to mix with water; paste—in jars ready to use.
   b. Home-made: Cooked—add ½ cup laundry starch (mix with a little water) to 1 quart boiling water (cook until thick, like pudding). Add ½ cup Ivory Flakes. Stir; cook; store in cool place (add a few drops of oil of wintergreen or peppermint to preserve it for several days). Uncooked—wheat paste, water, tempera.
   c. Directions for use: Finger paint is thick, applied directly with hands to glazed paper, the surface of which should be wet. Thumbtack paper to heavy cardboard. Wet shiny surface of paper with sponge. Add about 2 teaspoons of finger paint. Spread over entire surface with hands. Use a variety of movements and use fists, flat hand, etc. The homemade paint is clear, so that any easel color may be added while working.
3. Enamel paint: A permanent paint used for painting wood objects, sometimes used on other surfaces in small quantities to achieve a particular effect. Removable from hands with turpentine, with which it is also thinned.

C. Crayons: Used most satisfactorily on manila paper, preferably large (18 × 24 inches); used in a variety of ways on many different surfaces; experimentation is important; children need space, freedom to be expansive with own ideas. Remember that mimeographed sheets of pictures to color have no place in a kindergarten-primary program.

D. Adhesives.
1. Rubber cement: Spread cement on both surfaces, let dry before joining. For mounting, paperwork; not for joining wood pieces.
2. Wheat paste: Add wheat paste to water, beating hard; should be smooth. Purchased in hardware stores; commonly used for paperhanging.
3. Library, or "school paste": Available in many sizes. If purchased in gallon jars, small baby food jars may be filled from it. This is the paste children eat! Paste should be applied to object, not to surface on which it is to be pasted.
4. Glue: Usually used in woodworking but may be used for adhering some articles to cardboard, oak tag, etc.

Art activities

Kindergarten-age children enjoy many of the following art activities: finger painting, tempera painting, buttermilk chalk painting, working with clay and other molding materials such as sawdust, salt and flour dough, etc. They also enjoy other art activities such as making collages, string paintings, and wood sculptures, and making pictures and objects with construction paper. They are delighted when they can construct a puppet or help make a diorama. Woodworking, using good-quality tools, can be a very satis-

fying experience for young children. The possibilities are almost endless.

According to Brittain (1979, p. 18), "Noncreative tasks are mistakenly called 'art' by many nursery schools [kindergartens included]. Such activities include pasting macaroni into some sort of predetermined patterns, spilling sand onto wet glue, sticking toothpicks into Styrofoam, dipping string into wet paste and wiggling it over paper, painting over doilies on a sheet of paper, threading together paper plates . . . ." Teachers can and do use some of the above-named activities with children for other purposes, such as to improve their eye-hand coordination, to help them learn to follow directions, to reinforce other areas of the curriculum, and the like; they are not, however, to be considered under the category of "true art."

Painting with tempera

Painting is one of the favorite art activities of young children. Extreme care should be taken in selecting the proper painting materials and supplies. Equal care needs to be taken in presenting painting materials to five-year-olds. Tempera paints (liquid and powdered) are the most satisfactory for children and are universally liked. According to Cherry, "Since it (tempera paint) is water soluble, its density can be varied by the amount of water or other liquid added to it.

One color can be readily mixed with another to produce new colors. Tempera paint is opaque, which permits the child to cover one color with another, thus making changes well within his control" (Cherry, 1972, pp. 68-69).

Tempera paints of better quality are richer and brighter. But care must be taken with some of the more expensive kinds, since they are sometimes more difficult to wash out of children's clothing. In some instances they even stain the hands. The children will enjoy the experience more if they do not have to worry about stains getting on their clothing. *Note:* When children are wearing long sleeves, be sure and help them push them up on their arms. Also, have plenty of smocks or other protective coverings around to protect clothing.

Finger painting

By the time children reach kindergarten, they have generally had some type of finger-painting experience. Commercially prepared finger paints are good to use. Powdered finger paints can be mixed with water and used, but the colors are generally not as brilliant and rich looking. For variety, one might mix liquid soap, liquid starch, and the like, in with the paint. Finger paint paper, butcher paper, glazed shelf paper, waterproof wallpaper, and other types of paper may be used for the painting surface. Children also like to finger paint on formica-top tables and shelves. To make a monoprint, place a large sheet of paper on top of the completed fingerpainting. With the hand, press over the entire piece of paper. Take hold of the two top edges of the paper and lift it off carefully. The result should be a lovely print.

Dignifying the child's picture

Many teachers take the time to make frames for their children's artwork out of colored art board or colored construction paper. (Picture frame shops sometimes give away their framing samples.) We need to dignify some of the children's pictures by caring enough to set them into a frame before we hang them on the walls about the room. These pictures are special to the children who made them, and we should take the time to help the youngsters display them.

Using crayons

Crayons are an excellent tool for children's beginning artwork. They are inexpensive, generally easy to manipulate and control, and are long lasting. Moving crayons rhythmically back and forth and making sweeping movements with them helps prepare children for the time when they will need the more controlled motions for writing.

Crayons should be stored in containers and on shelves where children can readily reach them. Colors should be kept in groups of the same color for easy recognition. When crayons are being purchased, the nonroll kind are preferable. Crayons should be waxy but strong enough to resist breaking.

The following is a suggestion for using the stub ends of old crayons: Peel off the remaining paper. Place several stubs of crayons in a muffin tin cup. Put the muffin tin in a warm oven. Turn off the oven and permit the crayons to melt slowly. When melted, remove from the oven. *Note:* If the muffin cups are lined with foil, the hardened lump of crayon is removed more easily and the muffin tin is easier to clean. When the melted crayons are cooled sufficiently, the pan may be placed in the refrigerator to hasten the hardening process. If you mix the colors, the cookie crayon can be used to make a lovely multicolored picture.

Working with clay

Clay is one of the basic art materials and a material that most kindergarten children thoroughly enjoy using. Clay should be readily available for use by five-year-olds. In their studies, Brittain's group found that some kindergarten teachers were quite reluctant to have clay available. Brittain (1979, p. 216) reminds us that "young children are fully capable of handling clay. They can help prepare it for use, and then experiment with it in many ways." Hardened products of clay can be reused if the clay products are put into a tight container and water added to soften them.

The following material offers additional suggestions on the use of clay:

Clay

Ethelouise Carpenter*

SOME THINGS WE SHOULD KNOW ABOUT CLAY

Clay is a natural material. Like mud, dirt, water, and sand, children use it directly with their hands and it is a part of our natural environment. Clay has the advantage of staying where you put it, of yielding to punching, pushing, and poking without springing back into a mass by itself. It also has its limitations. Children must learn to accept these too.

In many areas children can use clay found in their own back yards. Soaked in a bucket and then poured through screen to eliminate sticks and stones, it soon becomes soft and pliable. Different areas of our country produce different kinds of clay:
1. *Red clay* is cheap and used commonly. It does not glaze well, however.
2. *Buff firing clay* is most adaptable; it is pliable and relatively inexpensive. It can be glazed and fired satisfactorily.
3. *Terra cotta* is a mixture of red and buff clays. It has pieces of fired clay ground in. It has a rough texture, is strong, and is often used for outdoor sculpture.

USING CLAY AND UNDERSTANDING IT

Children should have satisfying experiences with clay. Learning experiences cannot all be frustrating ones. Learning the limits of a material—and how to live with these—will help. Techniques become a part of the children's learning experiences and understandings:
1. Clay dries when exposed to air or heat. Even the heat of one's hands dries it. Extreme heat, as in a kiln, removes moisture and makes clay hard and durable.
    a. A pan of water for dipping fingers will help keep clay moist and pliable while working. If a piece is not finished in one "sitting," it should be wrapped in moist paper toweling or placed in a plastic bag.
    b. As clay dries, some parts may break off. While working, one should blend parts carefully into each other and into the body of the piece. Pulling parts out from a main chunk or ball of clay will help keep a one-piece kind of solidity. Very thin watery clay, called "slip," will help hold pieces.
    c. Hardened clay no longer wanted may be returned to a clay container, watered copiously, and left to become pliable again in a week or two. This is not recommended for painted pieces.
    d. Clay should always be stored in a tight container or plastic bag. Stone crocks are very satisfactory, but new special containers are available from supply houses. Many have rollers or lift-out bins. It is wise to purchase clay in plastic bags, since it will keep, ready for use, indefinitely.

---

*Formerly Associate Professor of Education, Kent State University, Kent, Ohio.

Continued.

Clay, cont'd

2. As with many manipulative materials, to a very young child the process of working with clay is often more satisfying than the product itself. When pieces sit around on shelves for several days, children often no longer identify themselves with the pieces. They can then be returned to the container.
3. It is usually the extra touch, special twist, or pleasant discovery of "what happened when I did this with my fingers" that gives the child a feeling of belonging to a clay piece. How much more delighted a parent should be with a simple punch bowl or interesting shape a child worked out himself than with a heavy hand print to hang precariously—and usually unattractively—on the wall. It takes no real creative imagination to press one's hand into a piece of clay and leave it as such. Unfortunately, so many children have *only this* experience with clay. It is wasteful and certainly unimaginative for both teacher and child.
4. Form is more important than detail. Children's first attempts "to produce" usually result in a multitude of marbles, snakes, pies, birds' nests with eggs, etc.—all of which are examples of a definite form that comes through certain basic motions children use with manipulative materials: rolling 'round and 'round; making a ball motion; rolling toward and away from oneself as with snakes and piecrust; flattening, pounding, then pulling clay up away from the flat piece as nests and bowls appear. As children discover that it can be pulled up from the working surface and that it stays up, then more shapes and forms appear. They learn that it sticks to itself when moist, so they try to push "legs" into "bodies." The next day comes the realization that when hard, clay has different tendencies.
5. When a clay piece is to be kept, it should be fired in a kiln if at all possible. In many school systems today, a kiln is shared by many elementary grades; or a high school may allow use of its kiln once in a while during the school year.
    a. Unfired clay is called "green clay." It is very fragile. It usually breaks either before a child gets it home or soon after. Children need to be alerted to this possibility.
    b. Painting of clay pieces has often been questioned. It does not make them more durable. They may seem more attractive to the teacher or to the child, but this may cause even greater heartbreak when the piece is broken. It also seems to be a waste

---

Silly putty (homemade)

MATERIALS NEEDED: Liquid glue, liquid starch, bowl, measuring cup, tablespoon, and tempera paint or food coloring.

LIMITS: Child should clean up when finished and put away silly putty for use next time.

DIRECTIONS: Mix 1 cup of liquid glue, ½ cup of liquid starch and 2 teaspoons of tempera paint or other coloring. Stir immediately, since putty will start to set. Knead until putty is soft and smooth. If too sticky, add more starch until you achieve the desired consistency.

Collage

Collage gives children the opportunity to interact more directly with materials in their environment. Collage is an art activity composed of pasting on a surface materials generally not associated with one another. When arranging a collage, children develop concepts of texture, shape, space, design, and size.

Collages can be made from all kinds of materials, but some of the most interesting

of materials. Another reason for not painting clay is that since it is a natural material, it should be kept as near that state as possible if facilities are not available to improve that state or preserve it.

c. Green clay can be kiln fired once (bisque firing), then glazed and fired again. Bisque firing makes it hard and as durable as any pottery or dish. The glaze adds gloss and color.

d. Glaze is usually purchased in powder form resembling tempera paint. It should be mixed with water and made about the consistency of custard. It should be applied roughly to the bisque-fired clay, not smoothed with the brush as in painting. Powdered glaze is very pale in comparison with the finished glaze.

e. Children need to know what is happening and to see it as much as possible. When applied, a glaze looks very pale; but it is a beautiful, rich, bright color after being fired. The glazed piece has a thick powdery appearance before going to the kiln. Possibly children could help load the kiln or at least watch while someone loads it. The causes and effects are very fascinating to children, and they should have as much opportunity as possible to see them in operation.

POINTS TO REMEMBER

1. Solid thick pieces may have air pockets, which will cause that piece and other pieces to blow up in the kiln. (Poke pencil holes up through the bottom while the clay is soft or hollow out from the base.)
2. Pieces of good, smooth, uncluttered design, without small appendages, will be most apt to come through the firing well.

MODELING CLAY

Sold under different trade names such as Plasticine, this clay does not become hard. It has value as another type of material that can be pushed, rolled, and shaped. It is reusable and is never painted or fired. Children can easily employ the additive method of construction preferred by young children in art beginnings. They add parts to wholes, both in two- and three-dimension expression.

---

materials are collected from the out-of-doors. Seeds, dried flowers and weeds, pieces of bark, driftwood, shells, and cones make lovely collages.

Scraps of paper and cloth materials make a good beginning for collage work. Scraps should be cut or torn to workable sizes.

Collage materials need to be sorted and put into attractive containers. Children can then make their own choices of materials for use in their collages. Cherry (1972, p. 118) makes these suggestions:

Present a small quantity of materials at one time. Too many different colors, sizes, and shapes can be as frustrating to the child as no variety at all. Giving the child too little material will hinder his developing the idea of selecting those pieces he prefers rather than just grabbing the first one he comes to. About three or four times as many pieces as each child might be able to use on one collage should be an approximate guide to quantity.

Encourage children to follow a theme when making their collages by using materials that are related in their original environment, such as materials from the seashore, the woods, or a flower garden. Also, suggest that they arrange the materials (in different ways) before pasting them onto the flat surface.

WOODWORKING
Establishing a woodworking area

It has been reported that working with wood and tools, to make first unplanned and later planned projects, has a beneficial effect on young children in establishing values and attitudes that carry over into other areas of their development.

Values and attitudes:
1. Develops large-muscle control
2. Provides eye-hand coordination
3. Develops use of imagination and self-expression
4. Provides experiences that increase the attention span
5. Provides sharing experiences with other children

In the process of establishing these values and attitudes by the use of woodworking, children progress through a pattern of growth. The first use of woodworking tools will be completely unplanned. Children may just nail two pieces of wood together. They may drive many nails into a piece of wood just for the satisfaction of hammering. Or, they may attempt to saw a piece of wood with no real purpose in mind. This is the stage of experimentation.

Children may then progress into the stage wherein they make something that is roughly identifiable, but still with very little plan or scale to its identity. They may in time, and with experience, get to the point of developing some order or plan to each project. They may use some means of measuring the pieces and will use only enough nails to hold the pieces together. While going through these stages, each child will develop at his own individual pace and will benefit in value and attitude development accordingly.

The benefits derived in most cases will be in direct proportion to the planning that goes into the:
1. Selection of the area
2. Selection of the equipment
3. Introduction and explanation of the use of the tools
4. Guidance given as the projects are being made

Selection of the area

The area must be large enough to provide safe handling of wood pieces, tools, etc. It must have plenty of light as well as storage shelves or cabinets for the tools and wood supplies. The area should be out of the traffic pattern, away from the other activities, but in full view of the supervising teacher.

Selection of the equipment

Equipment should be selected for durability, function, and safety. Good-quality tools will pay dividends as the program goes on, since they can be resharpened and reused for many years. The following items should be considered for a minimum complement of equipment:

Heavy table, workbench, or sawhorse
Wood vise with table clamps
Saws (crosscut) (16 inches is the best size)
Small claw hammers
Brace and bits
Ruler
Small square
Pliers
Small block plane

Along with the tools selected, it is necessary to provide some basic materials to work with:

Soft pine wood (new or scraps from lumberyard)
Variety package of nails
Paint (poster paint is advised)

Sandpaper (variety pack)
Wood spools, bottle caps, etc.

Introduction of the equipment

In the introduction of the tools and equipment, the stress should be on the proper care and use of them and on the fact that these are *not toys* but tools to build with. In order to become familiar with the details for this introduction, the instructor should study a good home repair book or refer to a book such as *Carpentry for Young Children* (Leavitt, 1971). These references will give a much more detailed explanation of the care and use of tools than can be allotted in this book.

Guidance

The amount of guidance given to each child will need to be tailored to fit the child. However, general points should be stressed and expanded from the previous introduction to equipment. As the child selects a tool to work with, the instructor has an opportunity to illustrate and demonstrate its proper handling and use, its individual hazards, and safety precautions that must be taken with it. This should be done in a low-key, casual manner in order to make the points, but also not to thwart the child's creativity or activities. By making these points on safety and handling, teachers are also impressing on children that tools are different from toys.

By continuing this practice of illustration and demonstration over a period of time, teachers can provide for children a safe, meaningful, learning experience from their participation in working with wood.

Example of a program utilizing woodworking

For several years the kindergarten classes at Evamere School, Hudson, Ohio, have been involved in a technology program in which the children learn about the world of technology. They work with many different kinds of materials and equipment, and have the opportunity to use real woodworking tools. Under careful supervision, the children learn how to use power tools such as power drills and power saws.

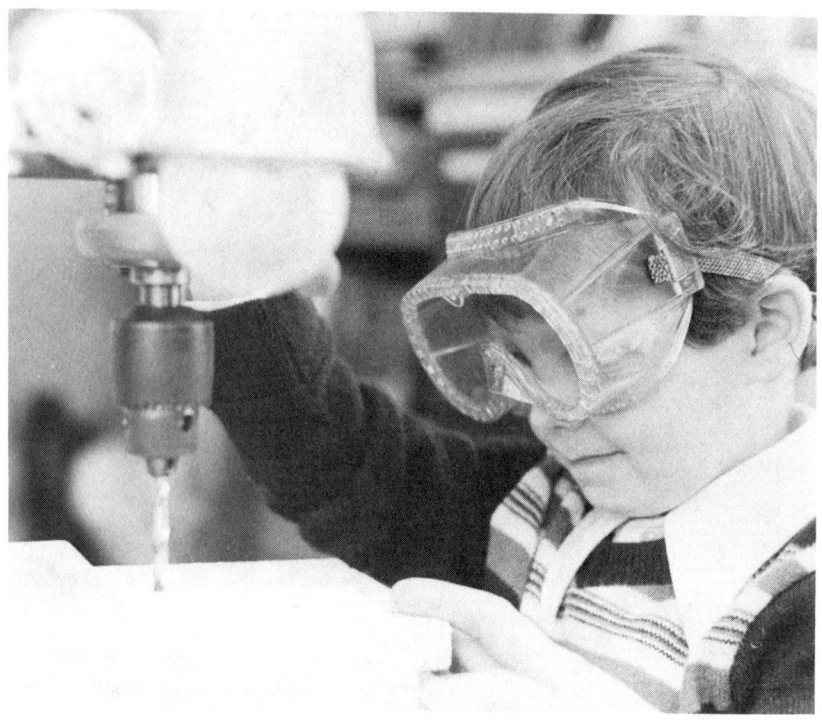

The Technology Exploratorium program not only introduces the children to the world of technology, but also serves as reinforcement and enrichment for the ongoing units of study in the kindergarten program. In the past, the children have worked on many projects, such as designing and building their own miniature airplanes and bird feeders. During their study of Indian life, making use of natural resources, the children made clay beads and other articles. In connection with this unit, as the children made leather bracelets, they learned all about assembly line procedures.

Motivation is high in this program. Discipline problems are practically nonexistent while the children are involved with these hand-on materials. The values and benefits of the program have been so rewarding that it is likely that the technology program will continue to be a part of the Hudson kindergarten program.

Teacher-made wooden puzzles

Children enjoy teacher-made materials. Not only is it a gratifying experience for the teacher to design and construct classroom materials, but it is meaningful for the children to know that their teacher cares enough about them to create learning materials for their enjoyment and use. Wooden puzzles can be easily constructed using the following process:

1. Select a map or picture for the puzzle.
2. Secure two identical pieces of Masonite.
3. Make the puzzle cutting lines on the picture.
4. Trace the puzzle onto the Masonite with carbon paper, including puzzle cutting lines, so that the puzzle will fit on the wood with at least an inch to an inch and a half for a border.
5. Drill a hole just large enough for the blade of the jigsaw to fit through some-

where on a cross line of the puzzle.
6. Remove the jigsaw blade from the saw, put it through the hole, and reattach the blade to the jigsaw.
7. Saw carefully along the puzzle cutting lines. Put the sawed pieces on the paper in order to know where they belong.
8. Remove the blade again to get the frame out when all the pieces are cut.
9. Sand all edges of the puzzle pieces and frame. Round the edges somewhat. The paint will be less apt to chip.
10. Using Elmer's glue, glue the puzzle frame to the other piece of Masonite that is the same size. Use clamps to hold it tightly in place for 24 hours.
11. When dry, sand the outside edge so that the joining of the two pieces is unnoticeable.
12. Paint all pieces, including sides, with enamel. Several (two to four) coats may be needed.
13. Lettering for maps can be put on with rub-on letters available in many sizes from extremely small to large. These are available at office supply stores.

• • •

There are many fine books on young children's art and art activities for teachers who work with kindergarten children. We suggest that you consult the books that are listed in the References and Suggested Readings. Brittain (1979), Cherry (1972), and Haskell (1979) are excellent sources.

The following, from the Pennsylvania Department of Education (1977, p. 113), applies not just to art and woodworking but to all of the expressive arts:

A particularly important reason for an emphasis upon fine arts in the kindergarten is that children tend to apply these qualities to any work they do. In later life, for example, the attributes that help a child become a creative painter, writer or musician also can make the child an equally productive scientist. Certainly it is true that children who are exposed to and participate in the fine arts, find new ways to work, play and live.

Summary

Some of the most delightful and rewarding experiences for the kindergarten child and the teacher come through sharing in the expressive arts. Truly we come to know and appreciate one another more fully as we sing, tell stories, paint and draw, and reveal ourselves through creative endeavor. In too many classrooms (and in too many homes), the expressive arts are neglected or give way to more "academic" pursuits. Yet all of us succeed and grow affectively through the arts. Begin today to add to your repertoire from the richness of the arts.

REFERENCES AND SUGGESTED READINGS
Music and movement

Andrews, Gladys. *Creative rhythmic movement for children.* Englewood Cliffs, N.J.: Prentice-Hall, Inc., 1954.

Austin, Virginia. I am my own instrument. In *Creativity in the elementary school.* New York: Appleton-Century-Crofts, 1959, pp. 53-61.

Bayless, Kathleen, and Ramsey, Marjorie E. *Music: a way of life for the young child.* St. Louis: The C. V. Mosby Co., 1978.

Block, Susan Diamond. *Me and I'm great.* Minneapolis: Burgess Publishing Co., 1977.

Chenfeld, Mimi Brodsky. *Moving movements for wiggly kids.* Phi Delta Kappan, 1976, 58(3), 261-263.

Cherry, Clare. *Creative movement for the developing child* (Rev. ed.). Belmont, Calif.: Fearon Publishers, Inc., 1971.

Clark, Carol E. *Rhythmic activities.* Dansville, N.Y.: The Instructor Publications, Inc., 1969.

Cole, Natalie. *The arts in the classroom.* New York: The John Day Co., 1940.

Hildebrand, Verna. *Introduction to early childhood education.* New York: Macmillan Publishing Co., Inc., 1971.

Hughes, Langston. *The first book of rhythms.* New York: Franklin Watts, Inc., 1954.

Jaye, Mary Tinnin. *Making music your own.* Morristown, N.J.: Silver Burdette Co., 1966.

Landreth, Catherine. *Preschool learning and teaching.* New York: Harper & Row, Publishers, Inc., 1972.

Margolin, Edythe. A world of music for young children.

In *Young children: their curriculum and learning processes*. Belmont, Calif.: Wadsworth Publishing Co., Inc., 1976.

McCall, Adeline. *This is music for today—kindergarten and nursery school*. Boston: Allyn & Bacon, Inc., 1971.

McDonald, Dorothy T. *Music in our lives*. Washington, D.C.: National Association for the Education of Young Children, 1979.

McLaughlin, Roberta, and Wood, Lucille. *Sing a song of people*. Glendale, Calif.: Bowmar, 1973.

Nye, Vernice. *Music for young children*. Dubuque, Iowa: William C. Brown Co., Publishers, 1975.

Petzold, R. Auditory perception by children. *Journal of Research in Music Education*. 1969, *17*, 82-87.

Scott, Louise Binder. The wonderful world of play and make-believe. In *Learning time with language experiences for young children*. New York: McGraw-Hill Book Co., 1968, pp. 123-183.

Seeger, Ruth Crawford. *American folk songs for children*. New York: Doubleday & Co., Inc., 1948.

Sheehy, Emma D. *Children discover music and dance*. New York: Teachers College Press, 1968.

Shelley, Shirley J. Music. In Carol Seefeldt (Ed.), *Curriculum for the preschool-primary child—a review of the research*. Columbus, Ohio: Charles E. Merrill Publishing Co., 1976.

Sinclair, Caroline B. *Movement of the young child ages two to six*. Columbus, Ohio: Charles E. Merrill Publishing Co., 1973.

Smith, Robert B. *Music in the child's education*. New York: The Ronald Press Co., 1970.

The dramatic arts
Stories and dramatic play

Andersen, B. E. *Let's start a puppet theatre*. New York: Van Nostrand Reinhold Co., 1973.

Bates, E. *Potpourri of puppetry*. Canyon: West Texas State University, 1974.

Crosscup, Richard. *Children and dramatics*. New York: Charles Scribner's Sons, 1966.

Dictionary of education, 1973.

Giles, Emily. *Creative dramatics for all children*. Washington, D.C.: Association for Childhood Education International, 1972-1973.

Hanford, R. T. *The complete book of puppets and puppeteering*. New York: Drake Publishers, Inc., 1976.

Heimig, Ruth, and Stillwell, Lyda. *Creative dramatics for the classroom teacher*. Englewood Cliffs, N.J.: Prentice-Hall, Inc., 1974.

Henry, Mabel Wright. *Creative experiences in oral language*. Champaign, Ill.: National Council of Teachers of English, 1967.

Jones, Anthony, and Buttrey, June. *Children and stories*. Oxford, Eng.: Blackwell Scientific Publications, 1974.

McCaslin, Nellie. *Creative dramatics in the classroom*. New York: David McKay Co., Inc., 1974.

Pierini, Mary. *Creative dramatics*. New York: Herder and Herder, 1971.

Richter, D. *Fell's guide to hand puppets*. New York: Frederick Fell Publishers, Inc., 1970.

Sawyer, Ruth. *The art of the storyteller*. New York: Dover Publications, Inc., 1951.

Schwartz, Dorothy Thames, and Aldrich, Dorothy (Eds.). *Give them roots and wings—a guide to drama in the elementary school*. Washington, D.C.: American Theatre Association, 1972.

Shedlock, M. L. *The way of the storyteller*. New York: The Viking Press, 1941.

Smith, Charles A. Puppetry and problem-solving skills. *Young Children*, 1979, *34*(3), 4-5.

Stewig, John. *Spontaneous drama*. Columbus, Ohio: Charles E. Merrill Publishing Co., 1973.

Tooze, Ruth. *Storytelling*. Englewood Cliffs, N.J.: Prentice-Hall, Inc., 1959.

Torrance, Ellis. *Encouraging creativity in the classroom*. Dubuque, Iowa: William C. Brown Co., Publishers, 1970.

Tyas, Bill. *Child drama in action*. Canada: Gage Educational Publishing Ltd., 1971.

Wagner, Joseph. *Children's literature through storytelling*. Dubuque, Iowa: William C. Brown Co., Publishers, 1970.

Wall, L. V., White, G. A., and Philpott, A. R. (Eds.). *The puppet book—a guide to drama in the elementary school*. Washington, D.C.: American Theatre Association, 1972.

Werner, Peter H., and Burton, Elsie C. Art. In *Learning through movement*. St. Louis: The C. V. Mosby Co., 1979, pp. 279-307.

Poetry

Bissett, Donald (Ed.). *Poems and verses to begin on* (Book 1). San Francisco: Chandler Publishing Co., 1967.

Bissett, Donald (Ed). *Poems and verses about animals* (Book 2). San Francisco: Chandler Publishing Co., 1967.

Chukovsky, Kornei. *From two to five*. Berkeley: University of California Press, 1968.

Ciardi, John. *I met a man*. Boston: Houghton Mifflin Co., 1961.

Ciardi, John. *You read to me, I'll read to you*. Philadelphia: J. B. Lippincott Co., 1962.

Counting out rhymes. New York: Dover Publications, Inc., 1970.

Dunning, Stephen, Lueders, Edward, and Smith, Hugh. *Reflections on a gift of watermelon pickle*. New York: Scholastic Book Services, 1966.

Eenie, meenie, minie mo. New York: Dover Publications, Inc., 1970.

Frostic, Gwen. *These things are ours*. Benzonia, Mich.: Presscraft Papers, 1960.

Greer, Mary, and Rubinstein, Bonnie. *Will the real teacher please stand up?* Santa Monica, Calif.: Goodyear Publishing Co., Inc., 1972.

Hassett, Jo, and Whisnant, Charleen. *Poetry power: ideas for creative writing*. Charlotte, N.C.: Red Clay Books, 1973.

Henry, Mabel Wright. *Creative experiences in oral language*. Champaign, Ill.: National Council of Teachers of English, 1967.

Hoberman, Mary Ann. *Nuts to you and nuts to me*. New York: Alfred A. Knopf, Inc.

Howard, Caralie. *The first book of short verse*. New York: Franklin Watts, Inc.

Kean, John M., and Personke, Carl. *The language arts: teaching and learning in the elementary school*. New York: St. Martin's Press, Inc., 1976.

Koch, Kenneth. *Wishes, lies, and dreams*. New York: Vintage Books, 1970.

Lawrence, Marjory. *A beginning book of poems*. Reading, Mass.: Addison-Wesley Publishing Co., Inc., 1967.

Lawrence, Marjory. *An invitation to poetry*. Reading, Mass.: Addison-Wesley Publishing Co., 1967.

Lewis, Richard. *Miracles*. New York: Simon & Schuster, Inc., 1966.

Mother Goose melodies. New York: Dover Publications, Inc., 1970.

One misty, moisty morning. New York: Farrar, Straus, & Giroux, Inc., 1971.

Painter, Helen W. *Poetry and children*. Newark, Del.: International Reading Association, 1970.

Peter Piper. New York: Dover Publications, Inc., 1970.

Sendak, Maurice. *Chicken soup with rice*. New York: Scholastic Book Services, 1962.

Shepard, Ernest, and Milne, A. A. *Now we are six*. New York: E. P. Dutton & Co., Inc., 1961.

Steiner, Violette G., and Pond, Roberta Evatt. *Finger play fun*. Columbus, Ohio: Charles E. Merrill Publishing Co., 1970.

Stevenson, Robert Louis. *A child's garden of verses*. London: Henry Z. Walck, Inc., 1947.

Voices of man series. Reading, Mass.: Addison-Wesley Publishing Co., 1969.

Wyndham, Robert, and Young, Ed. *Chinese Mother Goose rhymes*. New York: World Publishing Co., 1968.

Art and woodworking

Betts, Victoria Bedford. *Exploring finger paint*. Worcester, Mass: Davis Publications, Inc., 1963.

Bland, Jane Cooper. *Art of young child*. Greenwich, Conn.: New York Graphic Society, Ltd., 1968.

Brittain, W. Lambert. *Creativity, art, and the young child*. Belmont, Calif.: Fearon Publishers, Inc., 1979.

Cherry, Claire. *Creative art for the developing child*. Belmont, Calif.: Fearon Publishers, Inc., 1972.

Haskell, Lendall L. *Art in the early years*. Columbus, Ohio: Charles E. Merrill Publishing Co., 1979.

Leavitt, Jerome E. *Carpentry for children*. New York: Sterling Publishing Co., Inc., 1971.

Linderman, Earl W., and Heberholz, Donald W. *Developing artistic and perceptual awareness* (3rd ed.). Dubuque, Iowa: William C. Brown Co., Publishers, 1974.

Lindstrom, Miriam. *Children's art*. Berkeley: University of California Press, 1975.

Lowenfeld, Viktor, and Brittain, W. Lambert. *Creative and mental growth* (6th ed.). New York: Macmillan Publishing Co., Inc.

Margolin, Edythe. *Young children: their curriculum and learning processes*. New York: Macmillan Publishing Co., Inc., 1976.

Payne, G. C. *Adventures with clay*. New York: Frederick Warne & Co., Inc., 1969.

Pennsylvania Department of Education. *Kindergarten guidelines*. Revised, 1977.

Torrance, E. Paul. *Rewarding creative behavior*. Englewood Cliffs, N.J.: Prentice-Hall, Inc., 1964.

Werner, Peter H., and Burton, Elsie C. Art. In *Learning through movement*. St. Louis: The C. V. Mosby Co., 1979, pp. 279-307.

OTHER RESOURCES
Music and movement
Some favorite songbook collections to use with five-year-olds

American Folk Songs for Children
Ruth Crawford Seeger
New York: Doubleday & Co., Inc., 1948
   Includes 90 favorite folk songs with guitar chording. The introductory chapters explain how to sing the songs, how to improvise on the words, how to use the songs at home and at school, how to use the rhythm and repetition, and how to use the humor and tone play of folk songs.

The Big Book of Favorite Songs for Children
Dorothy Berliner Commins
New York: Grosset & Dunlap, Inc., 1951
   Contains 29 favorite songs of early childhood.

Clementine
Robert Quackenbush
Philadelphia: J. B. Lippincott Co.
   Favorite old songs illustrated with humor. The music is included

Every Child's Book of Nursery Songs
Donald Mitchell
New York: Crown Publishers, Inc., 1968
   A collection of old favorites and some new ones—musical games and simple accompaniments.

Eye Winker, Tom Tinker, Chin Chopper
Tom Glazer
New York: Doubleday & Co., Inc., 1973
  Contains 50 finger plays. There are familiar finger play songs, and also familiar finger plays newly set to music, as well as some beautiful new songs and famous folk songs with brand-new finger plays.

The Fireside Book of Children's Songs
Marie Winn
New York: Simon & Schuster, Inc., 1966
  The book is divided into five sections: *Good Morning and Good Night, Birds and Beasts, Nursery Songs, Silly Songs,* and *Singing Games and Rounds.*

The Fireside Songbook of Birds and Beasts
Jane H. Yolen
New York: Simon & Schuster, Inc., 1972
  The songs in this book are grouped into sections; the piano accompaniments are not difficult, and many old favorites are included.

Jim Along Josie
Nancy and John Langstaff
New York: Harcourt Brace Jovanovich, Inc., 1970
  Collection of folk songs and singing games for young children. The book contains traditional singing games that involve the child in singing, dancing, and acting out words. There are many action songs especially suited to the youngest child. Included are piano accompaniments, guitar chords, and some optional percussion accompaniments for use with simple instruments.

Music Activities for Retarded Children
David R. Ginglend and Winifred E. Stiles
New York: Abingdon Press, 1965
  An excellent handbook to assist parents or teachers in initiating a developmental music program for retarded children or young "normal" children.

Music for Fun

Music for Learning
Lois Birkenshaw
Toronto: Holt, Rinehart & Winston of Canada Ltd., 1977
  For regular and special classrooms.

Petatonic Songs for Young Children
Mary Helen Richards
Belmont, Calif.: Fearon Publishers, Inc., 1967
  Songs have voice ranges of six tones or less.

Selected list of recordings

Birds, Beasts, Bugs and Little Fishes
Pete Seeger,
Folkways/Scholastic Records

Chicken Fat
Lyons Band

Dance-a-Story Records
Anne Lief Barlin
Ginn & Co.

Easy Does It
Hap Palmer
Educational Activities, Inc.

Folk Song Carnival
Hap Palmer
Educational Activities, Inc.

Folk Songs for Little Singers
Bowmar

Getting to Know Myself
Hap Palmer
Educational Activities, Inc.

The Hokey Pokey and Other Favorites
A.B. LeCrone Co.

Ideas, Thoughts and Feelings
Hap Palmer
Educational Activities, Inc.

Learning Basic Skills through Music
Hap Palmer
Educational Activities, Inc.

Lullabies from 'Round the World
Tom Thumb Records

Movement Exploration
Educational Activities, Inc.

Nursery Rhymes for Little People
Kimbo Educational

Nursery Rhymes—Rhyming and Remembering
Ella Jenkins
Folkways Records

Patriotic and Morning Time Songs
Hap Palmer
Educational Activities, Inc.

Play Your Instruments and Make a Pretty Sound
Ella Jenkins
Folkways Records

Sea Gulls
Hap Palmer
Educational Activities, Inc.

Simplified Lummi Stick Activities
Kimbo Educational

The Small Dancer
Bowmar

The Small Player
Bowmar

The Small Singer
Bowmar

You'll Sing a Song and I'll Sing a Song
Ella Jenkins
Folkways Records

Records for appreciation

Ballet of the Unhatched Chicks
Moussorgsky

Carnival of the Animals
Saint-Saens

Children's Corner Suite
Debussy

Dance Macabre
Saint-Saens

Nutcracker Suite
Tchaikovsky

Peer Gynt Suite No. 1
Grieg

Peter and the Wolf
Prokofiev

Sources of records

Bowmar
4563 Colorado Blvd.
Los Angeles, Calif. 90039

Capital Records, Inc.
1290 Avenue of the Americas
New York, N.Y. 10019

Childcraft
Education Corp.
20 Kilmer Rd.
Edison, N.J. 08817

Children's Book & Music Center
5373 West Pico Blvd.
Los Angeles, Calif. 90019

Columbia Records
51 West 52nd St.
New York, N.Y. 10019

Decca Records
445 Park Ave.
New York, N.Y. 10022

Educational Activities, Inc.
Freeport, N.Y. 11520

Folkways Records
43 West 61st St.
New York, N.Y. 10023

Folkways/Scholastic Records
50 West 44th St.
New York, N.Y. 10036

Ginn and Co.
191 Spring St.
Lexington, Mass. 02173

Kimbo Educational
P.O. Box 477
86 South 5th Ave.
Long Branch, N.J. 07740

A. B. LeCrone Co.
819 N.W. 92nd St.
Oklahoma City, Okla. 73114

Lyons Band
530 Riverview Ave.
Elkhart, Ind. 46514

RCA Records
Educational Sales
P.O. Box RCA 1000
Indianapolis, Ind. 46291

Rhythms Productions
Whitney Bldg.
Box 34485
Los Angeles, Calif. 90034

Tom Thumb Records
Rhythms Productions
Whitney Bldg.
Box 34485
Los Angeles, Calif. 90034

Sources for ordering instruments

Children's Music Center, Inc.
5373 West Pico Blvd.
Los Angeles, Calif. 90019

Lyons Band
530 Riverview Ave.
Elkhart, Ind. 46514

Oscar Schmidt-International, Inc.
Garden State Rd.
Union, N.J. 07083

Peripole, Inc.
P.O. Box 146
Brown Mills, N.J. 08015

Rhythm Band, Inc.
P.O. Box 146
Fort Worth, Tex. 76101

CHAPTER 8

The communication arts

Language

> Words can sparkle and spin, or whistle and whine, and children should have numerous experiences in tuning their ears in to the glory and mystery of a Wonderland of Words. (Carlson, 1970, p. 46)

The kindergarten child is at the threshold of acquiring the key to a lifelong storehouse of words—words that become available through listening, speaking, reading, writing, and complex thinking—the integration of skills we know as the communication arts. The five-year-old is entranced by words—nonsense words, slang, limericks, riddles, "big" words, noisy words, rhymes, and even the absurd and profane. To begin to sort out and capture these words for daily use and power, the child looks to the adult for direction, stimulation, and interpretation.

Throughout the first three years of life, all of this mysterious language and sound surrounded the child and was acquired with little effort. Learning to talk was a part of a socialization process stimulated by everyone in the immediate environment. From the first babbling and cooing sounds, the child learned that the listening adults encouraged and enjoyed language and supported its production. No one worried about not being able to talk; rather there was a natural flow of words and sounds, a kind of circular participation *with* others.

I (M.R.) listened with delight as a 26-month-old gleefully completed line after line of nursery rhymes recited by his mother. This had been a household game for many months. The mother chanted or sang, "Jack and Jill went," and he, "up the hill," and she, "to fetch a pail," and he, "of water." After each successful completion of a verse, the child would clap and chortle, "Good, good!" He was reveling in pleasing the adults as well as himself. This same small boy, when accompanying his mother shopping, would remind her, "Mastercharge, Mommy!"

A father related a similar experience with his small daughter. As the father shaved in the morning or prepared for work, he would sing songs of every kind. The little girl would clap and complete the lines or call out the titles of the songs. Language development and enjoyment of the beauty of words was at its best.

In another family, a three-year-old stood in her crib and informed all of those around her, "I say naughty words"—and she did, many of them, with no thought of meaning but clearly understanding the startled reactions of the adults.

Meanings and intent are learned early. A

twenty-nine–month–old child after successfully opening a package of frozen squash, told his grandmother, "Good job, Grandma." And, as he, his mother, and his grandmother got into the car, "Seatbelt, Grandma!"

As King (1975) states, "It is a strange paradox that what occurs with seemingly little effort before school requires so much work and generates so much stress and anxiety in school."

We know that before the child enters kindergarten, a language system, complete with its own rule-governed grammar, has been acquired. We also know that this language, learned without compulsion, is a highly personal system, reflecting the heritage of a particular family and deeply rooted particular subculture. The child speaks the way he does because the language is an integral part of a strong background of experiences. Most of the language skills (but not most of the vocabulary) have been acquired by age four or five. Yet, how the child learns to put sentences together and learns language rules is unknown. Also, the role of the adult in the development of the child's language is not fully understood or appreciated.

The gift of language is indeed unique. As the child enters kindergarten, the ability to listen, think, speak, and perhaps read and write some words is operational. The early stages of true communication are awaiting development, expansion, and refinement. Each child is offering, at a particular maturational level, what we choose to think of as "the essence of the human spirit"—language. In the ensuing years, how well that language is developed could determine and have impact on all the years of life remaining—career choices, life-style, and continuation of productive learning—since we define ourselves to others in large part through language.

The kindergarten teacher has the challenge and exciting privilege of beginning the exploration with the five-year-old of what Carlson has called the "glory and mystery of words." We have much to consider. If, indeed, communication is the "essence of the human spirit," the teacher or caregiver of the five-year-old bears a considerable responsibility in guiding that five-year-old in the beginnings of mastery of the art of communication—an art that will undergird all future endeavor and span a lifetime.

PLANNING A LANGUAGE PROGRAM

Planning experiences and activities in the communication arts for the kindergarten child is a vital concern for the teacher. The communication arts are integrative; there should be no artificial separation of the skills in their presentation to the child. However, with that understanding, we have chosen to discuss each component separately for clarity and specificity. A blending of skills is then sought in the activities and other materials suggested.

As we consider listening, speaking, writing, and reading, keep in mind the interdependence and interaction of learnings involved. Also keep in mind that most of the five-year-olds already possess some degree of skill in the communication arts—they have not been living in a vacuum prior to entering kindergarten! There are few nonverbal children.

There are, however, children of differing backgrounds, children with differing speech needs, children who may have experienced little dialogue with adults, "only" children who may exhibit highly sophisticated vocabularies, twins who may communicate only with each other, children who are non–English speaking, children with varied dialects or immature speech, children with limited listening skills, and children already reading at fourth-grade level. All of these children enter the kindergarten door in September, bringing a gift of language and anticipating nurturance.

According to Dallman (1969, p. 20), the following points need to be kept in mind in planning:

1. A favorable socioeconomic background seems to be beneficial to language development.
2. The extent of the child's experience determines, in part, language development.
3. The "only" child is likely to be more advanced in language.
4. Twins are inclined to be less advanced in language development.
5. The quality of the language of the adults with whom the child comes in contact will affect the power of communication of the child.
6. In homes where a language other than English is spoken, a child upon entrance to school is likely to be handicapped in his ability to communicate in English.
7. In general, girls excel boys in various language abilities.
8. A critical attitude toward a child's communication skills helps determine the extent of language development.

Another consideration in planning effective and productive communication programs for the kindergarten is the wealth of materials, both commercial and "found," that are available. Pressures from parents and commercial interests are not insignificant. All want children to enhance communications skills, as does the teacher. How to satisfy the expectations of all involved and choose wisely and well requires judgment, familiarity with the needs of the children and with the materials, and expertise of presentation.

With the philosophy that language is the carrier of learning and the key to social adjustment, and as guidelines for planning a well-balanced program in the Communication Arts, the (Ohio) Ad Hoc Kindergarten Guidelines Committee (1978, pp. 13-15) recommends that the teacher:

1. Plan experiences based on how students learn language.
2. Plan a variety of trips, experiments, and experiences which will expand the child's knowledge as well as his vocabulary.
3. Provide a variety of ways for children to respond to literature—visual arts, discussions, role playing.
4. Provide an atmosphere conducive to conversation, both planned and unplanned.
5. Arrange an environment which will encourage sociodramatic play.
6. Provide time, and the environment for each child to investigate and to be himself.
7. Plan many walks and other experiences to help the young child identify with "his world" and build a common base with others for talking these over.
8. Provide a variety of materials which will contribute to finer eye-hand coordination and small muscle development and help children when they manifest a desire to write.
9. Offer many opportunities for recording information as a way of showing the relationship between talking and writing.
10. Focus attention on reasons for listening during and through individual, small, and large group activities.

Teacher-pupil planning can be done on various levels. Overall planning for the year should be considered by the teacher in light of the needs and abilities of the children. Planning for a single activity, such as a field trip or visit to the library or for a storyteller to visit the kindergarten room, is another approach. Even daily planning can be a joint endeavor, with children selecting books and materials or costumes for an impromptu presentation. Because the communication arts undergird virtually every activity, the opportunities for incidental learning are vast and the "teachable" moment comes into focus.

Planning also involves consideration of purpose, of individual differences of children and grouping patterns. Specific attention needs to be directed to children with learning difficulties and to the hearing-impaired child. Language is the base for learning. For the "special" child, skill in communication is absolutely essential.

Effective planning should reflect the models and functions of language. Halliday (1969, pp. 26-38) suggests that by age five the child should have internalized the following models:

1. Instrumental—"I want," "I need."
2. Regulatory-control—"Do this."
3. Interactional—"Who can?" "Who can't?" "Let's do this."
4. Personal—"I am," "I can."
5. Heuristic—"Why?"
6. Imaginative—"Let's pretend."
7. Representational—"I've something to tell."

As considerations for planning the language growth of the kindergarten child, Hendrick (1980, pp. 232-238) offers seven ways to foster language development. What are the implications?

I. Listen to the children. . . .
II. Give the children something real to talk about. . . .
III. Encourage conversation and dialogue. . . .
IV. Use questions to generate and develop language. . . .
V. Provide auditory training for the children. . . .
VI. When necessary, seek professional assistance promptly. . . .
VII. Become acquainted with research-based language development programs, and draw on these for resource materials.

Perhaps the most significant aspect of planning a language program in the classroom is the present level of attainment of the children in the kindergarten. Pflaum (1974, p. 68) suggests that:

1. Those children who are acquiring language should be identified and encouraged to engage in prereading and later, if their interest remains high, in beginning reading experiences.
2. Children whose language development is progressing normally should be identified, and their individual needs met so that the program helps them to increase their language knowledge.
3. Those children whose language acquisition is slow but in the regular sequence will require recognition and attention so that full development is ensured before they are required to engage in reading and other complex learning activities.
4. In addition, teacher assessment ought to locate those nonverbal children who need to be referred to specialists for further diagnosis.

The use of observation, informal checklists, or measures such as the Peabody Picture Vocabulary Test will provide some measure of vocabulary strength and facilitate overall program planning.

What are the goals to consider in planning a communication arts program in the kindergarten? A general overall goal might be to help the child develop and improve communication skills or develop fluent and appropriate language skills. Or a general goal might be to encourage vocabulary growth in terms of quantity of words as well as enhancement of the understanding of word meanings. A major goal would be the establishment of an environment conducive to optimal syntactic development as well as continual assessment of each child's growth in communication. Because children often learn more effectively when they have a part in planning their activities, one might also have a general goal of pupil participation in choice making. Self-satisfaction and the enhancement of self-concept could be a goal for all children as they acquire additional vocabulary words and further their communication skills. Children need to realize that language is a social tool and that there are many kinds of language.

Kindergarten children enjoy playing with and inventing language. They can learn, too, that language is a system of sounds and that language changes. (Think of the words that exist today that we did not have even ten years ago!) Words from other languages and cultures also fascinate these children.

Development of listening skills and better comprehension of what is heard should be part of the overall objectives in each of the communication arts components.

As teacher and kindergartners work together on a daily basis, more specific goals to suit a particular activity can be articulated. If the group has returned from a field trip to a bakery, a specific goal might be to develop a group summary of the experience through sharing and recording impressions. After a nature walk, individual children may wish to tape comments about their discoveries that later could be heard by other children. Small books could also be produced complete with pictures and captions descriptive of the nature walk.

Whatever the activity or larger framework of the communication arts, one needs to have in mind purpose and intent. The more clearly articulated the goal, the more effective the planning and the greater the ease of evaluation and modification on completion of an activity.

LISTENING

Listening is the child's first effort in making meaning with the world. How can listening skills be developed? In a world defined by a myriad of sounds and noises, including television, stereo, attention-centered commercials, and voices—the clatter of a technological society—the listening skills of the five-year-old may be very inadequate to the expectations of the school setting. Before the age of five, most children have lived in a very egocentric world where "I" is most important and the role of *listener* is secondary.

The differing backgrounds and cultures of children must also be considered. What has been their "listening quotient"? In some cultures, silence is accepted behavior; in others, a "wall of sound" blots out the chirp of a bird or the rustle of leaves.

However, most activity in the school assumes effective listening as the beginning point. Most of us do not realize how much classroom time must be spent in listening by children ill equipped to listen. Informal research reveals that in many classrooms, teachers talk 75% of the time and children 25%. (Think of the implications of such a situation. As you work with kindergartners, tape part of the day's activities. Replay the tape and discover how much talking *you* do.)

All of the while, children within the class may silently be thinking, "Listen to *me*." Unless parents and teachers listen to children, act as role models for listening behavior, and provide opportunities for listening activities, children may well be deficient in speaking, thinking, and reading skills.

What is listening and how can we help the five-year-old develop more efficient listening habits? Many people feel that to hear is to listen. Landry (1969, p. 601), however, cites the complexity of listening: "Listening implies more than just hearing. It involves giving active and conscious attention to the sounds for the purposes of gaining meaning. Listening involves the comprehension of meaning heard, as well as relating these sounds to our experience."

We know that many factors influence listening—the child's maturity, health, vocabulary, intellect, family background, motivation, ability to attend, auditory abilities, and opportunities. Hansen (1974, p. 278) states unequivocably that "the first environmental contact a child has with language is through listening, and it remains a major factor throughout life."

Obviously, the child's mental maturity and capacity, vocabulary, and home environment, as previously mentioned, play a vital role in overall language development. It is for the teacher, then, to assess the capacity of each child and build opportunities for listening. Significantly, instruction in listening (verbal comprehension) is only slowly gaining ground as an important element in the language curriculum—research in this area is vital.

Dialogues between children and their classmates, between teacher and children, between parents and children, and between other adults and children are essential. To develop, we must be able to listen to the ideas of others and be able to express our ideas to them. Listening is the key. The ideal listener maintains eye contact, mentally sorts out the words of the speaker, interprets what is said, and relates this to other ideas and events—the ideal listener thus attempts to understand the motivation and the very spirit of the speaker. Listening—*good* listening—is an intensely personal experience.

As one small kindergartner said, "My teacher never really listens to me—even when she is looking at me, I know she doesn't listen!" A child can intuitively feel rejected or realize that the exciting event being related is not actually important to a teacher busy "checking" other children in the room or perhaps concerned about a personal problem. Listening is often *caught,* not taught.

Special note needs to be taken of the hearing-impaired child in the kindergarten. Listening skills for this child are doubly significant. Placement in the classroom, direct eye contact with the child, monitoring the child's use of a hearing aid (if one is used), and careful listening *to* the child are important. Meers (1976) offers useful suggestions for the teacher of young hearing-impaired children.

The emotionally impaired kindergartner may also have difficulty attending, and specific activities may be needed for this child as well.

The following are general suggestions for improving listening skills in kindergartners:

Keep in mind that the "listening span" of most five-year-olds is relatively short. Inventory your own listening and talking. If you talk a great deal more than you listen to the children, try to bring the situation into closer balance. Children imitate listening. In all activities try to avoid repeating instructions. Too much repetition encourages "tuning out" and lazy listening. Provide activities and topics of interest to the children: offer story reading, poetry, rhythms, puppetry, records, tapes, and dramatics; take nature walks and listen to the sounds about you; develop and use exercises that demand concentration—memory exercises and games; and give specific directions. Create a classroom environment wherein listening and speaking are prized. Provide a balance between oral and aural activities.

A creative teacher, open and receptive to the conversation of kindergarten children and with an awareness of the many ways to develop opportunities for listening, can stimulate better listening habits. The development of listening cannot be left to chance. Some time needs to be scheduled each day for listening training. Each day should include conversation and discussion, jokes, riddles, anecdote and story telling, listening games, adventures, and explanations and announcements—these are the many ways in which listening is incorporated into the fabric of living.

The following activities may be helpful in promoting skill in listening:

1. The children watch while the teacher strikes three objects that produce different sounds. They then close their eyes; the teacher strikes one of the objects, and the children identify the object struck. At first, the sounds should be very different from each other (e.g., a bell, a glass, and a cardboard box).
2. The children try to identify which of

two, three, or four containers an object is shaken in. Containers can be cardboard, plastic, tin, or aluminum. The teacher demonstrates the sounds each container makes before asking the children to turn their backs and give the response.

3. The teacher rings a bell. The children raise their hands when they hear the sound; they lower their hands when the sound stops.
4. The children stand close together in a group. The teacher demonstrates the difference between near and far sounds by producing identical sounds near the children, then from a far corner of the room. This is done first with the children's eyes open, then with their eyes closed.
5. The children close their eyes while the teacher produces sounds from various parts of the room. The children point in the direction of the sound.
6. The teacher rings two bells. One has a clapper taped to the side. The children identify which bell is ringing. The teacher change hands, then holds one bell high and one low. The children name the direction of the sound: up or down.
7. One child with eyes closed pretends to be a mother cat. Three children pretend to be her kittens. As the mother cat sleeps, the kittens run away and hide in different parts of the room. The children who play kittens should not move after they hide. The mother cat wakes up and calls the kittens. They meow; she finds them from the direction of their sounds.
8. Each child picks a farm animal to imitate. When the children hear the

rooster crow (teacher), they make the sounds of a barnyard waking up. They continue until they hear the owl hoot (teacher). Then they become quiet, put their heads down, and pretend to be asleep. Children who respond rapidly take turns being the owl.

9. The teacher drops a certain number of beads into a metal can. The children repeat the sequence by dropping the same number of beads into their own containers. The teacher uses music as a background. The same task is done with the children's eyes closed, the volume of music increased, and the number of beads dropped increased to further the development of this skill.
10. Children sit in a circle, holding bells. One child sits in the center with eyes closed. The teacher points to one child, and he rings his bell. The child in the center points to the direction of the sound. The child who rang the bell gets the next turn. This activity develops ability to discriminate among *front*, *back*, *left*, and *right*.
11. Potato chip can shakers: An even number of cans are covered with contact paper. Small amounts of rice, buttons, rocks, etc., are put in the cans so that two cans will have identical sounds. Each child takes turns shaking a can in front of other children with cans until he finds the same sound as his own.

SPEAKING

All of us have our own unique "talking quota." At five, the child is still very much in the exploratory world of sound and word play. The five will grope for words to present an idea, will stutter ("you know" and "and-uh-and"), will miss endings, will misuse words or use multisyllabic words, will

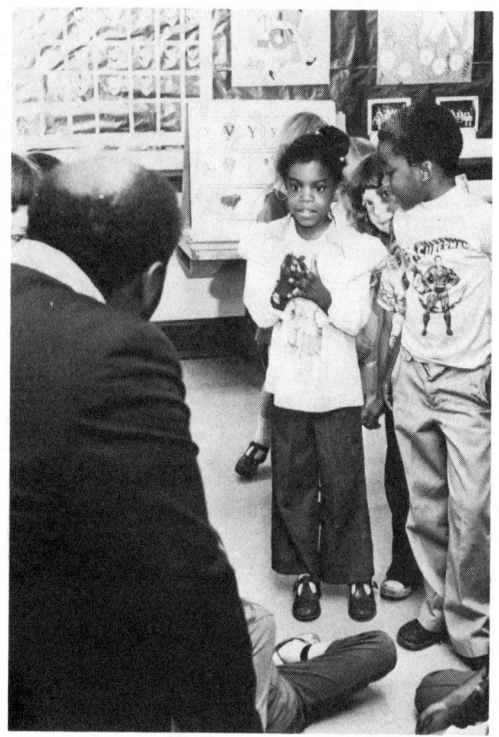

be easily distracted from a thought pattern, will chatter incessantly or talk not at all, will invent new words, will repeat or chant completely nonsensical phrases, or will delight in the big words that pop up in daily conversation. Differences are the norm.

The kindergarten teacher will encounter the bilingual child, the non–English-speaking child, the "perpetual talking machine," the silent child, the early talker, and the late talker. Regional dialects will be present, as will "secret" words, slang, "street" words, and colorful words. Yet, somehow, all of these children will be heard. Perhaps the most wonderful aspect of spoken language is the growth of vocabulary and the uniqueness of each child's speech. Each child's speech is creative, and that creativity needs to be encouraged. "Blum, blum, blum" is as appropriate to the five as is "supernumerary" or "rappelling"! The five is anything but predictable in speaking. I (M.R.) remember a precocious five-year-old who requested information about *quasars* and sent me on a merry chase to the university library and ultimately to *Fortune* Magazine.

Each five-year-old has a certain speaking style—a certain flair. Usually baby talk has disappeared, and the tongue experiments with words such as "delectable," "gloppy," "squishy," or "Fire, one!" (Stand aside in the classroom and listen to the flow of words, the interaction of children in a learning center, or a child requesting a committee meeting to find a solution to a problem. On a rainy day, eavesdrop on children playing school and hear your tone of voice, use of words, and even your inflections imitated to perfection!) Words can be tools or weapons as the child engages in dramatic play.

In a kindergarten one day, the "mother" was preparing the evening meal and directed the "father" to walk the "dog" until the food was ready. The "father" visited with neighbors along the street, commented on the weather and, in general, *was* an adult.

In the same kindergarten, an office had been set up and the "secretary" was busy typing a letter being dictated orally to her by her "employer." The words were most adult and appropriate to a thriving business. Telephone skills were being developed as well.

A healthy verbal ventilating can also occur in a classroom as sharp words are exchanged or anger is expressed in dramatic play. Children understand that words can hurt; and often, troubled family situations are revealed through puppetry or role playing.

The selection of words tells "Who I am" or establishes a role. One small kindergarten girl wanted to "evaluate" the puppet show just presented. One needs to keep in mind that "no matter how simple or complex it is, the child will learn (speak) the language heard most often spoken by the significant adults around him" (Spodek, 1972, p. 61).

Continuing, Spodek (p. 62) states:

> The speech patterns of children may differ in many ways. There can be differences in the pronunciation of words or in speech inflections. There may be differences in the labels ascribed to familiar things, so that what is called a "sack" in one area may be called a "bag" elsewhere. There may be syntactical differences among dialects. Syntactical differences make understanding difficult across dialects, for the structure of statements carries much of their meaning.

Bilingualism and a second language

With increasing mobility of our population comes the likelihood that many kindergartens will include bilingual children or children of non–English-speaking families. In both instances the children themselves are the greatest resource. Young children have a facility for language, enjoy word play, love to imitate, and want to communicate, to become part of the group.

Again, the teacher is the key—a model of clear, precise speech and a receptive, helping individual. If the classroom is flexible and provides opportunities for interchange and interaction for *all* children, the non–English-speaking child, with the help of other children, rapidly begins to learn the names and labels appropriate to the surroundings. Music, poetry, dance, choral verse, and nursery rhymes all contribute to the learning of new words.

Todd and Heffernan (1977, p. 413) remind us:

> The non–English-speaking child should be helped to understand that his "mother tongue" is another language spoken by many people in the world, but that he really needs to speak *two* languages—one to use in speaking to his family and friends at home, and another to use in school, where his teacher and most of his other friends speak English and help him have experiences with both his native language and English.

I (M.R.) remember walking to school daily with a boy from a Swedish-speaking family. Interests of young farm children being similar, it was not long before the boy was learning the English equivalents for his words and I was learning Swedish—in fact, we were both becoming quite adept in the other's language by the end of the year!

In another instance, a family where the mother was German and the father Indian delighted in the ability of their small son, who spoke German, Indian, and English and served as interpreter to each parent, neither of whom knew the other's native language. The boy was well aware of his capability and sometimes, mischievously, would interpret incorrectly!

Capitalizing on the many cultures and languages represented in a class can add much to the understanding of each child. Some teachers will post lists of words with English and other equivalents or label an object in two languages. As an extension of this, even in English, objects have different names, such as:

Elevator—lift
Radio—wireless
Vacation—holiday
Policeman—bobby
Car trunk—boot

A Vietnamese child shared a native song with English-speaking children, then went on to learn the English translation. The song was taped by the father of the child and played many times to the delight of all.

Many children's books and songs are available in other languages and with English translations. What better way to develop language capability than through sharing folk songs and dances of many ethnic groups in a kindergarten or in a school?

One of the best practical resources we have found for use with the non–English-speaking child is a manual by Nina Phillips (1968). The approach described was originally planned for volunteers in the Conversational English Program in New York, but teachers will find excellent suggestions in the manual. Phillips describes an audiovisual-lingual program that is associative in nature. The child *hears* the words, simultaneously *sees* and recognizes the objects, or observes the action and *says* the accompanying sentences. Key words are presented immediately, and concrete objects illustrate the key words. Key vocabulary words are always taught in the context of simple sentences.

Among the teaching aids described by Phillips (pp. 97-98) are the object box, picture games, action routines ("stand up," "come here," "raise your hands," etc.), instructional pictures, a picture file, and a category word list. To be kept in mind is the basic tenet that acquisition of a language may, in some ways, be compared to physical growth, since there are spurts of activity and intervals of rest. Progress is rapid at certain times; at other times, which may be called plateaus, improvement is not as apparent. Although improvement may be uneven, the length of time required to learn the language must be considered as a whole.

Another kind of useful resource is the foreign language films of outstanding children's books produced by Weston Woods. Films are available in Danish, Dutch, French, German, Italian, Russian, Spanish, Swedish, Turkish, and Welsh. Several captioned films, nonverbal films, and sing-alongs are also available. These films are a delightful way for the kindergarten child to make the transition from one language to another.

In planning for the bilingual child, the reader will find excellent help in Valverde's (1978) *Bilingual Education for Latinos*, in which the following conceptual framework (pp. 7-8) is suggested:

1. The learning of one's mother tongue takes place in the intimacy of one's family and carries with it memories, feelings, and emotions which become part of the self.
2. The acceptance and valuing of the pupil's native tongue nurture feelings of acceptance and valuing of self and family.
3. Human beings learn to listen and to speak before they learn to read and write. Thus, the natural order of language learning is listening, speaking, reading, and writing.
4. It is imperative that the student read first in the language which has been orally mastered at home.
5. There is an important relationship between oral language and its written form, for writing depends on the prior existence of speech.
6. Use and refinement of one's native language open up the content areas of math, science, literature, and all other facets of the curriculum which demand the processing of information presented through print.
7. A broad base of oral language should support any writing system to be learned if both oral and written language proficiency are the goals.

As kindergarten teachers, we are reminded that "the native language a child brings to his or her first school experience is a precious possession, and it is equal to the English language. No child is alingual. The school must use the child's native language as the mediator between the child's culture and that of the school and larger society" (Valverde, 1978, p. 9).

We have already indicated many ways in which a positive attitude and approach can help the bilingual or non-English-speaking child become a part of the kindergarten group. Another way to further this acceptance is through festivals, arts and crafts, and cooking. Sharing native foods and recipes develops appreciation for the heritage of others (and who has not enjoyed pizza, tacos, french bread, torte, shrimp tempura, and other marvelous and delicious foods!).

The five-year-old is a consumate imitator—skill in language is quickly developed.

Summary and additional thoughts

In a typical kindergarten, the teacher will encounter a variety of speech patterns and regional dialects reflecting the mobility of the present-day life-style of families. But most important to keep in mind is the fact that the fives need and want to communicate and share in the life of the classroom. The attitude, resourcefulness, and receptivity of the teacher are crucial in providing a setting for all children to develop appropriate language for every situation. Corcoran (1976), Meers (1976), and Pflaum (1974) speak to the concern of language development across social and cultural groups.

We know that adult recognition, a rich variety of experiences, encouragement of sensory activities and verbalization, a genuine respect for each child, active listening to each child, flexibility, and allowing a free rein of imagination and ample time for talk will do much to spur lively speech and communication. When speech development is the goal, silence is *not* golden.

The alert teacher will note early speech difficulties, immature speech, or divergent speech patterns and seek the counsel of the speech therapist or refer parents of the child to appropriate specialists.

Words and how we use them define the boundaries of our lives and our potential. Cultural differences of children can enrich the kindergarten. The five-year-old enjoys learning new words and phrases. Foreign words can be introduced informally through children's stories of their experiences or through songs, games, and stories. Adults from many cultures might serve as resource persons to the kindergarten. Holidays provide a natural way to introduce children to the pluralistic nature of the class. Puppetry and choral speaking can help children who are hesitant or afraid to discuss their backgrounds. Dance can often spur speech and sharing of experiences. The camera and pictures of "ourselves" can break down reserve and promote talking.

The Spanish-speaking child might share the music and vocabulary of the family and, in turn, acquire the English equivalent.

In this age of television, of instant replay, most kindergartners have access to the exciting world of "The Muppet Show" "Battlestar Galactica," "Wonder Woman," and "Roots"—and endless array of opportunities for conversation. Capitalizing on the moving scene of newspapers, movies, and television, one kindergarten teacher has introduced "News and Views" to supplant the old "Bring and Brag."

It is amazing how quickly, in a "helping" environment, the kindergarten child will understand, empathize, and acquire a working vocabulary and delight in the process—and come to appreciate *all* others and their contributions.

Appropriate speech patterns and the ability and desire to participate verbally should be the right of every child in kindergarten. A healthy personality and a feeling of "groupness" result when children express ideas and share with each other their accomplishments and interests.

"Speaking" ideas

Announcements
Choral verse
Dictation
Directions
Dramatic play
Filmstrips (being narrator)
Finger plays
Flannel board stories
Introductions
News
Original poetry
Original stories
Pictures that encourage discussion
Reports
Riddles, jokes, anecdotes
Social conversation
Telephone conversations
Topical concerns
  Clubs
  Families
  Favorite books
  Favorite foods
  Favorite movies
  Feelings
  Friends
  Hobbies
  Holidays
  Make-believe
  Personal experiences
  Pets
  Secrets
  Surprises
  Trips
  TV programs
  Unusual happenings
  Vacation
  Weather
  When I Grow Up
  Wishes

WRITING

Writing has always held fascination for the young child. From the first scribbles on newsprint or scrap paper to the triumph of doing one's name and then numbers and letters, writing has seemed a perfectly natural, "grown-up" process to the child—a process associated with school. It is a skill at once coveted and within the expectation of every kindergartner.

Handwriting is a tool—a means of effecting communication of ideas. Here again, differences in interest and abilities of the group will vary. Some fives are well coordinated and have long used clay, paints, scissors, crayons, felt-tipped pens or markers, and pencils. Others have not been permitted access to such common materials. Some may have had Magic Slates and even small chalkboards. Some may even have attempted another kind of writing—typewriting.

Most kindergartners have received letters or cards—valentines, birthday cards, and similar notes—that have been read to them. Printed invitations are within the experience of most, as are labels, signs, and other messages. Television, too, through programs and commercials, has heightened the child's awareness of the alphabet.

Some children, prior to kindergarten, may have had alphabet letters and magnetic boards or may have attempted to copy letters or signs they have seen. Others are disinterested.

Keeping the differences of the children in mind, the kindergarten teacher can find many spontaneous ways to provide experiences that extend readiness for writing to those who are mature enough for such activities. Capitalizing on the kinesthetic approach, the teacher might offer sandpaper letters or trays containing cornmeal or sand. For many children, it is a real delight to "write" on the blackboard.

Whatever techniques are used, most schools use manuscript form (a b c) for the young child because of the ease of formation of the letters and the later transition to cursive by merely connecting lines (*abc*). Children who have learned printing at home have little difficulty with the manuscript form.

We have seen primary typewriters in several kindergarten rooms. Children with poor eye-hand coordination and muscle control find the typewriter a useful tool for recording

their ideas. One classroom had an office corner, and the "secretary" could be observed typing while another child dictated a message. Would-be reporters enjoy the flow of words made possible by the typewriter.

Kindergarten teachers usually begin the writing experience with captions under pictures, announcements and notices posted about the room, newsletters, group stories, and poetry. Individual books about "me" are also popular. The child might dictate to the teacher or to an aide personal anecdotes that are then placed in a book format. Or the child might be helped to write a sentence describing an experience. One teacher encouraged the production of individual storybooks by placing them in the reading center for all to enjoy.

Perhaps the most imaginative display of a child's story was found in a classroom where the teacher had exhibited a child's story, "The Pink Puppy" by writing on newsprint and mounting it on one entire wall—as the story continued, it eventually covered the space from floor to ceiling. On the reading table was a dittoed copy of "The Pink Puppy" on pink paper! Needless to say, the five-year-old authoress proudly read her entire story and the class chimed in, in unison.

Class dictionaries are often developed in kindergartens, and "favorite word" boxes are kept by some children. As additional words are chosen, a card is placed in the box for easy reference.

Informality is the rule when one is presenting writing skills to the five-year-old—and this is done only for those who are ready. Spelling should not be an issue. However, when two kindergarten children were questioned in one primary school, the girl correctly spelled 28 words orally and the boy 22! Both initially said that they did not know how to spell.

Some children (such as the two mentioned above) seem to be intuitive spellers; and, of course, television has built an awareness of words. Children who accompany their mother shopping often know the names of cereals, various kinds of cookies, and other foods and extend their knowledge to toy labels and the like. We know of one three-year-old who demonstrated an ability to identify major brands of gasoline and, of course, also Pepsi, Coca-Cola, and Sprite.

In all writing and spelling activities, praise works wonders. The kindergartner likes to have papers displayed and enjoys showing others how to form the letters. If the teacher uses name tags early in the year, some children will quickly learn the names of friends—including how to write and spell them correctly.

Pressure is inappropriate. The varying maturity rates of children make handwriting difficult for some and easy for others. The kindergarten child is learning many skills simultaneously and often will reach a plateau in one skill area while spurting ahead in another. We need to realize, also, that copying from the chalkboard presents problems for some children, since their eye-hand development is unequal.

Margolin (1976, p. 110) reminds us that "the goals and objectives in writing programs for young children are directed toward helping them understand the purposes of writing, the worthiness of effectiveness, and the interesting forms of writing employed to express precisely what is intended."

In a relaxed, open kindergarten environment where the ideas and communication of all children are valued, writing skills grow naturally. When the five-year-old realizes that those "squiggles" on the page came from within "me" and convey the message intended, it is a moment to be enjoyed and celebrated.

You might try the activities in the following learning center on writing readiness:

Writing readiness

Susan Jenkins

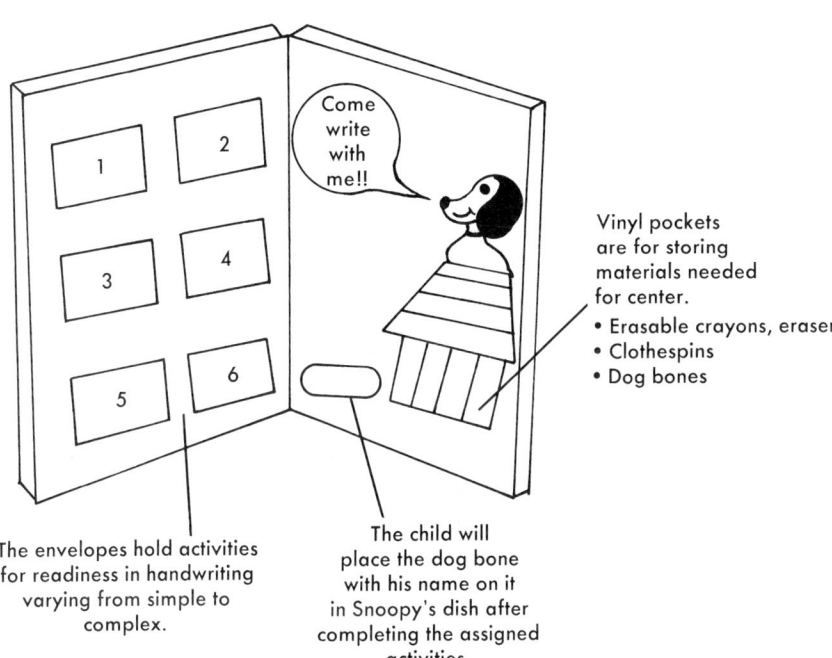

Vinyl pockets are for storing materials needed for center.
• Erasable crayons, eraser
• Clothespins
• Dog bones

The envelopes hold activities for readiness in handwriting varying from simple to complex.

The child will place the dog bone with his name on it in Snoopy's dish after completing the assigned activities.

ACTIVITY 1

OBJECTIVE: To reinforce visual discrimination of shapes.
ACTIVITY: The basic writing readiness shapes (triangle, square, and circle) are cut out of construction paper, laminated, and placed in an envelope. The child will take out the shapes one by one and place the correct shape on the sheet provided, which contains outlines of the shapes and are color coded.

ACTIVITY 2

OBJECTIVE: To reinforce visual motor responses.
ACTIVITY: The child will be provided with a set of heavy cardboard shapes that have been laminated and are outlined with sandpaper.
Example:

The child will first run a finger over the sandpaper, tracing the outline of the shape. Next the child will trace around the shapes with erasable crayons on a sheet provided.

Continued.

Writing readiness, cont'd

In the next activity, the child will trace over the same size shapes on laminated sheets; this time the shapes will appear as broken lines to be connected to form the shape.
Example:

ACTIVITY 3

OBJECTIVE: To reinforce visual discrimination, left-to-right progression, and fine motor coordination.
ACTIVITY: The child will be provided with a laminated sheet with 2-inch rulings, with shapes that have been cut from Masonite.
Example:

The child will place the shape on the designated line and trace around the shape with erasable crayons. Progressing from left to right, the child will trace as many shapes as possible on the line provided.

The child will then trace the same size shapes with erasable crayon. As in Activity 2, this time the shapes will appear as broken lines to be connected.

ACTIVITY 4

OBJECTIVE: To reinforce left-to-right progression.
ACTIVITY: The child will be provided with three sets of sequencing cards that involve knowing what happens first, second, and third. The child will select the card he thinks should appear first and attach the card to a clothesline with a clothespin. The child will continue the activity until all the cards are hung from the line.
Example:

The child can check his accuracy by turning the card over to see if the numeral and position of the card correspond.

The next two activity sheets involve having the child practice making straight lines and left-to-right progression by connecting arrows and broken lines from the left side of the paper to the right side.

Example:

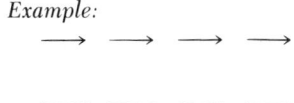

___ ___ ___ ___

ACTIVITY 5

OBJECTIVE: To match lowercase manuscript letters of the alphabet with capital letters.

ACTIVITY: The child will be provided with a card in which capital letters can be dialed on the left and lowercase letters on the right. The child will dial the card until the capital and lowercase letters match. The child can check this activity by turning the card over. If the child has successfully matched the capital and lowercase letters, the pictures will match on the back.

Example:

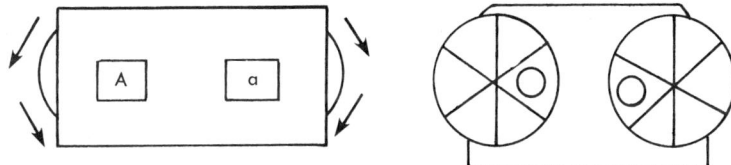

There are four cards, the letters are not in any order, and several of the letters are repeated twice.

ACTIVITY 6

OBJECTIVE: To reinforce visual discrimination and to provide practice in tracing and writing capital and lowercase manuscript letters.

ACTIVITY: The child will be provided with a laminated sheet with letters—capital and lowercase. The letters are ones that are often confused.

Example:

MN, EF, bd

The child will circle the letter that is different.

Next there are laminated sheets with capital letters on one side and lowercase ones on the other side. The child will first look at how the letter is formed—shown with arrows.

Example:

The child will follow the directions of the arrows by tracing the letter with his finger on fine-grade sandpaper. He will then trace the letter with his finger on the laminated sheet, following the directions of the arrows. The child will then connect the broken lines to form the letter. Finally, the child will attempt to write the letter himself.

Reading

No area is as replete with advice to teachers, research data, commercial interests, and varying instructional systems as is beginning reading. (Pflaum, 1974, p. 164)

Reading is a skill, part of the chain of the communication arts. Reading is the interpretation of writing, just as listening (or better, understanding) is the interpretation of speech (Walden, 1969, p. 43). Reading should be a natural process, as natural as speaking; yet, untold numbers of children and teachers, as well as parents, struggle to facilitate mastery of reading for each child.

We know that some children appear to learn to read without ever being taught and that some children learn to read through television or through a specific reading system, whether word by word, phonetic, linguistic, programmed, or ITA. Some children fail to learn to read whatever the materials or the method used.

In kindergarten, however the printed word is introduced, our concern must be for communication, for sharing, and for enjoyment. And we must be doubly concerned that no child be pressured through workbooks, "canned" programs, or well-meaning individuals to experience failure at a task too difficult for a particular maturational level.

Experts agree that the purpose of the reading program in kindergarten is to encourage positive attitudes toward reading. We would hope that all children might have access to many and varied books and other visual materials, begin to realize the many purposes of reading, and above all find pleasure in reading.

The issue at stake in many kindergartens and in many communities is that of readiness for reading and whether reading should be taught in kindergarten. The answer in many classrooms has been the introduction of dittoed sheets, specially prepared "readiness materials" or packaged programs, and, in some, formal reading instruction. The issue is a heated one, and often the child bears the brunt of the indecision and lack of information.

Historically, most of the professional education organizations have been concerned about practices in pre–first-grade reading instruction. National and regional conference programs have reflected symposia, speakers, exhibits, materials, and study groups with reading a major focus. In February of 1977, a representatives' committee from seven influential professional groups issued the following "Joint Statement of Concerns":

Reading and pre–first grade*
A joint statement of concerns about present practices
in pre–first-grade reading instruction and
recommendations for improvement

PRE–FIRST GRADERS NEED: Opportunities to express orally, graphically, and dramatically their feelings and responses to experiences;
    and
Opportunities to interpret the language of others whether it is written, spoken, or nonverbal.

---

*From International Reading Association, February 1977, in conjunction with the associations listed on p. 210.

TEACHERS OF PRE–FIRST GRADERS NEED: Preparation which emphasizes developmentally appropriate language experiences for all pre–first graders, including those ready to read or already reading;
   and
The combined efforts of professional organizations, colleges, and universities to help them successfully meet the concerns outlined in this document.

CONCERNS
1. A growing number of children are enrolled in prekindergarten and kindergarten classes in which highly structured pre-reading and reading programs are being used.
2. Decisions related to schooling, including the teaching of reading, are increasingly being made on economic and political bases instead of on our knowledge of young children and of how they best learn.
3. In a time of diminishing financial resources, schools often try to make "a good showing" on measures of achievement that may or may not be appropriate for the children involved. Such measures all too often dictate the content and goals of the programs.
4. In attempting to respond to pressures for high scores on widely used measures of achievement, teachers of young children sometimes feel compelled to use materials, methods, and activities designed for older children. In so doing, the teachers may impede the development of intellectual functions such as curiosity, critical thinking, and creative expression, and, at the same time, promote negative attitudes toward reading.
5. A need exists to provide alternative ways to teach and evaluate progress in pre-reading and reading skills.
6. Teachers of pre–first graders who are carrying out highly individualized programs without depending upon commercial readers and workbooks need help in articulating for themselves and the public *what* they are doing and *why*.

RECOMMENDATIONS
1. Provide opportunities for reading experiences as an integrated part of the broader communication process that includes listening, speaking, and writing. A language experience approach is an example of such integration.
2. Provide for a broad range of activities both in scope and in content. Include direct experiences that offer opportunities to communicate in different settings with different persons.
3. Foster children's affective and cognitive development by providing materials, experiences, and opportunities to communicate what they know and how they feel.
4. Continually appraise how various aspects of each child's total development affect his/her reading development.
5. Use evaluative procedures that are developmentally appropriate for the children being assessed and that reflect the goals and objectives of the instructional program.
6. Ensure feelings of success for all children in order to help them see themselves as persons who can enjoy exploring language and learning to read.
7. Plan flexibly in order to accommodate a variety of learning styles and ways of thinking.
8. Respect the language the child brings to school, and use it as a base for language activities.
9. Plan activities that will cause children to become active participants in the learning process rather than passive recipients of knowledge.

Continued.

Reading and pre–first grade, cont'd

10. Provide opportunities for children to experiment with language and simply to have fun with it.
11. Require that preservice and in-service teachers of young children be prepared in the teaching of reading in a way that emphasizes reading as an integral part of the language arts as well as of total curriculum.
12. Encourage developmentally appropriate language learning opportunities in the home.

THE COMMITTEE

Jeanne Corbin, Virginia Plunkett—American Association of Elemetary-Kindergarten-Nursery Educators
Dell Kjer, Alberta Meyer—Association for Childhood Education International
Barbara Day—Association for Supervision and Curriculum Development
Dolores Durkin, Joanne Nurss, Lloyd Ollila, Dorothy Strickland—International Reading Association
William Pharis—National Association of Elementary School Principals
Georgiana Engstrom, Marilyn Smith—National Association for the Education of Your Children
Jessie Roderick—National Council of Teachers of English

We concur emphatically with the recommendations as stated and urge that individuals working with kindergartens consider thoughtfully each of the recommendations and work toward implementation.

Other authorities have also expressed deep concern. In *Reading: A Conversation with Kenneth Goodman* (1976), Goodman shares a number of thoughts. Defining reading as a *process* that demands a reader attempting to get at meaning and using whole language to do so, Goodman states that we need to find simple, natural ways of letting print talk to children. Furthermore, he believes that we have underestimated the amount of natural learning to read that takes place in society because we have been looking in the wrong places. Goodman also believes that the key factor in early stages is to create a "literate" environment wherein children are constantly exposed to print and made aware of its functions, how it works, and its subtle differences and similarities.

Speaking of the importance of environment, Durkin (1976, p. 96) also considers the teacher whose own language provides children with a model worthy of admiration and imitation as well as with a positive attitude toward words.

We know that parents who read tend to encourage children to read. We know that teachers who cherish words develop children who appreciate and enjoy words. Indeed, kindergarten is too late to begin developing reading skills. Communication—reading, if you will—begins in the cradle!

READINESS

Entire articles and entire volumes have been written about readiness. Definitions of readiness abound, and most underrate the concept presented. Characteristics involved in being able to read attract attention. Authors offer comments on progression into reading, and countless reading readiness games can be found on the commercial market. Teachers are asked, "When and how do you *do* your readiness?"

Readiness is multidimensional—a state of being, unique to the individual child and to the task at hand. Readiness cannot be hurried; neither should it be ignored. Readiness must be measured in many ways—readiness is maturational. Readiness cannot be taught or practiced through devices, paper-and-pencil techniques, walking balance beams, or bouncing balls for eye-hand coordination. Neither is readiness automatic or equal throughout a group of kindergarten children. No single criterion will pinpoint readiness for all children; neither can we predict that all children will be "ready" to read if exposed to the same experiences in the same classroom situation.

In 1976 the Ohio Department of Education offered the following considerations for teachers. *Reading readiness:*

... does not surface at the time of the sixth birthday nor coincide with the young child's coming into a school situation.
... is a cultivated trait.
... is necessary before formal reading can be taught.
... is structured upon the relationships between learning to talk and learning to read.
... involves all aspects of human development: cognitive, physical, social, and emotional growth.
... is structured on the principle of individual differences.
... comes about through multisensory experiences.
... provides experiences for children to think verbally.
... develops sequentially in an ongoing spiral.
... is a total learning experience.
... as expressed in the measurement of child development, indicates that the child is ready for instructional reading when a mental age of six is evidenced.

An excellent, definitive source that merits careful study is Downing and Thackray's *Reading Readiness.* These authors (1967, p. 37) believe that the investment of time in talking with children and in sharing the content of books with them is probably the most certain method of helping them get ready for learning to read. This applies at school as well as at home.

Downing and Thackray (p. 98) provide a checklist for the teacher that is easily used. However, their strongest stance is taken in regard to the readiness of the *teacher*, checked by such questions as:

1. How am I fitting my demands in reading to the child's level of readiness?
2. Do the reading books fit the child's experiences of life in his particular environment?
3. Do the books fit his language or dialect?
4. Do the teaching methods fit the child's level of ability?
5. Does the alphabet in which the child's books are printed fit his needs in cognitive development?

A very positive statement is made by Downing and Thackray (p. 99) in their closing discussion: "Reading readiness is a state of the teacher as well as of the child. She will take care, not only to fit the child for reading, but also to fit the reading to the child."

Another highly recommended source for those working with the fives is Ollila's (1977) *The Kindergarten Child and Reading*, a collection of essays discussing interest, achievement, readiness, scheduling, and kindergarten reading materials.

For the teacher working with linguistically and culturally different children, Zintz (1977, p. 322) prefers materials written by teachers themselves and culturally related materials. Language problems, suggestions, and assessment of readiness factors are included.

APPROACHES TO READING

There are probably as many approaches to and materials for beginning reading as there are children in the kindergarten class. Because this text does describe *programs and practices*, brief descriptions of the seven major approaches follow.

The widely used *basal reading programs* (1) control vocabulary in terms of frequency of word usage. Children usually begin with a "big book" that is aimed at developing readiness and then proceed to levels of preprimers and sometimes primers. Most basal programs for kindergarten feature readiness activities of various kinds centered on auditory discrimination, visual discrimination, the alphabet, left-to-right progression, and similar skills. Since the early seventies, programs have a stronger phonics orientation and greater variety in terms of stories and content. These systems also provide extensive teachers' manuals, workbooks, and related materials.

Phonetic reading systems (2) control vocabulary in terms of sound/symbol correspondence. Critics of the program label the content as artificial and contrived in that natural speech patterns of children are not followed.

Individualized programs (3) utilize programmed materials or trade books that offer pupil options. Usually experience charts or pupil-dictated stories precede the use of either type of material. A wide variety of books must be readily available in the classroom. Students progress at their own rate, and small-group discussion may be used for sharing of books mutually selected.

ITA (Initial Teaching Alphabet) (4) adapts the printed symbols to provide one-to-one correspondence between sound and print. A gradual adjustment to conventional orthography is necessary.

Similar in philosophy to ITA are the *rebus systems* (5), which are pictorial in nature and then adjust to conventional orthography. In the kindergarten, labeling with pictures symbolic of words would begin such an approach.

Systems such as *DISTAR* (Science Research Associates) (6) involve a highly structured, decoding approach.

The *language experience approach* (7) promotes use of children's dictated and written stories as reading material. (Lee and Allen's [1963] *Learning to read through experience* is useful here.) Sometimes called the language arts approach, this system, when and if one begins reading for some children in kindergarten, is our preference because it encompasses all aspects of verbal communication. We have said earlier that the communication arts are interrelated and interdependent—the quality of "wholeness" must be maintained. By using the language of the kindergarten child as a beginning, one can help each child develop uniquely in listening, speaking, writing, and reading.

As an aside, the reader is urged to acquire a copy of Sylvia Ashton-Warner's (1971) *Teacher* and learn the firsthand experience of a creative individual as she guided native children into reading through individualization and language experiences.

Among the "givens" in the implementation of the language arts approach Durkin (1976, pp. 166-175) suggests:

1. Flexible scheduling
2. Pervasive language arts concern
3. Small-group instruction
4. Teacher aides (volunteers) who
   - Direct practice and review
   - Assist with materials
   - Guide conversations and read stories
   - Help with clerical duties

The more salient features of language experience as stated by Pflaum (1974, p. 190) are:

1. Use of children's oral language for reading material; the child's written language therefore parallels his spoken language.
2. Built-in provision for dialect and experiential variation.
3. A personalized instructional approach; the

teacher and child share important thoughts, experiences, and observations.
4. A natural means for an integrated language arts program; reading, writing, listening (to others' stories), and speaking (dictating) are all involved in the production of language-experience stories.
5. An open enough system to encourage creativity in children and in teaching.
6. Ease in combining the system with other methods of teaching reading.

Further elaboration of the language experience system is offered by Durkin (1976), Lee and Allen, and Pflaum. A very cogent point is made by Durkin (1976, p. 162) in a brief statement regarding an advantage of the language arts approach that we might seldom recognize:

> The broader perspective becomes a means of steering away from the label "early reading program." This could be of monumental importance because such a label too often results in the expectation that every child participating in the program will read. Whenever this happens, pressure is put not only on the children but also on their teacher. The result all too often is exactly what nobody should want for potential beginners in reading: routine and uniform instruction.

Available reading materials in the form of periodicals for and about children are listed at the end of the chapter. Pflaum (pp. 187-188) provides a listing of the major commercially available reading programs.

Remember, no one reading system is best for all children; children learn to read in a variety of situations and often teach themselves.

SUMMARY

Do we teach reading in kindergarten? What, then, is the answer to this exceedingly complex question? No, if we are referring to memorization, dittoed sheets, word drills, routine exercises on workbook pages, uniform expectations, a premium on quiet—and the expectation that every child complete all exercises on the page or all levels of commercial materials. Yes, if we are creating interest and awareness in words and in books, if we are creating personalized materials, building a background of experiences, and responding to questions about words—if there is "wanting to read."

A widely respected authority in the field of reading, Dolores Durkin (1978) states it best: "Reading instruction can begin in kindergarten—but conditions must be right." Durkin's article, reprinted on pp. 214-217, warrants thoughtful consideration by all those privileged to work with and know the five-year-old.

Text continued on p. 222.

Pre-first grade starts in reading: where do we stand?*
Reading instruction can begin in kindergarten — but conditions must be right.

Dolores Durkin**

Recently, a mother of four children expressed bewilderment about school practices related to the timing of beginning reading instruction. She commented, "My oldest child, who happens to be the brightest of our children, was not taught to read until about the second month of first grade. The youngest is now in kindergarten, and reading instruction has already begun. Why the difference?"

Those who think that the difference can be explained with carefully documented facts had better take another look at the research literature. If they do and are patient enough to examine relevant publications from about 1920 to the present, they will be forced to reach the following conclusion: Acceptance of proposals for the timing of beginning instruction in reading depends less on their quality than on when they are made. With a few details, let me explain why this disquieting conclusion just happens to be correct.

From approximately 1900 until the late 1950s, notions about child growth and development were overwhelmingly influenced first by G. Stanley Hall and then by his student, Arnold Gesell (Durkin, 1968). Because of their prominence and prolific publications, the two were able to convince the educational world for a very long time that hereditary and maturational factors determine when and how quickly children reach and pass through developmental stages.

READINESS FOR READING

Initial ideas about readiness for beginning reading, which were proposed in the 1920s, fit in perfectly with this view of development. They were quickly accepted even though facts to support them were missing. Essentially, this first interpretation saw readiness as something that occurred automatically at a given stage of development, which was later defined as a mental age of about 6.5 years (Morphett and Washburne, 1931). Although research by Arthur Gates in the 1930s (Gates, 1937; Gates and Bond, 1936) repeatedly showed that initial success with reading is affected more by the quality of instruction than by mental age, the first interpretation of readiness continued to enjoy unquestioning acceptance. Why?

The facts uncovered by Gates did not fit in with the stream of popular thought, which is why they were frequently quoted in the 1960s, not the 1930s.

EFFECTS OF SPUTNIK

What was popular in the 1960s was clearly linked to the dramatic effects of the launching of Sputnik I by the Russians in 1957. Among the more apparent effects was national insecurity followed by the push not only to do everything better in our schools, but also to do it sooner. "Doing it sooner" attracted attention to quite different theories about development—for

---

*From *Educational Leadership*, 1978, 36(3), 174-177. Reprinted with permission of the Association for Supervision and Curriculum Development and Dolores Durkin. Copyright © 1978 by the Association for Supervision and Curriculum Development. All rights reserved.
**Professor of Education, University of Illinois at Urbana—Champaign, Urbana, Ill.

example, the theories found in Hunt's *Intelligence and Experience* (1961), and in Bloom's *Stability and Change in Human Characteristics* (1964). Both books emphasized not only the importance of experiences for development, but also their unique importance during the pre–first-grade years.

If publications like these had appeared at another time, only graduate students would have known of their existence. Their appearance in the 1960s, however, made them so widely attractive that nobody seemed to notice or care that they offered only hypotheses to be tested, not facts to be implemented. And so the rush was on to teach everything sooner—including reading.

CURRENT KINDERGARTEN PRACTICES

It is unfortunate that educators who made decisions to start teaching reading in kindergarten rather than in first grade overlooked the details of Gates' research. As was mentioned, his studies showed that a child's success with beginning reading is largely determined by the quality of the instruction made available. However, because it has been the timing rather than the quality of beginning instruction that has won attention, it is now exceedingly common to find kindergarten reading programs being rooted in whole class drill on phonics.

Why such an unfortunate practice is common can be explained by a number of factors, the most important of which is the kindergarten teacher's lack of preparation to teach reading. Unprepared teachers who are put in the position of *having* to teach it find great comfort in workbooks and ditto sheets, many of which focus on phonics. The large number of children typically found in kindergartens makes it very tempting to use these materials with an entire class; and so we have whole class drill on phonics. Seeing the drill tempts one to say, "No reading in the kindergarten—please!" However, certain facts suggest that this is not the best response.

One such fact is that many five-year-olds are more than ready to read; some, indeed, have already begun (Durkin, 1966, 1974-75). Another important fact is that individual kindergarten teachers are able to demonstrate year after year that five's can be taught to read in ways that are not only productive, but also enjoyable for the children. Since space does not allow for detailed descriptions of what they do, let me just outline what is essential for any reading program designed for young children.

ESSENTIALS OF SUITABLE PROGRAMS

Underlying the essentials to be described here is a basic assumption; namely, that it is impossible to know whether any given child is ready to read until he/she is given an opportunity to learn. Since children arrive in kindergarten with different abilities and interests, it follows that learning opportunities ought to be characterized by variety in methodology. At the start, whole words of special interest can be featured. Later, opportunities for the children to learn to print should be available, because research indicates that some pre–first graders are more interested in printing than in reading and, in fact, become readers through their efforts with printing and spelling (Durkin, 1966).

Later, as reading vocabularies begin to grow, known words can be used to help children understand the alphabetic nature of our writing system. However, only if children demonstrate the ability to understand and remember letter-sound relationships should phonics instruction be pursued. To do otherwise is to foster negative attitudes toward reading, and perhaps toward school itself.

Continued.

Pre–first grade starts in reading, cont'd

Since oral language is the foundation of ability in reading, every kindergarten—whether it does anything with reading or not—is obligated to do everything possible to enhance that. Among other things, interesting experiences should allow for acquisition of knowledge, for concept development, and for enlarged listening-speaking vocabularies.

All this can be summarized by saying that the best of kindergarten programs will have a language arts orientation.*

EXPECTATIONS FOR KINDERGARTEN PROGRAMS

Because of the great differences found in any group of five's, preestablished expectations about how much all should learn are indefensible. Ideally, a kindergarten language arts program will neither impede a child's progress nor will it make unrealistic demands. Consequently, when the ideal is achieved, different children can be expected to have different kinds and amounts of abilities by the end of the year.

This suggests another important point—the need for kindergarten and first-grade teachers to be in close communication. In fact, it is only when first-grade teachers are both willing and able to build on what is accomplished in the kindergarten that it makes any sense to even consider the possibility of starting reading earlier.

PREPARATION OF KINDERGARTEN TEACHERS

Clearly, what has been described as an appropriate way to ease kindergartners into reading is not for the amateur teacher. Yet, even today, many who are attempting to teach reading at that level have had no preparation to do so. Unfortunately, some who seek help in a reading methods course often find that what is available on college and university campuses covers the entire elementary school. While the broad focus provides perspective, it does not allow for the detailed attention to the beginning level that kindergarten teachers require. So we have another need if the best of programs is to be assembled: reading methods courses that are designed especially for nursery school, kindergarten, and first-grade teachers.

NEW GOALS REQUIRE NEW SETTINGS

Even expertly prepared kindergarten teachers cannot put what they know into practice when the class is too big. Although it may have made sense in days gone by to assign as many as 25 children to a kindergarten in the morning and another 25 in the afternoon, changed expectations demand something different. Fewer children in each group is one needed change. The assistance of an aide is another, once a teacher has both the knowledge and the motivation required for a really good program. Admittedly, both changes will add to school budgets that are already too small. However, if expectations for teaching reading in the kindergarten continue, it is unfair to provide kindergarten teachers with settings that only allow for babysitting. Besides, the kind of program that has been briefly sketched is one possible way to reduce the high cost of remedial instruction later on.

As has been pointed out, the decision to teach reading in the kindergarten should not be taken lightly. Nor should it be made without regard for the fundamental importance of

---

*How these recommendations can be implemented is described in detail in one of the references (Durkin, 1976) listed at the end of the article.

oral language. While the readiness of a particular group of five's must always be considered, so too must the readiness of the kindergarten faculty to teach reading.

If taught well, kindergarten reading will have a positive effect on five-year-olds not only in terms of their abilities, but also in the way they feel about themselves and about going to school. If taught well, kindergarten reading should also have an immediate impact on the first-grade program and an eventual one on all other grades. Without such a ripple effect, kindergarten reading becomes little more than an isolated event—perhaps not worth the effort it takes.

REFERENCES

Benjamin S. Bloom. *Stability and Change in Human Characteristics.* New York: John Wiley and Sons, 1964.

Dolores Durkin. *Children Who Read Early.* New York: Teachers College Press, Columbia University, 1966.

Dolores Durkin. *Teaching Young Children to Read.* Boston: Allyn and Bacon, Inc., 1976.

Dolores Durkin. "When Should Children Begin to Read?" In: *Innovation and Change in Reading Instruction.* Sixty-seventh Yearbook of the National Society for the Study of Education, Part II. Chicago: University of Chicago Press, 1968.

Dolores Durkin. "A Six-Year Study of Children Who Learned to Read in School at the Age of Four." *Reading Research Quarterly* 10(1):9-61; 1974-75.

Arthur I. Gates. "The Necessary Mental Age for Beginning Reading." *Elementary School Journal* 37(7):497-508; March 1937.

Arthur I. Gates and Guy L. Bond. "Reading Readiness: A Study of Factors Determining Success and Failure in Beginning Reading." *Teachers College Record* 37(9):679-85; May 1936.

J. McVicker Hunt. *Intelligence and Experience.* New York: The Ronald Press Co., 1961.

M. V. Morphett and C. Washburne. "When Should Children Begin to Read?" *Elementary School Journal* 31(7):496-503; March 1931.

One teacher has suggested the following learning center in relation to reading readiness:

Reading readiness
Gayle Hottell

BEFORE A CHILD IS READY FOR READING HE MUST BE:
1. Aware of language
2. Physically able to hear and see symbols
3. Intellectually and emotionally mature
4. Able to use vocabulary and body concepts as a social exchange
5. Able to perceive a printed page as a means of communication

Continued.

Reading readiness, cont'd

READING READINESS TASKS
1. Picture interpretation
2. A speaking vocabulary that enables the child to be understood in class
3. Left-to-right orientation
4. Family and neighborhood experiences
5. Desire to read
6. Ability to attend to the task at hand
7. A sense of sequence
8. Ability to follow directions
9. Ability to discriminate visual forms (letters and words)
10. Ability to discriminate similarities and differences in sounds (rhyme sounds and initial consonant sounds)
11. Ability to see spatial relations and other visual-motor perceptions*

ACTIVITIES
1. Tracking.
    a. Materials: Dittoed sheets.
    b. Procedure: The child uses his finger and traces the pathways.
2. Visual discrimination.
    a. Materials: Paste, picture, cardboard, and clear contact paper.
    b. Procedure: Paste the picture on cardboard. Put contact paper over the picture. Cut the picture into large pieces. Children put the pieces together as they would a jigsaw puzzle.
3. Left-to-right orientation.
    a. Materials: Cardboard, clear contact paper, marking pencil, and guide sheet.
    b. Procedure: The child draws a line from 1 to 2, 3 to 4, etc. Vary lines—wiggly, straight, zigzag etc.
4. Listening and visual skills.
    a. Materials: Record player, and record and book stories.
    b. Procedure: Let the child choose a story. The listening area should be a comfortable setting.
5. Visual discrimination game: "Spin and Win."
    a. Materials: Cardboard, clear contact paper, and pen.
    b. Procedure: Make a spinner with the numerals 1 to 10. Make cards with pictures having anywhere from one to ten objects. Each player spins in turn. If the pointer lands on a numeral, the player takes a card with that number of objects on it. If the pointer lands on "no turn," the player loses a turn. The game continues until all cards are taken. The player with the most cards wins. Two to four children can play.
6. Visual discrimination: color words.
    a. Materials: Cardboard, crayons, and clear contact paper.
    b. Procedure: The child matches the correct color word to the correct color. ("Coloring time is over in Miss Muffet's classroom. The crayons need to be put back in the crayon

---

*From Harris and Smith. *Reading instruction.* New York: Holt, Rinehart & Winston, 1978, p. 138.

box in the correct order. Can you help Miss Muffet by matching each crayon to the correct color word?")

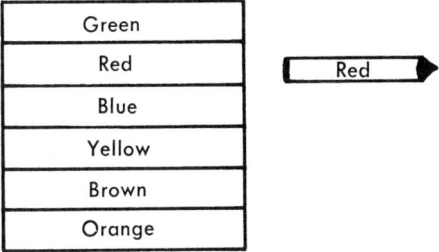

7. Visual discrimination: matching shapes.
   a. Materials: Cardboard and clear contact paper.
   b. Procedure: Have three long strips of cardboard containing the basic shapes. Make pictures containing these shapes. Cards are shuffled and played face down in a pile on the table. Each player in turn draws a card from the pile. If the card matches a shape, it is played next to the shape card. The first one to get two of each shape wins. Two to four children can play, or this can be done individually.

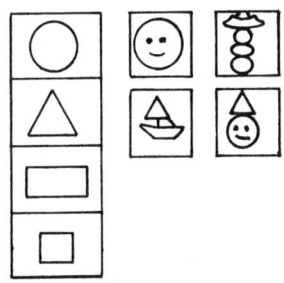

8. Visual memory: sequencing.
   a. Materials: Catalog pictures, tagboard, clear contact paper, and pen.
   b. Procedure: Put a variety of pictures on the tagboard. Write the names of the pictures on the back of the tagboard. Vary the number of pictures on the tagboard. Have the child look at the pictures for a brief period of time. Take the pictures away and ask the child what pictures he saw—in order.
9. Fine motor skills and letter identification.
   a. Materials: Tagboard, pen, clear contact paper, and damp paper towel.
   b. Procedure: Put letters of the alphabet on the tagboard and cover with contact paper. Have the child make his own letter beneath the one already printed. Erase with a wet paper towel.
10. Letter identification: capital and lower case.
    a. Materials: Tagboard, felt-tipped pens or markers, and clear contact paper.
    b. Procedure: Print letters on the tagboard. Color code with shapes on the back. Cover with contact paper. The child matches capital with lowercase letters. The child self-checks by looking at the shapes on the back. This can also be done in reverse by matching the shapes and checking the letters.

Continued.

Reading readiness, cont'd

11. Letter identification.
    a. Materials: Egg carton, pen, and buttons.
    b. Procedure: Print letters of the alphabet in each cup of the egg carton. Put a button in the carton. Close the carton and have the child shake, then open it. The child is to say the letter where the button lands.
12. Tactile and mental images.
    a. Materials: Old sock, can, and objects.
    b. Procedure: Slip the sock over the can and cut off the toe. The can contains objects that start with the same letter sound. The child must put his hand through the sock, feel the objects, and identify them. He checks by pulling the object out of the can.
13. Tactile and visual discrimination: slow-moving shapes.
    a. Materials: Tagboard, crayon, and clear contact paper.
    b. Procedure: Draw turtles with shapes on the bodies. Color and cover with contact paper. Make matching shapes and cover with contact paper. The child matches shapes that vary in size. ("Tim, Ted, and Tommy turtles are ready to begin a race. Before they are allowed to start, they must match all the shapes on their shells. Can you help them find their correct shapes so they can begin the race?")
14. To build meaningful sight vocabulary: "Laugh-in."
    a. Materials: Tagboard, clear contact paper, and pen.
    b. Procedure: Cover pictures that show feelings. On pieces of tagboard write words that name feelings—angry, sad, funny, happy. After the word is pronounced by either teacher or child, the child is asked to match the word with the picture that depicts that feeling.
15. Sight words.
    a. Materials: Tagboard, pen, and tape.
    b. Procedure: Write each child's name on tagboard and place on the table in front of the child. The child learns to recognize his name. In early stages the child can trace his name using his finger.
16. Listening skills: comprehension.
    a. Materials: interesting books.
    b. Procedure: Read a story to the child on a one-to-one basis or to the class. Ask questions pertaining to the story.
17. Weaving place mat: left-to-right orientation, fine motor skills.
    a. Materials: Construction paper strips, construction paper cut with slits.
    b. Procedure: Show the child how to start from the left and go over and under all the way to the right side.
18. Interest in reading.
    a. Materials: Books.
    b. Procedure: Have a collection of children's books out where the child can use them readily.

CHECKLIST

Each activity is color coded by a shape. When a child completes an activity, he places an identical shape next to his name.

	★	○	□	▭	△	〜
Tom	★	○	□	▭		
Sue	★	○	□			
Bob	★	○				
Ann	★					

FEELING AWARD

For every three activities done, the child receives an award.

Television

Television is a fact of life. Television is seen and heard in virtually every American household. The five-year-old in kindergarten will be as familiar with the characters on the TV screen as he is with the child next door. We know that both children and adults spend large amounts of time watching television, perhaps as much as 20 to 30 hours per week. We are, indeed, the television generation. In fact, only sleeping takes up more time than TV viewing!

Television is extremely influential in the realm of communication; thus, we need to consider its impact on the five-year-old.

It is appropriate for those of us concerned with the young child to heighten our level of awareness regarding not only the programs watched by young children but also how we might capitalize on the positive aspects of TV viewing and ameliorate the negative.

Perhaps the simplest way to make a beginning would be to listen to children as they discuss favorite programs and characters, and observe their actions and reactions modeled from those characters. Another approach might be to survey the group as to viewing habits. (Certainly the teacher's responsibility would include reviewing the Saturday morning cartoons—the programs that seem to appeal most to children—and discussing with parents the TV-viewing habits of their children. Access to a television set in the classroom could also provide a beginning.

Kindergarten children like to be entertained. They enjoy action, thrills, humor, slapstick, family situations, animal stories, and variety shows. Often they are using television to live out a fantasy, to escape from the home situation, to "have something to do," to try out roles, to gain information, to dispel loneliness and boredom, and as a parent substitute. That the child can also "tune in and out" is evident. I (M.R.) observed a class of five-year-olds one day watching "Sesame Street." Little attention was being directed to the dialogue, but when the jingles and commercials were interjected, everyone chimed in enthusiastically and everyone *knew* the content! And to the extreme, even our snacks and comfort breaks are synchronized to TV schedules.

CONCERNS

The five-year-old is vulnerable and impressionable and, as we have said before, a consumate imitator. Thus, the concerns regarding TV viewing are many. Television is essentially a passive activity, almost addictive to the young viewer. Playtime and family-related activities become second choice, and simple contemplative solitude is a rarity. In some households, "good talk" does not exist. Television also provides many instant solutions and instant gratification—an unrealistic world.

One colleague spoke of information overload—of constant input with little need to "do" anything. Much of the concern centers about excessive violence in the programs presented. Studies have shown that watching violence tends to produce more aggressive behavior, especially among young children— a kind of desensitizing to feelings occurs. Fear is also generated, as is confusion between fact and fantasy. Unrealistic expectations may also be stimulated. Teachers report that children are impatient with long or involved tasks. Parents report that young children are particularly vulnerable to commercials—a fact all of us can attest to when a child accompanies us to the supermarket! Faulty perceptions of the world at work also result, with a distorted picture of women, minorities, police, etc.

A very pointed question is asked by Singer and Singer (1979, p. 52): "Is human imagination going down the tube?" The position they take is that it is entirely possible that our capacity for sustained attention—for imaginative and deliberate thought—is being altered by TV viewing.

Singer and Singer suggest that the rapid pace and the constant intrusion of new material on the screen seem to interfere with learning. In their experimentation, children seemed to benefit more from slower paced programs, such as "Mister Rogers' Neighborhood," because time was allowed to "savor" the material. Children tended to become more imaginative and more cooperative, and they smiled and concentrated more than children watching "Sesame Street" during the same experimental time period.

Could it be, as these authors suggest, that we need time to mentally replay materials just witnessed and also to link pictures and sounds to word labels?

Both researchers believe that the human imagination is one of the great miracles of evolution, and they recommend slower moving programs, more sustained images, and less frenetic activity. Both also posit that emphasis on shorter commercials and continuous chopping up of material has gone too far even for commercial interests. Television, they say, could stimulate thought rather than produce a kind of mindless staring.

BENEFITS

Certainly, the five-year-old is also the beneficiary of television. The vocabulary and store of knowledge is expanded—skill in reading can result. One four-year old garnered the rudiments of reading while sitting before the television set, munching dry cereal and asking from time to time of his mother, "What does _____ spell?" Reading, for him, was effortless, at will, and a completely natural process facilitated by television.

The panorama of the world is revealed through television. The multiplicity of cultures, life-styles, and possibilities are on display.

Educational television offers a wide variety of worthwhile programs to tempt the child and the family. Television can also provide a way of "trying on life" without the risks and hazards of reality. Another benefit to the homebound or institutionalized is accessibility of the world shared by others in a more active role.

TV viewing can spark dialogue, researching, questioning, reading, and travel, as well as writing. In the kindergarten classroom, communication skills can be practiced through basing an activity on a shared viewing experience.

Much incidental learning can be accrued from television, particularly if adult and child view a program together. Values, taste, and appreciation can build from such shared episodes. Programs using puppets, fantasy, and make-believe can all foster prosocial values and behavior. We must not discount the role model effect as the five-year-old observes the athlete, the sports figure, or the humanitarian at work. Good, wholesome entertainment is a legitimate offering of television.

GUIDELINES

We must accept the fact that television is here to stay. Rather than deplore the amount of viewing time of young children, ask how we can capitalize on such time and build on it. Parents and teachers, in concert, must offer guidance in the choice of programs viewed and must be aware of fatigue factors and of total time spent—in fact, must be aware that a flick of the off knob is often the best solution to the overstimulated young child. TV viewing can be limited to a reasonable period, can be a shared enjoyable interlude, and can indeed be a reward.

In many families, young children watch television as much as they want and when they want, with little adult intervention or supervision. Compromises can be effected, and discussions of programs, values portrayed, and activities suggested can result in a mutual feedback system.

Television can be positive or negative, depending on what the teacher or parent does with it. The use of television as an educational tool needs to be expanded. Bridges to other human experience can be built. Children can be helped to become very effective consumers after an experience with a defective product obtained through TV advertising. Product comparison can be stimulated.

Good literature, drama, and music can become a part of everyday life as adult and child together share TV offerings. (Try sitting down with a five-year-old before the screen; respond to the questions, which may come rapidly, exclaim together over the wonders of nature being portrayed, or sing together the melodies heard.) Once such an experience is shared, both the adult and the child will seek other such opportunities. Often a live performance or a trip to observe a phenomenon viewed on television can extend learning and enjoyment. Watching the Monte Carlo circus might provoke expressions of desire to see the "real" circus, or watching "The Muppet Show" or "Charlie Brown" might suggest real-life situations the child would enjoy. Certainly, the imagination flourishes, and the laughter that ensues binds the viewers together.

Kindergartners need guidance from adults in television viewing. Consider:

1. What is the purpose of the program?
2. Is the pace appropriate to allow appreciation and absorption?
3. Has the child experienced a balance of activities for the day? Is it time to curtail viewing? Is fatigue a factor?
4. Are positive role models portrayed and accurately presented?
5. Is the program suited to the age of the child?
6. Does the program overstimulate?
7. Does the program display wholesome problem solving—is it relevant to the child's experience?
8. Is the humor childlike?
9. Are experiences extended beyond the immediate environment? Does the program offer further opportunities to explore, to investigate?
10. Is the content of the program appropriate? Can the child relate to the issues presented?
11. Is the advertising excessive?
12. Are the speech patterns acceptable and vocabulary appropriate to the kindergarten viewer?
13. Does the program have entertainment and/or information value?
14. Does the child view a balanced "menu" of programs—comedy, situational, etc.—or is it a steady diet of science fiction, cowboys and Indians, or cartoons?

Finally, how much time do you, as significant adult, devote to jointly viewing television with the child? What positive impact do you make on program selection? Perhaps of even greater importance, what influence have you had on commercial interests featured on television or on programers' scheduling of objectionable materials? Have you taken an active role in the improvement of TV offerings for children by expressing opinions about programs or withholding purchase of shoddy merchandise of sponsors?

SUMMARY

The issue of television in the lives of children is a complex one. There is no single best way. We must try to involve ourselves directly—this is a media generation and a media world. Our impact must be made through evaluation and guidance—through knowing what is being programmed and being willing to share the television experience with the five-year-old.

REFERENCES AND SUGGESTED READINGS
Language and reading

Ad Hoc Kindergarten Guidelines Committee. Language arts. In *Recommended kindergarten guidelines, state of Ohio,* Columbus, Ohio, 1978, pp. 13-15.

Ashton-Warner, Sylvia. *Teacher.* New York: Bantam Books, Inc., 1971.

Brogan, Peggy, and Fox, Lorene K. *Helping children read.* New York: Holt, Rinehart & Winston, 1961.

Carlson, Ruth Kearney. *Enrichment ideas: sparkling fireflies.* Literature for children series. Dubuque, Iowa: William C. Brown Co., Publishers, 1970.

Cazden, Courtney B. Preschool education: early language development. In Benjamin S. Bloom et al. (Eds.), *Handbook on formative and summative evaluation of student learning.* New York: McGraw-Hill Book Co., 1971, pp. 345-398.

Cazden, Courtney B. *Language in early childhood education.* Washington, D.C.: National Association for the Education of Young Children, 1972.

Chenfield, Mimi Brodsky. *Teaching language arts creatively.* New York: Harcourt Brace Jovanovich, Inc., 1978.

Cohen, Dorothy H., and Rudolph, Marguerita. The three R's: reading and writing. In *Kindergarten and early schooling.* Englewood Cliffs, N.J.: Prentice-Hall, Inc., 1977, pp. 292-312.

Coody, Betty. *Using literature with young children.* Dubuque, Iowa: William C. Brown Co., Publishers, 1974.

Corcoran, Gertrude B. *Language experiences for nursery and kindergarten years.* Itasca, Ill.: F. E. Peacock Publishers, Inc., 1976.

Cowe, Eileen Grace. *A study of kindergarten activities for language development.* Saratoga, Calif.: R and E Research Associates, 1974.

Dallman, Martha. *Teaching the language arts in the elementary school.* Dubuque, Iowa: William C. Brown Co., Publishers, 1969.

Downing, John, and Thackray, Derek. *Reading readiness.* London: Hodder & Stoughton, Ltd., 1976.

Dunn, Lloyd M. *Peabody picture vocabulary test.* Circle Pines, Minn.: American Guidance Service, 1965.

Durkin, Dolores. *Teaching young children to read* (2nd ed.). Boston: Allyn & Bacon, Inc., 1976.

Durkin, Dolores. Pre-first grade starts in reading: Where do we stand? *Educational leadership,* 1978, 36(3), 174-177.

Eliason, Claudia Fuhriman, and Jenkins, Loa Thomson. *A practical guide to early childhood curriculum.* St. Louis: The C. V. Mosby Co., 1977.

Engel, R. C. *Language motivating experiences for young children.* Van Nuys, Calif.: DFA Publishers, 1968.

Ervin, Jane. Communication starts in the cradle. *Akron Beacon Journal,* May 6, 1979, p. G1.

Fastenau, Michele S. *A procedure for diagnosing and remediating difficulty in listening in detail in five-year-olds.* Unpublished master's thesis, Kent State University, 1975.

Fisher, Carol J., and Terry, Ann. *Children's language and the language arts.* New York: McGraw-Hill Book Co., 1977.

Fromberg, Doris Pronin. Reading and language teaching. In *Early childhood education: a perceptual models curriculum.* New York: John Wiley & Sons, Inc., 1977, pp. 141-176.

Glaus, Marlene. *From thoughts to words.* Champaign, Ill.: National Council of Teachers on English, 1965.

Goetz, Elizabeth M. Early reading: a developmental approach. *Young Children,* 1979, 34 (5), 4-11.

Gleason, Jean Berko. Language development in early childhood. In James Walden (Ed.), *Oral language and reading.* Champaign, Ill.: National Council of Teachers of English, 1969, pp. 15-30.

Haberman, Martin. The meaning of reading readiness for young children. *Childhood Education,* 1979, 55 (5), 288.

Halliday, Michael. Relevant models of language. *Educational Review,* 1969, 22 (1), 26-38.

Hansen, Halver P. Language acquisition and development in the child: a teacher-child verbal interaction. *Elementary English,* February 1974, 51, 278.

Heilman, Arthur W. *Phonics in proper perspective.* (2nd ed.). Columbus, Ohio: Charles E. Merrill Publishing Co., undated.

Hendrick, Joanne. Fostering the development of language skills. In *The Whole Child* (2nd ed.). St. Louis: The C. V. Mosby Co., 1980.

Henry, Mabel Wright. *Creative experiences in oral language.* Champaign, Ill.: National Council of Teachers of English, 1967.

Herrick, Virgil E., and Nerborig, Marcella. *Using experience charts with children.* Columbus, Ohio: Charles E. Merrill Publishing Co., 1964.

Hildebrand, Verna. Language arts. In *Introduction to early childhood education* (2nd ed.). New York: Macmillan Publishing Co., Inc. 1976, pp. 239-261.

John, V. P., and Horner, V. M. *Early childhood bilingual education.* New York: Modern Languages Association of America, 1971.

Karnes, M. B. *Helping young children develop language skills: a book of activities.* Washington, D.C.: Conference for Educational Development and Research, 1968.

Kean, John M., and Personke, Carl. Oral language. In *The language arts: teaching and learning in the elementary school.* New York: St. Martin's Press, Inc., 1976, pp. 111-146.

King, Martha L. Language: insights from acquisition. *Theory into Practice,* 1975, *14,* 283-298. College of Education, Ohio State University.

Kingman, Lee (Ed.). *Newberry and Caldecott Medal Books, 1966-1975.* Boston, Mass., The Horn Book, Inc., 1975.

Kovalcik, Alfred L. Another look at reading readiness. *Education Digest,* 1977, *42*(1), 48-50.

Landry, Donald L. The neglect of listening. *Elementary English,* May 1969, *46,* 601.

Language use and acquisition. *Theory into practice,* 1975, *14*(5). College of Education, Ohio State University.

Lavatelli, C. S. *Language training in early childhood education.* Urbana, Ill.: ERIC, 1971.

Lee, Dorris M., and Allen, R. V. *Learning to read through experience* (2nd ed.). New York: Appleton-Century-Crofts, 1963.

Leeper, Sarah Hammond, et al. Language arts; and growth through language arts experiences and activities. In *Good schools for young children* (2nd ed.). New York: Macmillan Publishing Co., Inc., 1969, pp. 153-211.

Lunsteen, Sara W. *Listening: its impact on reading and other language arts.* Urbana, Ill.: ERIC Document Reproduction Service No. LC 79-173390, October 1971, p. 12.

Marbach, Ellen. Language development. In *Creative curriculum: kindergarten through grade three.* Provo, Utah: Brigham Young University Press, 1977, pp. 35-80.

Margolin, Edythe. Children need to communicate. In *Young children: their curriculum and learning processes.* New York: Macmillan Publishing Co., Inc., 1976, pp. 93-144.

Meers, Hilda J. *Helping our children talk.* New York: Longman, Inc., 1976.

Motion pictures related to outstanding children's books. Weston, Conn.: Weston Woods, Spring 1979.

National Association for the Education of Young Children. *The idea box.* Washington, D.C.: The Association, 1973.

Ollila, Lloyd O. (Ed.). *The kindergarten child and reading.* Newark, Del.: International Reading Association, 1977.

Ohio Department of Education, Division of Educational Redesign and Renewal. *Teaching early reading.* Columbus, Ohio, 1976.

Pflaum, Susanna Whitney. Implications for early childhood education. In *The development of language and reading in the young child.* Columbus, Ohio: Charles E. Merrill Publishing Co., 1974, pp. 66-82.

Phillips, Nina. *Conversational English for the non-English speaking child.* New York: Teachers College Press, 1968.

Pitcher, Evelyn Goodenough, et al. *Helping young children learn* (2nd ed.). Columbus, Ohio: Charles E. Merrill Publishing Co., 1974, pp. 172-176.

Pre-kindergarten curriculum guide. Curriculum Bulletin No. 11. Board of Education of the City of New York, 1965-1966.

Reading: a conversation with Kenneth Goodman. Chicago: Scott, Foresman & Co., 1976. (Monograph)

Scientists making progress on dyslexia. *Akron Beacon Journal,* February 19, 1978, p. G9.

Scott, Louise Binder. *Developing communication skills.* New York: McGraw-Hill Book Co., 1971.

Scott, Louise Binder. *Talking time.* New York: McGraw-Hill Book Co., 1971.

Shane, Harold G., and Walden, James (Coordinators). *Classroom-relevant research in the language arts.* Washington, D.C.: Association for Supervision and Curriculum Development, 1978.

Spodek, Bernard. Language learning in early childhood education; and Issues and activities. In *Teaching in the early years.* Englewood Cliffs, N.J.: Prentice-Hall, Inc., 1972, pp. 59-85; 87-111.

Steen, Arleen. Reading in the kindergarten. *The McGuffey Reader,* 1973, *2*(2). Oxford, Ohio: McGuffey Laboratory School, Miami University.

Strickland, Dorothy S. On reading. An ACEI position paper. *Childhood Education,* 1979, *56*(2), 67-74.

Sutherland, Zena (Ed.). *The best of children's books.* Chicago: University of Chicago Press, 1973.

Sutton-Smith, B. *Child psychology.* Englewood Cliffs, N.J.: Prentice-Hall, Inc., 1973.

Taylor, Barbara. *A child goes forth.* Provo, Utah: Brigham Young University Press, 1970.

Todd, Virginia Edmiston, and Heffernan, Helen. Developing communication skills. In *The years before school* (3rd ed.). New York: Macmillan Publishing Co., Inc., 1977, pp. 409-444.

Trubowitz, Sidney. Books for children; and books for teachers. In *A handbook for teaching in the ghetto school.* Chicago: Quadrangle/The New York Times Book Co., Inc., 1968, pp. 147-162.

U.S. Department of Health, Education, and Welfare. *Learning to talk: speech, hearing and language problems in the preschool child*, Washington, D.C., 1969.

Valverde, Leonard (Ed.). *Bilingual education for Latinos*. Washington, D.C.: Association for Supervision and Curriculum Development, 1978.

Walden, James (Ed.). *Oral language and reading*. Champaign, Ill.: National Council of Teachers of English, 1969.

Weiss, Curtis E., and Lillywhite, Harold S. *A handbook for prevention and early intervention: communicative disorders*. St. Louis: The C. V. Mosby Co., 1976.

Winsor, Charlotte B. (Ed.). *Dimensions of language experience*. New York: Agathon Press, Inc., 1975.

Woods, Margaret. Readiness for reading. In *Creative experiences in oral language*. Champaign, Ill.: National Council of Teachers of English, 1967, pp. 59-63.

Zintz, Miles V. Teaching the linguistically and culturally different child. In *Corrective reading* (3rd ed.). Dubuque, Iowa: William C. Brown Co., Publishers, 1977, pp. 293-337.

Television

Chamberlin, L. J., and Chambers, N. How television is changing our children. *The Clearing House*, 1976, *50*(2), 53-57.

Childers, P. R., and Ross, J. The relationship between viewing television and student achievement. *Journal of Educational Research*, 1973, *66*(7), 317-319.

Clinton, S. TV as a behavior model. *American Education*, 1975, *11*(6), 40.

Cohen, Dorothy H. Through a glass darkly: television and the perception of reality. *National Elementary Principal*, 1977, *56*(3), 22-29.

Cohen, Dorothy H. *The media and the climate of the school*. Report of Centennial Educational Conference. New York, 1979, pp. 27-45.

Comstock, G. The second teacher: recent research on television. *National Elementary Principal*, 1977, *56*(3), 16-21.

Edgar, P. Families without television. *Journal of Communication*, 1977, *27*(3), 73-77.

Eron, L. D., Huesmann, L. R., Lefkowitz, M. M., and Walder, L. O. How learning conditions in early childhood—including mass media—relate to aggression in late adolescence. *American Journal of Orthopsychiatry*, 1974, *44*(3), 412-423.

Fox, S., and Huston-Stein, A. Television's hidden curriculum. *National Elementary Principal*, 1977, *56*(3), 62-68.

Frank, J. *Television: how to use it wisely with children* (Rev. ed.). New York: Child Study Association of America, Inc., 1969.

Garry, R. *Television's impact on the child*. Washington, D.C.: Association for Childhood Education International, 1967.

Ingles, R. L. *A time to learn*. New York: The Dial Press, 1973.

Kronick, D. Television, the opiate of our children. *Academic Therapy*, 1971, *6*(4), 399-403.

Kuhmerker, L. When Sesame Street becomes Sesamstrasse: social education for preschoolers comes to television. *Social Education*, 1976, *40*(1), 34-37.

Lyle, J., and Middleton, J. Television, the uncommon common medium. *National Elementary Principal*, 1977, *56*(3), 8-15.

Morris, N. S. *Television's child*. Boston: Little, Brown & Co., 1971.

Schramm, W., Lyle, J., and Parker, E. B. *Television in the lives of our children*. Stanford, Calif.: Stanford University Press, 1961.

Siegel, A. E. A nation of vidkids. *National Elementary Principal*, 1977, *56*(3), 54-59.

Singer, D. G., and Singer, J. L. Family television viewing habits and the spontaneous play of preschool children. *American Journal of Orthopsychiatry*, 1976, *46*(3), 496-502.

Singer, D. G., and Singer, J. L. Is human imagination going down the tube? *The Chronicle of Higher Education*, April 23, 1979, *18*, 52.

Steur, F. B., Applefield, J. M. and Smith, R. Televised aggression and the interpersonal aggression of preschool children. *Journal of Experimental Child Psychology*, 1971, *11*(3), 442-447.

Study claims TV impact on kids' view of violence. *Akron Beacon Journal*, April 23, 1979, p. 1.

Waters, H. F. What TV does to kids. *Newsweek*, February 21, 1977, pp. 62-70.

Wiles, J., and McNamera, D. From "Bionic Woman" to "Ultra Man": TV's new stereotypes. *National Elementary Principal*, 1977, *56*(3), 60-61.

OTHER RESOURCES
Language and reading
Periodicals on children's literature

The Booklist
American Library Association
50 East Huron St.
Chicago, Ill. 60611

The Calendar
Children's Book Council
175 Fifth Ave.
New York, N.Y. 10011

Guide to Children's Magazines, Newspapers, Reference Books
Association for Childhood Education International
3615 Wisconsin Ave., N.W.
Washington, D.C. 20016

The Horn Book Magazine
Horn Book
585 Boylston St.
Boston, Mass. 02116

Language Arts (formerly *Elementary English*)
National Council of Teachers of English
704 South Sixth St.
Champaign, Ill. 61820

School Library Journal
R. R. Bowker
1180 Avenue of the Americas
New York, N.Y. 10036

Periodicals for children

Children's Digest
Parents Institute of Parents Magazine
52 Vanderbilt Ave.
New York, N.Y. 10017

Ebony Jr.!
820 South Michigan Ave.
Chicago, Ill. 60605

Highlights for Children
2300 West Fifth Ave.
P.O. Box 269
Columbus, Ohio 43216

Humpty Dumpty's Magazine for Little Children
Parents Institute of Parents Magazine
52 Vanderbilt Ave.
New York, N.Y. 10017

Jack and Jill
Saturday Evening Post Co.
1100 Waterways Blvd.
Indianapolis, Ind. 46202

Ranger Rick
National Wildlife Federation
1412 16th St., N.W.
Washington, D.C. 20036

Sesame Street Magazine
North Rd.
Poughkeepsie, N.Y. 12601

Television

National organizations to promote change in TV programming

Action for Children's Television
46 Austin St.
Newtonville, Mass. 02160

American Council for Better Broadcasts
111 King St.
Madison, Wis. 53703

Council on Children, Media, and Merchandising
1346 Connecticut Ave., N.W., Room 523
Washington, D.C. 20036

National Association for Better Broadcasting
Box 53630
Los Angeles, Calif. 90043

Radio-TV Council of Greater Cleveland, Inc.
P.O. Box 5254
Cleveland, Ohio 44101

Sources of information for TV evaluation

But First, This Message
Action for Children's Television, Inc.
46 Austin St.
Newtonville, Mass. 02160
   A 15-minute 16-mm sound color film about the nature and extent of advertising on children's TV programs. Recommended for parent-teacher meetings. Among other material available from ACT is an information packet.

The Family Guide to Children's Television
Evelyn Kaye
New York: Pantheon Books, Inc., 1974
   What to watch, what to miss, what to change, and how to do it by one of the founders of Action for Children's Television, Inc. Paperback.

National Instructional Television Center
606 West Wisconsin Ave.
Milwaukee, Wis. 53203
   Write for evaluation guidelines.

Prime Time School TV (PTST)
Dept. T.
100 North LaSalle St.
Chicago, Ill. 60602
   A nonprofit organization that provides subscribers with materials to help make the most of good evening TV for middle-schoolers and beyond.

Television: How to Use It Wisely with Children
Josette Frank
New York: The Child Study Press, revised edition, 1969
   Pertinent and perceptive suggestions. Paperback.

CHAPTER 9

Discovery: order and form, science and numbers

Science

> We must be careful not to smother a child's tender sparks of inquiry with a heavy blanket of directions and facts. (Harlan, 1978, p. 15)

As we think back to the earlier discussion of the five-year-old, perhaps the best way to describe what happens as the kindergartner approaches the world is that there is a freshness, a sense of wonder, of marveling, of newness. The "why-er" is curious, eager, and wanting to know. The adult who is privileged to share in this stage of development is indeed a critical element in how the child is led to discovering and in the child's continuation of this sense of awe and excitement. Indeed, as the child examines a flower, a leaf, or the seeming magic of a magnet, the adult is often left breathless by the spate of questions, the sharpness and range of inquiry, and, yes, inability to respond adequately to some of the child's investigations.

Accompany the kindergartner on a walk of the school yard or neighborhood and note that the smallest bug, that odd-shaped acorn, the puffy clouds, the garter snake, a field mouse, or green apples have not escaped notice! Often the young child *is* the teacher as the adult rekindles lost curiosity or long-forgotten puzzling about natural phenomena.

Holt (1977, p. 2) states that "with young children, science is continuous wondering, finding out, knowing. Science is thinking and doing and making the two go together."

Another point of view, expressed by Dietz and Sunal (1976, p. 127), is that "science is mainly a product for some, a process for others, and both a product and a process for others. Science for the young child is defined as being mainly a method of achieving. . . ."

PLANNING

The responsibility of participating with the child in seeing and making order in the world is a delightful one as well as a serious undertaking. Capitalizing on that elusive asset—curiosity—in the pursuit of science can be a rare and special adventure for adult and child together. According to Holt (p. 3), we need to realize that the best sources of early learning experiences are those nearest at hand and of the child's own making (Holt, 1977, p. 3).

It is virtually impossible to misjudge or to err in the selection of activities that encourage the five-year-old to observe, to explore, and to question if we keep Holt's directive in mind. The child is a part of science, as are we. Harlan (1976, viii) reiterates a similar feeling:

> When we present science experiences in the early childhood years, we are not introducing

new activities to children. We are merely defining a process they began at birth: making sense of their world with the intellectual processes currently available to them.

Spodek (1972, p. 128), in a review of basic science programs, states:

At the kindergarten and primary levels, teachers have available to them a number of newly developed science programs from which to choose.... Often the decision of what to teach under such circumstances is not the individual teacher's, for a school system may adopt a single textbook series or program in order to insure continuity of learning through the grades with a minimum duplication of experiences.

Others, not being satisfied to follow a very prescribed content, prefer to offer informal "hands on" experiences for the eager five-year-old. Guidelines suggested often include meaningful encounters with the environment, including materials, forces, and people.

As reported by Dietz and Sunal (p. 139), when the child enters kindergarten, he appears able to grasp semiabstract concepts without handling materials. The child's ability to understand scientific ideas appears to be influenced by socioeconomic factors, his logical reasoning ability, his memory, and his self-image. What children consider part of science and how much interest they have in science are two additional elements to be considered in planning a program.

In selecting experiences or setting the stage for "sciencing," Eliason and Jenkins (1977, p. 220) offer "do's and don'ts":

Do have actual materials for the children to explore.
Do use the water trough or similar container for science materials and equipment. . . .
Do frequently use science tools such as magnifying glasses, thermometers, magnets, and scales. . . .
Do develop an interested, curious, and enthusiastic attitude toward science yourself. . . .
Do relate science activities and units to the child's environment. . . .
Do perform experiments and activities ahead of time to have confidence in what is being done. . . .
Do scale ideas and concepts down to the child's understandings. . . .
Don't make science activities magic—make them a part of the real world; and help children see the cause-and-effect relationship. . . .
Don't be afraid to say, "I don't know.". . .
Don't let children use equipment, materials, or substances that are dangerous. . . .
Don't just teach scientific facts—assist children in learning to solve problems. . . .

The Eliason and Jenkens text contains a wealth of ideas and activities in relation to food experiences; smell and taste; sound and pitch; texture, weight, and balance; temperature, weather, and seasons; and plants and animals.

Many activities of the kindergartner might be viewed as pre-science. As children manipulate, explore, and find out, they become "natural" scientists.

In the planning of experiences for the five-year-old, play, biological phenomena, physiology, and botany are logical sources. Many authors cite the value of cooking as a basis for scientific learning. We have enjoyed with kindergartners fresh-baked bread, vegetable soup, and even a Thanksgiving turkey!

As planning for science for the five-year-old proceeds, the processes of learning are emphasized. Observation, description, problem solving, classification, logical reasoning, seeing relationships, and inferring are included.

In an informal interview, Alfred Friedl (1978), an authority in science for the young child, stated that science is "more than leaves in the fall" and went on to discuss the need for a systematic program as well as exploration of events and children's ideas. Friedl also felt that what went on in many kindergartens was a travesty in the teaching of science. He recommended that teachers accumulate their own materials, since often the usual science kits found in schools have items missing or are being used by others, or are inappropriate.

Many states have very stringent time requirements for science in the kindergarten, but probably very few are being met. The "paper requirements are good but in practice do not work."

Another delight about science, according to Friedl, is that the activities are marvelous for "special" kids. "In fact, you don't even need to know how to read!"

Both short-range and long-term planning are important, as is provision for those "serendipities" that occur in the company of all young children. I (M.R.) clearly remember one eventful morning when, pulling open the desk drawer, my hand encountered a field mouse family, probably lovingly placed there by a mischievous *and* curious five-year-old! To ignore the opportunities inherent in that happening would have been shortsighted.

On another occasion during a visit to a kindergarten, the children proudly explained the family tree (pedigree) of the resident guinea pigs. An astute teacher had charted the entire genealogy—the "roots"—of the classroom mascot.

In that same kindergarten, the children demonstrated that a tall, towerlike contraption was an elevator, newly constructed—and quite well understood in terms of scientific principle.

Careful planning for maximized scientific learning includes knowledge of the children and of resources available within the community, understanding of the processes of science, openness to many approaches, and flexibility of thinking. Careful planning also assumes participation on the part of the children and acceptance of their points of view.

From reading the research literature on

science for young children, it becomes apparent that we need to know more about children's powers of observation, inference, communication, and concept formation. Teachers will need to sharpen their own skills in these areas as they work with the kindergarten child.

GOALS

Four generally recognized goals in teaching science to young children appear in much of the literature:

1. Problem solving through the use of methods of science
2. Developing a scientific attitude
3. Gaining knowledge and information
4. Developing an interest and appreciation of scientific learning

Other goals might include:
1. Open encounters with the environment
2. Interaction of materials, forces, and organisms
3. Investigations into the "how" and "why" of phenomena
4. Repeated experiences illustrating consistent effects
5. Organized inquiry skills

Robison (1977, p. 211) makes a strong statement on the values and goals of exploring and discovering:

Major outcomes of active participation in exploratory learning are the child's secure feelings that *he* is finding out for himself what the world is like, that he *is* discovering how things work, and that nobody knows everything so there are some things nobody knows at all.

Surely, this is a major discovery in itself and rather challenging to the five-year-old! Robison continues in saying, "A child who has such a 'can-do' attitude engages problems at home and at school without wasting time in false starts or attempts to escape self-testing situations."

Additional considerations cited by Robison (p. 212) include:

1. That the activities be multisensory and active.
2. That the children have sufficient familiarity or interest in the materials to want to work with them at length.
3. That the materials can take the child manipulations expected without causing problems of high cost of replacement.
4. That the children can find some ways to pattern their observations and the results of their manipulations.

The science curriculum for the kindergartner should include an introduction to the different sciences of chemistry, physics, mechanics, magnetism, electricity, light, rockets and spaceships, bacteriology, conservation, and pets. The child needs to know the natural environment intimately.

An excellent source of activities is *Science and Children*, a periodical designed to provide science learning experiences and activities suited to the young child. Taylor's (1970) *A Child Goes Forth* offers a wealth of ideas and resources and is highly recommended. A partial listing of materials suggested for a science center is given on pp. 238-241.

ACTIVITIES AND EXPERIENCES

Accurate observation is a must. "Children often *look* but do not see because they need to learn how to observe and what kinds of things they ought to be observing" (Sciara and Walter, 1974, p. 24).

Keeping in mind the expansion and enhancement of the primary skill of observation, one can develop many experiences. Whenever feasible, the actual object should be used. Then learning can be extended with pictures, films, and resource people.

1. Bring in seeds of all kinds, including nuts, grain, and fruit. Children can taste, touch, and plant.
2. Provide buckeyes. Talk about shape, color, feel, and growing conditions. Do the same with acorns and hickory nuts.
3. Make vegetable soup, but first carefully examine all the raw ingredients. What does celery look like? How does it grow? Does it grow underground or above? Ask similar questions about potatoes, carrots, turnips, etc.
4. Visit a potato farm. See how potatoes grow. Pick potatoes and wash, peel, and prepare them in many ways. Enjoy eating and tasting.
5. Obtain cuttings of various flowers. Place them in water and observe the development of the root structure. Later, plant them in pots and plot the growth.
6. Open different kinds of fruit. Examine

the seeds. Prepare the fruit in different ways.
7. Have the children keep growth charts of themselves and of pets. Make this a year-long project.
8. Plan a variety of cooking experiences. Talk about changes that occur. Bake bread and cupcakes. What has happened? (Recipes are included later in this chapter.)
9. Study of soil fascinates. Bring in several kinds. Experiment with growing seeds. In what soil do seeds thrive? What other conditions are necessary to accelerate growth? Why is sunlight essential?
10. Select a pumpkin. Keep it indoors all year. Observe what happens. One kindergarten group learned with delight that what had been a 30-pound pumpkin at Halloween could easily be lifted in the spring! Extend the learning by making custard, baking pumpkin, etc.
11. Study snowflakes and ice crystals as well as icicles.
12. Bring in samples of fabrics. With an eyedropper and water find out which fabrics absorb water and which do not. Wash the fabrics. Which fade, shrink, pucker, etc.?
13. Discover that substances have different odors (vinegar, perfume, cinnamon, furniture polish, etc.).
14. In how many different ways can eggs be prepared (fried, dried, boiled, scrambled, baked, etc.)? How does the taste differ?
15. Investigate water. What can water do? In what form does it appear? Discuss conservation, energy, and recreational use of water.
16. Experiment with magnets and various metals. What happens?
17. Collect a variety of simple machines and discover how each works (eggbeater, scale, pulley, padlock, doorknob, etc.).
18. Develop cause and-effect situations (ice and water, friction experiments, soap dissolving, wood and ash, leaves in the fall, fog, mold, milk souring, etc.).
19. Encourage collections (seed pods, dried flowers and weeds, rocks, feathers, illustrations of footprints, etc.). Compare, share.
20. A worm farm is fun and informational. Start a small soil frame with earthworms. An ant farm can be fascinating to children and provide hours of observation. Children will ask innumerable questions and eagerly look for changes each day.
21. A bee frame also provides hours of ob-

servation. One kindergarten had a bee frame built through the wall to the out-of-doors!
22. Take a field trip to the supermarket vegetable and fruit sections. Perhaps salads could be made by the children, followed by a recipe book.
23. Capitalize on the environment—where you live (desert, mountains, plain, etc.).
24. Children discovering themselves is also scientific learning. Children revel in comparing, measuring, and talking about:
    - Height and weight.
    - Body structure and movement.
    - Teeth and bones.
    - Joints and muscles.
    - Hair and nails.
    - Body parts and image.
    - Age and relative strength.
    - Athletic prowess and skill.
    - Autobiographical data.

    Coupled with these activities can be discussions on appropriate clothing and adaptation to the seasons.
25. Pollution is an excellent theme for kindergartners. Observe factories, cars, garbage fills, etc. What solutions do the children suggest?
26. Energy concerns everyone. What sources are there? Visit a solar house, a windmill, a grist mill, etc.
27. Bird feeding in winter safeguards the bird population. Become a bird watcher. Listen to the songs in the spring. Bird song records are available.
28. Hang gliding can be observed in some parts of the country. A unit about air can provide much scientific learning. Make kites. Experiment with balloons.
29. Take a tree walk. Observe the kinds of leaves, the bark, and the rings.
30. A weather vane, thermometer, and sundial are accessible and fascinating to children.
31. The weather is rich in opportunities. Winter storms, summer heat and lightning, hail, and clouds—what changes occur?
32. An electrical board is useful. Christmas lights, bulbs, and switches prompt questions, as does static electricity.

As sources for integrating science with music, poetry, mathematics, and creative movement, the works by Eliason and Jenkins (1977) and Harlan (1978) are invaluable.

Science is a continuous process for the five-year-old, interwoven into the fabric of daily living.

Also appropriate is the drama of a scientific experiment (carefully planned) or an ongoing project such as a garden.

Find opportunities to sing about the world of nature, read stories about animals, or find poetry that extends scientific learning. The potential for capturing and enhancing curiosity of the young child is everywhere.

The five-year-old enjoys the drama and vitality of science. Science in kindergarten is not a hit or miss kind of learning; neither is it a lesson to be learned. It is not just watering plants, feeding goldfish, and carrying small turtles around. It requires a day-by-day alertness of teachers/adults and an awareness of the many opportunities to make children discoverers of the *whys* and *whats* and *what-happens-ifs* all around them. (Carpenter, undated, p. 1)

Search out the adventures and wonders of the world about you with the kindergartner. Sharpen your awareness and powers of observation. Both of you will thrive.

Both science learning centers presented here have been used with kindergartners. Adapt the ideas to your own classroom.

Magnets

Fran Durham

This learning center will give children an opportunity to expand their awareness of the world around them by observing and classifying. Magnets have a particular fascination for children. For many children, magnets remain a mystery. This center will help children focus on specific concepts about magnets and will help organize them into a meaningful whole.

OBJECTIVES

Children will:
1. Be able to tell how magnets act in different ways by experimenting with different magnets.
2. Separate objects that a magnet will pick up from those it will not.
3. Discover that a magnet's force can go through some materials and not others.
4. Learn how magnetic power can be turned off and on.

ACTIVITIES

1. Magnet types: Place three different types of magnets on a table so that children can explore with each one (touching metal and nonmetal objects, etc.).
2. Magnetic attraction: On the table place two trays, one with a "smile face" on it and the other with a "frown face" on it. Between the trays place several items, some that are attracted by a magnet and some that are not. Permit children to use a magnet and discover which items it will pick up. Have children put the items that are attracted on the "smile face" tray and the ones that are not, on the "frown face" tray.
3. Fishing game: Make several fish out of paper. On the paper fish, draw pictures of items that magnets will pick up and also items that magnets will not pick up. Place paper clips on the fish and place them in a container. With a pole made from a dowel rod and a magnet attached to it by a string, children can take turns fishing. As they pick up a fish, they tell what picture is on the fish and if that object could be picked up by the magnet.
4. Magnetic mystery boat: Make a mystery boat by placing a row of tacks on the underside of a piece of cork. On the top of the cork, place a pin and made a paper sail. Put water into a long glass cake pan and set the glass pan on top of two solid boxes near the edges. Put the sailboat into the water and hold the magnet against the underside of the glass pan near the boat. When the magnet is moved, the boat will move also. (Be sure children are supervised when doing this experiment because of the glass pan.)
5. Electromagnet: Secure a large nail and scrape the covering off each end of a piece of bell (thin) wire. Wind the wire about 25 times around the nail. Take a dry cell battery and tape one end of the wire tight to the flat bottom of the battery. Place a pile of paper clips on a table. Pick up the loose end of the wire and hold it down on the button (opposite end) of the battery. Put the point of the nail into the pile of clips and slowly lift. Let go of the wire, and the pulling power will be turned off.

Foods

Donna Gardner

This learning center would be suitable as a supplement to a unit on foods. The activities offered at the center will be extended and reinforced by other class experiences. The focus on the center is on handling and preparing real foods, especially natural foods, but the scope of learning possibilities goes beyond this.

OBJECTIVES

Children will:
1. Identify a variety of common foods in their different forms by sight, taste, and smell.
2. Determine which foods are nutritionally valuable to them.
3. Handle a variety of kitchen utensils in preparing simple dishes.
4. Match initial sounds of food names with the letter that makes that sound.

PROCEDURE

Introduce the center to the entire class through discussion and demonstration. Each day, introduce the new food to be prepared and the utensils. Include new vocabulary words, concepts, and explicit instructions on handling the utensils and foods. Children sign in for their time at an activity and record it on a chart when completed. Whatever children begin, they must finish before going on to another activity.

ACTIVITIES

1. Puzzle cards: Recognition of basic foods in various forms (e.g., a whole red apple matched with a half apple showing pulp and seeds).
2. Collage station: Children create with magazine pictures, scissors, and paste. Use different themes (e.g., dessert foods).
3. Sorting: Children classify and categorize dried foods (nuts, beans, macaroni, etc.).
4. Smell jars: Small plastic cups contain odorous foods under cover. Children identify and match them to the chart.

Science materials

Absorbent cotton
Aluminum foil
Aquariums with glass covers and some with screen covers (any glass tank or large-mouthed jar may be used as an aquarium or terrarium)
Autoharp
Baking soda
Balloons
Balls of various sizes
Binoculars or field glasses
Blocks of all sizes and shapes
Blotting paper
Boards of various lengths and sizes
Bottles
Bricks
Broomsticks
Brushes
Bubble pipes
Bulletin board (steel)
Buttons
Cages for animals
Calendar
Candles (assorted)
Canned heat
Cans
Caps (aluminum)

5. Planting station: Small pots of soil and containers of water for growing seeds and vegetable tops.
6. Felt board: Children can arrange nutritious meals with an assortment of felt-backed food pictures.
7. Lotto game: Five lotto cards, each with a food source depicted and five spaces for little food pictures. (Foods come from trees, gardens, farm animals, and the sea.) Small food cards fill the spaces.
8. Magnetic fishing: Children fish for food pictures. They identify and name the food they catch and match the name to a letter square for the initial sound of the word. Letters are on a large vinyl sheet.
9. Foods for preparation.
    a. Celery: Wash, dry, and cut (do not use sharp knives); stuff with peanut butter or cream cheese.
    b. Apples and bananas: Wash, dry, slice, and remove seeds from apples (a butter knife is good for coring apples); for bananas, peel and slice.
    c. Carrots and cucumbers: Wash, pare if necessary, and slice. Sour cream may be provided for dipping.
    d. Toast: Place bread (whole wheat preferably) in a toaster; toast and spread with butter, jelly, peanut butter, or honey.
    e. Cheese and crackers: Provide cookie cutters for fancy shapes and provide an assortment of crackers. (Use natural cheeses.)
    f. Fruit-flavored gelatin or instant pudding: Children measure, mix, and put in the refrigerator. Use for snack the next day.
    g. Tuna sandwiches: Tuna may be mixed with a variety of things and spread on bread or crackers.
    h. Vegetable soup: Use hamburger as a base and add consommé, fresh or frozen vegetables, barley, and noodles. Children all help by bringing in foods and preparing them. Soup can be cooked on an electric hot plate.

Carbon tetrachloride
Cardboard
Cellophane (assorted colors)
Cereals
Cheesecloth
Clay
Cloth (assorted scraps)
Clothespins
Cocoons and cocoon holders
Combs
Compass
Containers (assorted bowls, boxes, bottles, cooking utensils, dishes, jars, pails, tin cans)
Corks (assorted)
Corrugated cardboard
Crepe paper (fireproofed)
Darts
Doll furniture
Dolls
Door bells
Drinking straws
Dry cells
Egg timer
Electric fan
Electric hot plates and oven
Electric lamps
Electrical invention kit (batteries, bells, wires, switches)

Fasteners (hooks, nails, nuts and bolts, paper clips, pins, screws, staples, thumbtacks)
Feathers
Flashlights
Flower holders and flowerpots
Flowers
Food coloring
Fossils
Fruit jars
Funnels
Garden tools
Garden twine
Gears
Glass tumblers
Globe
Glue
Hammers
Hand lenses or magnifying glasses
Hourglass
Inclined plane
Insect containers
Insects
Iron filings
Jack-in-the-box
Kaleidoscope kit
Knitting needles
Lamp chimneys
Level
Light bulbs
Magnets, bar, U, V, and preferably of alnico
Magnifying glass
Marbles
Measuring cups and spoons
Measuring tape
Medicine droppers
Metal scraps
Mirrors (small)
Modeling clay
Musical tops
Needles (darning)
Newspaper
Noisemakers (bells, horns, whistles)
Paints, shellac, varnish, and turpentine, alcohol
Paper bags
Papier-mâché
Paraffin
Pegs, beads, tiles
Pet food
Petroleum jelly

Pets: chicks, ducks, canaries, fish, hens (for setting), turtles, etc.
Ping pong balls
Plants
Plaster of Paris
Plastic bags
Plastic toys (for play with water)
Plasticine
"Plumber's" force cups
Pot holders
Prisms
Pulleys, ropes
Rocks
Rubber bands
Rubber tubing
Ruler or tape
Salt
Sand
Sandpaper
Sawdust
Scales (household), weights, balances
Scissors
Seeds and seed catalogs
Snails
Soil
Sponges
Sprinkling can
Stones
Straws
String
Sugar
Syringe
Talcum powder
Teakettle
Terrarium
Thermometers (inside and outside, Fahrenheit and Celsius)
Thread
Tire or ball pump
Tongs
Tools (bit and brace, chisels, files, hammers, saws, screwdrivers, shovels, wire, shears)
Toothpicks
Tops (spinning)
Toy animals
Toy cars
Toy fruits and vegetables
Toy musical instruments
Toys, mechanical

Tubing
Tuning fork
Turf (clumps)
Vinegar
Wagon or wheelbarrow
Watering can
Waxed paper
Wheat paste
Wheels
Whistles
Wind vane
Wire (insulated copper, picture, and screening)
Wooden beads
Yardsticks

Numbers

The young child of five lives with one foot in the real, concrete, sensory world and the other in the abstract, symbolic world. While he is always doing, doing, doing, he is also thinking about what he is doing and developing thinking structures (abstract and symbolic). (Ad hoc Kindergarten Guidelines Committee, 1978)

Young children seek order. The world of numbers has a fascination from toddlerhood through adulthood. The five-year-old becomes aware of mathematical ideas very early. As an infant, toes may have been counted with "This Little Piggy," "Ten Little Indians," or "One, Two, Buckle My Shoe." Also birthdays were (and are) extra special.

As the child grows, experience to the world of numbers intensifies and broadens. Through counting, signs, measuring, cooking etc., application of numbers begins to take on significance. The young child goes shopping, and "value" enters the stream of experience.

Research indicates that of children entering kindergarten:

1. Many children can count and find the number of objects to ten, and some are able to count to at least 20.
2. Some can say the number name of tens in order (that is, 10, 20, 30), but far fewer can say the names when counting by twos and fives.
3. Most know the meaning of "first," and many can identify ordinal positions through "fifth."
4. Many can recognize the numerals from 1 to 10, and some can write them.
5. Most can give correct answers to simple addition and subtraction combinations presented verbally either with or without manipulative materials.
6. Most have some knowledge about coins, time, and other measures; about simple fractional concepts; and about geometric shapes. (*Mathematics in Early Childhood*, 1975, p. 49)

However, there is a real need for research in the area of affective factors of mathematical learning. The attitude of the teacher may be particularly important. How adults view mathematics may be how children view learning mathematics. What teachers say and how they say it could be influential. Continual attention toward reinforcement of positive experiences and attitudes should be a goal in mathematics for the kindergartner.

For further study of research in mathematical learning, the reader is referred to Suydam and Weaver's presentation in the Thirty-seventh Yearbook of the National Council of Teachers of Mathematics.

Many questions regarding all areas of mathematical learning still need investigation. "Action" research initiated in the classroom can prove informational and productive for both children and teacher.

Mathematics at the kindergarten level is very much a part of daily living as children acquire mathematical understandings in varying degrees from opportunities provided by alert adults.

I (M.R.) realized early in a kindergarten situation that one child, Dale, was already very aware of time. It was not long after the opening of school that Dale would say, "Isn't it time for snacks?" or "I think it is time for a story!" Time and clocks, today and tomorrow, were no mystery to Dale, and he insisted on routines *on time!*

Another child, seeing his aunt reading a magazine, said, "I know what page that is—73!" Further checking revealed that the four-year-old could identify all double-digit numerals with ease and could identify several in the hundreds.

As we think back to the characteristics of the five-year-old, it becomes apparent that the teacher must know each child well, informally assess the "number readiness" of each, listen with care to the vocabulary that indicates mathematical knowledge, and capitalize on the curiosity, the eagerness, the wanting to be "big," and the appeal of numbers to the child of this age. Also, because children vary in intelligence in terms of rate of growth and ability, programs in mathematics need to be varied and multilevel; and they should allow for different approaches to solution.

A rather precise discussion of research in early mathematics and a review of several projects in this area can be found in the work by Johnson and Wilson (1976). The reader may wish to investigate specific studies in more detail.

PLANNING

Most authorities agree that mathematics programs in kindergarten should include both incidental and structured activities because children are still learning to use and sophisticate their senses. Development of abstract, symbolic thinking results from real, concrete experience. We also know that what the child feels about mathematics is often a direct result of the teacher's behavior. In addition, the maturity level of the children involved is critical. Mathematics can become an anathema if this area of learning is not adapted or carefully planned.

According to Piaget (1965, pp. 147-157) the child's conception of numbers takes place in terms of three stages:

1. Perception which is coordination only within the field of perception.
2. Operations which go beyond the field of perception.
3. Transition from perception to deduction, progressive combination of operations and gradual developmental reversibility.

The readiness of the child in terms of developmental stages must be recognized.

Again, keen observation of the children is essential. Some fives can:

1. Count objects and people.
2. Tell their age, house, and telephone number.
3. Use money to buy milk or snacks.
4. Understand *big, little, high, low, wide, circle, round, on, under, between, tall, short,* etc.
5. Recognize small groups of objects without counting.
6. Find six *more* blocks.

Flexibility of planning is necessary, and thoughtful provision must be made for situations that will require the use of mathematics and quantitative thinking. Planning should include provisions for real, manipulative, pictorial, and symbolic materials.

Many kindergartens also have available Cuisenaire rods (wooden rods of different lengths and colors that allow children to explore number relationships by fitting the rods together), Stern structured mathematics materials, Montessori beads, and other formal commercial programmed materials. School supply houses usually carry the materials mentioned. (Suggested materials are also listed on pp. 254-255.)

In fact, "found" materials, contributed either by children or the teacher, can provide a base for rich mathematical experimentation and learning. A mathematics center offers variety as well as challenge to the kindergarten child. Often we tend to think so traditionally about mathematics that we overlook the world about us and the abundance of mathematical serendipities!

Mathematics is a special language system—developed in small incremental steps. Children need to learn to use the system with precision and also to appreciate the usefulness of this "new" language. Helping to find mathematics at home as well as at school is part of the responsibility of the teacher in developing individualized programs.

GOALS

In short- and long-range planning for mathematical experiences, one needs to keep the following in mind:

If a student is to develop tenacity, if he is to take delight in problem solving, he must be free to choose his own problems and his own way of attacking them. He must be free to change the approach, to leave a problem, to return to it, to dwell on one problem at a time, to reject another. (Alberti and Davitt, 1974, p. 96)

The attitude and approach of the teacher to mathematics sets the stage.

In the Thirty-seventh Yearbook, (1975, p. 29) Trafton cites general instructional goals:

Developing a problem-solving mind set
Showing the relationship between mathematics and the real world
Creating an orientation toward finding patterns and relationships
Making children active participants in learning experiences

A balanced emphasis on concepts, skills, and application is vitally important in programs for young children. Trafton (p. 33) emphasizes three distinct areas:

Learning the mathematical content—the ideas, the concepts, the relationships
Learning specific techniques and skills that are necessary in everyday experience
Applications that relate mathematics to a variety of other situations

Goal setting can also be informal—a child planning a task, such as "I'll need seven cubes for this," or "How many more will I need?" or "My building needs more blocks than I have." The teacher might have developing and extending the mathematics vocabulary of the kindergarten group as a long-term goal and deliberately select materials from other curricular areas, such as music, dramatic arts, expressive arts, cooking, mapping, etc.

Goals must, of necessity, also be highly individualized within the concept building the teacher intends for each child. The advanced learner who comes to kindergarten with knowledge and understanding of one-to-one correspondence should be encouraged to take the next step; the child who counts by rote but who does not understand meaning needs a different kind of experience. Thus, informally, the teacher is assessing and observing while establishing goals not only for the kindergarten group but also for each child within that group. We have noted in a large proportion of kindergartens that whereas teachers individualize or work with small groups in reading readiness activities, they are likely to present mathematical situations in a total-group instructional framework. How can such a practice be justified given the wide range of learning styles and experiential backgrounds represented in a kindergarten class? We note with increased concern the many commercial materials, kits, programs, and the like, for mathematics being introduced into the kindergarten and the corresponding total-group instruction resulting—also the tendency and pressure to complete "a lesson" each day even though many children are unable to comprehend and master the material when they are paced in such fashion.

Mathematical problem solving lends itself particularly well to pairs working together or to groups of three or four children working together, with all working on the same problem or with each group working on a different problem; or the child may work alone or with the teacher in specific situations. Goal setting should reflect approaches best suited to teacher interest and capability as well as the children's learning patterns and needs. Experiment as you plan and work with children. Find your own best ways.

ACTIVITIES AND EXPERIENCES

Most kindergarten mathematics programs provide experience with classifying, comparing, ordering, measuring, determining shape and space, seeing patterns, and organizing data. Others specify, in addition, vocabulary development, counting, money, money values, and fractions.

Spodek (1972, pp. 148-153) suggests the following topics: grouping; counting; the number system; number operations; geometry; linear measurement; measurement of weight, volume, and time; fractions; graphs and charts; and money.

Many kindergarten programs, whether incidental or planned, include activities built around:

1. *Classification:* The ability to group objects, actions, feelings, and events on the basis of *similarities* (physical attributes—color, shape, size—and function—things you eat, things to ride).
2. *Seriation:* The ability to arrange items on the basis of *differences* (one dimension—color, size, height, weight).

Discovery: order and form, science and numbers

3. *Correspondence:* Four identical candies put into four identical dishes—one candy to each dish.
4. *Conservation:* Certain attributes remain the same while others undergo transformation. (A mass of clay rolled, pulled apart, etc., is still the same amount; a quart of water poured in equal amounts into different-sized containers is still the same total amount of water.)

Far too many programs consist of formal, total-class learning experiences and work with workbooks. Programs must be based on what children know (Spodek, 1972, p. 107).

Some teachers organize the mathematics program into a kind of laboratory, such as a store, a bakery, a bank, a supermarket, or a post office. Usually this is a total-class endeavor (useful for some children and not for others, we might add). Mathematics learning centers, such as those described at the end of this section, are another approach.

In the Thirty-seventh Yearbook, Gibb and Castaneda (1975) and Payne and Rathmell (1975) offer extensive suggestions for mathematical experiences for the kindergartner.

Cooking is an excellent activity that builds mathematical skills in measurement and vocabulary. Try the following with your class:

Aggression cookies

3 c brown sugar	6 c oatmeal
3 c margarine or butter (or 1½ c each)	1 tbs baking soda
	3 c flour

Put all this in a huge bowl; mash, knead, and squeeze. Then form into small balls, midway between filbert size and English walnut size, and place on an ungreased cookie sheet. Butter the bottom of a small glass, dip it in granulated sugar, and mash the balls flat. Keep doing it. (You need butter the glass bottom only once or twice, but redip it in sugar for each ball.) Then bake at 350° F for 10 to 12 minutes. (*Note:* The temperature may need to be a bit higher and the baking time longer, depending on your oven.) When cool, cookies should be crisp.

Variations of the following recipe appear in many cookbooks. Or use a prepared mix.

Gingerbread men

Simmer 15 minutes:	1 c molasses and 1 c shortening
Cream together:	1 c sugar, 1 egg, and 1 tsp vanilla
Dissolve:	2 tsp soda in ½ c hot water
Add hot water and soda mixture to sugar and egg. Sift together:	6 c flour, ½ tsp cloves, 1 tsp cinnamon, 1 tsp salt, and ½ tsp ginger

Add to other mixture and stir until flour is well mixed. Roll thin and cut with a cookie cutter. Bake 10 minutes at 375° F. Decorate. (This dough does not stick to the pan. Even a child can handle it.)

Homemade ice cream (uncooked)

8 eggs	3½ pt milk
4 c sugar	4 tsp vanilla
2 pt whipping cream	

Beat eggs slightly, and then add sugar and beat. Add the cream (as it is, do not whip) and beat just until well mixed. Add the milk and vanilla, and mix well. Pour into a freezer can and freeze according to directions. Makes 1 gallon.

Jello is simple to make, as are the following:
  Instant pudding
  Instant cereal
  Scrambled eggs
  Cupcakes (follow package directions)
  Applesauce
  Vegetable soup
  Baked beans
  Baked potatoes
  Rice

Noodles and spaghetti
Chili

Baking or cooking offers many opportunities to teach math. Use a measuring cup and spoons. Talk about *dozen* and *half dozen;* look at the size of containers, of fruits, of vegetables. Note oven and meat thermometers, as well as scales. Introduce *sticks* or *ounces* of butter and *pounds* of meat. Count out eggs and oranges. Cut pieces of cake or pie into eighths or halves. Use *less* milk than sugar. Your imagination helps!

Extending mathematics even further at home or school, children can set the table for snacks. How many napkins are needed, how many straws, and how many cups? Ask the child to divide portions equally. Count out loud.

The element of time looms large. What time is breakfast? Leaving for school? Dinner? Where are the hands on the clock? How soon will the cookies be baked? Talk about morning, afternoon, and night.

Shopping also reinforces mathematics. The supermarket offers a wealth of opportunity. Take a field trip to select items for salad or some other ingredients for a baking project in the classroom. I (M.R.) remember when a kindergarten boy contributed a roll of cookie dough to be baked at school. He and four delighted little girls proceeded to slice the dough and place the fat slices on a cookie sheet (without checking instructions!). The smells from the oven were tantalizing. When the timer bell rang, signaling that the cookies should be ready, there was one *giant* cookie, covering the entire cookie sheet! Very nonchalantly, as though he had intended all this from the beginning, the "cook" broke off generous pieces and bestowed them on his helpers for munching.

At another school, morning and afternoon groups of kindergartners prepared an entire Thanksgiving dinner and then shared the excellent meal proudly with parents and teachers.

Refer also to the recipes suggested in Chapter 7 for clay, finger paint, etc.

Mathematics *is* real life experience.

In addition to the activities already described, the Ad hoc Kindergarten Guidelines Committee (1978, pp. 20-22) recommends the following experiences:

a. Recognizing physical characteristics of objects
b. Grouping by physical properties
c. Discriminating items not belonging to groups
d. Recognizing groups that have no members (empty, zero)
e. Working with equivalence, greater than, equal to
f. Introducing cardinality (how much), ordinality (in what order)
g. Writing symbols
h. Graphing, tally marks
i. Combining groups (adding), taking groups apart (subtracting)
j. Mathematical labels and language

Extend mathematical learning through selecting books that introduce mathematical concepts. Selections such as *Anno's Counting Book; The Very Long Train; My Very First Book of Shapes; One, Two, Where's My Shoe?; James and the Rain; One Was Johnny: A Counting Book;* and *Seven Little Monsters* will add spice to the program. Your school library should yield many such books.

Remember:

You, the teacher, hold the key. You must determine the best approach to your class, you should be sensitive to each student's ability and should help him discover a working level high enough to intrigue him but not so high that it will overwhelm him. With experience you will learn when to introduce new problems, when to dwell longer on one problem, when to review, and when to suggest free play. (Alberti and Davitt, 1974, p. 96)

The mathematics activities presented here have been used successfully with the five-year-old.

Number sets

Barbara Mancine

OBJECTIVES

1. Children will be able to recognize the number sets 1 to 10.
2. Children will be able to recognize the numerals 1 to 10.
3. Children will understand the number sequence 1 to 10.

ACTIVITIES

1. Flannel apple trees and apples: Make ten apple tree cards out of poster board and number from 1 to 10. Glue green felt on the poster board to represent the leaves. Make the trunk of the tree and numerals with a felt-tipped pen or marker. Cut apples out of red felt. The child puts the correct number of apples on each tree. (This will be checked by the teacher or aide.)
2. Apple man game: Cut large apple shapes out of red tagboard. Glue felt on the apples where the eyes, ears, nose, mouth, and tie should be. Then cut eyes, ears, nose, mouth, and a tie for each apple out of poster board. Paint and number the pieces and glue felt on the backs. Make a die by covering a wooden block with contact paper. Each child takes a turn throwing the die and adds the numbered part to his apple that matches the numeral thrown on the die. Whoever completes the apple man first wins the game. The children can look at a set of cards showing the numerals and sets to check themselves.
3. Matching: Make a game board that pictures the sets through 9. Prepare cards that have the numerals on one side and the sets on the other. The child matches the numerals on the cards to the sets pictured on the game board. He can turn the cards over to check the answer.
4. Felt board: Glue felt on a lightweight board. Cut out felt shapes in sets of ten each. Make a set of flannel-backed numeral cards. The child puts a piece of yarn around the correct number of felt shapes so as to form a specified set.
5. Carpet squares: Cut the numerals 1 to 10 out of contact paper and stick each one on a carpet square. Put the sets 1 to 10 on cards. The child picks a card from 1 to 10, finds the matching carpet square, and hops or jumps on it as many times as the numeral indicates. This would be a good activity for an aide and a small group of children.
6. Sequence cards (bunnies:) Make cards out of poster board using a felt-tipped pen or marker. Glue felt on the backs of the cards so that they could also be used on the flannel board. Draw one bunny on the first card, two on the second, etc. The child arranges the bunnies in the proper sequence starting with 1 and continuing through 10. He then matches flannel-backed numeral cards to each line of bunnies.
7. Magic box: Make a box out of a gallon milk carton. Cut two slits in one side and attach a strip of tagboard on the inside so as to look like this:

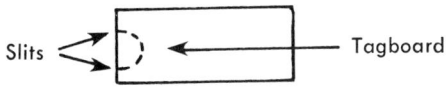

Continued.

Number sets, cont'd

Then cover the carton with contact paper. Make cards with numerals on one side and sets on the other. The child inserts a card with the numeral side showing in the top slit, and it will come out the bottom slit with the set side showing.

8. Counters: Cut about 150 squares out of poster board and put in a container. The child makes sets on a table top by using these counters. This would also be a good activity for an aide and a small group of children.
9. Count the beans: Print the numerals 1 to 10 in the cups of an egg carton. The cups on the end are used for storing the beans or other counters. The child drops the correct number of beans in each cup.
10. How many: Fold a paper into four sections and put a numeral in each section. The child draws a set of objects for each numeral.

Number skills

Robert Robinson

DEFINITION: The ability to count and use simple numbers to represent quantity.

PSYCHOEDUCATIONAL RATIONALE: Arithmetic understanding and usage begins with basic number concepts and is preliminary to mastery of more advanced basic processes.

BEHAVIORAL OBJECTIVES: The child will be able to count forward to 25, use simple numbers to represent quantity, and group simple quantities.

ACTIVITIES

1. Have the child hold up both hands. Starting at the child's left, fold back each finger as you say the numerals. Repeat several times and encourage the child to count with you.
2. When the child is counting with you, let him count alone as you fold back his fingers.
3. Reverse roles. Let the child count your fingers from left to right.
4. Counting.
    a. Materials: None.
    b. Procedure: Clap and count, or march and count.
5. What number comes next.
    a. Materials: None.
    b. Procedure: Begin counting. Stop and tap the child. He supplies the next number. Then keep counting and tap someone else for another number.
6. Kerplunk.
    a. Materials: Metal pan or cup plus ten washers or corn kernels, etc.
    b. Procedure: Let the child drop the objects one at a time into the cup. As it goes "kerplunk," count for each one: "one-two-three," etc.
7. Counting.
    a. Materials: Ball plus horn or two sticks.
    b. Procedure: Have the child bounce the ball and count as he bounces (can also jump). Or have him announce the number of times he will bounce.

8. Bounce the ball.
   a. Materials: Large ball.
   b. Procedure: One child stands in front of a group and bounces the ball. He then calls on another child to clap the same number of times the ball was bounced. If he succeeds, he may be the new leader.
9. Ten pins.
   a. Ten blocks, etc., and ball.
   b. Procedure: Start with four or five blocks. Have the child roll the ball to knock down pins. He then counts the number of pins he knocked over.
10. Simple sets.
    a. Materials: Buttons, beads, candy, or pictures of objects.
    b. Procedure: Give the child a number of objects (two). Have him tell you how many he has. Give him more (one). Then ask how many he has. Take away (one or two). Then ask him how many he has.
11. Pass the beans.
    a. Materials: Small box of beans, buttons, etc.
    b. Procedure: Have one child take (seven) beans from the box and give them to the next child. The next child must determine if he received (seven) beans. Then he returns the beans to the box and the teacher gives another number.
12. Clap, clap.
    a. Materials: None.
    b. Procedure: Have one child listen while you clap. When you finish, ask how many times. Warn him you may clap, then stop and clap again. Ask him how many times you clapped altogether. (Examples: Clap . . . clap, clap . . . clap; *or* clap, clap, clap . . . clap; *or* clap . . . clap, clap, clap . . . clap).
13. Whistle game.
    a. Materials: Whistle (or clap hands, ring a bell, etc.).
    b. Procedure: Blow the whistle and have the child take as many steps forward or backward as the number of times the whistle blows.
14. One-to-one correspondence.
    a. Materials: Crayons and any one of the three dittoed sheets below.

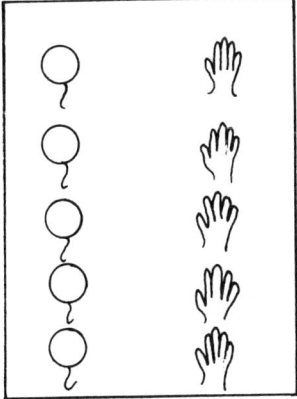  

Number skills, cont'd

b. Procedure: Have the child follow directions. Stress left-to-right movement. (Examples: "Each balloon needs a string so it won't fly away from the hand; draw a line from the balloon to the hand"; *or* "Draw a line from one dog to one bone; now draw lines to give each of the other dogs one bone"; *or* "Draw a line from one boy to one cookie." Stress counting and point out the same number of balloons as hands, etc.

15. Cookie tray.
    a. Materials: Crayons and dittoed sheet.
    b. Procedure: Have the child find how many cookies there are on the dittoed sheet. Direct attention to the empty tray. Have the child draw the same number of cookies on the empty tray.

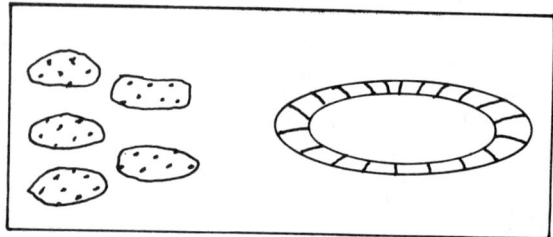

16. Equal sets.
    a. Materials: Crayons and paper.
    b. Procedure: With three children, direct each child to draw a set (two or three birds, four trees, etc.) on a piece of paper. Have the children trade papers. Then ask each child to draw a set equivalent to the set on his paper.
17. Drawing game.
    a. Materials: Crayons and paper folded into four sections.
    b. Procedure: Have the child start in the first square. Ask him to draw two umbrellas. In the next square have him draw three suns, etc.
18. Find it.
    a. Materials: Two sets of cards with objects drawn on the cards (one to ten).
    b. Procedure: Set five (or ten when the child can do it) cards on a ledge. Give a card from the second set to the child. He must match it to one of the five cards. This can be played with two or three children; each child scores a point if he can correctly match the number of objects.
19. Order.
    a. Materials: Picture cards or dots.
    b. Procedure: Give cards to children (one per child). Instruct them to line the cards up in order on the chalk ledge (card that has one more than this set).
20. Buying balloons.
    a. Materials: Construction paper circles with numbers on them and strings attached.
    b. Procedure: Place "balloons" on the table. The child may "buy" one if he knows the number.

21. Count the beans.
    a. Materials: Egg carton, beans, or other counters.
    b. Procedure: Have numerals 1 to 10 written in each cup of the egg carton. Store beans in the two extra cups. Have the child look at the number in the first cup. He then puts the same number of beans in that cup. Do the same for each cup.

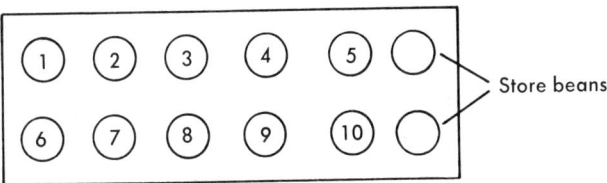

22. Macaroni or bead stringing.
    a. Materials: Elbow macaroni or beads, string, and tags with numerals 1 to 10 written on them.
    b. Procedure: Have the child thread one bead on his string with the appropriate tag, then two, etc.
23. Matching.
    a. Materials: Numeral cards and cards with dots.
    b. Procedure: Have the child count the dots and find the matching numeral.
24. How many?
    a. Materials: Numeral cards, crayons, and paper.
    b. Procedure: Show the child a numeral. Have him make that many circles on the paper.
25. How many?
    a. Materials: Crayons and paper folded into four sections.
    b. Procedure: Put a numeral in each box. The child draws that many objects.

★ ★ ★	
3	4
6	5

26. Find the number.
    a. Materials: Crayons and picture covered with acetate or dittoed sheet.
    b. Procedure: Have the child look at the first row. ("What number is at the beginning of the row?") The child then looks at the objects. He finds a group of three objects and draws a circle around them.

Continued.

Number skills, cont'd

27. Matching and counting.
    a. Materials: Fifteen red hearts (etc.), dittoed sheet with heart outlines, and paste.
    b. Procedure: Ask the child how many hearts he sees in the top row (one). Then have the child paste one red heart on top of the outline on the paper. Next, the child pastes one red heart on the second row and then one more to make it two, etc. Then return and ask how many in each row.

28. Matching.
    a. Materials: Crayons and picture covered with acetate or dittoed sheet.
    b. Procedure: Have the child read the numerals, then look at the objects at the right and count them. The child finds the numeral that tells how many.

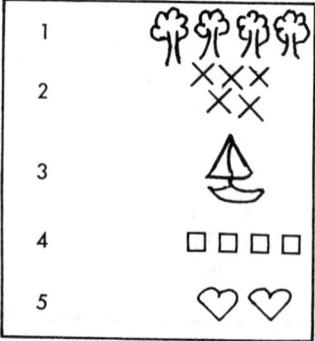

Discovery: order and form, science and numbers

29. Color the number.
    a. Materials: Crayons and dittoed sheet.
    b. Procedure: Have the child look at the first square. ("What is the number? In that square color only three of the houses.")

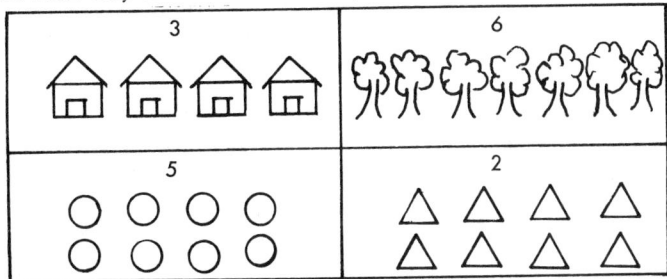

30. Dominoes: Play to improve counting and matching skills.
31. How many more?
    a. Materials: Crayons and dittoed sheet or numeral cards with colored shapes.
    b. Procedures: Have the child look at the first box. ("What is the numeral? How many triangles are there? How many more do you need? Draw them.")

32. Which number?
    a. Materials: Crayons and picture covered with acetate or dittoed sheet.
    b. Procedure: ("Name the numerals in the first square. Count the objects in the square. Find the matching numeral.") Numbers can be increased as the child gains skill in this area.

Number skills, cont'd

33. How many more (less).
    a. Materials: Any group of objects that can be counted.
    b. Procedure: Present a group of objects to the child. Have him count them. Then the child closes his eyes as you remove or add objects. When the child opens his eyes, he tells what has happened.
34. Greater than and less than.
    a. Materials: Cutouts or dittoed sheet as below.
    b. Procedure: Have the child compare the group on the left with the group on the right. Is the set on the left greater than or less than the one on the right? The child then compares the set on the right with the set on the left.

35. Parts.
    a. Materials: Apples, other fruit, paper, knife, and scissors.
    b. Procedure: Provide opportunities for the child to cut objects into halves, quarters, etc. ("How many parts are there?")
36. Number skills: Use number songs and number books.

Mathematics materials

Abacus
Adding machine
Articles for making sets
Artificial fruit
Attribute blocks
Balls
Beads
Bean bags
Beans
Bingo cards
Blocks
Calendar
Cash register
Ceiling tiles
Chart holder
Clock
Clothespins
Counters (many kinds)
Counting frames and sticks
Crayons
Cuisenaire rods
Dice, buttons
Dominoes
Drum
Egg timer
Electric board
"Feel" box
Finger paint
Fingerplays
Flannel or felt board and cutouts
Flash cards

Floor tiles
Games
    Concentration
    Dice game
    Fishing game
    Magnetic board and materials
    Magnetic fish game
    Match Me
    Measuring and weighing materials
    Notation cards
    Numb
    Order rummy
    Perception cards
    Rhyming games
    Show Me
    Skunk
Geoboards
Geometric shapes
"Greater than" chart
Height chart
Hourglass
Index cards (3 × 5)
Jars (pint, quart, half-gallon, and gallon sizes)
Jump ropes
"Less than" chart
Loops
Macaroni
Magic slate
Magnetic board and numerals
Marbles
Measuring cups
Measuring spoons
Measuring tape
Money
Newspapers and magazines
Number lines with numbers and blank
Numeral cards
Oaktag
Overhead projector
Paper clips
Paper plates
Parquetry blocks
Paste
Pegboards, golf tees
Pegs
Pencils
Perception cards
Picture dominoes
Pipe cleaners
Place value chart
Plastic numerals
Play money
Pocket calculator
Popsicle sticks
Practice wheels
Puzzles
Rhythm instruments
Rings
Rubber bands
Ruler, yardstick
Sandpaper
Scales
Scissors
Seesaw balance pans
Set cards
Shoe boxes
Sorting trays
Stop watch
Straws
Thermometer
Tooth picks
Transparencies
Yarn

REFERENCES AND SUGGESTED READINGS
Science

Ad Hoc Kindergarten Guidelines Committee. *Recommended kindergarten guidelines, state of Ohio.* Columbus, Ohio, 1978.

Blake, Jim, and Ernst, Barbara. *The great perpetual learning machine.* Boston: Little, Brown & Co., 1976.

Broman, Betty L. Science. In *The early years in childhood education.* Chicago: Rand McNally & Co., 1978, pp. 245-277.

Carmichael, Viola S. *Science experiences for young children.* Los Angeles: Southern California Association for the Education of Young Children, 1977.

Carpenter, Ethelouise. *Science in the kindergarten.* Undated statement.

Cohen, Dorothy H., and Rudolph, Marguerita. Science experiences for children and teacher. In *Kindergarten and early schooling.* Englewood Cliffs, N.J.: Prentice-Hall, Inc., 1977, pp. 180-209.

Dietz, Maureen A., and Sunal, Dennis W. Science. In Carol Seefeldt (Ed.), *Curriculum for the preschool-primary child: a review of the research.* Columbus, Ohio: Charles E. Merrill Publishing Co., 1976, pp. 125-150.

Eliason, Claudia Fuhriman, and Jenkins, Loa Thomson. Science experiences. In *A practical guide to early*

childhood curriculum. St. Louis: The C. V. Mosby Co., 1977, pp. 217-242.
Friedl, Alfred. Informal interview, Kent State University, Kent, Ohio, December 5, 1978.
Harlan, Jean Durgin. *Science experiences for the early childhood years.* Columbus, Ohio: Charles E. Merrill Publishing Co., 1976.
Hill, Dorothy M. *Mud, sand, and water.* Washington, D.C.: National Association for the Education of Young Children, 1977.
Holt, Bess-Gene. *Science with young children.* Washington, D.C.: National Association for the Education of Young Children, 1977.
Keyes, Carol R. A science open house is worth copying. *Young Children,* 1976, *31*(5), 346-349.
King, W. H. Science for the young. In Belen Collantes Mills (Ed.), *Understanding the young child and his curriculum:* selected readings. New York: Macmillan Publishing Co., Inc., 1972, pp. 347-380.
Kolson, Clifford J., et al. The oral science vocabulary of kindergarten children. *Science Education,* 1963, *47*(4), 408-415.
Lay, Margaret Z., and Dopyera, John E. Resourcefulness with animals. In *Becoming a teacher of young children.* Lexington, Mass.: D. C. Heath and Co., 1977, pp. 246-272.
Leeper, Sarah Hammond, et al. Science. In *Good schools for young children* (3rd ed.). New York: Macmillan Publishing Co., Inc., 1974, pp. 301-315.
Mindess, David, and Mindess, Mary. Utilizing the outdoor environment. In *Guide to an effective kindergarten program.* Englewood Cliffs, N.J.: Parker Publishing Co., 1972, pp. 63-74.
Neuman, Donald. Sciencing for young children. *Young Children,* 1972, *27*(4), 215-226.
Pitcher, Evelyn Goodenough, et al. Understanding the physical and social world. In *Helping young children learn.* Columbus, Ohio: Charles E. Merrill Publishing Co., 1974, pp. 109-128.
Robison, Helen F. Exploring and discovering: causing things to happen. In *Exploring teaching in early childhood education.* Boston: Allyn & Bacon, Inc., 1977, pp. 206-231.
Roche, Ruth L. *The child and science.* Washington, D.C.: Association for Childhood Education International, 1977.
Sciara, Frank J., and Walter, Richard B. *Social studies and science activities with the tape recorder.* Dansville, N.Y.: The Instructor Publications, Inc., 1974.
Spodek, Bernard. Science in the early years. In *Teaching in the early years.* Englewood Cliffs, N.J.: Prentice-Hall, Inc., 1972, pp. 113-135.
Taylor, Barbara J. Science. In *A child goes forth.* Provo, Utah: Brigham Young University Press, 1970, pp. 75-89.
Todd, Vivian Edmiston, and Heffernan, Helen. Building science concepts. In *The years before school: guiding preschool children* (3rd ed.). New York: Macmillan Publishing Co., Inc., 1977, pp. 322-373.
Wills, Clarice, and Lindberg, Lucile. Science for children under six. In *Kindergarten for today's children.* Chicago: Follett Publishing Co., 1967, pp. 131-148.

Numbers

Ad Hoc Kindergarten Guidelines Committee. Mathematics. In *Recommended kindergarten guidelines, state of Ohio.* Columbus, Ohio, 1978, pp. 20-22.
Alberti, Del, and Davitt, Robert J. *Attribute games and problems.* Teacher's guide. New York: McGraw-Hill Book Co., 1974.
Blake, Jim and Ernst, Barbara. *The great perpetual learning machine.* Boston: Little, Brown & Co., 1976.
Broman, Betty L. Mathematics. In *The early years in childhood education.* Chicago: Rand McNally Co., 1978, pp. 279-300.
Copeland, Richard W. *How children learn mathematics: teaching implications of Piaget's research.* London: Collier-Macmillan Ltd. 1970.
Davis, Robert B. *The changing curriculum: mathematics.* Washington, D.C.: Association for Supervision and Curriculum Development–National Education Association, 1967.
Dawes, Cynthia. *Early maths.* New York: Longman Inc., 1977.
Eliason, Claudia Fuhriman, and Jenkins, Loa Thomson. Numbers. In *A practical guide to early childhood curriculum.* St. Louis: The C. V. Mosby Co., 1977, pp. 44-68.
Gibb, Glenadine, and Castaneda, Alberta. Experiences for young children. In *Mathematics in early childhood.* Thirty-seventh Yearbook. Reston, Va.: National Council of Teachers of Mathematics, 1975, pp. 96-124.
Johnson, Martin L., and Wilson, John W. Mathematics. In Carol Seefeldt (Ed.), *Curriculum for the preschool-primary child: a review of the research.* Colombus, Ohio: Charles E. Merrill Publishing Co., 1976, pp. 153-174.
Johnson, Stanley W. *Arithmetic and learning disabilities.* Boston: Allyn & Bacon, Inc., 1979.
Leeper, Sarah Hammond, et. al. Mathematics. In *Good schools for young children* (3rd ed.). New York: Macmillan Publishing Co., Inc., 1974, pp. 233-257.
Marbach, Ellen S. Number concepts and skills. In *Creative curriculum: kindergarten through grade three.* Provo, Utah: Brigham Young University Press, 1977, pp. 237-254.
Margolin, Edythe. Mathematics in children's lives. In *Young Children: their curriculum and learning proces-*

ses. New York: Macmillan Publishing Co., Inc., 1976, pp. 176-205.

Mathematics in early childhood. Thirty-seventh Yearbook. Reston, Va.: National Council of Teachers of Mathematics, 1975.

Mcintyre, Margaret. Books which give mathematical concepts to young children: an annotated bibliography. *Young Children*, 1969, 24(5), 287-291.

Mills, Belen Collantes. Teaching mathematics to young children. In *Understanding the young child and his curriculum*: selected readings. New York: Macmillan Publishing Co., Inc., 1972, 332-346.

Payne, Joseph, and Rathmell, Edward. Number and numeration. In *Mathematics in early childhood*. Thirty-seventh Yearbook. Reston, Va.: National Council of Teachers of Mathematics, 1975, pp. 126-160.

Piaget, Jean. *The child's conception of number*. New York: W. W. Norton & Co., Inc., 1965.

Scott, Louise Binder. *Mathematical experiences for young children*. New York: McGraw-Hill Book Co., 1978.

Spodek, Bernard. Mathematics for young children. In *Teaching in the early years*. Englewood Cliffs, N.J.: Prentice-Hall, Inc., 1972, pp. 137-153.

Steffe, Leslie P. (Ed.). *Research on mathematical thinking of young children*. Reston, Va.: National Council of Teachers of Mathematics, 1975.

Suydam, Marilyn N., and Weaver, J. F. (Eds.). Developing computational skills. In *Mathematics in early childhood*. Thirty-seventh Yearbook. Reston, Va.: National Council of Teachers of Mathematics, 1975.

Todd, Virginia Edmiston, and Heffernan, Helen. Exploring time, space, and numbers. In *The years before school* (3rd ed.). New York: Macmillan Publishing Co., Inc., 1977, 374-408.

Trafton, Paul. The curriculum. In *Mathematics in early childhood*. Thirty-seventh Yearbook. Reston, Va.: National Council of Teachers of Mathematics, 1975, pp. 28-41.

Weikart, David P., et. al. *The cognitively oriented curriculum*. Washington, D.C.: National Association for the Education of Young Children/ERIC, 1971, pp. 94-145.

OTHER RESOURCES
Science
Periodicals

Childhood Education
Association for Childhood Education International
3615 Wisconsin Ave. N.W.
Washington, D.C. 20016

*Highlights for Children**
2300 West Fifth Ave.
P.O. 269
Columbus, Ohio 43216

*National Geographic World** and *National Geographic*
National Geographic Society,
P.O. Box 2330
Washington, D.C. 20013

Ranger Rick† and *National Wildlife*
National Wildlife Federation
1412 16th St., N.W.,
Washington, D.C. 20036

Young Children
National Association for the Education of Young Children
1834 Connecticut Ave., N.W.
Washington, D.C. 20009

Children's books

Baylor, Byrd. *Everybody needs a rock*. New York: Charles Scribner's Sons, 1974.

Golden Guide Books (12 titles). Racine, Wisc.: Western Publishing Co.

Life Nature Library (25 titles). Morristown, N.J.: Silver-Burdett Co.

Piercewicz, Ann Thomas. *See what I caught*. Englewood Cliffs, N.J.: Prentice-Hall, Inc., 1974.

Pollard, Barbara Kay. *The sensible book: a celebration of your five senses*. Milbrae, Calif.: Celestial Arts, 1974.

Provensen, Alice, and Provensen, Marion. *Our animal friends at Maple Hill Farm*. New York: Random House, Inc., 1974.

Rinkoff, Barbara. *Guess what trees do*. New York: Lothrop, Lee & Shepard Co., 1974.

Numbers

The Newsletter of Parenting
2300 West Fifth Ave.
P.O. 2505
Columbus, Ohio 43216

Nuffield Mathematics Project
New York: John Wiley & Sons, Inc.
   Extensive ideas and activities incorporated in guides.

---

*For children.
†For older children but could be adapted for younger ones.

CHAPTER 10

Parents and the teacher

> Nowhere in the long educational continuum is the parent-teacher relationship more important than in the child's early years.
> (Hildebrand, 1976, p. 425)

Parents and teachers are active partners in the life, well-being, and education of the kindergartner. To the degree that the partnership between parent—or caregiver—and teacher flourishes, the five-year-old flourishes.

Here, we are considering as parent any adult who has assumed the responsibility for the total welfare and protection of the child.

PARENTS AS PARTNERS

A strong position on the issue of parent involvement in the schooling of young children is expressed by a number of authorities. In *Good Schools for Young Children*, Leeper and her associates (1974, p. 401) state that the happiest and most successful teacher is the one who regards parents as partners and friends in the program of educating the child.

Gordon (1976, p. 173) states that the pressures of parenting and teaching have much in common. What we do as teachers and parents—as adults—makes a difference in what happens to the children. It behooves all those in the caregiver role to create a learning environment with the child as central. The school and the home need each other. The kindergarten child needs both.

Leeper and her associates state further that in order to provide a complete program for the child, the parent and the teacher need to see the *whole* child as he reacts in his life at school and at home.

A mutual goal should be continuity and extension in the life of the child—a freedom of movement from home to school and from school to home with each enriching and supporting the other.

Evans (1975, p. 340) cites three primary reasons for parent involvement:

1. Even a minimal effort to involve parents in their children's education can bridge the continuity gap which often exists between home and school.
2. Properly informed and equipped parents can provide home practice opportunities for their children in many school related activities
3. By contributing in meaningful ways to their children's development and education, many parents may achieve an improved sense of self-worth and respect. If so, the general affectional relationships among parents and children may also improve.

Among the other benefits of parent involvement in the business of the school, parents report that they feel an improved sense of competence and self-esteem regarding parental skills; they also report that verbal interactions with their children are strengthened.

Parents need to become active agents in their children's care and education. The creation of a successful and mutually satisfying partnership of home and school demands effort and compromise. It also demands mutual respect and the belief that parent and teacher have much to share. The common concern of both is the child.

An effective partnership enhances the optimal development of the child—physical, social, intellectual, and emotional growth is maximized.

PATTERNS OF INVOLVEMENT

Several forms and programs of parent involvement are found in schools. In some communities there is minimal contact—parents are bystanders or observers in an audience role and educators are the experts. The kindergarten teacher may meet with parents at the beginning and end of the year to present the overall instructional program, expectations, needs, and progress of the children.

Other situations find parents in a direct and active teaching role with their children. The classroom climate may be one of reciprocal sharing and problem solving, and parents may share in decisions and policy making.

Evans (1975, p. 347) and most other early childhood authorities believe that whatever the dimension of parent-teacher-child interaction, parent involvement is fast becoming a top priority in education.

Parents as paraprofessionals

Involving parents as paraprofessionals or aides in the schoolroom demands careful consideration and planning. The involvement follows the establishment of the climate of parents as partners in the education of the kindergarten child. Another assumption is that the teacher has organized the classroom and planned the instructional program so as to capitalize on the help parents can give.

There is no one or best way to initiate a program for parents wishing to serve as paraprofessionals. We begin with an awareness of the individual differences of parents. "Parent participation also requires adjustment by the parents to the role of learner and modification of their relationship with the child," (Levitt and Cohen, 1976, p. 271).

The paraprofessional role may entail home visitation, working with small groups of children, working with a child with special needs, or sometimes serving as a substitute or ally on field trips and activities away from school.

How do parents, as primary teachers, teach their children? According to Gordon and Breivogel (1978, p. 173), "They teach essentially the way teachers teach. They provide the learning environment, model behavior, and engage in direct instruction with the child. These two means are common to parents and teacher."

A parent in the role of paraprofessional is particularly well suited to enlist support of skeptical parents since not only may they be similarly situated economically, but they also share a personal stake in the program of the classroom.

There is much evidence that many parents and children of all socioeconomic backgrounds suffer from a degree of isolation unique to our modern, mobile society. Another parent who has experienced similar mobility and isolation can do much in the paraprofessional capacity to orient a new family into the community and to the kindergarten child's school world. With the numbers of mothers of preschool children in the work force expected to increase to 1.5 million this year, there is an increased need for strong, cooperative relationships between home and school. (U.S. Senate Committee on Finance, 1971).

A parent serving as an aide in the kindergarten classroom should not be dealing with sensitive information. Rather, the parent might function as a tutor to a child needing additional practice on a skill, listen and record an individual story, perhaps tape a favorite storybook for use in the listening center, or work with a child needing help in constructing a puppet.

Other activities could well encompass preparation of materials of instruction according to teacher direction, inventory of resources available to the children, categorization of individualized activities, and replenishing supplies.

Parents as volunteers

Perhaps the easiest way to involve parents in the activities of the kindergarten is through the many volunteer contributions that enhance the program. From helping with initial "roundup" days to reading stories, collecting resource materials, helping with special days, working with the library, making games and instructional devices, publishing a cooperative newsletter, or serving as a resource visitor, foster grandparent, or listener, the parent may play a vital role.

Parents could well participate, after careful orientation, in the screening procedures usually scheduled in late spring or early fall. Small groups or individual children being tested for motor skills, hearing, and vision might work with one parent or rotate from station to station, where parents serve as "checkers."

Many kindergarten teachers enlist the help of a volunteer parent in the construction of instructional materials such as puppets, games, or charts. And all of us recall the mother of the kindergarten child who brought delicious cupcakes on an exciting birthday! In some situations parents as volunteers and parents as aides function very similarly, although usually the aide deals with professionally oriented activities. An aide might well be a fully certified teacher who has elected to be involved with young children on a limited, less responsible level.

Parents as resources

Parents can offer significant help to the kindergarten teacher because they *are* parents—with a fund of information about the five-year-old. Special interests of the child, significant events and accomplishments, personal anecdotes, the health history and habits, and behavior styles shared with the teacher can contribute much to the planning of a program for the child. The parent is the first teacher of the child, and five years of information (resources) can be invaluable.

Parents as resources can also be those with special travel experience; collections of dolls, toys, posters, or pictures; musical talents; skill in athletics and sports; interesting professions; or training in dramatics, story telling, or abilities and hobbies of all kinds.

In *Educating for Parenting*, Lane (1975, p. 52) includes a fascinating listing of benefits derived from parents as resources at Hartmann School in New Jersey. The "didjuever" list suggests in part:

Didjuever have a parent who . . .
- Stood on his head in his child's class—then went on to somersaults
- Showed home movies of a trip to the zoo
- Made a gingerbread house and brought it to school
- Went on a hike with the class—backpack and all
- Was a dentist and came to school to "play dentist"

Lane's book also includes an excellent listing of resources the reader might explore for further ideas to develop parent involvement.

However, a word of caution is in order. We need to be sure that any adult—or parent—serving as a resource can relate effectively to the five-year-old. The presentation must be at the child's level and within the sphere of interest. The kindergarten curriculum can be vastly expanded and enriched through the wise use of resource people, but only if those individuals can communicate with the young child.

Extensions of involvement

There are many additional ways in which the kindergarten teacher and the parent can come together for the betterment of the child. Brief descriptions of such possibilities follow. All could also be expanded to school-wide participation.

Study groups

Often parents indicate a need or desire to learn more about the kindergarten learning styles, behavior patterns, and the like. The teacher might well sponsor a series of "coffees" or periodic meetings with those parents who might be interested.

Workshops

In a workshop, parents might provide valuable skills in toy construction, furnishing of centers of interest, puppetry, or cooking, or the teacher might delegate specific tasks to be completed in a workshop.

Such workshops could be scheduled at midday, as was one where a Spanish-speaking parent, through music and speech, added an enriching experience to the kindergarten. Other sessions could be available immediately following the school's afternoon session, in early evening, on Saturday, or even on Sunday afternoon, as in one school we know of. The Sunday session attracted several fathers.

The parents' room

The kindergarten might well share in the benefits of a parents' room that the school provides as a place for parents to meet informally in small groups to read current professional literature, to work on a project of benefit to the children, for planning sessions, and for general fellowship. Parents freely discussing with other parents topics of mutual concern can extend understanding and create a wholesome environment for all. Parents of children with handicapping conditions gain support and information from others facing similar anxieties. A parents' room can make a difference!

Programs, fairs, and exhibits

All of us have experienced at some time the enjoyment and excitement of participating in a program, fair, or exhibit in "our" classroom. The kindergarten child is thrilled when the parent can observe firsthand the child's play or musical event, exhibition of work completed, circus, puppet show, or fair. In such a setting, parent and teacher can talk spontaneously of Mary's or Billy's contribution and progress.

Home visits

Careful groundwork and mutual consideration should precede visits to the home of a kindergarten child. In some school systems, home visits are expected and are an integral part of orientation to the child's entrance into school. In other situations, parents accompany children to a "roundup" before school begins or during the first week of school activity, as in staggered-entrance programs.

Initial home visits usually center on personal characteristics and needs of the child, with the parent sharing with the teacher. Such visits should be brief and informal and at the convenience of the parent. Sensitivity to the home situation is essential. Low-income parents or one-parent families are often hesitant to extend an invitation for a home visit; thus, there is a need for openness, objectivity, and a nonjudgmental attitude on the part of the teacher. A classroom aide who lives in the community and accompanies the teacher can often ease a first visit. Subsequent home visits could be scheduled late in the year and focus on the child's progress, collections of the child's work, or possible summer activities and experiences for the child (to be supervised by the parent) that would strengthen specific skills.

Home visits initiated by the kindergarten teacher may include activities for parent and child that extend the school experience. Perhaps, because of illness, the child wishes to complete projects begun at school; or the child may choose to work with a personal story or diary. Creative endeavor, such as crafts, poetry, music, or collections, lend themselves to home activities that later are taken to school.

Incidental contacts

Whether the contact with the parent is made by telephone or in the supermarket or at parents' night, the kindergarten teacher can capitalize on the incidental and informal character of the event. The telephone message might be one of sharing an important learning—a kind of serendipity for the child—or one of sharing a problem or concern that the child is experiencing; or it might even be a reminder of an upcoming event of importance to the child. The parent appreciates the thoughtfulness of such gestures, and a stronger bridge results between home and school.

Contacts in the community reveal more personal dimensions of the parent and of the teacher. From this can result greater ease and honesty of communication about the child.

PRINTED COMMUNICATIONS

Newsletters, notes, anecdotal records, observation checklists, handbooks, comments on a child's papers, and written grade cards or evaluations are all means of symbolically communicating vital information about the five-year-old. Such communication should be a two-way process between kindergarten teacher and parent. The reader is referred to the earlier discussion of "beginning days" in Chapter 3 and to Appendix B for examples of initial communications.

Periodic newsletters could contain news, notes, stories, and poems by the children, notices of upcoming events, items of personal achievement, explanations of curricular projects—whatever concerns the children and parents.

Kindergarten news features

Book club notes
Large-muscle activities
A new pet
New staff and helpers
Pictures are needed for . . .
A recipe to try
A tear-off for parents to indicate interest areas
We need parents for. . .
What the insurance policy covers . . .

Has your child been *vaccinated*?

Your child should have an *immunization card* the first day of school.

Try to have your child vaccinated in the spring!

Check local requirements for polio, tetanus, diphtheria, smallpox, measles, and pertussis *immunizations*.

About your child's *clothing*

Please put your child's name on each article of *outside* clothing.

Clothes should be simple, washable, sturdy, not too tight, safe, easy to manage—and *labeled*. Overshoes should be large enough for the child to put on himself.

What are the rules for *attendance*?

A written excuse is required from you each time your child is *absent* or *tardy* or *dismissed*.

What about *money*?

IF you give your child money for milk or other reasons, please put it in an *envelope* and write on the envelope your child's name and the *purpose* for which the money is sent.

Physicals due

If your child's physical has expired or he or she is new to school, the deadline for turning in the completed form is *September 30*.

News needed

If you have items for the newsletter, drop them off in the mailbox in each classroom.

Seesaw Book Club

Orders for books are due by *September 30*. Orders must be accompanied by payment either in cash or by check payable to Carol Jones (who writes one check to cover all orders).

The following books being offered are particularly good literature for young children.

Clifford at the Circus
Curious George Rides a Bike
Georgie

For every five books ordered by parents, our room receives one free book for its resource library.

Large-muscle activities

We have the use of the school gym every day this year from 11:00 to 11:30 AM. This should help us to provide more gross motor activities—especially on rainy days.

Please tear off and return to school

Check those you are interested in.
☐ Share with children an interest, talent, etc. Describe: _____
☐ Read stories, or do music or creative dramatics with children.
☐ Help put together the newsletter.
☐ Go on field trips with children. Ideas for field trips: _____
☐ Help with construction of playground equipment
☐ Repair toys.
☐ Participate in parent discussion groups. Topics I would like to have discussed: _____

Other suggestions for parent involvement: _____

Name _____
Date _____

Anecdotal records are ongoing reminders to the teacher and can provide an objective basis for conferences with the parent. *Observation checklists* often serve a similar purpose, although the teacher may develop guidepoints within specific areas for personal use. A checklist is of distinct value to the teacher.

OBSERVATION CHECKLIST

	Good	Fair	Poor
Motor behavior			
Posture	☐	☐	☐
Sense of balance	☐	☐	☐
Effective skipping	☐	☐	☐
Basic command of tools (crayons, scissors)	☐	☐	☐
Handedness	☐	☐	☐
Rhythm	☐	☐	☐
Language behavior			
Speech clarity	☐	☐	☐
Vocabulary	☐	☐	☐
Sentence structure	☐	☐	☐
Questioning strategies	☐	☐	☐
Speech patterns	☐	☐	☐
Health habits			
Safety habits	☐	☐	☐
Adequate rest	☐	☐	☐
Adequate diet	☐	☐	☐
Overall health	☐	☐	☐
Emotional health	☐	☐	☐
Toileting habits	☐	☐	☐
Social behavior			
Independence	☐	☐	☐
Friendliness	☐	☐	☐
Cooperation	☐	☐	☐
Adaptability	☐	☐	☐
Patience	☐	☐	☐
Stability	☐	☐	☐
Poise	☐	☐	☐

Handbooks are often school-wide endeavors, yet the kindergarten teacher may wish to prepare one designed to aid the transition from home to school. *Welcome to Kindergarten* might be the title of such a handbook, which would contain:
Statement of goals or philosophy
Schedule
Fees
Suggestions about clothing
Outdoor play expectations
Attendance
Library regulations
Home habits
Immunization
Materials that could be donated
The format for a handbook could also discuss and include:
Superintendent's message
Administrative requirements
Kindergarten program
Helping your child get ready
Health guide
Suggested reading for parents
Vital information

A handbook designed to provide basic information such as the above and also brief sections on the first weeks of school could meet the needs of parent and kindergarten teacher alike. Parents have a need to know expectations and procedures. A kindergarten handbook can become a useful reference and communication bridge.

When initiating a handbook project, one might include a parent advisory group, since often excellent ideas for materials and activities can result. The amount of time and effort spent in preparing a kindergarten handbook is well worth it. Parents often remark that use of the handbook effected a smoother transition into school for their child.

Representative of the kind of handbook now being developed is the Hudson Evamere School's WELCOME TO KINDERGARTEN. The text of the handbook follows:

Welcome to kindergarten

KINDERGARTEN HOURS

Morning session: _____ to _____   *Afternoon session:* _____ to _____
If your child is a walker, he should not arrive before:
_____ for morning children   _____ for afternoon children

TRANSPORTATION

The *morning group* comes to school with the other grade school children. At _____ AM the buses leave with the morning group to take them home.

The *afternoon group* is then picked up by the buses. They return home with the other grade school children at _____ PM.

Please notify the teacher when there is any change in your child's routine procedure for returning home. This is very important. Do not rely on your child to tell the teacher; a note *must* be written. If it is necessary to take a child out of class and you have not sent a note, you must get a permit from the office to present to the teacher.

Continued.

Welcome to kindergarten, cont'd

CLOTHING

Recommendations for parents in regard to child's clothing:

1. Clothe your child simply so that he may be comfortable in school activities and handle his clothing by himself.
2. Each outer piece of clothing should be plainly and permanently marked with your child's name. (Name tapes, magic markers or indelible pens are excellent for this purpose.)
3. Provide galoshes and rubbers large enough to go on easily over his shoes and mark them.

PREPARING FOR KINDERGARTEN

Kindergarten for most children is the first independent adventure away from home. It is here that a child develops lasting attitudes toward school, his teacher, and his classmates. It is here he learns to accept other children and to be accepted by them.

While this adjustment appears to be a natural one, it is by no means an accidental one. It is a very complicated process for little folk. It takes place best when love, patience and understanding are present in the home and in the school. For this reason, cooperation between teachers and parents is so very important. The parents and teacher have an opportunity to pool their understanding of the child and to work out harmonious ways of helping him.

When your child enters kindergarten, it is desirable that he should have sufficient emotional stability to be free of temper outbursts and excessive fears. He should be able to speak understandably, to take care of his bathroom requirements, and to use a handkerchief when needed.

HEALTH

At school your child will be closely associated with many children. Be alert for signs of contagious disease or communicable skin infection. If symptoms are present, keep him home for his own protection and that of his classmates. Please notify the school if he is ill with any contagious disease or will be absent from school for an extended period due to reasons of health.

Let the teacher know if your child is going to have an operation of any kind and when it is to be. Also, should any member of the family be ill or hospitalized, it is helpful if the teacher is informed.

If your child becomes ill in school, you will be notified as quickly as possible.

Please report any changes of address or telephone number promptly to the secretary so that you may be reached if needed.

Required duration of absence from school for the following:

Measles: For 7 days from the appearance of the rash.
German measles: Until recovery is complete; 4-5 days usually.
Mumps: Until recovery and swelling of glands has subsided.
Chicken pox: At least 7 days from the appearance of the first crop of blisters.
Tonsils, adenoids. appendicitis: Return to school only after permission from your doctor.

GOALS AND THE SCHOOL PROGRAM

We hope to provide a rich, full, happy environment promoting the development of each child to his fullest potential in relation to his needs and age by doing the following:

1. Offer a liaison experience between home living and primary-grade entrance.

2. Promote parent-school cooperation in helping the child make satisfactory adjustments to the school situation.
3. Help him learn to live and work happily in a group and observe group rules.
4. Develop manual and physical coordination.
5. Develop acceptable forms of self-expression and encourage creativity.
6. Give him practice to develop skill in thinking.
7. Strengthen habits of:
    a. Courtesy
    b. Cooperation
    c. Self-confidence
    d. Responsibility
    e. Neatness
    f. Punctuality
8. Enrich background through exchange of ideas and interests.
9. Develop the ability to listen to and follow directions.

Activities of a kindergarten day designed to accomplish these goals include:

Activity or free play	Art and craft work
Conversation and planning	Reading readiness
Music and rhythms	Modern math
Organized games	Physical education
Stories and poems	Motor-perceptual development

ESPECIALLY FOR PARENTS

Attendance

Punctuality and regular attendance in kindergarten are extremely important. It is an important part of your child's character training and sets the pattern for attitudes toward school absence in the years ahead.

Birthdays

We enjoy celebrating with the children. Please make arrangements with the teacher by note or phone if your child wishes to bring a treat on his birthday.

Milk money

There is a nominal weekly charge for the milk and cookies eaten at snacktime. This fee is due every Friday as advance payment for the coming week and should be sent in an envelope marked on the front with the name of your child, his teacher, and the amount of money enclosed.

Parent conferences

Parents should feel free to initiate a parent-teacher conference if desired. Such conferences should be scheduled with the teacher in advance and will be arranged for hours when the children are not in the room. In addition to parent initiated conferences, there will also be two regularly scheduled conferences for reporting student progress.

Visitors

Parents are always welcome. It will be necessary to check with the teacher to avoid any days that would not be a normal kindergarten day. School policy does not permit children visitors to attend a kindergarten session.

SCHOOL VISITATION IN KINDERGARTEN

Often the key to a successful relationship between parent, teacher, and child lies in the many times when all three are together within the school environment or in the kindergarten classroom.

This coming together clarifies and resolves many misconceptions. Cohen and Rudolph (1977, p. 400) state:

> Some mothers tell their children at the kindergarten door "to behave," other mothers tell them "to learn," and many mothers seem uncertain of what to tell their children about school. Despite the differing perceptions of teacher and parent, children remain themselves throughout. They do not leave parts of themselves inside or outside the schoolroom door. All of them enters, all of them reacts, all of them feels, all of them leaves in one piece.

Prejudgment or misjudgment on the part of any of the three participants can create obstacles. How often, prior to an initial visit to the dentist, a child is told, "Now this won't hurt," when *that* particular idea had never entered the child's consciousness! Some children and some parents feel the same about school. Many parents may well be recalling traumatic experiences from school days or even their own failures as young children attempting to succeed in school.

We need to realize that "when parents are not familiar with the purpose and plan for the activities of the school, they may be suspicious of the total program" (Leeper et al., 1974).

Reiterating in a similar vein, Almy (1975, p. 183) writes:

> When parents "see with their own eyes," they can more readily understand how a program furthers or perhaps hinders their child's learning. The words the teacher uses take on added meaning when the parents' picture of the program in operation is based on observation or participation.

What will parents want to know and what might prompt interest in school visitation? Developmental patterns of five-year-olds; children's interests; and guidelines for selecting learning materials, monitoring TV viewing, choosing suitable playthings, and contributing to reading readiness are all concerns of parents. Research indicates that particular aspects of kindergarten life—discipline, reading, and play—provoke more questions than any other area. The effective kindergarten teacher will find a willing participant in most parents in discussion of these many aspects of the life of the five-year-old.

Observation

Planned observations can be most revealing and productive for the parent. Certainly parents should be encouraged to make periodic visits to the classroom specifically to observe their children in a work situation—perhaps during the activities portion of the program or even the outdoor segment. Relationships with other children can be observed, as well as working styles, areas of participation, behavior, patterns, and strengths and weaknesses.

A brief preliminary discussion between teacher and parent is recommended. The teacher might state the purpose of the particular activity, the levels of achievement, and expected outcomes. An opportunity for questions following the session could lead to suggestions for child and parent cooperative effort on home projects. Planned observations help establish benchmarks for the child and foster understanding and appreciation for progress made in skill areas. Fromberg (1977, p. 314) cautions that if, as sometimes happens, retention of a child in kindergarten becomes a necessary decision, observations by the parent throughout the year should eliminate surprises and facilitate a wiser choice. Carefully planned and sequenced observations provide a rich opportunity for the teacher to interpret both short- and long-range significance of visible activity.

A provocative statement made by Leavitt and Cohen (1976, p. 263) is a useful reminder:

A new view of parent-child interaction has developed—one suggesting that demarcation between experts and parents vis-a-vis the development of children is a simplistic one. This new view recognizes that parents make a unique contribution to the affective and cognitive development of their children. This contribution stems from their intimate interaction with these children in their role as informal and/or formal instruction.

Whether in casual encounters, observations, or the conference setting, the kindergarten teacher would do well to acknowledge the multifaceted role of the parent.

Conferences

Conferences between parent, teacher, and sometimes other support personnel are rapidly becoming the preferred mode of communication about the child. If kindergarten is the first formal school experience for the child, the conference is preferred over all other methods previously discussed. The printed word can be cold and impersonal, permitting little interaction between reader and sender—and poorly structured written messages can often intensify problems.

Values of the conference are many:
1. The likelihood of misunderstanding is reduced in face-to-face conversation.
2. The conference is a *mutual* process, with each participant receiving assurances and essential advice and/or suggestions.
3. The child is the focal point, with all participants concentrating on enhancing development.
4. Unfair comparisons among children can be eliminated.
5. Mutual respect and understanding as well as personal growth of each participant can flourish.
6. The child develops a greater feeling of security when he knows both teacher and parent are working together for his benefit.
7. Both teacher and parent are stimulated to provide a better environment for the child at home and at school.
8. Areas of deficiency and proficiency in achievement can be established specifically, qualified, and explained.
9. The public relations value of the conference cannot be underestimated.
10. Conditions, both short range and long term, can be established for greater esprit de corps.

Conference planning

Productive conferences do not just happen; they are carefully planned. The teacher must keep in mind that many parents have special needs, such as the "single" parent; the parent of a handicapped child; the migrant parent; the rootless, mobile, middle-class parent; or the inexperienced parent.

The conference should be tailored to the parent and child involved.

The teacher should also recognize that there may be differences of opinion and philosophy regarding discipline (permissiveness versus conformity), play and the work ethic, whether to begin reading, and attitudes toward the responsibility of home and school for the child. In addition, some parents may have no desire for involvement beyond the routine.

Prior to the conference, the teacher will have determined a schedule through contacts with all parents. A brief form will suffice to obtain desired information (see Appendix B for example). The schedule should be confirmed when all details are known.

In some instances with working parents, it may be necessary to schedule conferences early in the morning or in the late afternoon or evening. Some school systems allow special conference days for kindergarten. Flexibility and a cooperative approach will help teacher and parent arrive at a mutually satisfactory time for the session.

A folder for each child that contains samples of work, as well as teacher notes and "jottings" about possible points for discussion provides a basis for initiating the conference. Materials collected should be supportive of statements to be made. A note card (recipe file) system with periodic entries about the child is favored by many kindergarten teachers as a means of remembering salient points. A thoughtful organizational scheme will facilitate and ease even the most stressful situation.

Anticipating questions that might be concerning the parent is also useful. Most parents want to know:

1. How does my child get along with other children?
2. How does my child "behave"?
3. Is my child working up to ability and, in general, in comparison with others?
4. What interests or special abilities have you noted?
5. Does my child participate and contribute to the entire class?

Remember, the child is the extension of the parent. Objectivity may be difficult for the parent, and criticism may be viewed as personal.

An often neglected or overlooked aspect in planning for the conference is the kindergarten classroom environment itself. Teachers might ask themselves the following questions concerning the surroundings parents will enter:

1. Is the room neat, attractive, and welcoming?
2. Is informal, comfortable seating provided? (Sitting *behind* a desk should be avoided.)
3. Will there be freedom from interruption?
4. Is there space for all materials (folders, books) that may be used?
5. If a parent needs to wait, is a "waiting space" available, perhaps with current magazines or even coffee? (This place should be out of range of the discussion.)
6. Do all arrangements facilitate confidentiality and relaxation, yet a professional attitude?

Conducting the conference

Early childhood authorities suggest the following techniques for successful conferences:

1. Keep the child's welfare central to the discussion—convey mutuality of interest.
2. Be straightforward, honest, and tactful in your evaluation.
3. Confidentiality is expected. Individualize the comments; comparisons with other children or references to other teachers or parents is unprofessional.
4. Realize that the conference is a two-way experience; cultivate the art of listening and take cues from the parent's concerns.
5. Document your comments; offer suggestions for improvement and follow-up. *Together* work out a plan.
6. Concentrate on the most important needs of the child and on the positive aspects—too much information only confuses.
7. If additional counsel appears necessary, refer the parent to the principal or supervisor.
8. Summarize briefly to close the conference—learn to pace discussion—encouragement and reassurance are positive notes.

WADE ELEMENTARY SCHOOL
Conference Record

Child's name _____ Grade _____

Teacher _____ Date _____

Type of conference: ☐ Personal ☐ Telephone ☐ Letter
Participating in conference: ☐ Mother ☐ Father ☐ Child ☐ Principal ☐ Teacher

Concerns:

1. _____
2. _____
3. _____
4. _____
5. _____
6. _____

Suggestions:

Follow-up:

BIRD ELEMENTARY SCHOOL
Kindergarten Conference Guide Sheet

Child's name _____

Teacher _____

Person at interview: ☐ Mother ☐ Father ☐ Other _____

	First conference (Date:)	Second conference (Date:)
Motor activities 1. Skipping 2. Balance beam 3. Ties shoes 4. Ball throwing		
Social skills 1. Participates in activities 2. Gets along with others 3. Speech 　a. Speaks clearly 　b. Talks in sentences 　c. Has speech problem 4. General attitude toward school		
Readiness 1. Knows colors 2. Can count objects one to ten 3. Prints name 4. Knows right and left 5. Recognizes shapes 6. Can cut and paste—uses scissors 7. Is attentive 8. Enjoys books		

Follow-up:

Health

1. Good physical appearance
2. Posture
3. General well-being

Work habits

1. Uses time wisely
2. Quality of work is good
3. Stays at task
4. Is flexible
5. Has good interest span
6. Cares for materials
7. Follows directions
8. Is responsible

Follow-up:

9. Plan how to inform parents who do not attend the scheduled conference.
10. A conference guide sheet can be very useful and provides a record of the discussion as well as follow-up plans. Two examples are shown on pp. 271-273.

Broman (1978, p. 426) offers a time line for recording a child's development:

September—Evaluate individualized skills and performances on rating form.

October through December—Make anecdotal records for each child.

January—Re-evaluate individualized skills and performances. Summarize anecdotal records. Hold individual conferences with parents.

February through April—Add more anecdotal records to child's folder.

May—Re-evaluate individualized skills and performances. Summarize anecdotal records. Write a report of progress. Hold individual conferences with parents.

The listing of techniques is not exhaustive. Consider the individual school situation and remember—in the conference setting, you are a learner also.

As we recall the original thesis of "parents and the teacher," we know that parental support of school programs can be a vital factor in the achievement of the five-year-old. Parents as partners with the school are better able to guide their children's growth and provide the needed support system.

Bronfenbrenner (1974) found that not only did parent intervention sustain developmental gains, but the involvement of parents in day-to-day activities and in the decision-making process led to increased awareness of school programs, a larger number of school visits, and more instances of work in the schools.

For the kindergartner, parents, teacher, and "me" becomes a powerful, satisfying triad.

REFERENCES AND SUGGESTED READINGS

Almy, Millie. *The early childhood educator at work.* New York: McGraw-Hill Book Co., 1975.

Andrews, Palmyra. What every parent wants to know. *Childhood Education,* 1976, 52(6), 304-305.

Broman, Betty L. *The early years in childhood education.* Chicago: Rand McNally & Co., 1978.

Bronfenbrenner, Uri. *A report on longitudinal evaluation of preschool programs: Is early intervention effective?* (Vol. 2.) Washington: D.C.: U.S. Department of Health, Education, and Welfare, 1974.

Cohen, Dorothy. *The learning child.* New York: Pantheon Books, Inc., 1972.

Cohen, Dorothy H., and Rudolph, Marguerita. *Kindergarten and early schooling.* Englewood Cliffs, N.J.: Prentice-Hall, Inc., 1977.

Comer, James P., and Poussaint, Alvin F. *Black child care.* New York: Simon & Schuster, Inc., 1975.

Evans, Ellis D. *Contemporary influences in early childhood education* (2nd ed.). New York: Holt, Rinehart & Winston, Inc., 1975.

Fromberg, Doris Pronin. *Early childhood education: a perceptual models curriculum.* New York: John Wiley & Sons, Inc., 1977.

Gordon, Ira, J. Parenting. teaching and child development. *Young Children,* 1976, 31(3), 173-183.

Gordon, Ira J., and Breivogel, William F. *Building effective home/school relationships.* Boston: Allyn & Bacon, Inc., 1978.

Greenberg, Kenneth R. *Tiger by the tail: parenting in a troubled society.* Chicago: Nelson-Hall, Publishers, 1974.

Hildebrand, Verna. Teacher-parent relations. In *Introduction to early childhood education* (2nd ed.). New York: Macmillan Publishing Co., Inc., 1976, pp. 425-444.

Hogan, Jane. Getting parents involved in their children's education. *News, Notes, and Quotes,* July-August 1978, 22. Newsletter, special research issue, Phi Delta Kappa.

Honig, Alice C. *Parent involvement in early childhood education.* Washington, D.C.: National Association for the Education of Young Children, 1975.

Lane, Mary B. *Education for parenting.* Washington, D.C.: National Association for the Education of Young Children, 1975.

Lay, Margaret, and Dopyera, John E. *Becoming a teacher of young children.* Lexington, Mass.: D. C. Heath & Co., 1977.

Leeper, Sarah Hammon, et al. Involving parents as partners. In *Good schools for young children* (3rd ed.) New York: Macmillan Publishing Co., Inc., 1974, pp. 389-405.

Levitt, Edith, and Cohen, Shirley. Educating parents of children with special needs—approaches and issues. *Young Children,* 1976, 21(4), 263-272.

Lille, David L. Planning a parent program. In *Early childhood education: an individualized approach to developmental instruction.* Chicago: Science Research Associates, Inc., 1975, pp. 191-205. Also excellent annotated bibliography, pp. 199-204.

Margolin, Edyth. *Sociocultural elements in early childhood education.* New York: Macmillan Publishing Co., Inc., 1974.

Markum, Patricia M. *Parenting.* Washington, D.C.: Association for Childhood Education, International, 1973.

Mattox, Beverly, and Rich, Dorothy. Community involvement activities: research into action. *Theory Into Practice,* 1977, 16(1), 29-34.

Nedler, Shari. Working with parents on the run. *Childhood Education,* 1978, 53(3).

Saylor, Mary Lou. *Parents: active partners in education*. Washington, D.C.: American Association of Elementary-Kindergarten-Nursery Educators, 1971.

Taylor, Katherine Whiteside. *Parents and teachers learn together*. New York: Teachers College Press, 1968.

U.S. Senate Committee on Finance. *Child care data and materials*. Washington, D.C.: U.S. Government Printing Office, 1971.

Wills, Clarice Dechant, and Lindberg, Lucile. Parent-teacher partnership; and Working with the parent group. In *Kindergarten for today's child*. Chicago: Follett Publishing Co., 1967, pp. 335-358.

OTHER RESOURCES

American School Health Association
1740 Broadway
New York, N.Y. 10019

Bank Street College of Education
610 West 112th St.
New York, N.Y. 10025

Child Study Association of America
9 East 89th St.
New York, N.Y. 10028

Children's Bureau
U.S. Department of Health, Education, and Welfare
Washington, D.C. 20002

Early Childhood Council of New York City
220 Waverly Pl.
New York, N.Y. 10014

National Congress of Parents and Teachers
700 North Rush St.
Chicago, Ill. 60611

CHAPTER 11

The state of the art

> Kindergarten is a beginning, a beginning of school experience. It must be just that—a beginning. Kindergarten is not first grade; it is not supposed to "hurry up" the maturation process so that children will be able to perform at a superior level when they reach first grade. Kindergarten should be a place where each child is recognized as an individual and where individual needs are met. (Ad hoc Kindergarten Guidelines Committee, 1978, p. 5)

What have we learned of today's kindergarten and the children and teachers who work there? What are the problems still to be resolved—the unanswered questions? What concerns appear to be emerging? As professionals intimately involved with caring about and planning for the educational programs of the five-year-old, where should our efforts be directed?

In the early chapters of the text, we discussed "beginnings," as well as the infinite variety of settings and experiences that kindergartners will encounter. Plans, suggestions, activities, and ideas from curricular areas have followed. Hopefully, you, the reader, have already begun to test, adapt, expand, and explore the many approaches we have presented. You may have been stimulated to compare notes with colleagues and discuss further the implications of what you have read.

You may feel comfortable about your relationships with the fives and your role as a teacher in the immediate setting. You may have an extensive collection of instructional materials, ranging from pictures to manipulative materials to a curriculum guide or two.

However, in a larger sense, as professionals, we must consider the kindergarten within the framework of the total educational environment and heighten our awareness and understanding of the many issues and problems to be confronted. Trends too are worthy of study.

The "classic" questions to be answered are, of course:

1. What should be appropriate curricular content for the fives?
2. Who is qualified, and how is certification met for the kindergarten teacher?
3. When should concepts be introduced in the various disciplines?
4. What is the appropriate setting for the kindergarten?
5. How—or by what methodology—can we ensure effective and efficient learning?

Each of these questions must be addressed in terms of the specific children, group, and setting involved, with resources, personnel, and expectations of the community in mind. Local and regional emphases must be considered, as must experiential backgrounds of children and adults.

Issues and concerns surrounding the kindergarten are many.

ORGANIZATION

What is the best organizational plan for kindergarten? As discussed in earlier chapters, organizational patterns in kindergarten are several. The daily half-day session with the same teacher responsible for two groups of children for approximately 2½ hours each has been traditional. The alternate-day full-day program has proponents in many areas, partly predicated on transportation and budget decisions rather than programmatic issues. Extended-day programs are available to some five-year-olds. Daily full-day kindergarten sessions are still relatively rare. Research on the desirability and educational results of each pattern has been limited. Pigge and Smith (1978) compared the achievements, attitudes toward school, and peer acceptance of kindergarten students in daily half-day kindergartens with those in alternate-day full-day kindergarten sessions. The students who attended kindergarten on a daily half-day basis earned a significantly higher set of means on the Metropolitan Reading Readiness Test than did a group of statistically matched students who attended school on an alternate-day full-day schedule. The daily half-day schedule was more advantageous for boys than girls. No differences were apparent in attitudes toward school or in peer acceptance or isolation.

The Minnesota State Department of Education (1972) compared children who attended kindergarten on a daily half-day basis with those who attended on an alternate-day full-day basis. Children who attended kindergarten daily had significantly higher scores on tests of ability to name numerals 1 to 10 and on knowledge of sounds of the letters of the alphabet. On all measures used, the children in the alternate-day full-day program had lower scores and greater group variability.

Cleminshaw (1977) investigated academic and social effects of kindergartens with differing time and structure formats. She found positive academic and social effects to be associated with the alternate-day full-day kindergarten, as well as positive parental attitudes toward the program. Unusual fatigue was not a finding. This research encourages the implementation of alternate-day full-day programs for kindergartens.

Wenger (1978, pp. 164-167) studied the effectiveness of alternate-day full-day kindergarten classes as compared with the effectiveness of daily half-day programs of instruction and concluded:

1. The type of kindergarten organization in which the child was enrolled was a significant factor contributing to observed differences in achievement among children.
2. Sex differences, within levels of organization, were not a significant factor contributing to the observed differences in achievement among kindergarten pupils (overall, girls, regardless of the type of organization, often achieved significantly higher scores than boys).
3. Age differences, within levels of organization, were not a significant factor contributing to the observed differences in achievement among kindergarten pupils.
4. Sex differences and age differences were found to interact significantly on some measures of academic achievement.

Wenger summarizes the study with the caution that public school personnel should evaluate carefully the reasons for altering daily half-day kindergarten programs and that substantive aspects of schooling should take precedence over concerns for administrative and financial matters.

In related studies, Bagley (1974), Johnson (1974), Lysiak and Evans (1976), and Mouw (1974) provide conflicting conclusions and recommend further research.

As might be expected, finances (budgets) are often the overriding concern, with bus transportation costs a significant factor, in the decision of organizational structure of the kindergarten, However, we would hope that as more communities consider the educational implications of decisions, more extended-day and daily full-day programs will become available for the five-year-old.

As we consider the opportunities for learning and the quality of learning experienced by the kindergartner, we tend to forget the intangibles. Attendance is impacted by the energy crisis, the weather, teacher strikes, bus problems, illness, holidays, school facilities, in-service days for teachers, and parent conferences, to list the most common factors. If all holidays are on Monday and the kindergarten child is programmed for a Monday–Wednesday–half-day Friday program, think what happens to the quality of learning!

ENROLLMENT

New statistics released by federal and private agencies disclosed that the number of children enrolled in kindergarten declined last year by the largest number since the government began keeping records 130 years ago. The plunge in kindergarten enrollment—about 300,000—is expected to continue for three more years. ("Washington Briefs," 1978, p. 723)

The decline in the birth rate has strongly impacted on school systems with the resulting closing of several elementary buildings, larger classes, and/or transporting of children to schools other than the neighborhood one. Kindergarten children are often traveling more miles and spending more hours away from home.

In some school systems declining enrollments may also mean that former intermediate-level teachers are assigned to kindergarten and may not have the requisite skills to deal with the younger child.

Children of the mobile, middle-income family may change location in mid-year; the migrant child moves often; the inner-city child may move several times a year. Dramatic changes from northern cities to cities of the Sun Belt occur daily, with kindergarten children experiencing many stresses. Teachers too experience stress as new children enter the class throughout the year and program individualization becomes necessary.

Fluctuations in class size demand adjustments, as does "learning" new children or preparing records for the five-year-old who is leaving. Changing schools may also be traumatic and create pressures for the teacher.

Of concern is what the effects are of stress and change on kindergarten children and teachers.

EVALUATION

Evaluation sometimes seems mysterious, yet it is a necessary process in determining whether the kindergarten program is succeeding with all children and achievement of goals is being accomplished. The tools of evaluation are many, including observation, interviews, accurate records, standardized tests, parent conferences, and child conferences. We might think in terms of "outcome" evaluation—the before and after—by looking at the five-year-old at the beginning and at the end of the kindergarten year and assessing the changes. In one sense, we are creating a profile of the assets and liabilities of the child in a particular setting at a particular time. Some educators discuss the "ecological" approach to the child, or the ecological system of the kindergarten—the child, the teacher, siblings, caregivers, and others. In simpler terms, this is the study of the relationship between the kindergarten child and his unique set of environmental circumstances. Characteristics and settings described in the early chapters of the text provide baseline data for program planning and evaluation.

The following criteria for evaluation of the kindergarten has been contributed by a former kindergarten teacher, Joan S. Jones:

Please use the following as guidelines only and be kind to future children by adding your own suggestions. Constant input is surely necessary if we are to offer improved programs rather than, year after year, a watered-down diet of gruel.

1. Relationship between teacher-child, child-child, and teacher-children:
   - Are children noticed?
   - Are language experiences occurring?
   - Are children accepted?
   - Are problems occurring naturally so that realistic problem solving can occur?
   - What kinds of nonverbal expressions can you pick up?
   - Are children purposefully involved?
   - How do they use materials within the environment?
   - Is anything socially productive occurring?
   - Are there signs of human warmth and affection?
2. Choices:
   - Can children, indeed, make choices?
   - Can you see a balance of teacher-directed choices and child-directed choices?
3. Materials:
   - Are they appropriate?
   - Are there more of some?
   - Are there less of others?
   - Which ones are needed?
   - Is there a variety?
4. Learning:
   - Are any examples visible?
   - Are there planned provisions for learning?
   - Does the atmosphere encourage exploring, discovering, generalizing, and concluding?
   - Are affective and cognitive domains in evidence—relatively balanced?
   - Are there opportunities and encouragement for play?
5. Space:
   - Is the spatial arrangement conducive to social groupings?
   - How could space be rearranged?
   - Are there any open space areas that appear to be troublesome ones?
   - Is there evidence of public property?
   - Is there evidence of private property?
6. General:
   - How do you feel about this kindergarten generally?
   - It is mentally healthy for adults and children?

The following reports to parents illustrate what evaluation of individual children might reveal:

Kari has enjoyed her year in kindergarten. She has made much growth in the social-emotional areas. Her earlier contacts with children were sometimes fraught with physical and verbal conflicts—sharing and taking turns was hard for her—she had one friend whom she clung to. It is now much easier for her to give and take with others—she has a wider circle of friends and is, herself, a better friend—she is more open about what she does and how she feels. Kari is very reserved and may study a new person or situation for a long time before she gives of herself—once she accepts, she reveals an affectionate nature—loves to talk to adults—in fact, has many adult-like qualities—is a mature, poised child.

She excels in physical activities—has excellent coordination that reflects itself in games of physical skill—her graceful movements in rhythms and dance—her precise handling of tools, brushes, crayons, scissors, and pencils—and her successful handling of paper-and-pencil activities. Intellectually capable, she should do well in academic areas. She has revealed a genuine talent in her paintings, and this area could be encouraged outside of school.

Kari has a good atittude toward school—is a good student—is now a comfortable child who is quite happy with her school—is quite happy with her new daddy and told us about him—talks about her activities outside of school more now than before. She is a talented little girl with a great deal of potential—she is very ready for "formal" schoolwork.

Tina—the child of gentle spirit and deep thoughts—a late-blooming perennial—economical with her speech and saying only what is necessary—affectionate—compassionate—a lover of animals—a quiet observer of life, absorbing it all and making her own internal conclusions.

Sad feelings at times caused tears—it was a great comfort for her to be able to "go up and see my mom." (Mothers are very special people as Tina tells it.) Shy and fragile in outward appearance, Tina possesses a steely determination and can close her mind like a steel trap—loud noises, violence, rough people disturb her. She gives of herself carefully, but once she accepts you, her loyalty is unsurpassed.

Tina slowly became a "whole" part of her group—is now willing to try out new situations and people—has made many friends—is well liked and accepted by others—is still hesitant about contributing to group discussions (she is so well behaved and quiet that you must be careful that she does not become that "good little girl who sits over in the third seat," as she has much potential that must be drawn out). She is an excellent listener—a good taker of turns—has good work-study habits—a well-developed attention span—above average mental equipment in excellent working order—she has delighted herself and me with her success in reading—is off to a good start—is highly motivated—handles paper and pencil well—has good small-muscle and eye-hand coordination—should have no difficulty with reading.

Her ability to create should be constantly encouraged—she is a lover of stories, poems, music, plays, etc., and should have much exposure to these areas in time to come. Tina worked with many materials well this year (clay, paint, wood, cloth, cooking, paper, crayons, etc.)—become totally absorbed for long periods of time—manipulated messes till they became what she wanted—was responsible about cleaning up and caring for those things she used. Her paintings, in particular, represent a high level of maturity, and her dynamic use of color and line is further evidence of her talent.

Her year in kindergarten has been rich in experiences and growth. Tina is rather like a poem—once you've read her, she always remains part of you. Her uniqueness has been her special gift to me—thank you for making the world brighter by having had her.

Reporting to parents is indeed an art!
We must remember, of course, that evaluation is daily, weekly, and long-term. We evaluate accomplishment of group goals as well as goals for individual children; and, just as important, we evaluate ourselves—our performance, our impact, and our outreach on the kindergarten.

RETENTION AND PROMOTION

To retain or promote in kindergarten is a critical component of evaluation, since in many instances it is the program that has failed or succeeded in meeting the individual needs of the child. Any kindergarten teacher knows what a sensitive issue retention is. Unless careful counseling, periodic evaluation, and sharing of all information has occurred, retention of the child can be devastating for all concerned.

For the parent, guilt feelings, shame, anger, denial, and refusal are common reactions. For the child, lack of self-confidence, self-esteem, misunderstanding, and confusion become evident. If kindergarten has been a mutual relationship for parents, child, and teacher, retention should be a *reasoned* decision.

In most instances, immaturity or the need for more growing is the basis for retaining the child for additional kindergarten experiences.

Symptoms of immaturity include "youngness," easy distractibility, lagging social development, short attention span, and poor coordination and control. Some children are late bloomers and, with proper nurturing and understanding, suddenly blossom and spurt ahead. Retention can be a positive approach for many children.

Acceleration is much less common for the five-year-old. Most educators would agree that early placement in first grade taxes the social adaptation of most kindergartners. Adjustment of the instructional program in terms of early reading or work with numbers for those ready for these skills is a more acceptable decision. If the primary education department of the school is organized as a continuous-progress unit, bright children move ahead at individual rates according to individual talents.

LEGISLATION

The passage of Public Law 94-142 has mandated the acceptance, planning for, and integration of children with handicaps into the regular classroom. As a result, severely handicapped children and those with lesser disabilities will be included in most kindergarten groups unless the nature of the handicap is such that aids and services of special classes are required.

The kindergarten teacher, already committed to the developmental approach—the individualized approach—can work with these "special" children with equanimity. Consideration of handicapped children as *whole* children with strengths and weaknesses helps focus attention on careful program planning.

Study of handicapping conditions also adds depth of understanding of each child. Dickerson and Davis (1979) write of implications to all teachers in their excellent article in *Young Children*. In *Childhood Education* Quisenberry (1979) summarizes the unanswered questions regarding the mainstreaming of young children and presents an excellent review of the research. Again, teachers' attitudes toward mainstreaming and handicapped children appear to be a critical factor for success of this approach.

Another excellent resource for further study is the November-December 1978 issue of *Journal of Teacher Education*.

Sometimes overlooked are the concerns evolving about children with socially maladaptive problems. Earlier discussion of such concerns in Chapter 5 should build awareness of these children. The migrant child and the child of the inner city also merit attention in terms of more effective approaches to classroom and school adjustment.

The kindergarten teacher is in the unique position of being able to aid in early identification of possible handicapping conditions and make proper referrals. Most universities offering teacher preparation programs now include course work relative to the new legislation and the subsequent knowledge base and program modifications necessary for children with all types of handicapping conditions.

THE CURRICULUM

What should constitute the curriculum for the kindergarten child is of critical concern to all those confronted with the deluge of published commercial materials and the pressures of special interest groups. Guidelines to selection of content and materials can be reviewed in earlier chapters.

The broader concern rests with decisions regarding early reading, the use of commercial workbook materials and total–content area programs, the work-play dichotomy, the inclusion of esthetic education, the integration of out-of-school activities, the question of balance within the various curriculur areas, and how best to use the time that the five-year-old is in school.

A cyclic approach to the study of curriculum is a healthy one. Including the kindergarten within the primary or early education unit will allow for continuity, sequence, integration, and proper pacing of instruction. Articulation of all curricular area profits everyone and eases the burden many kindergarten teachers face in decision making. Within an early education unit, language arts may be studied in depth by staff one year, science and mathematics the next, and so on, until all content areas have been treated. Teachers come to know one another and appreciate the contributions of all; knowledge

of children can be exchanged; and the administrative staff and instructional group work together to enhance learning for all ages. So often the kindergarten is a separate entity within the total school framework, and teachers feel isolated. Long-term curricular decisions and the selection of instructional materials must be made within the context of developmental stages of children.

RESEARCH DIRECTIONS

Research efforts in the kindergarten have already been effected in many areas. Other questions need answers. Research findings regarding *organizational patterns* and achievement are reported earlier in this chapter. What organizational structure will facilitate the most effective learning and provide the best "match" for community and school resources? This area needs further investigation in a variety of settings.

Models of kindergarten practice—"open," "traditional," Montessori, "follow-through," and "eclectic"—are discussed in Chapter 1. Here again, comparative studies would be useful in the decision-making process.

Learning styles of the kindergarten child need to be studied. Ideally, if we are to effect a "match" with teaching styles or even with particular organizational patterns, we need to investigate individual learning styles further. Optimal learning for each child is the goal. For a broader discussion of learning styles, the reader is referred to the January 1979 issue of *Educational Leadership*.

The concept of *readiness* needs expansion and investigation. How does a teacher determine the readiness quotient of each kindergarten student? How effective are the so-called readiness materials? When does a five-year-old become ready for formal instruction? What instructional approaches enhance readiness? Do grouping practices affect readiness?

Evans (1975, pp. 385-386) asks:

1. What, exactly, must the child know to be capable of doing in order to learn whatever it

is I plan to teach and in the manner I plan to teach it? (Teacher analysis)
2. To what degree does the child have at his command these prerequisite or subordinate skills and knowledge? (Assessment)
3. Is this child capable of attending sufficiently to this task so that he can master it? (Motivation)
4. Can efficient learning be accomplished at this time? (Economy)

Class size impacts on the performance and achievement of kindergarten children. What is the optimum class size for a group of five-year-olds? We know of groups of 45 and 50 children per kindergarten class, as well as groups of 10. Do some children thrive in the large-group environment? Within a class, what is the optimum grouping arrangement? In Phi Delta Kappan, Glass (1979) reports a major finding that as class size decreases, student achievement climbs. Would there be similar results with kindergarten children?

Program content, program methodology, and *timing* are other major issues cited by Evans as problems for study. Each of these issues holds implications for the kindergarten, with the way in which teachers present material being most critical.

The teacher within the kindergarten setting will have many opportunities to pose questions about each of the issues mentioned. Informal and formal research, both short and long term, could be designed to provide data for more effective teaching and learning.

TRENDS IN KINDERGARTEN EDUCATION

Several trends are observable in kindergarten programs throughout the country. As discussed in earlier chapters, the use of screening and assessment measures for diagnostic and placement purposes is increasing. Organizational patterns are undergoing closer scrutiny. There is a greater awareness of individual differences of children, and adaptations are being made for the child with a handicap, the gifted child, and the bilingual/multicultural child. More parents are expecting individualized planning for their children. Legal action has been brought to place the child with a physical handicap as well as the learning-disabled student in the regular classroom.

The curriculum for the kindergarten child is becoming more comprehensive, with a wealth of resources being marshaled for richer instruction. However, we would be remiss if we did not cite the increasing use of commercially packaged kits and materials in total-group instruction, the increasing number of workbooks being used in kindergarten classrooms, the press toward early reading and structured phonics programs, the lack of experiences in music and art, the meager opportunities for scientific learning, the unrealistic standards for performance placed on some children by the materials being used, and the general lack of excitement about learning.

Again, on the other hand, we are seeing changes in the *role of the teacher;* more involvement in decision making, referral of services, and the team concept are being promoted.

The *health needs* of the five-year-old are receiving increased attention. Nutrition, diet, rest, physical neglect, immunization, dental care, family status, and emotional health, as well as disease control, are coming under the direct influence and concern of the school. Early detection is the goal. Suchara's (1977, pp. 291-296) forthright position statement on "The Child's Right to Humane Treatment" in *Childhood Education* pertains particularly to the kindergarten child.

Increased parent education and *involvement* is another general trend specific to the kindergarten. A major emphasis of Chapter 10 is the home-school-community triad.

The kindergarten teacher is becoming increasingly more aware of changes in the family structure and the effects of such changes on children. Parent groups and parent volunteers within the kindergarten are becoming the rule rather than the exception. This move should be applauded.

Each teacher, each school, and each community must confront the issues and concerns in ways appropriate to the immediate environment.

Thus, we return to the beginning: kindergarten as a beginning, kindergarten in ferment, kindergarten for today, kindergarten for the product of the multimedia age, kindergarten in infinite variety, but most important, kindergarten for that "symphony of movement and sound," the five-year-old!

SUGGESTED READINGS

Ad Hoc Kindergarten Guidelines Committee. *Recommended kindergarten guidelines, state of Ohio.* Columbus, Ohio, 1978.

Bagley, Janice Prickette. *A study of half-day and full-day public school kindergartens in three northern Texas counties* Ph.D. thesis, Texas Woman's University, 1974.

Center for the Study of Families and Children, Vanderbilt Institute for Public Policy Studies. *The futures of children, categories, labels, and their consequences.* Nashville, Tenn.: Vanderbilt University, 1975.

Cleminshaw, Helen K. *Academic and social effects of all-day alternate-day kindergarten versus half-day, everyday kindergarten in traditional and open-classroom settings.* Doctoral dissertation, Kent State University Graduate School of Education, 1977.

Dickerson, Mildred C., and Davis, Michael D. Implications of P.L. 94-142 for developmental early childhood teacher education programs. *Young Children*, 1979, 34(1), 28-31.

Educational Leadership, 1979, 36(4), entire issue.

Evans, Ellis D. Changing patterns of early education; and Major issues in perspective. In *Contemporary influences in early childhood* (2nd ed.). New York: Holt, Rinehart & Winston, 1975, pp. 1-40; 365-401.

Glass links small class size to increased student achievement. *Phi Delta Kappan*, 1979, 60(6), 411.

Johnson, Edith W. *An experimental study of the comparison of pupil achievement in the all-day kindergarten and one-half–day control group.* Ph.D. thesis, Walden University, 1974.

Journal of Teacher Education, 1978, 29(6), entire issue.

Karnes, Merle. Exemplary early education programs for handicapped children: characteristics in common. *Educational Horizons*, January 1979, 56, 47-54.

Lysiak, Fae, and Evans, Charles L. *Kindergarten—fun and games or readiness for first grade: a comparison of seven kindergarten curricula.* Paper read at the American Educational Research Association (AERA) annual meeting, San Francisco, April 19-23, 1976.

Minnesota State Department of Education. *Kindergarten evaluation study: full-day alternate-day programs.* St. Paul: Minnesota State Department of Education, 1972.

Mouw, Annabelle J. *The description and evaluation of the alternate-day full-day kindergarten program.* Master's thesis, Wisconsin State University, 1976.

Pigge, Fred L., and Smith, Robert A. Daily half-day versus alternate-day full-day kindergarten sessions. Unpublished research study, Bowling Green State University, 1978.

Quisenberry, Nancy (Ed). Mainstreaming of young children: unanswered questions. *Childhood Education*, 1979, 55(3), 186-191.

Scott, Myrtle, and Grimmett, Sadie. *Current issues in child development.* Washington, D.C.: National Association for the Education of Young Children, 1977.

Suchara, Helen T. The child's right to humane treatment. *Childhood Education*, April-May 1977, 53, 290-296.

Umansky, Warren, and Cryan, John R. Mainstreaming of young children: unanswered questions. *Childhood Education*, 1979, 55(3), 186-191.

Washington briefs. *Phi Delta Kappan*, 1978, 59(10), 723.

Weber, Evelyn. Toward new theoretical positions; and Curricular issues. In *The kindergarten: its encounter with educational thought in America.* New York: Teachers College Press, 1969, pp. 211-241.

Wenger, Eugene B. *The effects of time on the achievement of kindergarten pupils.* Unpublished dissertation, Ohio State University, 1978.

Zigler, Edward, and Hunsinger, Susan. Look at the state of America's children in the year of the child. *Young Children*, 1979, 34(1), 2-3.

Zimiles, Herbert. Early childhood education: a selective overview of current issues and trends. *Teachers College Record*, 1978, 79(3), 509-527.

APPENDIX A
Children's books

ALPHABET BOOKS

Anno, Mitsumasa. *Anno's alphabet.* New York: Thomas Y. Cromwell Co., Publishers, 1975.
 An alphabet book with letters that look as if they were made of wood. Unusual objects are on facing pages.

Buringham, John. *John Burningham's ABC.* The Bobbs-Merrill Co., Inc., 1967.
 An alphabet book that uses traditional format. Lettering is satisfying in design. 4-6 years.

Grossbart, Francine. *A big city.* New York: Harper & Row, Publishers, Inc., 1966.
 An alphabet book that uses familiar objects for the urban child. 3-6 years.

Matthiesen, Thomas. *ABC: an alphabet book,* New York: Platt and Munk Publishers, 1966.
 An alphabet book with each page of text having an opposite page of full-color photographs. 3-6 years.

ANIMAL STORIES

Aruego, Jose. *Look what I can do.* New York: Charles Scribner's Sons, 1971.
 Very little text needed, since pictures tell the story of two caraboo in a frantic follow-the-leader game that exhausts both of them. Grades K-2.

Carle, Eric. *The very hungry catepillar.* Cleveland: Collins + World, 1970.
 A caterpillar eats his way through the days of the week and the pages of this book.

DuBoise, William Pine. *Bear circus.* New York: The Viking Press, 1971.
 When an army of grasshoppers strip the leaves from the trees that the koala bears eat, they are moved to a new park by the kangaroos—a journey that takes 12 years. 4-7 years.

Fatio, Louise. *The happy lion's vacation.* New York: McGraw-Hill Book Co., 1967.
 The zoo keeper's son takes the happy lion along for a day at the seashore and finds no one wants a lion as a traveler, Grades K-2.

Fatio, Louise. *The happy lion's treasure.* New York: McGraw-Hill Book Co., 1970.
 The happy lion decides to write a will, then discovers he owns nothing. His friends, the animals in the zoo, convince him that his treasure is his loving heart. Grades K-2.

Freeman, Don. *Dandelion.* New York: The Viking Press, 1964.
 Dandelion is invited to a come-as-you-are party, but he doesn't follow the suggestion; in the end he learns it is better to be yourself.

Goodall, John S. *Jacko.* New York: Harcourt Brace Jovanovich, 1972.
 A story in pictures about a monkey, Jacko, who escapes his owner and sails away on a sailing ship. 2-5 years.

Heide, Florence Parry: *Maximillian.* New York: Funk & Wagnalls Book Publishing, 1967.
 Maximillian, who is a mouse, decides he would rather be a bird, so he stows away in a bird's nest, much to the embarrassment of Mother Bird. 4-6 years.

Hoban, Russell C.: *Best friends for Frances.* New York: Harper & Row, Publishers, Inc., 1969.
 A sequel to several popular picture books about a small badger who has gone through problems familiar to young children. Grades K-2.

Hurd, Edith Thacher: *Johnny Lion's bad day.* New York: Harper & Row, Publishers, Inc., 1970.
 A familiar situation when Johnny Lion, in bed with a cold, begs his mother not to give him any medicine. Grades K-2.

Jackson, Jacqueline. *Chicken ten thousand.* Boston: Little, Brown & Co., 1968.
 A picture book that traces the life of a chicken in the mechanized world of big-business egg packing and

combines it with the story of a chicken heroine who escapes. Grades K-2.

Jackson, Jacqueline. *The orchestra mice*, Chicago: 1970, Reilly and Lee.

This family of mice so loved music that they lived with a symphony orchestra. Each of the 12 offspring were trained to play a musical instrument, and this saved their lives. Grades K-3.

Keith, Eros. *Rrra-ah*. Scarsdale, N.Y.: Bradbury Press, Inc., 1969.

Poor Rrra-ah, a toad, is mistaken for a frog and taken home by children, put in a box, and fed turtle food. Grades K-3.

Kraus, Robert, *Leo the late bloomer*. New York: Windmill Books, Inc., 1971.

All the animals can read and write and draw neatly except Leo—he can't even talk. 3-5 years.

Lionni, Leo. *Fredrick*. New York: Pantheon Books, Inc., 1967.

All through the summer the field mice collect food for the winter, but Fredrick collects the warm sun rays and colors that he shares with them in the winter. 5-7 years.

Lionni, Leo. *The biggest house in the world*. New York: Pantheon Books, Inc., 1968.

The biggest house in the world is the shell that belongs to a proud snail and, hampered by it, he dies. 3-7 years.

McCloskey, Robert. *Make way for ducklings*. New York: The Viking Press, 1941.

When a duck family tries to cross a busy Boston street, a policeman comes to their rescue. 3-5 years.

Newmann, Rudolf. *The bad bear*. New York: Macmillan Publishing Co., Inc., 1967.

The bear is the nastiest bear ever born until he learns to sing and dance so he can become the childrens' playmate. Grades K-2.

Ormondroyd, Edward. *Theodore*. Emeryville, Calif.: Parnassus Press, 1966.

An aging toy bear, Theodore accidentally gets caught in a load of wash at the laundromat and is not happy getting so clean. 3-6 years.

Ormondroyd, Edward: *Broderick*. Emeryville, Calif.: Parnassus Press, 1969.

An industrious mouse seeks and finds a path to fame and fortune through initiative and diligence when he becomes a champion surfer. Grades K-2.

Ormondroyd, Edward. *Theodore's rival*. Emeryville, Calif.: Parnassus Press, 1971.

Lucy, Theodore's mistress, gets a new bear for her birthday; and Theodore is very jealous until he realizes that the new bear is really a panda and not another bear! 4-6 years.

Potter, Beatrix: *The sly old cat*. London: Frederick Warne & Co. Ltd., 1972.

The cat invites the rat to tea, and the rat is offended when he gets only crumbs. He outwits the cat and eats the last muffin. 3-5 years.

Steig, William. *Sylvester and the magic pebble*. New York: Simon & Schuster, Inc., 1969.

A Caldecott Award (1970) winner, this is the story of a young donkey who finds a magic pebble and his adventures because of it (see p. 297). K-2.

Steig, William. *Amos and Boris*. New York: Farrar, Straus & Giroux, Inc., 1971.

Amos is a mouse who falls off a ship he is sailing; and Boris, the friendly whale, rides him back to land. During their adventure they become good friends who hate to part when the journey is over. K-2.

Stolz, Mary. *The story of a singular hen and her peculiar children*. New York: Harper & Row, Publisher, Inc., 1969.

The silly, endearing story of a hen who has no children and her amazing adoption plan for acquiring some. Grades K-3.

Titus, Eve. *Anatole and the piano.* New York: McGraw-Hill Book, Co., 1966.

There is only one piano great enough for Anatole, the magnificent mouse, to play on; and he is given it when he has done a noble deed that benefits all orphans and music lovers. Grades K-3.

Titus, Eve. *Anatole and the thirty thieves.* New York: McGraw-Hill Book Co., 1969.

Anatole, the mouse of distinction, turns sleuth and solves a robbery in the cheese factory where he works. Grades K-2.

Waber, Bernard. *A firefly named torchy.* Boston: Houghton Mifflin Co., 1970.

Torchy is a misfit firefly whose light is too bright, and only through trying to outshine the night lights of a city does he learn to only twinkle. Grades K-2.

CIRCUS

Aldridge, Josephine Haskell. *Reasons and raisins.* Emeryville, Calif.: Parnassus Press, 1972.

A nonsensical story with a circus setting and colorful pictures. A box of raisins tempts the little fox, and adventures begin when he takes it. Grades K-2.

Wildsmith, Brian. *Brian Wildsmith's circus.* New York: Franklin Watts, Inc., 1970.

Brilliant pictures showing jugglers, acrobats, big cats, and clowns describe this circus with very little text. 2-5 years.

COLORS

Reiss, John J. *Colors.* Scarsdale, N.Y.: Bradbury Press, 1969.

A first book for learning and practicing colors with the use of familiar objects. 2-5 years.

Tison, Annette: *The adventures of the three colors.* New York: World, 1971.

A slight plot about a boy experimenting with colors and a lesson on how secondary colors are obtained. Grades K-3.

ECOLOGY

Mizumura, Kazue. *If I built a village.* New York: Thomas Y. Crowell Co., Inc., 1971.

This book gives an unstated message of conservation in its dreaming of "what it would be like if I built a village or a town or a city." 4-6 years.

Olsen, Ib Spang. *Smoke.* New York: Coward, McCann & Geoghegan, Inc., 1972.

A family bent on a country outing discovers that the air is polluted with smoke. What they do to control it gets the message across about what we can do to control the quality of air. Grades K-2.

Parnall, Peter. *The mountain.* New York: Doubleday & Co., Inc., 1971.

A mountain is inhabited by peaceful animals and beautiful flowers until it becomes a national park. The change it undergoes is a lesson in preserving ecological balance. Grades K-3.

Peet, Bill. *The Wump world.* Boston: Houghton Mifflin Co., 1970.

The planet of Wumps is invaded by the Pollutions, who destroy the quiet world and move on!

Tresselt, Alvin: *The beaver pond.* New York: Lothrop, Lee and Shepard Co., 1970.

A description of the cycle of a beaver colony, this book introduces the aspects of ecological balance in simple terms by telling how, because of the beavers, the pond was begun. Grades K-2.

FAIRY TALES

Adams, Adrienne. *Hansel and Gretel.* New York: Charles Scribner's, Sons, 1975.

Both the text and illustrations are good in this edition of the old story. For reading aloud.

Briggs, Raymond. *Jim and the beanstalk.* New York: Coward, McCann & Geoghegan, Inc., 1970.

A sequel to the original tale. Silly and engaging, the story is enhanced by the illustrations, for example, Jim struggling under a huge set of false teeth. 4-7 years.

Godden, Rumer. *The old woman who lived in a vinegar bottle.* New York: The Viking Press, 1972.

The old woman, who is poor but happy, returns a fish to the sea instead of eating it. The fish is a prince and tells her he will grant her every wish. Then the troubles begin until she is returned again to her former life—poor but happy! Grades K-3.

Grimm, Jakob Ludwig Karl. *The four clever brothers.* New York: Harcourt Brace Jovanovich, Inc., 1967.

A Grimm fairy tale about four brothers sent into the world by their poor father. They learn a trade, rescue the king's daughter, and outwit the dragon. Grades K-3.

La Fontaine, Jean de. *The hare and the tortoise.* New York: Franklin Watts, Inc., 1967.

The familiar tale of the hare and the tortoise is illustrated beautifully in this oversized picture book. Grades K-2.

McGowen, Tom. *Dragon stew.* Chicago: Follett Publishing Co., 1969.

The king was always losing his cooks because he kept giving them advice. Finally, the new cook lets the king do the cooking using a recipe the king got from a dragon. Grades K-3.

Ungerer, Tomi. *Zeralda's ogre.* New York: Harper & Row, Publishers, Inc., 1967.

A hungry ogre raids a village and eats his favorite food: children. Zeralda tames the ogre by becoming his cook and teaching him to eat other things. Grades K-2.

Winn, Marie. *The fisherman who needed a knife.* New York: Simon & Schuster, Inc. 1970.
The book explains why people use money as it tells how the fisherman had to make many trades before he got the knife he needed. 4-7 years.

FAMILY LIFE*

Ardizzone, Edward. *The wrong side of the bed.* New York: Doubleday & Co., Inc., 1970.
A story in pictures. A small sullen figure at the breakfast table—his hands need scrubbing, his manners are atrocious, he teases his sister, and he is scolded by his father. But the story has a happy ending. 3-6 years.

Ets, Marie Hall. *Bad boy, good boy.* New York: Thomas Y. Crowell Co., Inc., 1967.
Roberto speaks only Spanish, and he is unable to adjust to his neighbors, family, or friends. Finally, at the Children's Center he learns skills and confidence. Grades K-3.

Goodall, John S. *Naughty Nancy.* New York: Atheneum Publishers, 1975.
Nancy is to be the flower girl at her sister's wedding, but she finds more interesting things to do.

Hill, Elizabeth Starr. *Evan's corner.* New York: Holt, Rinehart & Winston, 1967.
The setting for this book is Harlem. Eight people in a two-room apartment doesn't provide much privacy, so Evan's mother gives him a corner of his own. Grades K-2.

Hoban, Russell C. *A birthday for Frances.* New York: Harper & Row, Publishers, Inc., 1968.
Frances will not give her sister, Gloria, a birthday present until her mother gently persuades her to. Grades K-2.

Keats, Ezra Jack. *The snowy day.* New York: The Viking Press, 1962.
Peter is a black child having fun in the snow. He finds that the snowball he tries to save melts.

Kellogg, Steven. *Can I keep him?* New York: The Dial Press, 1971.
Arnold brings home every stray animal he can find, asking the usual question, "Can I keep him?" 4-6 years.

Lexau, Joan M. *Me Day.* New York: The Dial Press, 1971.
Me Day is Rafer's birthday, but he is not very happy, because his mamma and daddy are divorced. He wonders if they will ever become undivorced. Grades K-3.

Mahy, Margaret. *A lion in the meadow.* New York: Franklin Watts, Inc., 1969.
When the little boy tells his mother there is a lion in the meadow, she gives him a match box with a dragon inside to chase the lion away. (Parent copying with an imaginary situation.) 5-7 years.

McCloskey, Robert. *One morning in Maine.* New York: The Viking Press, 1952.
Warm family life is depicted in this story of how Sal lost her first tooth. (P)

Neumeyer, Peter F. *The faithful fish.* Reading, Mass.: Young Scott Books, 1971.
Two episodes: one black and one white family vacation at the same cottage and tell their impressions of the delights of fishing. Grades K-3.

Parsons, Ellen. *Rainy day together.* New York: Harper & Row, Publishers, Inc., 1971.
A loving family and the pleasures of everyday routine are described as a small girl tells about her rainy day at home alone with her mother. 3-5 years.

Scott, Ann H. *Sam.* New York: McGraw-Hill Book Co., 1967.
When Sam's mother sends him out to the kitchen, his brother and sister scold him and his father yells at him. Some attention and a job to do makes Sam happy. A story about a middle-class black family. 3-6 years.

Sharmat, Marjorie. *Goodnight, Andrew, goodnight, Craig.* New York: Harper & Row, Publishers, Inc., 1969.
Two small boys go to bed peacefully; but the younger brother, Andrew, is not sleepy. As the boys become noisier and noisier, their father finally goes in to quiet them. 4-6 years.

Sonneborn, Ruth. *Seven in a bed.* New York: The Viking Press, 1968.
Mama, the baby, and seven children get off the plane in America; and because their home isn't quite ready, all the children must sleep in one bed. Grades K-2.

Sonneborn, Ruth. *Friday night is Pappa night.* New York: The Viking Press, 1970.
A small Puerto Rican boy, Pedro, asks his mother why his father comes home only on Friday nights; she explains that Pappa must work two jobs to support his family. Grades K-2.

Steptoe, John. *Stevie.* New York: Harper & Row, Publishers, Inc., 1969.
Robert, a small black boy, isn't very happy when he finds out he will have Stevie as a boarder in his house; but then when Stevie leaves, Robert misses him. 5-7 years.

Viorst, Judith. *Alexander and the terrible, horrible, no good, very bad day.* New York: Atheneum Publishers, 1972.

---

*Other stories on family life can be found under "Grandparents" and "Siblings."

The youngest of three boys, Alexander wakes up to a day of disasters. The day ends with his mother telling him that some days are just like that, even in Australia. Grades K-3.

Zolotow, Charlotte. *When I have a son*. New York: Harper & Row, Publishers, Inc., 1967.

John, on his way to his piano lesson, tells his friend all the things his son will not have to do when he is a father. There is a companion book titled *When I Have a Little Girl*. Grades K-2.

Zolotow, Charlotte. *A father like that*. New York: Harper & Row, Publishers, Inc., 1971.

A boy without a father wishes for one, and he lists all the wonderful things his father would do if he had one. Grades K-2.

FOLKTALES

Aliki, Ed. *Three gold pieces*. New York: Pantheon Books, Inc., 1967.

A simple retelling of the Greek folktale about Yannis, a poor peasant who leaves home to serve a rich man and how he trades his three gold pieces for some good advice. Grades K-2.

Ambrus, Victor G. *Brave soldier Janosh*. New York: Harcourt Brace Jovanovich, Inc., 1967.

There is history for even the small child in the story of Janosh, a Hungarian folk hero, and his defeat of Napoleon. Grades K-3.

Anderson, Lonzo. *Two hundred rabbits*. New York: The Viking Press, 1968.

Based on a French folktale, this is a humorous picture book in which the author is a rabbit. Grades K-2.

Brown, Marcia. *Stone soup*. New York: Charles Scribner's, Sons, 1947.

Three French soldiers talk the villagers into contributing their hidden vegetables to make stone soup. Grades K-2.

Daniels, Guy. *The tsar's riddles*. New York: McGraw-Hill Book Co., 1967.

A retelling of a Russian folktale. Faced with a difficult legal decision, the tsar sets a series of riddles that can only be answered by a seven-year-old girl. Grades K-2.

Daniels, Guy. *Foma the terrible*. New York: Delacorte Press, 1970.

Foma, the squinty-eyed, bulbous-nosed peasant, becomes a national hero by his many deeds and misdeeds. Grades K-3.

Dayrell, Elphinstone. *Why the sun and the moon live in the sky*. Boston: Houghton Mifflin Co., 1968.

A story of the beginning of time based on an African folktale. Grades K-2.

Emberley, Barbara. *Drummer Hoff*. Englewood Cliffs, N.J.: Prentice-Hall, Inc., 1967.

A Caldecott Award winner (1968), this is an adaptation of a folk verse. It describes Drummer Hoff and the firing of a cannon (see p. 297). 5-7 years.

Haley, Gail E. *A story, a story*. New York: Atheneum Publishers, 1970.

The story explains the favorite African folk material, the spider tale (see p. 297). Caldecott Award winner (1971). Grades K-2.

Hogrogian, Nonny. *One fine day*. New York: Macmillan Publishing Co., Inc., 1971.

A Caldecott Award winner (1972), this picture book is based on an Armenian folktale about a fox who needs a favor—to have his tail sewed back on (see p. 297). Grades K-3.

Jacobs, Joseph. *Munachar and Manachar*. New York: Thomas Y. Crowell Co., Inc., 1970.

A Celtic folktale to be read aloud about Munachar and how everything he does is undone by Manachar. Grades K-2.

Lester, Julius. *The kneehigh man and other tales*. New York: The Dial Press, 1972.

A rural background is the setting for this collection of six animal stories from black folklore. Grades K-2.

Lipton, Betty Jean. *The one-legged ghost*. New York: Atheneum Publishers, 1968.

Based on a Japanese legend. Yoshi finds a one-legged ghost with no purpose until he discovers it will keep him dry when it rains. Grades K-3.

McDermott, Gerald. *Anansi the spider*. New York: Holt, Rinehart & Winston, 1972.

An African folk tale from the Ashanti, this story is about the six sons of Anansi, who each possessed a special talent, and how they used these talents to rescue their father. Grades K-2.

Mosel, Arlene. *Tikki, tikki, tembo*. New York: Holt, Rinehart & Winston, 1968.

A good book to read aloud, since rhyme and rhythm are maintained by the repetition of the title. This is an adaptation of an Oriental folktale. Grades K-2.

Ransome, Arthur. *The fool of the world and the flying ship*. New York: Farrar, Straus & Giroux, Inc., 1968.

A Caldecott Award winner (1969), this is a retelling of the Russian folktale of how a group of men, each with magical powers, outwit the czar (see p. 297). Grades K-3.

Rees, Ennis. *Brer Rabbit and his tricks*. Reading, Mass.: Young Scott Books, 1967.

Three Brer Rabbit stories are told in rhyming verse without dialect: "Brer Rabbit and the Tar Baby," "Winnianimus Grass," and "Hello, House." Grades K-3.

Rees, Ennis. *More of Brer Rabbit's tricks.* Reading, Mass.: Young Scott Books, 1968.

Three more Brer Rabbit stories without dialect but in rhyme. Grades K-3.

Shivkumar, K. *The king's choice.* New York: Parents' Magazine Press, 1971.

A retelling of the Eastern Indian folktale of the fox, the vulture, and the leopard, who wish to eat the camel after he has carried them on their journey. The lion (king) tells the story. Grades K-3.

Sleator, William. *The angry moon.* Boston: Little, Brown & Co., 1970.

An adaptation of a legend of the Tlingit Indians of Alaska. The moon becomes angry when it is laughed at and disappears. Grades K-2.

Tamchina, Jurgen. *Dominique and the dragon.* New York: Harcourt Brace Jovanovich, 1969.

A German folktale, this tells of the much-feared dragon that turns out to be the model of friendship as Dominique tells the dragon that all animals are nice. Grades K-3.

Ushinsky, K.: *How a shirt grew in a field.* New York: McGraw-Hill Book Co., 1967.

The story of a Russian child, Vasya, whose father tells him that he is planting shirts in the field. The child is amazed to see only flax come up from the seeds his father planted. Grades K-2.

Yulya. *Bears are sleeping.* New York: Charles Scribner's Sons, 1967.

Set in a quiet snowbound forest, this tale gives the musical phrases and words of an old Russian lullaby. 4-7 years.

Zemach, Harve. *The speckled hen.* New York: Holt, Rinehart & Winston, 1966.

This is a Russian nursery rhyme about grandparents who have a speckled hen that lays a speckled egg. 4-6 years.

FRIENDSHIP

Campbell, Peter. *Harry's bee.* New York: The Bobbs-Merrill Co., Inc., 1971.

How Harry and the bee become friends and decide to travel together. 4-7 years.

Carle, Eric. *Do you want to be my friend?* New York: Thomas Y. Crowell Co., Inc., 1971.

A picture book with only a few words. Small children will have fun guessing what is on each page as the small mouse asks the question. 2-5 years.

Cohen, Miriam. *Will I have a friend?* New York: Macmillan Publishing Co., Inc., 1967.

Jim, brought to kindergarten the first day by his father, wonders if he will make a friend. The locale is a city neighborhood that is racially mixed. 4-6 years.

Cohen, Miriam: *Best friends.* New York: Macmillan Publishing Co., Inc., 1971.

The setting is in a busy kindergarten, and the making of a friendship between Paul and Jim is an experience the children can identify with. 3-5 years.

de Regniers, Beatrice Schrenk. *May I bring a friend?* New York: Atheneum Publishers, 1964.

A boy is invited to have tea with the king and queen; and each time he goes, he takes a different animal friend.

Lionni, Leo. *Alexander and the wind-up mouse,* New York: Pantheon Books, Inc., 1969.

Friendship triumphs over self-interest in a story about a real mouse and his friend Willy, a toy mouse. 4-6 years.

Kantrowitz, Mildred. *I wonder if Herbie's home yet?* New York: Parents' Magazine Press, 1971.

The story of a small boy whose best friend has gone off to play with someone else. Grades K-2.

Shecter, Ben. *Conrad's castle.* New York, Harper & Row, Publishers, Inc., 1967.

Conrad's castle grows and grows in his head while his friends try to distract him. Grades K-2.

Udry, Janice May. *Let's be enemies.* New York: Harper & Row, Publishers, Inc., 1961.

John decides James is much too bossy and doesn't want to be his friend anymore.

Waber, Bernard. *Ira sleeps over.* Boston: Houghton Mifflin Co., 1975.

Ira is spending the night at his friend's house, and his sister plants some seeds of doubt.

GRANDPARENTS

Borack, Barbara. *Grandpa.* New York: Harper & Row, Publishers, Inc., 1967.

A monologue by a small girl, describing her grandfather and their relationship. Tender, humorous illustrations. 3-7 years.

Buckley, Helen E. *Grandfather and I.* New York: Lothrop, Lee and Shepard Co., 1959.

A young boy and his grandfather like to take walks together because neither is in a hurry.

Lexau, Joan M. *Benjie.* New York: The Dial Press, 1964.

Benjie, a small black boy in Harlem, forgets his shyness when he tries to find the lost earrings of his beloved grandmother. Grades K-2.

Lexau, Joan M. *Benjie on his own.* New York: The Dial Press, 1970.

Benjie is in school now and doesn't need his grandmother to pick him up, but he does worry when she doesn't appear. Grades K-3.

Stanek, Muriel. *Left, right, left, right.* Chicago: Albert Whitman & Co., 1969.

Bespectacled Katie must learn to tell her left hand

from her right hand. Her grandmother helps her solve her problem when she gives her a ring to wear on her right hand. Grades K-1.

Udry, Janice. *Mary Jo's grandmother*. Chicago: Albert Whitman & Co., 1970.

After Christmas, Mary Jo's family leaves Mary Jo at her grandmother's in the country. When her grandmother falls and hurts her leg, Mary Jo must find help. A country setting involving a middle-class black family. Grades K-2.

Zolotow, Charlotte. *William's doll*. New York: Harper & Row, Publishers, Inc., 1972.

Grandmother understands why William wants a doll, even though his father prefers for him to play with a basketball. (Someday William will be a father and will need to know how to love a baby.) Grandmother takes William shopping for the doll he wants and explains to his father why it is important for him to have it. 4-8 years.

HEALTH

Raskin, Ellen. *Spectacles*. New York: Atheneum Publishers, 1968.

Unaware of her need for glasses, Iris sees strange creatures where familiar objects really exist. When she gets spectacles, the world around her becomes clear. Grades K-2.

Rockwell, Harlow. *My doctor*. New York: Macmillan Publishing Co., Inc., 1972.

Large, clear illustrations show a doctor's equipment and procedures.

HOLIDAYS

Coopersmith, Jerome. *A Chanukah fable for Christmas*. New York: G. P. Putnam's Sons, 1969.

This adaptation of Moore's poem incorporates Moshe Dayan, flying saucers, and brotherhood. To be read aloud. Grades K-3.

Hoban, Russell C. *The mole family's Christmas*. New York: Parents' Magazine Press, 1969.

Delver Mole did not know what Christmas was until one of the house mice told him about it. Grades K-2.

Kraus, Robert. *How Spider saved Christmas*. New York: Simon & Schuster, Inc. 1970.

The humorous story of how Fly and Ladybug invite Spider to their house for Christmas and the gifts he brings to help celebrate. 3-5 years.

Moore, Clement Clarke. *A visit from St. Nicholas*. New York: Simon & Schuster, Inc., 1971.

A facsimile of the 1848 publication, this edition contains the old-fashioned engravings unlike our traditional Santa Claus. All ages.

Tresselt, Alvin. *The world in the candy egg*. New York: Lothrop, Lee and Shepard Co., 1967.

A picture book for Easter about the toys in a toy shop looking through the window of a candy egg and how the egg is finally given to a small girl. 3-7 years.

MISCELLANEOUS

Burningham, John. *Mr. Gumpy's outing*, New York: Holt, Rinehart & Winston, 1971.

Good story to read aloud. Mr. Gumpy goes for a boat ride and takes along two children, a rabbit, a cat, a dog, and other animals. Of course, the boat tips over. 4-7 years.

Caudill, Rebecca. *Contrary Jenkins*. New York: Holt, Rinehart & Winston, 1969.

Contrary Jenkins stops to see his brother in the mountains and stays three years. A tall tale to be read aloud. Grades K-3.

Gag, Wanda. *Millions of cats*. New York: Coward, McCann & Geoghegan, Inc., 1928.

A lonely old man goes off to find a cat for himself and his wife. He returns with millions of cats.

Goodall, John S. *Shrewbettina's birthday*. New York: Harcourt Brace Jovanovich, 1971.

This story of a shrew's gala day is set in an English village of Victorian times. 3-5 years.

Hermann, Frank. *The giant Alexander in America*. New York: McGraw-Hill Book Co., 1968.

Alexander is called to America by the President to help land a man on the moon. When something goes wrong with the pickup crew, Alexander rescues the astronauts and becomes a hero. Grades K-2.

Hutchins, Pat: *Rosie's walk*. New York: Macmillan Publishing Co., Inc., 1968.

A very funny picture book depicting Rosie's walk across the yard, over the haystack, past the mill, under the beehive, and back home for dinner—all the time she is being followed by a fox. 3-6 years.

Hutchins, Pat. *Clocks and more clocks*. New York: Macmillan Publishing Co., Inc., 1970.

When Mr. Higgins' grandfather clock needs checking, he buys another clock, and another, and another, and so on, until he ends with a watch. 4-6 years.

Keeping, Charles. *Alfie finds "the other side of the world."* New York: Franklin Watts, Inc., 1968.

Alfie, a small Cockney boy, comes across the Thames to an amusement park that seems to him like the other side of the world. Grades K-2.

Lent, Blair. *John Tabor's ride*. Boston: Little, Brown & Co., 1966.

This tall tale is based on a New England legend about a shipwrecked sailor from Nantucket who takes a ride on the back of a whale. Grades K-3.

Lindgren, Astrid. *Springtime in Noisy Village.* New York: The Viking Press, 1966.

The story of Noisy Village (in Denmark) and the children who live there. Grades K-3.

Lipton, Betty Jean. *Kap and the wicked monkey.* New York: W. W. Norton & Co., Inc., 1968.

Kap, an elf, must have it out with the wicked monkey to save his sick father. Grades K-2.

Lipton, Betty Jean. *A dog's guide to Tokyo,* New York: W. W. Norton & Co., Inc., 1970.

A travel book with pictures of contemporary life in Tokyo as seen by dogs and explained by Jumblie, a poodle. Grades K-3.

Martin, Patricia Miles. *Rolling the cheese.* New York: Atheneum Publishers, 1966.

Maria visits her uncle Pasquale in San Francisco and enters a cheese-rolling contest. A story to be read aloud. Grades K-3.

Mayer, Mercer. *Frog, where are you?* New York: The Dial Press, 1969.

A picture story about a small boy and his pet frog. The boy goes to bed while his frog is in a jar and awakes the next morning to find the frog gone. 3-5 years.

McCloskey, Robert. *Lentil.* New York: The Viking Press, 1940.

Set in a small midwestern town, this story is about Lentil, a boy who substitutes for the town band on a special occasion. Grades K-2.

McCloskey, Robert. *Blueberries for Sal.* New York: The Viking Press, 1948.

Sal and a baby bear find themselves with the wrong mothers as they pick blueberries on the Maine hillside. 3-5 years.

McGowen, Tom. *The apple strudel soldier.* Chicago: Follett Publishing Co., 1968.

Maxl is the best baker in Glutenstern, and his delicious apple strudel wins the war. Grades K-3.

Ness, Evaline. *Sam, Bangs and moonshine.* New York: Holt, Rinehart & Winston, 1966.

A Caldecott Award winner (1967), this is the story of a small girl, Sam, and her cat, Bangs. Moonshine is what she calls all the fibs she tells (see p. 297). Grades K-2.

Raskin, Ellen. *Franklin stein.* New York: Atheneum Publishers, 1972.

The humorous story of Fred, the complicated junk structure made by Franklin while he was locked in the attic room. Grades K-2.

Rey,, Margret Elizabeth. *Curious George goes to the hospital.* Boston: Houghton Mifflin Co., 1966.

This book has the same light humor of all the Curious George books. Curious George pays a visit to the hospital after swallowing a piece of a jigsaw puzzle. Grades K-2.

Sendak, Maurice. *Where the wild things are.* New York: Harper & Row. Publishers, Inc., 1963.

Max wears his wolf suit, gets into trouble, and is sent to bed to dream about where the wild things are.

Sendak, Maurice. *In the night kitchen.* New York: Harper & Row, Publishers, Inc., 1970.

A fantasy that takes place when a small child falls asleep and wakes up in the night kitchen; then, when the cock crows, he tumbles back into his bed. Grades K-2.

Spier, Peter. *Hurrah, we're outward bound.* New York: Doubleday & Co., Inc., 1968.

A sixteenth or seventeenth century sea voyage is pictured from the old French port of Honfleur. The text consists of sea chanteys and rhymes as the ship travels from Honfleur to New York and back again. Grades K-2.

Taylor, Mark. *Henry explores the jungle.* New York: Atheneum Publishers, 1968.

Henry says goodbye to his mother and sets out through the jungle with his trusty hound to find a tiger. Much to Henry's surprise, he does, but the tiger turns out to have escaped from the circus. Grades K-2.

White, E. B. *Charlotte's web.* New York: Harper's Magazine Press, 1952.

A little girl who talks to animals and a spider who can write and talk save the life of Wilbur, a pig. To be read aloud to the class. (P)

Winn, Marie. *The man who made fine tops.* New York: Simon & Schuster, Inc., 1970.

A story about why people do different kinds of work. The concept of division of labor is introduced when the father makes a top for his son and trades it for raw materials he doesn't have. Grades K-2.

Winn, Marie. *The thief-catcher.* New York: Simon & Schuster, Inc., 1972.

A concept storybook that explains why we pay taxes by describing a busy community that because of a series of thefts needs a thief-catcher. Grades K-2.

Zemack, Harve; *A penny a look.* New York: Farrar, Straus & Giroux, Inc., 1971.

The tables are turned when a man and his brother journey to a land inhabited by one-eyed people in order to capture and bring back a specimen for exhibit. Grades K-3.

MOTHER GOOSE

Alderson, Brian. *Cakes and custard.* New York: William Morrow & Co., Inc., 1975.

A new collection of well-illustrated Mother Goose.

Briggs, Raymond. *The Mother Goose Treasury.* New York: Coward, McCann & Geoghegan, Inc., 1966.

Rhymes and illustrations are excellent, gentle, delicate, and grotesque. 3-6 years.

Tucker, Nicholas. *Mother Goose lost.* New York: Thomas Y. Crowell Co., Inc., 1971.

These nursery rhymes were collected by Nicholas Tucker while he was doing research on Mother Goose and for the most part are unfamiliar to adult and child. 2-5 years.

Wyndham, Robert. *Chinese Mother Goose rhymes.* New York: World, 1968.

This is a collection of universal rhymes—some familiar and some with the special charm of the unfamiliar. 4-6 years.

NATURE

Coatsworth, Elizabeth Jane. *Under the green willow.* New York: Macmillan Publishing Co., Inc., 1971.

Not a story, this book shows the water creatures in the crowded spot under the willow tree. Grades K-3.

Mari, Iela. *The apple and the moth.* New York: Pantheon Books, Inc., 1970.

A book for the young biologist. The story is told by pictures, from the larva feeding on the apple to the adult moth flying off to start the cycle again. 3-5 years.

Mari, Iela. *The chicken and the egg.* New York: Pantheon Books, Inc., 1970.

A book for the young biologist. Pictures show the egg being laid, the growth of the embryo, the brooding hen, and the hatching. 3-5 years.

Selsam, Millicent. *Is this a baby dinosaur?* New York: Harper & Row, Publishers, Inc., 1972.

A book for the young naturalist. The informal text gives much information about the plants and animals that are pictured. Grades K-3.

Stevens, Carla. *The birth of Sunset's kittens.* Reading, Mass.: Young Scott Books, 1969.

A series of photographs show every detail of kittens being born. The text explains the process from the first contraction to the kittens nursing. Grades K-3.

Tresselt, Alvin. *The dead tree.* New York: Parents' Magazine Press, 1972.

The text follows the life of a tree from full maturity to its return to rich humus on the forest floor. Grades K-2.

NUMBERS

Adler, Irving. *Sets and numbers for the very young.* New York: The John Day Co., 1969.

Big pages filled with multiple simple examples in words and drawings to make clear to the very young child the cardinal and ordinal numbers and the concept of sets. Adult help needed. Grades K-2.

Allen, Robert. *Numbers: a first counting book.* New York: Platt & Munk, 1968.

Big, clear photos of familiar objects and an introduction to the numbers one to ten. Does introduce some simple addition. 4-6 years.

Feelings, Muriel L. *Mojo means one.* New York: The Dial Press, 1971.

Swahili for the numbers one to ten is given in a counting book illustrated with pictures that show East African life. 4-7 years.

Grest, W. Cabell. *My pictionary.* New York: Lathrop, 1970.

A compilation of labeled actions and objects grouped as to people, animals, storybook characters, things, places, colors, and numbers. 3-6 years.

Hoban, Tana. *Count and see.* New York: Macmillan Publishing Co., Inc., 1972.

A counting book that moves from one to fifteen, then in tens to fifty, and then to one hundred. 2-5 years.

Kredenser, Gail. *1—One dancing drum.* New York: S.G. Phillips, Inc., 1971.

A counting book that is worked around a bandmaster, musicians, and instruments. 3-6 years.

Oxenbury, Helen. *Numbers of things.* New York, Franklin Watts, Inc., 1968.

A tall counting book from England; the shape is used to advantage for the contrasting facing pages. 4-7 years.

Reiss, John J.: *Numbers.* Scarsdale, N.Y.: Bradbury Press, Inc., 1971.

This book is distinguished for its big, bold pictures and colors. The numbers are one to twenty, moving by tens to one hundred. 2-5 years.

POETRY

Aldis, Dorothy. *All together: a child's treasury of verse.* New York: G. P. Putnam's Sons, 1952.

A collection of 144 poems for young children.

Clifton, Lucille. *Some of the days of Everett Anderson.* New York: Holt, Rinehart & Winston, 1970.

Poems for each day of the week explore the fears and pleasures of a black child, Everett Anderson. Grades K-2.

Fisher, Aileen. *Cricket in a thicket.* New York: Charles Scribner's Sons, 1963.

A collection of nature poems for young children.

Lewis, Richard W. *Miracles.* New York: Simon & Schuster, Inc., 1966.

A collection of poems written by children between the ages of 5 to 13 grouped by theme. All ages.

Lobel, Arnold. *On the day Peter Stuyvesant sailed into town.* New York: Harper & Row, Publishers, Inc., 1971.

Colonial history told in verse—how Peter Stuyvesant

cleaned up the colony by putting the people to work. K-3.

Prelutsky, Jack. *Toucans, two.* New York: Macmillan Publishing Co., Inc., 1970.

A collection of humorous and rhythmic poems about silly animals. Grades K-2.

RHYMES

DeForest, Charlotte B. *The prancing pony.* New York: Walker & Co., 1968.

Nursery rhymes from Japan of universal subject appeal: snow, springtime, butterflies, elves, and animals of all kinds. 3-7 years.

Domanska, Janina. *If all the seas were one sea.* New York: Macmillan Publishing Co., Inc., 1971.

The familiar nursery rhyme about a tree made of all the trees in the world falling into a sea made of all the seas in the world. 3-5 years.

Domanska, Janina. *I saw a ship a-sailing.* New York: Macmillan Publishing Co., Inc., 1972.

A well-known rhyme with exceptional illustrations of the ship, crew, and cargo. 3-5 years.

Hoffmann, Felix. *A boy went out to gather pears.* New York: Harcourt Brace Jovanovich, Inc., 1966.

An old rhyme illustrated with small sturdy figures who march across the pages, gradually filling the empty spaces with the cumulative characters of the rhyme. Grades K-2.

Kraus, Robert: *Whose mouse are you?* New York: Macmillan Publishing Co., Inc., 1970.

A rhyme-and-rhythm text that asks the question, "Whose mouse are you?" answered by, "My mother's mouse, she loves me so," and is easily memorized for reading along. 2-5 years.

Matterson, Elizabeth. *Games for the very young.* New York: American Heritage Publishing Co., Inc., 1971.

A selection of rhymes with diagrams for finger play. The material is divided into categories related to the interest of young children. 2-5 years.

Watson, Clyde. *Father fox's penny rhymes.* New York: Thomas Y. Crowell Co., Inc., 1971.

The pictures, some in comic strip format, show the activities of the fox world; and the rhymes are rhythmic and bouncy. 3-6 years.

SCHOOL

Bemelmans, Ludwig. *Madeline.* New York: The Viking Press, 1939.

Madeline is the smallest of 12 girls who live at Miss Clavels' boarding school. Her surprise appendectomy makes her different.

Caudill, Rebecca. *Did you carry the flag today, Charley?*, New York: Holt, Rinehart & Winston, 1966.

The story of a five-year-old boy and his first encounter with a classroom at a summer school in Appalachia. To be read aloud. Grades K-2.

Hurd, Edith Thacher. *The white horse.* New York: Harper & Row, Publishers, Inc., 1970.

Jimmie Lee is an introspective child but not a lonely one. His visit to the zoo with his class and the discovery of the white horse are part of the adventure. Grades K-3.

Krauss, Ruth. *I write it.* New York: Harper & Row, Publishers, Inc., 1970.

A text showing the many ways and places "I write it" and the happiness of achievement in learning to write your own name. 5-6 years.

Meshover, Leonard. *The guinea pigs that went to school.* Chicago: Follett Publishing Co., 1968.

A description of a school project—a child brings her pet to school, and the children learn from the situation. Grades K-2.

Simon, Norma. *What do I say?* Chicago: Albert Whitman & Co., 1967.

A simple book of etiquette with settings at home and in the classroom for an urban kindergarten child. Available in an English-Spanish edition. 3-6 years.

SHAPES

Freeman, Mae. *Finding out about shapes.* New York; McGraw-Hill Book Co., 1969.

An introduction to spatial conceptualization with simple definitions of shapes, lines, and forms. K-3.

Hoban, Tana. *Shapes and things.* New York: Macmillan Publishing Co., Inc., 1970.

This book, which has no text, is useful for encouraging observation. It uses silhouette pictures to show the shapes of familiar household objects. 2-5 years.

Ogle, Lucille: *I spy.* New York: American Heritage Publishing Co., Inc., 1970.

A picture book of objects in a child's home environment—some familiar, some not. 2-5 years.

Oppenheim, Joanne: *Have you seen roads?* Reading, Mass.: Young Scott Books, 1969.

All kinds of roads are included in this book: busy city streets, country lanes, mountain roads, riverways, bridges, and unmapped roads of space. K-2.

SIBLINGS

Alexander, Martha. *Blackboard bear.* New York: The Dial Press, 1969.

A book for the very young child who feels left out of older children's games. A simple and satisfying story of how the younger child copes. 3-6 years.

Alexander, Martha. *Nobody asked me if I wanted a baby sister.* New York: The Dial Press, 1971.

The new baby is getting all the attention, so Oliver puts Bonnie in his wagon and goes off to give her away. Not a brand-new theme, but direct and affectionate. 3-6 years.

Borack, Barbara. *Someone small.* New York: Harper & Row, Publishers, Inc., 1969.

Life is full when a baby sister comes along to disrupt things. A pet bird is acquired and then dies—lesson in the changes of life. Grades K-2.

Byars, Betsy C. *Go and hush the baby.* New York: The Viking Press, 1971.

Just as he is about to leave the house to play ball, Will is asked by his mother to pacify the baby. He tells the baby a story but is soon replaced by the baby's bottle. 2-5 years.

Greenfield, Eloise. *She came bringing me that little baby girl.* Philadelphia: J. B. Lippincott Co., 1974.

Written in black dialect, this is the story of a boy who dislikes the attention being paid to his new baby sister.

Keats, Ezra Jack. *Peter's chair.* New York: Harper & Row, Publishers, Inc., 1967.

Peter is upset when his father wants to paint his chair and crib pink, but he soon realizes he is too big for them. 3-6 years.

Reavin, Sam. *Hurray for Captain Jane!* New York: Parents' Magazine Press, 1971.

Jane refuses to share the three prizes she won at a birthday party with her little brother and happily goes off to a bath and dreams of adventures. Grades K-2.

Scott, Ann H. *On mother's lap.* New York: McGraw-Hill Book Co., 1972.

An Eskimo boy, Mick All, loves to cuddle on his mother's lap under the reindeer blanket, but he doesn't feel there is room for his baby sister. 3-5 years.

Zolotow, Charlotte: *If it weren't for you.* New York: Harper & Row, Publishers, Inc., 1966.

A small boy lists all the joys of life he enjoyed before he had a new brother, but in the end he admits it is not all bad. 3-6 years.

SONGBOOKS*

Emberley, Barbara. *One wide river to cross.* Englewood Cliffs, N.J.: Prentice-Hall, Inc., 1966.

The familiar song that begins "Old Noah built himself an ark" is illustrated with humor as the door to the ark becomes smaller and smaller as the pages go by. Grades K-5.

Ipcar, Dahlov. *The cat came back.* New York: Alfred A. Knopf, Inc., 1971.

A simple arrangement of an old folk song precedes the text, which sings itself as it is read aloud. Grades K-3.

---

*Songbook *collections* are listed at the end of Chapter 7.

Mother Goose: London bridge is falling down! New York: Doubleday & Co., Inc., 1967.

A version of the singing game—each verse is pictured with a double-page spread. There are words and music for the song and some historical notes about the bridge. Grades K-2.

Paterson, A. B. *Waltzing Matilda.* New York: Holt, Rinehart & Winston, 1972.

The words to the song "Waltzing Matilda" are illustrated in this book about Australia. 4-8 years.

URBAN LIFE

Hitte, Kathryn. *Mexicali soup.* New York: Parents' Magazine Press, 1970.

A Chicano family learns a lesson in changing too much when they move to the city. Grades K-3.

Keats, Ezra Jack. *Goggles.* New York: Macmillan Publishing Co., Inc., 1969.

Peter encounters a gang of big boys who demand the goggles he has found. A realistic story in an urban setting. 5-7 years.

Keats, Ezra Jack. *Hi, cat!* New York: Macmillan Publishing Co., Inc., 1970.

The setting is a city neighborhood. Archie finds a cat in a paper bag, and the cat eventually goes home with him. Grades K-2.

Keith, Eros. *A small lot.* Scarsdale, N.Y.: Bradbury Press, Inc., 1968.

Bob lives on one side of the lot, and Jay lives on the other. To keep the lot from being used for a business, they turn it into a park. Grades K-2.

Raskin, Ellen. *Nothing ever happens on my block.* New York: Atheneum Publishers, 1966.

Chester sits on the curb and complains that nothing ever happens on his block while behind him all sorts of wild adventures are taking place. Grades K-3.

Schick, Eleanor. *City in the winter.* New York: Macmillan Publishing Co., Inc., 1970.

Jimmy wakes up one morning and finds there is no school because of a blizzard. His mother goes to work, and he spends the day with his grandmother. An unusual event in a familiar, everyday environment. Grades K-2.

Segal, Lore. *Tell me a Mitzi.* New York: Farrar, Straus & Giroux, Inc., 1970.

Three tales set in an urban neighborhood tell the adventures of Mitzi: "Mitzi Takes a Taxi," "Mitzi Sneezes," and "Mitzi and the President." Grades K-2.

Shulevitz, Uri. *One Monday morning.* New York: Charles Scribner's Sons, 1967.

The setting is urban, inner city, and lower class, the story concerns a small, imaginative, solitary child who dreams of everyday as well as glamorous occupations. Grades K-2.

CALDECOTT AWARD WINNERS, 1966-1979

1966 Leodhas, Sorce Nic. *Always room for one more.* New York: Holt, Rinehart & Winston, 1965.

A story adapted from an old Scottish folk song. Music is included in the book. Lachie MacLachlan invites all passers-by into his wee house during a storm. After the catastrophe they all get together and build a new house so there is room for all.

1967 Ness, Evaline. *Sam, Bangs and moonshine.* New York: Holt, Rinehart & Winston, 1966.

A story of imagination and its consequences. The fisherman's little daughter learns that her tall tales can lead to real trouble.

1968 Emberley, Barbara. *Drummer Hoff.* Englewood Cliffs, N.J.: Prentice-Hall, Inc., 1967.

A free adaptation of a folk verse called "John Ball Shot Them All." Each step in the firing of a cannon and its consequences is described. A minor theme is the destruction of war.

1969 Ransome, Arthur: *The Fool of the World and the flying ship.* New York: Farrar, Straus & Giroux, Inc. 1968.

The traditional folk story of three sons seeking their fortunes. The third son, the Fool of the World, outwits the czar and marries the princess.

1970 Steig, William. *Sylvester and the magic pebble.* New York: Simon & Schuster, Inc., 1969.

Sylvester is an enterprising donkey who finds a magic pebble; adventures follow with tragedy and a happy ending.

1971 Haley, Gail E. *A story, a story.* New York: Atheneum Publishers, 1970.

Ananasi, the Spider Man, wants to tell stories to the children; but in order to do this, he must capture a leopard, a hornet, and a fairy for the Sky God, Nyame. The Spider Man succeeds. Effective for reading to a group.

1972 Hogrogian, Nonny. *One fine day.* New York: Macmillan Publishing Co., Inc., 1971.

The story of a fox who steals an old woman's milk and how she cuts off his tail. A cumulative tale wherein one situation leads to another, building suspense in repetition.

1973 Mosel, Arlene. *The funny little woman.* New York: E. P. Dutton & Co., Inc. 1972.

The story of a jolly little Japanese woman who is caught by the wicked Oni while chasing her runaway dumpling. With the help of a magic paddle, she escapes and becomes the richest woman in Japan. Humor and suspense with a different flavor.

1974 Zemach, Harve. *Duffy and the devil.* New York: Farrar, Straus & Giroux, Inc. 1973.

The Rumpelstiltskin-like story of Duffy, a lazy maid, and the pact she makes with the devil. Sly humor and an engagingly nasty devil.

1975 McDermott, Gerald. *Arrow to the sun.* New York: The Viking Press, 1974.

The story of a Pueblo boy and his search for his father, and the four trials he survives.

1976 Dillon, Leo, and Dillon, Diane. *Why mosquitos buzz in people's ears.* New York: The Dial Press, 1975.

A retelling of a West African folktale packed with action, varied animal characters, and humor.

1977 Musgove, Margaret W. *Ashanti to Zulu: African traditions.* New York: The Dial Press, 1976.

This picture book shows the variety of people and customs of Africa. The common people are the stars, and ordinary living situations are depicted.

1978 David, Peter Spier. *Noah's ark.* New York: Doubleday & Co., Inc., 1977.

Delightful and detailed color illustrations lend magic to the story of Noah's ark.

1979 Goble, Paul. *The girl who loved wild horses.* New York: E. P. Dutton & Co., Inc., 1978.

The legend of a Plains Indian girl and the tribe's horses. The story ends with a Navaho and Oglala Sioux song. To be read aloud to younger students. Grades 1-3.

APPENDIX B

Information forms for children entering kindergarten

WINTERGREEN LOCAL SCHOOL DISTRICT
Kindergarten Information Form

Date _____

Name of child: _____
                  Last name   First name   Middle name   Name used

Date of birth: Month _____ Day _____ Year _____ Phone _____

Parent or guardian: _____
                     Last name   First name   Middle name

HOME AND ACTIVITIES

Number of children in family _____ Child's rank _____

What previous group experience has child had?

☐ Nursery school   How long? _____

☐ Other   How long? _____

Child's special interests _____

What travel experiences has child had? _____

How does child get along with adults? _____

How does child get along with other children? _____

Does child have playmates of own age? _____

What forms of discipline are most often used in child's home? _____

_____

HEALTH

Health status _____

Serious illnesses or accidents _____

Allergies _____ Pertinent information concerning allergies _____

_____

Does child have any nervous habits? _____

Any special fears (storms, the dark, animals, insects, etc.) _____

Any eye, ear, speech difficulties, or physical problems _____

MY CHILD

My child:	Not yet	Needs a lot of help	Needs a little help	Needs no help
1. Puts on and takes off clothing (shirt, coat, sweater, pants, shoes)	☐	☐	☐	☐
2. Fastens clothing				
• Zippers	☐	☐	☐	☐
• Buttons	☐	☐	☐	☐
Ties shoelaces or buckles	☐	☐	☐	☐
3. Goes to the toilet by himself	☐	☐	☐	☐
4. Follows simple directions without being reminded	☐	☐	☐	☐
5. Tells what he wants or needs	☐	☐	☐	☐

My child:	Not available	Not interested	Sometimes	Very often
1. Likes to look at books	☐	☐	☐	☐
2. Enjoys being read to	☐	☐	☐	☐
3. Likes to listen to records	☐	☐	☐	☐
4. Watches television	☐	☐	☐	☐
5. Uses:				
• Scissors	☐	☐	☐	☐
• Pencil and crayons	☐	☐	☐	☐
• Paints	☐	☐	☐	☐
• Clay	☐	☐	☐	☐
• Paste or glue	☐	☐	☐	☐

My child:	Not yet	Just beginning	Does well
1. Talks in sentences	☐	☐	☐
2. Can tell color of things	☐	☐	☐
3. Says rhymes	☐	☐	☐
4. Sings songs	☐	☐	☐
5. Can tell "how many" of something	☐	☐	☐
6. Recalls and retells stories	☐	☐	☐

Please add any other information that would be helpful to the school in planning your child's program.

Information given by _____

Dale Public Schools
250 Evans Avenue

Dear Kindergarten Parents:

Your child is registered for kindergarten at _____ School. We have planned a program of parent-teacher-child conferences to acquaint you and your child with the school.

The conference will provide an opportunity for us to meet. While the child explores the kindergarten room, we will be able to talk about the child's experiences and interests, so that together we can work better for the child's development. The interview will only be approximately 15 minutes long. It would be helpful if all of us could spend a few minutes together in this first schoolroom.

Your conference will be held in Room A and has been scheduled for _____,
                                                                                                Day
_____ at _____.
   Date   Time

                                            Sincerely,

                                            _____
                                            Kindergarten teacher

----

Parent's reply

Please check one of the following and return this portion of the form to _____
_____ School.

☐ We will come to school as scheduled above.

☐ We would prefer another time and suggest _____

                                            _____
                                            Parent's signature

                                            _____
                                            Address

                                            _____
                                            Telephone

March 21, 19_____

Kindergarten registration
19 _____

Registration at Grant will be held on April 4.

WHAT: Registration for children who will be attending kindergarten at Grant School in September of 19 _____. To be eligible for kindergarten a child must be five years old before October 1, 19 _____, having been born before October 1, 19 _____.

WHEN: At 9:00-11:00 AM and 1:00-3:00 PM on Tuesday, April 4, 19 _____.

WHERE: Parents will take prospective kindergartners to our kindergarten (Room 101), where our kindergarten teacher, Mrs. Buxton, our speech therapist, Mrs. Hills, and a volunteer PTA mother will give them a peek at kindergarten life and treat them to cookies and punch. After leaving children in Room 101, parents will go to the multipurpose room (Room 105) to register them.

HOW: Volunteers from PTA will take registrations.

SPECIALISTS PRESENT: Principal, kindergarten teacher, nurse, and speech and hearing therapist.

PLEASE BRING*:
1. Birth certificate or baptismal record.
2. Proof of residency, such as a current utility bill, copy of a lease or purchase agreement, or a bank statement.
3. Immunization record. (State law requires that all children, before admission to school, be vaccinated or immunized against diphtheria, whooping cough, tetanus, poliomyelitis, regular measles, and three-day measles. In addition, it is also recommended that a tuberculin test be given. Smallpox immunization is left to the discretion of your pediatrician.)
4. Medical report from physician. This may be sent to the school office at a later date. Physical examinations prior to entrance into kindergarten are strongly encouraged.
5. Parents' employment: company, address, and telephone number.
6. Name, address, and telephone number of a neighbor, relative or friend who may be contacted in an emergency.
7. We would appreciate proof of custody if parents are divorced or separated.

NOTE: Our present kindergartners will not have school this day so that the teacher and kindergarten room can be used for the prospective 19 _____ kindergartners.

Please share this information with any neighbors who may have children starting school next year.

---

*Registration will not be completed unless the first three items are presented.

APPENDIX C

A brief annotated bibliography on kindergarten screening*

Bradley, Estelle. Screen them early! *Academic Therapy,* 1975, *10*(3), 305-308.

    This study focused on the effectiveness of a kindergarten screening program. The statistical results seem to confirm the need for such testing early in the school year. This can give the teachers a thorough understanding of each child's learning style. The specialists' stress of prescriptive remediation did not significantly improve pupil performance. The key to any successful educational program has been, and always will be, the classroom teacher diagnosing each child's area of weakness, and then remediating this problem in a meaningful manner. (Author abstract)

Chia, Thomas E. Parents as identifiers of giftedness, ignored but accurate. *Gifted Child Quarterly,* 1974, *18*(3), 191-195.

    This study reaffirms earlier reports that correct identification by teachers at the kindergarten level is below 25%. Results of this study indicate that at the kindergarten level parents are more able than teachers to assess their children's abilities.

Early identification of learning disabilities: a discussion and approach (ERIC Document Reproduction Service No. ED 089 837)

    Medvedeff's approach to identifying potential learning problems in young children. Six areas are evaluated: visual, visual motor, speech and hearing, physical and behavioral, psychomotor, and psychological.

Early prevention of school failure: Illinois Title III ESEA Project (ERIC Document Reproduction Service No. ED 115 052)

    Screening tests include evaluations of visual-motor integration as well as speech, language, and motor development.

Feshbach, Seymour. Early identification of children with high risk of reading failure. *Journal of Learning Disabilities,* 1974, *7*(10), 639-644.

    Two alternative models for identifying kindergarten-age children with a high risk of becoming reading failures are compared. One model places primary emphasis on psychometric test procedures assessing linguistic and perceptual-motor skills related to reading readiness. The alternative strategy is based upon the kindergarten teacher's evaluation of the child's skills and behavior, with particular emphasis on the discrepancy between a child's specific competencies and those required for success in a particular first-grade classroom. Significant and encouraging correlations were obtained between the various measures taken in kindergarten and reading achievement test scores obtained at the end of first grade. (Author abstract)

Hillerich, Robert L. *Kindergarten screening procedures: early identification or merely early labeling?* (ERIC Document Reproduction Service No. ED 103 825)

    This is a diagnostic instrument, rather than a predictive one, to diagnose for necessary skills. The screening battery (Prediction with Diagnostic Qualities—PDQ—) consists of nine tests: auditory discrimination, listening comprehension, general vocabulary, ability to categorize, knowledge of relationship of words, picture sequencing, oral language development, abilities to follow oral directions, and abilities to use oral context.

---

*Screening is not a one-time process or activity. Informally, the teacher engages in questioning, noting, diagnosing, and prescribing in a kind of cyclic approach throughout the year with individual children. A good program and good experiences rely on flexibility, adjustment, and the use of multiple resources. Only in this way are needs and expectations of the five-year-old met.

Jens, Dorothy. *Project genesis: final report* (ERIC Document Reproduction Service No. ED 049 820)

Clinics held in the spring test kindergartners on perceptual-motor abilities, hearing, speech and language development, vision, developmental maturity, and learning readiness.

Keah, Barbara K., et al. Teachers' perceptions of educationally high risk children. *Journal of Language Development*, 1974, 7(6), 367-374.

Fifty-eight kindergarten and primary-grade teachers were individually interviewed in order to determine their perceptions of children's behavior indicative of educationally handicapped pupils viewed as learning, behavioral, and personality problems, and potential retarded pupils viewed primarily as educational problems. Some differences in risk indicators were found relative to the socioeconomic status of the school district. Findings lend clear support to use of classroom teachers as a first-level screen for early identification of high-risk pupils. Teachers' observations of classroom performance provide insight into children's learning and behavioral styles which facilitate or interfere with their school success. (Author abstract)

Maitland, S., et al. Early school screening practices. *Journal of Learning Disabilities*, 1974, 7(10), 645-649.

To ascertain the prevalence of early school screening practices, the specific tests employed, and the use made of the test results, a survey was conducted of a representative sample of school districts in the United States. Responses indicated that a majority of districts do screen, and there is great variability in the measures they employ. Although there are many published measures for kindergarten and first grade, only the Metropolitan Readiness Tests are used by a high percentage of school districts. Tests given at the end of the kindergarten year are most often used for determining first-grade placement; tests given at the beginning of the kindergarten or first-grade year are used equally often to individualize instruction. (Author abstract)

APPENDIX D
Films

VARIOUS ASPECTS OF THE KINDERGARTEN*

Child Language: Learning without Teaching
Davidson Films, Inc.
   The viewer is encouraged to listen to children in their learning of an involved process. The film shows many problems children face as they learn to communicate. 20 minutes.

Child/Parent Relationships: Selected Segments from Look at Me Series
Perennial Education, Inc., 1975
   An overview of a series that deals with ideas about things parents and children can do together. The emphasis is on enjoyment; self-image; and learning in the areas of language, math, and science. 28½ minutes.

Child's Play
CRM—McGraw-Hill, 1978
   Explores the value of play in the overall growth of the child. Explores various kinds of play and notes the important role of adult interaction with children's play. 20 minutes.

Child's Play and the Real World
Davidson Films, Inc.
   Clearly demonstrates how essential play is to development. Examines the world of children at play as they become social beings who share ideas, solve problems, and cope with frustrations. 18 minutes.

The Child Watchers
CRM—McGraw-Hill
   Discovering the laws that govern the development patterns of children. 29 minutes.

Children's Aggression: Its Origin and Control
Davidson Films, Inc.
   Describes aggression in children and methods for managing this behavior. 17 minutes.

The Creative Kindergarten
Soundings
   Pilot study on intervention strategies. 40 minutes.

Foundations of Reading and Writing
Campus Film Distribution Corp., 1975
   Focuses on the learning of reading and writing as an integration of many skills and basic experiences. Showing children involved in painting, block play, story reading, etc., the film presents some examples of vocabulary with meaning, phonics, symbol recognition, and other concepts. 33 minutes.

Foundation of Science
Campus Film Distribution Corp., 1977
   Focuses on development of concepts as children investigate, observe, compare, and test. Activities with water, food, magnets, wood, blocks, outdoor equipment, plants, and animals are included. 17 minutes.

The Haunted Mouth
Modern Talking Pictures Service, Inc. 1975
   An approach to preventive dentistry that challenges viewers to brush and floss properly, and to see the dentist regularly. 13 minutes.

The Impact of the Classroom Environment on Child Development
Davidson Films, Inc.
   Shows how imaginative teachers create a fertile environment for preschoolers.

Jenny Is a Good Thing
Precision Films
   Nutrition film emphasizing eating patterns and food preparation. 18 minutes.

---

*These films are available through the film services of most universities.

Kindergarten: Twigs from a City Tree
Coronet
  Inner-city kindergarten. 22 minutes.

Learning in the Kindergarten
Anti-Defamation League of B'nai B'rith
  Follows a day's activities of children. 36 minutes.

Reading: The American Dinosaur
Media Five, 1976
  Views of a British educator regarding issues and problems in reading. 26 minutes.

Room to Learn
Association Films, Inc.
  Open environment based on Montessori philosophy. 22 minutes.

Teachers, Parents, and Children
Davidson Films, Inc., 1974
  The close relationship between families and their teacher clearly supports and encourages a child's growth, as shown in this film. 17 minutes.

TV: The Anonymous Teacher
Mass Media Ministries, 1976
  Gives a good view of how TV watching affects children. Shows children's focus while they are viewing various programs and discusses with children what they have seen. 15 minutes.

Time of Their lives
National Education Association
  Events in the daily routine of kindergarten. 25 minutes.

You're Not Listening
Modern Talking Pictures Service, Inc.
  Jonathan is a seven-year-old with a perceptual problem and hyperactive behavior. The problem is developed from the child's perception. 30 minutes.

FILMS ON CHILD ABUSE

A Chain to Be Broken
Memorial Hospital Medical Center
  Discusses child abuse and parenting skills in broadest forms. Offers alternatives and solutions for communities and individuals.

Child Abuse and the Law
Perennial Education, Inc., 1978
  Everyone who works with children will benefit from seeing this film, which shows flashbacks of incidents. 27 minutes.

A Cry of Pain
Mass Media Ministries
  Child abuse in America. Affirmative action film for caring communities. Shows families in distress and what can be done to help them.

SOURCES OF FILMS

Anti-Defamation League of B'nai B'rith
315 Lexington Ave.
New York, N.Y. 10016

Association Films, Inc.
600 Madison Ave.
New York, N.Y. 10022

Campus Films Distribution Corp.
2 Overhill Rd.
Scarsdale, N.Y. 10583

Coronet Films
Coronet Bldg.
65 East Water St.
Chicago, Ill. 60501

CRM—McGraw-Hill
110 Fifteenth St.
Del Mar, Calif. 92014

Davidson Films, Inc.
165 Funstead Ave.
San Anselmo, Calif. 94960

Mass Media Ministries
2116 North Charles St.
Baltimore, Md. 21218

Media Five
3211 Cahuenga Blvd.
West Hollywood, Calif. 90068

Memorial Hospital Medical Center
P.O. Box 1428
2801 Atlantic Ave.
Long Beach, Calif.
Attn. Paul Kleiter

National Education Association
1201 Sixteenth St., N.W.
Chicago, Ill. 60601

Modern Talking Pictures Service, Inc.
Film Scheduling Center
5000 Park St., North
St. Petersburg, Fla. 33709

Perennial Education, Inc.
1825 Willow Rd., Box 236
Northfield, Ill. 60093

Precision Films
Precision Film Laboratories, Inc.
630 Ninth Ave.
New York, N.Y. 10036

Soundings
2150 Concord Blvd.
Concord, Calif. 94520

APPENDIX E
Resource materials

PROFESSIONAL ORGANIZATIONS, NEWSLETTERS, AND JOURNALS

Organizations

ACEI
Association for Childhood Education International
3615 Wisconsin Ave., N.W.
Washington, D.C. 20016

ASCD
The Association for Supervision and Curriculum
  Development
225 N. Washington St.
Alexandria, Va. 22314

DCCDCA
Day Care and Child Development Council of
  America, Inc.
1401 K Street, N.W.
Washington, D.C. 20005

ERIC/ECE
Educational Resources Information Center/Early
  Childhood Education
805 West Pennsylvania Ave.
Urbana, Ill. 61801

IRA
International Reading Association
800 Burksdale Rd., Box 8139
Newark, Del. 19711

MENC
Music Educators National Conference
1902 Association Dr.
Reston. Va. 22091

NAEYC
National Association for the Education of Young
  Children
1834 Connecticut Ave., N.W.
Washington, D.C. 20009

NCSS
The National Council for the Social Studies
2030 M St., N.W., Suite 400
Washington, D.C. 20036

NCTE
The National Council of Teachers of English
508 S. 6th St.
Champaign, Ill. 61820

NCTM
The National Council of Teachers of Mathematics
1906 Association Dr.
Reston, Va. 22091

NSTA
National Science Teachers Association
1742 Connecticut Ave., N.W.
Washington, D.C. 20009

PTA
National Congress of Parents and Teachers
700 North Rush St.
Chicago, Ill. 60611

U.S. DHEW
U.S. Department of Health, Education, and Welfare
Office of Child Development
Children's Bureau
Washington, D.C. 20201

Newsletters

ERIC/ECE Newsletter
805 West Pennsylvania Ave.
Urbana, Ill. 61801

Report on Preschool Education
Capitol Publications, Inc.
Suite G-12
2430 Pennsylvania Ave., N.W.
Washington, D.C. 20037

Today's Child
Roosevelt, N.J. 08555

Journals

Child Development
Society for Research in Child Development
University of Chicago Press
5801 Ellis Ave.
Chicago, Ill. 60637

Childhood Education
Association for Childhood Education International
3615 Wisconsin Ave., N.W.
Washington, D.C. 20016

Children Today
U.S. Department of Health, Education, and Welfare
Office of Child Development
Children's Bureau
Superintendent of Documents
U.S. Government Printing Office
Washington, D.C. 20402

Elementary English
The National Council of Teachers of English
508 South 6th St.
Champaign, Ill. 61820

Exceptional Children
The Council for Exceptional Children
1920 Association Dr.
Reston, Va. 22091

The Mathematics Teacher
The National Council of Teachers of Math
1906 Association Dr.
Reston, Va. 22091

Merrill-Palmer Quarterly of Behavior and Development
Merrill-Palmer Institute
71 East Ferry Ave.
Detroit, Mich. 48202

Music Educators Journal
Music Educators National Conference
1902 Association Dr.
Reston, Va. 22091

The Reading Teacher
International Reading Association
800 Burksdale Rd., Box 8139
Newark, Del. 19711

Science and Children
National Science Teachers Association
1742 Connecticut Ave., N.W.
Washington, D.C. 20009

Social Education
The National Council of the Social Studies
2030 M Street, N.W., Suite 400
Washington, D.C. 20036

Young Children
National Association for the Education of
  Young Children
1834 Connecticut Ave., N.W.
Washington, D.C. 20009

APPENDIX F
Some programs used with kindergarten children

Alpha Time
New Dimensions in Education, Inc.
  Designed as a prereading program. Introduces children first to letters and then to letter sounds. Oral communication skills and vocabulary are developed through use of the materials and activities. Materials include:

Huggables (26)	Read-to-me books (4)
Records (5)	Filmstrips (6)
Professional guide	Picture cards (8)
Duplicating masters (2)	Picture books (6 titles, 30 each)
Puzzles (9)	
	Picture squares (144)

Beginning to Read, Write, and Listen
J. B. Lippincott Co.
  Designed to provide experiences and develop letter knowledge. Materials include:

Pupil's kit	Masters
Consumable letterbooks, (24)	Cassette tapes
Magic slates	Guides
Teacher's kit	Alphabet cards

Breakthrough to Literacy
Bowmar
  Coordinates children's work with language and leads from listening and speaking to reading and writing. Materials include:

Story figures (32)	Project folder (5 sets)
Classroom sentence maker	
Teacher's resource book	Student word maker (5 sets)

Communication Skills Program (Reading—Revised SWRL)
Ginn and Co.
  The major outcome areas are:
  1. Word recognition outcomes, which include learning decoding skills and a small proportion of sight words
  2. Comprehension outcomes, which include studying word and sentence meaning

  Materials include:
  Block I
    Activity packet (16 students)
    Storybook packet (16 copies of 16 titles)
    Teacher materials
  Block II
    Activity packet (16 students)
    Storybook packet (16 copies of 21 titles)
    Teacher materials

Goldman-Lynch Sounds and Symbols
American Guidance Service, Inc.
  Designed to stimulate production of the speech sounds in our English language and recognition of their associated symbols. Picture cards, puppets, character and letter cards, posters, sentence strips, and workbooks are among materials included.

Language Experience in Early Childhood
Encyclopaedia Britannica, Inc.
  Utilizes the oral language each child brings to school as a basis for developing the child's competency as a reader and as a writer. Materials include:
    Teacher's resource book
    Set of pupil-parent leaflets

Language and Thinking Program
Follett Publishing Co.
  Uses a "learning through experiencing" approach for teaching language, basic concepts, and critical skills. Materials include:
    Multimedia, multisensory packages (10)
      Let's Start (oral language)
      Colors
      Shapes
      Sizes
      Directions
      Blends

Action
Functions
Classification
Relevant learning experiences
 Student activity books
 Criterion test
 Spirit masters
Peabody Language Development Kits
American Guidance Service, Inc.
 Self-contained kits of lessons and materials designed to stimulate overall oral language and intellectual development. Cards, posters, puppets, recordings, and models are among materials included.
 Level P (3-5 years)
 Level I (4½-6½ years)
PRS (Pre-Reading Skills)
Encyclopaedia Britannica, Educational Corporation
 Teaches five basic skills necessary for learning to read effectively:
 1. Attending to letter order
 2. Attending to letter orientation
 3. Attending to word detail
 4. Sound matching
 5. Sound blending
 Materials may be purchased separately and include:
  Teacher file
  Management system
  Grouping cards
  Class charts
  Record
  Skill list
  Schedule book
  Children's games (50)
  Ditto masters (practice sheets, take-home games)
  Teacher guide folders
  Packet chart/flannel board
SELF
Silver Burdett Co.
 Designed to build a foundation of oral language development. Materials include:
  Self-told tales (36 picture books)
  Self-search (64 pictures and 2 records)
  Self-sound (10 records)
  Self-packs (picture cards)
  Gabby puppets (3)
  Self-pads (student worksheet, consumable)
  Together (parent-child activities, consumable)
  Teacher resource manuals

APPENDIX G

Transitions

Transitions:
1. Aid individuals or groups of children in changing from one activity to another.
2. Help move individuals or groups of children from one place to another.
3. Can be used during "waiting time," such as waiting until all children have gathered into a group.

Little has been written about using transitions in the classroom. Many teachers agree that using transitions promotes good daily living in the classroom if they are used wisely. The very best transitions spring from ideas generated from ongoing lessons and activities within a particular classroom. Transitions should not be used as gimmicks to quiet children, but should help them relax and "change gears" in productive ways.

Transition activities originate from songs, rhythms, singing games, exercises, games, finger plays, brain teasers, poetry, creative movement, creative drama, drawing ideas from the content areas, etc.

The following examples show how transitions may be used in different ways:
1. "Everyone wearing clothes with seven buttons may line up at the door." (Buttons must be showing.)
2. "All those who live in a brown house."
3. "Those who have the numeral 6 in their house number."
4. "Those whose last name begins with the letter *B*."
5. "Anyone who lives on Jackson Street."
6. "Everyone who worked on wood sculpture today."
7. "All those who ride on Mr. Barlow's bus."
8. "Everyone whose family has a green car."
9. Using some type of percussion instrument, play out the rhythm of the children's names. For example, *Mar-i-lyn*. Several children may have the same number of syllables in their names. (Do not try this until the children are familiar with each other's names.)
10. Mouth the child's name by syllables.
11. "Let's walk as if we were walking on a very narrow board."
12. "Let's go to the library like a sandwich today. Two slices of bread, please." The children may line up two by two. (Try to inject subtle humor into some of the activities. The children will thrive on it.)
13. "As we walk down the hall to the gym, let's count silently the number of steps it takes to get there."
14. "As we walk back to our room from the art room, let's think to ourselves about one kind deed that someone did for

each of us during the past week." (You may need to give an example.) The children should then have the opportunity to quickly relate "deeds" on returning to the room.
15. Hold up cards with the children's names (or initials) on them.
16. "Let's see how many different ways we can get to the door." *Examples:* Walking sideways, skipping, tiptoeing, etc.
17. "I'll say a number [or letter], and you say the number that comes after the number I say."
18. Give the children a simple riddle about anything you can think of. Have them raise their hands when they know the answer.
19. Have a child do a pantomime. Other children guess what the pantomime is about.
20. Play "Simon Says."
21. Play "Follow Me." Teacher or child is the leader. Cross legs, hold up hands, wiggle, clap hands, etc. Return to the position you want the children to be in for the next activity.
22. Child sits in a chair with back to other children. Child says:
    "Here I sit in my little chair,
    Listening to the cuckoo clock."
    Another child then strikes a triangle (or other instrument) a certain number of times. If the first child gives the correct answer, the second child sits in the chair and repeats the rhyme.
23. Draw a large tree on the board. Play a note on the piano. If the sound of the note is high, the child draws a leaf high up in the tree. If the note has a low sound, the child draws the leaf low on the tree.
24. Play "Who Am I? "It" is seated in the middle of the floor. A player stands behind "It," who has his eyes covered. The player says, "Who are you?" "It" replies, "I am Tommy." The player asks, "Who am I?" "It" is permitted three tries at guessing who is speaking. This game is more readily accepted after the group has been together a few months and the children's names are better known to each other.
25. Describe something. ("I am thinking of—")
    a. Someone in the room. (Describe that person—that object.)
    b. A place.
    c. An animal.
    d. An object.
26. "On the way to school I saw—" (Child gives other children a number of clues about something seen on the way to school. Children then guess.)
27. Tap out or clap the rhythm of a very

familiar song. Let children guess what song it is.
28. Play "Who Am I?" Have a child use a puppet. Have the puppet talk for some storybook character. Other children guess the character.
29. Have a child bounce a ball a certain number of times. Another child is chosen to guess the number of bounces.
30. Repeat nursery rhymes or poems known to the children. Leave out a word at the end or middle of a line. *Example:*
"Jack and Jill went up the _____
To fetch a _____ of water," etc.
31. Active transition: "The Hokey-Pokey" (may be sung or chanted).
32. Play "What Is Missing?" Draw pictures of objects on cards. *Example:* "Draw a lamp with the electric cord missing." Children guess the missing part.

Often, after practice, the children can suggest ideas for transitions or will express their favorite activities. As you develop sensitivity to the moods and nuances of the classroom, certain transition activities will be more appropriate than others, and the "flow" of the room will show subtle and steady improvement.

APPENDIX H
Guides*

Idaho Kindergarten Guide
State Department of Education
Boise, Idaho (1976)

Kindergarten, a Place to Get Ready
North Canton City Schools
North Canton, Ohio (no date)

Kindergarten Activities
Peoria Public Schools
Peoria, Ill. (no date)

Kindergarten Curriculum
East Hartford Public Schools
East Hartford, Conn. (1977)

Kindergarten Curriculum
North Valley Schools
Closter, N.J. (1977)

Kindergarten Guide
Hayward Public Schools
Hayward, Calif. (1970)

Kindergarten Science and Social Studies Guide
Wichita Public Schools
Wichita, Kan. (1976)

Kindergarten Teacher's Guide
Newark Public Schools
Newark, Ohio (1978)

Teaching in the Kindergarten
Houston Independent School District
Houston, Tex. (1975)

Teaching Kindergarten
Unified School District
San Francisco, Calif. (1975)

---

*These guides are representative of materials available from school systems and state departments of education.

Index

A

Abilities in social studies learning, 123-128
Abuse, child, 93-96
Action songs, 151
Activities
    art, 176-182
    to develop listening skills, 147-148
    to develop writing readiness, 205-207
    safety, 90-93
    storytelling, 162-163
    in teaching numbers, 244-255
    in teaching science, 234-241
Aggression cookies, 245
Allergies, 69
Animals, songs about, 152
Anxiety, separation, 24
Appreciation, music, development of, 148
Approaches to reading, 211-213
Arrangement of kindergarten room, 32-36
Art, 171-182
Art center, establishment of, 175-176
Arts
    communication, 191-229
    dramatic, 157-171
    expressive, 143-189

B

Balance, body, activities for development of, 74-75
Basal reading programs, 212
Basic planning for kindergarten, 21
"Bear Hunt," 166
"Beckoning," 55-56
Beginnings, 19-28
Behavior, 96-100
    democratic, 133-136
Beliefs, 118-119

Benefits of television viewing, 223
Bereiter-Engelmann model of kindergarten, 4
Bibliotherapy, 161
Bilingualism and a second language, 199-201
Body balance, activities for development of, 74-75
Body coordination, activities for development of, 78
Body localization, activities for development of, 73-74
Books for children, 161, 286-297
Books, choosing and using, with five-year-olds, 157-158
British infant school, 3-4

C

Caldicott Award winning books, 297
Call-and-response singing, 149
Causes of child abuse and neglect, 94-95
Causes of misbehavior, 100
"Chalk talk" in story presentation, 159
Change in human culture, 119-120
Characteristics
    of abused and neglected children, 95
    of five-year-old, 11-12
    of kindergarten teacher, 13-17
Children's books, 286-297
Churches, study of, 116
Cinquain, 171
Class dictionaries, 204
Clay, working with, 178-181
Collage, 180-182
Communication arts, 191-229
Communications, printed, to parents, 263-267
Community, songs about, 152
Community, teacher knowledge of, 20-21
Concepts
    acquisitions of, play and, 54
    complex, 125
    definition of, 124-125

Concepts—cont'd
  formation of, 123-124
  relational, 125-126
  of value of a democratic society, 132
Concerns regarding television viewing, 222-223
Conducting parent-teacher conference, 270-273
Conferences in handling misbehavior, 98-99
Conferences, parent-teacher, 269-273
Contacts, incidental, with parents, 263
Contributors to play, 52-53
Cooking in teaching numbers, 245-246
Coordination, body, activities for development of, 78
Counting songs, 152
Crayons, use of, 178
Creative dramatics, 164-165
Cubby, 32
Cultural heritage, 120-123
Culture, human
  geographic variations in, 120
  historical change in, 120
  knowledge about, 113-123
  variation and change in, 119-120
Curriculum for kindergarten child, 282-283
Curriculum, social studies, 107-141
Curriculum guides, 41-42

D

Day(s)
  first, of kindergarten, 21-24
  integrated—point of view, 104
  next, after first day of kindergarten, 24-25
Democratic behavior, 133-136
Democratic society, value concepts of, 132
Democratic values, 111-112
Denial of activity in handling misbehavior, 98
Development, Piaget's model of stages of, 105
Dictionaries, class, 204
Diet, proper, 70
Dignifying child's picture, 178
Dioramas in story presentation, 158-159
Diseases, communicable, chart of, 60-67
DISTAR reading systems, 212
Distortions in kindergarten, 5
Domain of knowledge in social studies, 108-123
Dramatic arts, 157-171
Dramatic play, 162-167
"Duck, Duck, Goose," 55

E

Eclectic model of kindergarten, 4-5
Education, kindergarten, trends in, 284-285
Education, moral, 132-133
Educators, early, and development of kindergarten, 6-7
Emergencies, 89

Emotional health, 71-72
Enrollment, kindergarten, 279
Equipment for instruction, 29-32
Equipment for woodworking, 182-183
Evaluating, child's skills in, 128
Evaluation of kindergarten program, 279-281
Exhibits for parents, 262
Expectancy, high, in handling misbehavior, 99
Experiences in teaching numbers, 244-255
Experiences in teaching science, 234-241
Expressive arts, 143-189

F

Fair play, 111
Fairs for parents, 262
Family, study of, 114-115
Feelings, exploring, 136
Feelings, songs about, 152
Felt board in story presentation, 159
Films for kindergarten teachers, 304-306
Finger painting, 178
Finger play, 169-170
Fire drills, 89
Fire safety, 90-92
"Five Little Monkeys," 149
Five-year-old
  characteristics of, 11-12
  kindergarten teacher and, 11-18
  well-being of, 51-105
Flannel board in story presentation, 159
Folk songs, 152
"Follow the Leader," 55
Follow-through model of kindergarten, 4
Follow-up of story, 160-161
Food(s), 70
  learning center on, 238-239
Form, discovery of, 231-257
Format for lesson planning, 43
Full-day schedule, sample of, 38-40

G

Games, group, 55-56
Games, singing, 152
Geographic variations in human culture, 120
Gingerbread men, 245
Goal planning, long- and short-term, 42
Goals
  of expressive arts, 143
  in teaching numbers, 243-244
  in teaching science, 233-234
"Goblin Lives in Our House," 168
Group(s)
  knowledge about, 111-112
  membership in, 111

Group(s)—cont'd
  study, for parents, 262
Grouping, 48
Growth, emotional, fostering of, by play, 53-54
Growth, physical, promotion of, by play, 53
"Guess Who," 169
Guidance in woodworking, 183
Guidelines for television viewing, 223-224
Guides, kindergarten, 314

H

Haiku, 171
Half-day schedules, samples of, 38
Handbooks to aid transition from home to school, example of, 265-267
Hazards, special, 89
Head Start, follow-through kindergarten and, 4
Health, 57-87
Health examinations, 58-59
Health forms, 58-59
Health problems, detecting, 59-70
Health problems, special, 68-70
Hearing problems, 59, 66-67
Heritage, cultural, 120-123
Historical change in human culture, 120
Historical views about play, 52-53
Holidays, songs about, 152
Home, songs about, 152
Home visits, 262-263
  before school begins, 20
"Hot Ball," 56
Human beings, knowledge about, 112-113
Hurricane drills, 89
Hyperactivity, 69-70
Hyperkinesis, 69-70
Hypothesizing, 127

I

Ice cream, homemade (uncooked), 245
Imagining, 127-128
Imitating, activities for development of, 79
Immunization, 58
Incidental contacts with parents, 263
Individual programmed instruction in follow-through kindergarten, 4
Individualization of instruction, grouping and, 48
Individualized reading program, 212
Individuals, knowledge about, 110-111
Inferring, 127
Information, gathering of, 123
Information forms for children entering kindergarten, 298-301
Initial Teaching Alphabet, 212
Institutions in a culture, 114-116

Instruction, organizing for, 29-49
Instructional materials, 29-32
Instruments, 153-155
Integrated day, 3
Introduction
  of equipment for woodworking, 183
  of instruments in music education, 153-154
  of story in storytelling, 160-161
Involvement, parental, patterns of, 260-263
Isolation in handling misbehavior, 99
ITA, 212

J

Judgment, moral, Kohlberg's stages of, 130-131
Jumping, activities for development of, 77

K

Kindergarten
  first day of, 21-24
  models of, 2-5
  orientation to, 19-20
  program of, 2
  purpose and philosophy of, 8
  screening for, 25-27
  timetable of, 5-8
  today's, 1-10
Kindergarten games, 55-56
Kinds of play, 54
Knowledge, domain of, in social studies, 108-123
Kohlberg's stages of moral judgment, 130-131

L

Language, 191-207
  in a culture, 116-118
  second, bilingualism and, 199-201
Language experience approach to reading, 212
Learning
  motor, activities for, 73-80
  purposes and domains of, in social studies, 109
  social studies, abilities and skills in, 123-128
Learning centers, 47
  on foods, 238-239
  on magnets, 237
  on number sets, 247-248
  on number skills, 248-254
Legislation affecting kindergartens, 282
Lesson planning, 42-44
Limits, setting of, on behavior, 98
Listening
  in communication, 195-198
  enhancement of experiences in, 148
  in musical experiences, 146-148
  skills in, activities to develop, 147-148
Localization, body, activities for development of, 73-74

M

Magnets, learning center on, 237
Mainstreaming, 282
Materials
  art, description of, 175-176
  to enhance movement, 156
  instructional, 29-32
  for teaching numbers, 254-255
  for teaching science, 238-241
Mathematics, 241-255
Media for art, 175
Membership in group, 111
Misbehavior, 98-100
Models, kindergarten, 2-5
Montessori model of kindergarten, 2-3
Motor learning, activities for, 73-80
Movement, 155-157
Movement exploration, tips for promoting, 157
Music, 143-155
Musical value in using instruments, 154-155

N

Nature, songs about, 152
Needs of five-year-old, 12-13
Neglect, child, 93-96
Non–English-speaking child, communication and, 199-201
Nonsense songs, 152
Number sets, activities for learning, 247-248
Number skills, activities for learning, 248-254
Numbers, 241-255
Nutrition, 70

O

Observation, parental, 268-269
"Old King Cole," 168
Open model of kindergarten, 3-4
Orchestrating with instruments, 154
Order, discovery of, 231-257
Organization
  for instruction, 29-49
  of kindergarten, 278-279
  room, 32-36
Orientation to kindergarten, 19-20
Outdoor environments, 36-37

P

Painting, finger, 178
Painting with tempera, 177-178
Pantomime, 165-166
Paraprofessionals, parents as, 260-261
Parents as partners, 259-260
Parents, teacher and, 259-275
Parents' room, 262

Partners, parents as, 259-260
Patriotic songs, 152
Patterns of parental involvement, 260-263
Perceptual problems, 67-68
Philosophy of kindergarten, 8
Phonetic reading systems, 212
Physical activity, 72-88
Physical fitness, 72-88
Piaget's model of stages of development, 105
Picture, child's, dignifying of, 178
Planning
  basic, for kindergarten, 21
  of language program, 192-195
  of parent-teacher conferences, 269-270
  of program, 40-48
  in teaching numbers, 242-243
  in teaching science, 231-233
Play, 51-57
  dramatic, 162-167
Poetry, 167-171
Power, sense of, provision of by play, 53
Pre–first grade starts in reading, Durkin's article on, 214-217
Presentation of new songs, 151
Presentation of stories, 158-161
Printed communications to parents, 263-267
Priority of safety, 89-90
Private kindergarten, 2-3
Problem solving, interpersonal, 137
Problem solving, nurturing of, by play, 53
Program(s)
  kindergarten, 2
  language, planning of, 192-195
  for parents, 262
  planning of, 40-48
  used with kindergarten children, 309-310
Promotion, 281-282
Props in story presentation, 159
Public Law 94-142, 282
Puppetry, 166-167
  in story presentation, 159
Purpose of kindergarten, 8
Purposes of play, 53-54
Puzzles, wooden, teacher-made, 184-185

Q

"Quiet Ball," 56

R

Readiness for reading, 210-211, 217-221
Readiness for writing, activities to develop, 205-207
Reading
  approaches to, 211-213
  in communication, 208-221

Reading—cont'd
  pre–first grade and, a joint statement of concerns, 208-210
  readiness for, 210-211, 217-221
Rebus reading systems, 212
Records, sources of, 189
Redirection in handling misbehavior, 99
Reinforcement, positive, in handling misbehavior, 99
Remarks of teacher in handling misbehavior, 99-100
Reporting of child abuse and neglect, 94
Research directions in kindergarten, 283-284
Resource materials, 307-308
Resources, parents as, 261-262
Rest, 70-71
Retention, 281-282
Rhythm instruments, 153
Role of teacher
  in art experiences, 173-175
  in child abuse and neglect, 95-96
  in controlling behavior, 96-98
  in guiding play, 56-57
  in teaching music, 145-146
Role playing, play as means of, 54
Room, arrangement and organization of, 32-36

S

Safety, 88-93
Safety activities, 90-93
Scalewise songs, 149-150
Scheduling for kindergarten day, 37-40
School, before beginning of, 19-21
School environment, safe, maintenance of, 88-89
Schools, study of, 115-116
Science, 231-241
  songs about, 152
Screening, kindergarten, 25-27
  annotated bibliography on, 302-303
Seasons, songs about, 152
Selection of equipment for woodworking, 182-183
Selection of songs, 150
Self-expression, play and, 54
Self-selection of activities, 45
Sensory-motor integration, activities for development of, 79-80
Separation anxiety, 24
Setting limits on behavior, 98
Shopping in teaching numbers, 246
Silly putty (homemade), 180
"Simon Says," 55
Singing, 148-152
Singing games, 152
Skills
  listening, activities to develop, 147-148, 196-198
  listening, in musical experiences, 146-148

Skills—cont'd
  in social studies learning, 123-128
  in thinking, 127-128
Snack time, 70
"Snowman," 149-150
Social participation, 138-141
Social studies, 107-141
Songs
  favorite, 151-152
  presenting new, 151
  scalewise, 149-150
  selection of, 150
  sources of, 150-151
  teaching of, 151
Sources
  of films, 305-306
  of records, 189
  of songs, 150-151
Speaking in communication, 198-202
"Speaking" ideas, 202
Special handicaps, 68-69
Speech problems, 59, 66-67
Spirituals, 152
Stages of development, Piaget's model of, 105
Staggered entrance to kindergarten, 20
Stories, 157-163
Storytelling activities, 162-163
Strategies for teaching values, 136-138
Study groups for parents, 262

T

Tasks of social studies curriculum, 108-110
Teacher
  account of first days as, 15-17
  characteristics of, 13-17
  five-year-old and, 11-18
  knowledge of community of, 20-21
  parents and, 259-275
  role of
    in art experiences, 173-175
    in child abuse and neglect, 95-96
    in controlling behavior, 96-98
    in guiding play, 56-57
    in teaching music, 145-146
  voice and remarks of, in handling misbehavior, 99-100
  wooden puzzles made by, 184-185
Teaching songs, 151
Teaching strategies for values, 136-138
Technology of a culture, 113-114
Television, 222-224
Tempera, painting with, 177-178
"Theodore," 169
Time in teaching numbers, 246
Time line for recording child's development, 273

Timetable, kindergarten, 5-8
Today's kindergarten, 1-10
Tornado drills, 89
Tour of classroom, 22
Tour of school building, 25
Traditional model of kindergarten, 2
Traffic safety, 92-93
Transitions, 311-313
Travel between school and home, safety in, 89
Trends in kindergarten education, 284-285
Typewriters in kindergarten, 203-204

V

Value(s), 118-119
  analysis of, 138
  basic, 129
  concepts of, of a democratic society, 132
  democratic, 111-112
  elements of, of democratic behavior, 133
  other, 129, 132
  of play, 53-54

Valuing, 128-138
Variation in human culture, 119-120
Vision problems, 59
Visitation in kindergarten, 268-273
Visits, home, 262-263
Visual discrimination, 81-87
Visual-motor integration 80-81
Volunteers, parents as, 261

W

Walking, activities for development of, 75-77
Well-being of five-year-old, 51-105
"Wiggles," 169
Woodworking, 182-185
Work time, teacher account of, 45-46
Work time–activity period, 44-46
Workshops for parents, 262
Writing, activities for readiness in, 205-207
Writing in communication, 202-207